A Search for Sovereignty

Law and Geography in European Empires, 1400–1900

A Search for Sovereignty maps a new approach to world history by examining the relation of law and geography in European empires between 1400 and 1900. Lauren Benton argues that Europeans imagined imperial space as networks of corridors and enclaves, and that they constructed sovereignty in ways that merged ideas about geography and law. Conflicts over treason, piracy, convict transportation, martial law, and crime created irregular spaces of law, while also attaching legal meanings to familiar geographic categories such as rivers, oceans, islands, and mountains. The resulting legal and spatial anomalies influenced debates about imperial constitutions and international law both in the colonies and at home. This original study changes our understanding of empire and its legacies and opens new perspectives on the global history of law.

Lauren Benton is Professor of History and Affiliate Professor of Law at New York University. Her book *Law and Colonial Cultures: Legal Regimes in World History, 1400–1900* (Cambridge University Press, 2002) won the Law and Society Association's James Willard Hurst Book Prize, the World History Association Book Prize, and the PEWS Book Award from the American Sociological Association.

A Search for Sovereignty

Law and Geography in European Empires, 1400–1900

LAUREN BENTON
New York University

CAMBRIDGE UNIVERSITY PRESS
Cambridge, New York, Melbourne, Madrid, Cape Town,
Singapore, São Paulo, Delhi, Tokyo, Mexico City

Cambridge University Press
32 Avenue of the Americas, New York, NY 10013-2473, USA

www.cambridge.org
Information on this title: www.cambridge.org/9780521707435

First published 2010
Reprinted 2011

A catalog record for this publication is available from the British Library.

Library of Congress Cataloging in Publication Data

Benton, Lauren A.
A search for sovereignty : law and geography in European Empires, 1400–1900 /
Lauren Benton.
p. cm.
Includes bibliographical references and index.
ISBN 978-0-521-88105-0 (hardback) – ISBN 978-0-521-70743-5 (pbk.)
1. Law and geography – Europe – History. 2. Europe – Boundaries – History.
3. Sovereignty. I. Title.
KJC1337.B46 2010
341.4′2–dc22 2009015844

ISBN 978-0-521-88105-0 Hardback
ISBN 978-0-521-70743-5 Paperback

For my mother,
Charlotte Russ Benton,
with love and appreciation

Contents

List of Illustrations — *page* ix
Preface and Acknowledgments — xi

1 Anomalies of Empire — 1
2 Treacherous Places: Atlantic Riverine Regions and the Law of Treason — 40
3 Sovereignty at Sea: Jurisdiction, Piracy, and the Origins of Ocean Regionalism — 104
4 Island Chains: Military Law and Convict Transportation — 162
5 Landlocked: Colonial Enclaves and the Problem of Quasi-Sovereignty — 222
6 Bare Sovereignty and Empire — 279

Bibliography — 301
Index — 329

List of Illustrations

2.1. "The Discovery of Six Other Rivers" (1591) *page* 47
2.2. Map of South America, by Levinus Hulsius (1599) 70
2.3. Map of Massachusetts and Merrimack Rivers (1678) 92
3.1. Navigation Map of the Atlantic (1545) 107
3.2. The World's Subterraneous Canals (1665) 109
3.3. A Map of the West Indies or the Islands of America (1709) 154
4.1. Map of Juan Fernández Island (c. 1750) 178
4.2. George Raper, Principal Settlement on Norfolk Island (1790) 199
5.1. Port Called Nombre de Dios (c. 1590) 230
5.2. Map of Baroda (1907–1909) 252

Preface and Acknowledgments

Several years ago, I mentioned to a friend that I had started working on a book about the history of European perceptions of oceans. I said it would take me only a year or two to research and write. I had come to this topic after reflecting on historians' reluctance to probe critically the spatial dimensions of early modern empires. We seemed often to assume that empires and states aspired to establish political and legal control over discrete, bounded territories. I thought we needed to learn more about how Europeans imagined unbounded, distant geographies and much more about the varied legal practices they relied on to project sovereignty into those spaces.

The sea seemed a logical place to begin. By definition, there could be no territorial control of the oceans, at least not in the ways conventionally imagined. This observation had already informed histories of the sea as a space trending from lawlessness to regulation under emerging international law. But it seemed to me that the usual narratives shifted attention away from the concerted efforts of empires to extend authority into the oceans, a process often carried out by mariners operating more or less on their own, beyond the range of close imperial oversight. To explore the history of the disorganized projection of imperial control over the oceans, I began by poring through accounts by and about pirates to find out whether and how even rogues might have acted as conduits of law. The good news, I soon realized, was that many of my hunches were borne out. Pirates held deeply entrenched ideas about the law and acted on them, even in the midst of seemingly lawless raiding. And there was plenty of evidence linking their legal strategies with the policies of European empires as they sought to extend their influence over trade routes, sea lanes, and ports. It was even more intriguing that mariners' perceptions of the sea as a space of interconnected passageways closely matched ideas about the extension of imperial jurisdiction into ocean space along narrow bands imaginatively marked by the passage of ships. Crisscrossed by legal corridors and dotted at their edges by competing colonial jurisdictions, the smooth oceans appeared to be legally very lumpy. The bad news – though perhaps I can now acknowledge that it was more good news – was that the story I wanted to explore turned out to be not "just" about oceans. If Europeans were beginning to identify parts of oceans as distinctive kinds of legal spaces through travel, and in contests over privateering and piracy, then it stood to reason that European imperial pursuits were producing other uneven legal geographies. It was important to understand these patterns to grasp the puzzles facing imperial officials, colonial polities, sojourners, settlers, conquered subjects, merchants, jurists, lawyers, and others engaged in struggles to define, establish, and challenge sovereignty in empire. A diverse array of actions and interpretations was shaping an interimperial legal regime whose contours did not always fit comfortably within past and present accounts of the foundations of international law.

I could see that exploring associations between geography and law would produce a story in tension with several familiar and seductive narratives in world history. One narrative portrays European expansion as acting to further the rationalization of space. Another story depicts the gradual consolidation of a global order based on agreements between political units enjoying territorial sovereignty. In both tales, the consolidation of empires appears as a force working to flatten space and to corral law into conventionally defined jurisdictions. Instead, I was finding repeating sets of irregularly shaped corridors and enclaves with ambiguous and shifting relations to imperial sovereignty. To trace the origins and significance of these fragments, I would have to explore a chronologically and spatially wider array of points of intersection between geographic imagination and imperial legal practices.

I wanted, of course, to draw connections between law and geography from the sources rather than to concoct associations out of theory or make educated guesses. After investigating pirates and jurisdiction at sea, I delved into early voyage chronicles from fifteenth- and sixteenth-century expeditions in the Atlantic world. In rather short order, an interesting and surprising correlation emerged. European sponsors and chroniclers were especially focused on rivers as the points of entry and pathways to trade and settlement in Africa and the New World, an observation that historians had sometimes noted in passing but rarely investigated in detail. As they moved through river regions, expeditions followed a familiar pattern of becoming embroiled in internal disputes; with surprising frequency, rivals devised and then broadcast accusations of treason. I began to understand these charges as part of a complex legal politics of subjecthood in early European settlements, a process that blended preoccupation with imperial claims and anxieties about membership in colonial political communities.

As I pursued this odd but illuminating association between dangerous upriver regions and treacherous colonial legal politics, I began also to read the accounts of colonial officials from later periods and other places, keeping an eye out for fresh connections, however quirky, between geographic discourse and legal practices tied to claims of sovereignty. Another story soon jumped off the pages: descriptions of hill and mountain regions depicted them as legally archaic places, and as zones of primitive sovereignty. This association had a long pedigree but attracted new attention in the context of late nineteenth-century efforts to define discrete, interior enclaves within colonies and to characterize them as areas of partial sovereignty. From hill country, I moved to consider the peculiar representations of islands in the context of intensifying interimperial competition in the late eighteenth century, when the imagination of islands became closely linked to the perceived utility and constitutional dangers of martial law. The representations of hill country and islands as particular kinds of legal spaces took me to British and Spanish imperial archives, where I investigated case studies highlighting problems associated with the peculiar and enduring lumpiness of imperial legal space.

As I thought about the definitions of sovereignty associated with these uneven configurations, I also pondered the implications of this perspective for an understanding of debates about international law and narratives about the origins and structure of a global legal regime. I used the material about geographic imagination and legal practices in empire to take a fresh look at some familiar texts and concepts within European legal writings. My earlier book on comparative colonial law had adopted a world history approach and had focused especially on the relation between imposed and indigenous law; there were good reasons to make this project on geography and law in empires similarly global in scope and to continue to study legal pluralism, this time from another angle. But there were more compelling reasons for limiting my analysis to European, and especially British and Spanish, empires, and for placing indigenous legal actors within the analytic framework but not at its center. I would then be able to examine more closely the discursive pairings of geography and law, and the relation of practices meant to mark and sustain sovereignty with metropolitan understandings of sovereignty. The dangers of producing a Eurocentric study seemed to me to be outweighed by the benefit of being able to trace the influence of a shared repertoire of (especially) Roman and canon law and to follow links between the fluid politics of empires and the texts of European jurists, including some of the leading figures in the history of international law: Gentili, Grotius, Bentham, Maine, and others. These writers responded very directly to the challenges of cataloging spatial and legal variations, and in the process they recognized inter- and intra-imperial legal politics as sources of international law.

The task of interweaving geographic discourse, legal politics, and international law turned my optimism about writing a quick book into a private joke. It also made the process of research and writing enormously entertaining and rewarding. Thankfully, I was able to benefit at every stage from the insights of many other historians. In my first full year working on the project, I had the good fortune to participate in a reading group at the School of Law at New York University. Meeting weekly, the International Law in Times of Empire group discussed a series of authors and problems, nearly all of which turned out to be relevant to the topic of territoriality in empire. I am grateful to the conveners, Benedict Kingsbury and David Armitage, and to the participants, especially Jane Burbank, Benjamin Straumann, Lisa Ford, Charles Beitz, and Jennifer Pitts, for discussions that helped me shape my ideas about the research in its earliest stages. The NYU History Department has been a wonderfully congenial intellectual home. In Atlantic history, Karen Kupperman and Nicole Eustace have offered bibliographic leads and insights on many occasions. I am lucky to have as colleagues Jane Burbank and Fred Cooper, who generously shared their ideas about imperial political imagination with me as they worked on an important book about empires in world history. Many other NYU historians responded promptly to my queries or commented on parts of the manuscript, including Thomas Bender, Zvi Ben-Dor Benite, Manu Goswami, William Klein, Sinclair Thomson, Joanna Waley-Cohen, Barbara Weinstein, and Larry Wolff. At the NYU School of Law, the Legal History Colloquium provided a stimulating forum for discussing draft chapters, and I benefited from the detailed constructive criticism provided by William Nelson and Daniel Hulsebosch. I made good progress on the book while in residence as a Fellow at the Shelby Cullom Davis Center at Princeton University, where

Gyan Prakash added to his duties as acting director by commenting on sections on India. Other opportunities to present parts of the book-in-progress were very valuable to me and are too numerous to list. With the sad certainty that I am forgetting the names of some scholars who extended invitations, contributed insights, or just provided moral support, I would like to thank Jeremy Adelman, David Armitage, Brian Balogh, Jerry Bannister, Christopher Bayly, Craig Buettinger, Christina Burnett, Paul Corcoran, Clifton Crais, Antonio Feros, Roquinaldo Ferreira, Lisa Ford, Eliga Gould, Alan Greer, Alexander Haskell, Peter Hoffer, Alan Karras, Amalia Kessler, Rande Kostal, Michael LaCombe, Peter Lake, Mark Mazower, Adam McKeown, Christian McMillan, Joseph Miller, Matthew Mirow, Peter Onuf, Brian Owensby, Carla Rahn Phillips, Richard Ross, Linda Rupert, James Scott, Rebecca Scott, Richard Sher, Aaron Slater, Miranda Spieler, Philip Stern, Taylor Stoermer, David Tanenhaus, Aparna Vaidik, Martine van Ittersum, Christopher Warren, and John Witt. I am indebted to Kären Wigen for reading the full manuscript carefully, offering invaluable advice, and not minding when I failed to take all of it. At Cambridge University Press, Frank Smith and Eric Crahan expertly guided the book's progress from the time it was just a notion to its completion. I thank Jerusha Westbury and Paul Sager for helping to organize the bibliography and illustrations, and Patricia Mouzakitis for expertly handling many small tasks related to the project.

Working on this book has been, in surprising ways, a real pleasure, and I give most of the credit for that to my family and friends. Victoria and Gabriela Garcia were disappointed when they learned the book would not be all about pirates, but it has taken long enough to write that they (unlike some historians) matured past the infatuation-with-pirates stage and rallied to encourage me, while also making sure that I stopped to have some fun. Eduardo Garcia steadfastly reminded me that I should take the time to get it right. Sustenance in the form of hilarious running commentary was provided by Susan Field, Stefanie Dimeo, Cristina Paul, Doris Sher, Janet Sabel, Cleo Kearns, and Deborah Gaines. I enjoyed strangely enlightening conversations with George Field about the similarities of legal fragments in empire and fragments of matter at the edges of the galaxy. In Princeton, London, Hunstanton, Pasadena, and Nashville, Sandy Solomon and Peter Lake endured detailed updates in between shared laughter and over good food. And, while traveling more widely than some of the global sojourners I write about, Charlotte Benton cheered me on as she has always done. The book is dedicated to her, in appreciation of her contagious, lifelong love of language, travel, and learning.

Parts of the following articles have been reprinted with permission: "From International Law to Imperial Constitutions: The Problem of Quasi-Sovereignty, 1870–1900," *Law and History Review* 26 (2008): 595–620; "Empires of Exception: History, Law, and the Problem of Imperial Sovereignty," *Quaderni di Relazioni Internazionali* (2007, December): 54–67; "Spatial Histories of Empire," *Itinerario* 30 (2006): 19–34; "Legal Spaces of Empire: Piracy and the Origins of Ocean Regionalism," *Comparative Studies in Society and History*, Vol. 47, no. 4 (2005): 700–724.

1

Anomalies of Empire

In his geographical treatise of 1537, the Portuguese cosmographer Dom João de Castro explained that it would be possible to correlate all newly discovered lands with astronomical markers to produce an accurate map of the world. The result would be, he wrote, a "true and perfect geography."[1] The movement toward this vision, from the cartographic revolution of thirteenth-century portolan charts to the use of surveying to map colonial territories in the nineteenth century, is a compelling narrative of the rationalization of space, and of the reinforcement of this trend by the pursuit of European imperial interests.[2]

[1] Quoted in Armando Cortesão and Avelino Teixeira da Mota, "General Introduction," in *Portugaliae Monumenta Cartographica*, ed. Armando Cortesão and Avelino Teixeira da Mota, (Lisbon: Imprensa Nacional-Casa da Moeda, 1960), 1:xvii.

[2] This narrative is presented piecemeal in works spanning the history of cartography, historical geography, colonial studies, and the literature of empire. In early colonial history, there has been a consistent emphasis on the erasure of the spatial understandings of non-Europeans; the best example remains J. B. Harley, "New England Cartography and the Native Americans," in *The New Nature of Maps: Essays in the History of Cartography*, ed. Paul Laxton (Baltimore: Johns Hopkins University Press, 2001), 169–96. In the construction of high colonialism, mapping is considered a reinforcement of social control; for example, see Matthew H. Edney, *Mapping an Empire: The Geographical Construction of British India, 1765–1843* (Chicago: University of Chicago Press, 1997). The general argument about an association between the transition to Cartesian representations of space and European empire is presented in Robert David Sack, *Human Territoriality: Its Theory and History* (Cambridge: Cambridge University Press, 1986), chap. 2. Bruce McLeod mines literary texts to emphasize connections between the management and manipulation of space in empire and the movement toward planned and geometrically regular spaces associated with social control in England. *The Geography of Empire in English Literature, 1580–1745* (Cambridge: Cambridge University Press, 1999), chap. 5.

This narrative needs to be placed alongside the history of imperfect geographies and the production in empire of variegated spaces with an uncertain relation to imperial power. Territorial control was, in many places, an incidental aim of imperial expansion. While an iconic association with empire is the pink shading of British imperial possessions in nineteenth- and early twentieth-century maps, that image, and others like it, obscures the many variations of imperial territories. Empires did not cover space evenly but composed a fabric that was full of holes, stitched together out of pieces, a tangle of strings. Even in the most paradigmatic cases, an empire's spaces were politically fragmented; legally differentiated; and encased in irregular, porous, and sometimes undefined borders. Although empires did lay claim to vast stretches of territory, the nature of such claims was tempered by control that was exercised mainly over narrow bands, or corridors, and over enclaves and irregular zones around them.

Maritime empires represented this pattern most clearly, with their networks of sea lanes connecting dispersed settlements or trading posts. But territorial expansion in Europe also occurred through the creation and protection of corridors and enclaves. The pattern extended to overseas reconnaissance, influenced settlement strategies, and helped shape systems of colonial rule. Imagining and enlarging empire sometimes appeared synonymous with efforts to gather information about corridors of control, including mapping and describing ocean passages, river networks, merchant roads, and other travel routes. Enclaves such as missions, trading posts, towns, and garrisons were strung like beads along interconnected corridors. These imperial outposts coexisted with other kinds of enclaves, including areas of partial or shared sovereignty within larger spheres of influence or rule. Such zones might form when peoples or polities fended off formal conquest, bargained for a measure of autonomy, or courted rival imperial sponsors for protection. Colonial powers found reasons to create semiautonomous spaces that were legally and politically differentiated from more closely controlled colonial territories. Together these patterns and practices produced political geographies that were uneven, disaggregated, and oddly shaped – and not at all consistent with the image produced by monochrome shading of imperial maps.[3]

[3] The emphasis on corridors and enclaves is consistent with a view promoted in other recent histories of European empires as webs or networks. My interest in the legal qualities of corridors and enclaves differs slightly in shifting attention from the movement of

Law represented a particularly important factor in the social construction of this variegated colonial world. Legal cultures traveled with imperial officials, merchants, sailors, soldiers, sojourners, settlers, captives, and even pirates – agents in empire who positioned themselves as subjects and often as representatives of distant sovereigns while interacting with locals and representatives of competing empires. Travelers' actions extended the reach of the law, helped to form new political communities, promoted challenges to imperial designs, and created variations of familiar legal practices. The administration of empire depended, meanwhile, on the exercise of delegated legal authority. This layered quality of imperial rule spawned contests over the prerogatives of officials, the definition and rights of subjects, and the articulation of colonial administration with the law of indigenous or conquered peoples. Together, these dimensions of imperial sovereignty – the portability of subjecthood and the delegation of legal authority – generated territorial variations. On one level, they contributed to the patterning of corridors and enclaves; delegated legal authorities extended their control over enclaves and the areas around them, while the movement of subjects left its own spatial imprint along networks of travel, trade, and provisioning. On another level, a fluid legal politics surrounding subjecthood and authority produced further variations within and across corridors and enclaves. A graphic representation of imperial power more accurate than the standard, multicolored maps would show tangled and interrupted European-claimed spaces and would represent, perhaps in colors of varying intensity, the changing and locally differentiated qualities of rule within geographic zones.

It is tempting to interpret such patterns as merely temporary formations on the way toward more evenly expansive territorial rule and settled sovereignties. But to do so is to project backward in time the post-nineteenth-century idea that territoriality was not just one element

goods and people through these webs and focusing on their place within the processes of imagining and constructing sovereignty. In merging these mainly compatible perspectives, it is helpful to refer to Kerry Ward's observation that the "nodes and networks" of empire had a "modular" quality deriving from an "incremental development of imperial sovereignty." *Networks of Empire: Forced Migration in the Dutch East India Company* (New York: Cambridge University Press, 2008), 56, 60. On webs and networks composing European empires, see also Alison Games, *The Web of Empire: English Cosmopolitans in an Age of Expansion, 1560–1660* (New York: Oxford University Press, 2008); David Hancock, *Oceans of Wine: Madeira and the Emergence of American Trade and Taste* (New Haven, CT: Yale University Press, 2009).

of sovereignty but its defining element.[4] Although control of territory formed an important part of early modern constructions of sovereignty, European powers often asserted and defended imperial dominion on the basis of strategic, symbolic, and limited claims while recognizing the incomplete and tentative nature of more expansive spheres of influence. Some legal practices, including rituals defining subjecthood and acts controlling criminality, had only an indirect relation to dominion over territory. Transitions to modern statehood in the long nineteenth century did not eliminate patterns of territorial unevenness.[5] Even – or especially – in polities advancing very explicit programs of territorial expansion and consolidation, new kinds of differentiated legal zones dotted the landscape. Their creation was a function of the routine operations of empire rather than the result of persisting, older irregularities.

The problem of bringing sovereign and territorial claims into alignment was a familiar one within Europe, and historians have recently begun to retell the history of sovereignty in European nation-states as a contingent and stubbornly incomplete process.[6] The search for sovereignty in empire presented some of the same problems, while also marking imperial sovereignty as distinctive in some ways and, at times, as especially elusive.[7] *Dominium*, most commonly thought of as the right to possess

[4] A fuller discussion of treatments of sovereignty is presented in Chapter 6.

[5] Here and elsewhere in the book where I refer to a *long century*, I am following Fernand Braudel's practice of using the convention to recognize continuities that disturb the usual periodization by century. Braudel's long sixteenth century stretched from about 1450 to 1640. Depending on the region and the trends being analyzed, some long centuries are longer than others. Most historians, for example, would define the long nineteenth century as the period from about 1780 until the beginning of World War I but would label the long eighteenth century as extending from roughly 1680 to about 1840 (British historians sometimes attach the precise dates of 1688 and 1832). I will provide a range of years when the dates are important to the topic under discussion; otherwise when I refer to a long century, the phrase should be taken to signify a period from several decades before the beginning of a century to several decades after its end.

[6] See especially recent writings on the Treaty of Westphalia that question its significance as a turning point in the development of territorial control as an integral element of modern sovereignty. For example, Stéphane Beaulac, *The Power of Language in the Making of International Law: The Word Sovereignty in Bodin and Vattel and the Myth of Westphalia* (Leiden: Martinus Nijhoff, 2004).

[7] Charles Maier argues that European imperial sovereignty differed from sovereignty within Europe precisely because empires depended not on the integrity of frontiers but on "the continuing manifestation of power" required to keep out rivals. *Among Empires: American Ascendancy and Its Predecessors* (Cambridge, MA: Harvard University Press, 2006), 101. We should note that some of the irregularities of imperial sovereignty can be explained by the high costs and communications problems posed by rule over distant territories. Certainly technological advances and the consolidation of colonial bureaucracies

territory, and *imperium*, associated with sovereign jurisdiction, remained imprecisely defined, especially in relation to one another, for a long time.[8] Territorial variations meanwhile resulted from conflicts over which legal instruments and prerogatives extended into which portions of empire and under whose local authority. Did all or some of metropolitan legislation apply? Did monarchs hold the same or greater authority overseas as in their immediate realms? Could new law, or novel interpretations of old law, issue from colonial officials or courts? Answering such questions often required imagining sovereignty as a divisible quality whose component parts could be apportioned in various combinations.[9] Imperial officials and legal writers found that the problem of configuring sovereignty could not be addressed separately from pragmatic and theoretical questions arising from the entanglements of local legal politics and the challenges of interimperial contests.

Recognizing the spatial variations of imperial sovereignty helps us to amend our understanding of the changing structure of the global legal regime. The history of international law has tended to be narrated as a shift from natural to positive law, beginning with the arguments of jurists in the sixteenth and seventeenth centuries about the centrality of natural law principles in regulating interimperial relations and leading to the

did change the possibilities for even distribution of effective imperial authority. But there is clearly more to the story than communications and cost constraints, and a focus on legal communications tends to encourage an emphasis on variations among empires, while I am more interested in exploring patterns of variation within imperial formations. On legal communications as a lens for viewing differences among empires, see Kenneth J. Banks, *Chasing Empire across the Sea: Communications and the State in the French Atlantic, 1713–1763* (Montreal: McGill-Queen's University Press, 2002); Richard Ross, "Legal Communications and Imperial Governance: British North America and Spanish America Compared," in *The Cambridge History of Law in America*, ed. Michael Grossberg and Christopher Tomlins (Cambridge: Cambridge University Press, 2008), 104–43.

[8] *Imperium* was often used as a synonym for sovereignty, while *dominium* was sometimes used more narrowly than defined here to designate lordship or property and sometimes more broadly to convey a vast domain that was claimed but not controlled. The definitions adopted here are not designed to be precise. Like *sovereignty*, whose shifting definition is discussed especially in Chapter 6, *dominium* and *imperium* were employed strategically, and their meanings in discourse on empire were influenced by changing definitions in domestic politics. David Armitage views "the problem of uniting *imperium* and *dominium*... as the fundamentally and ultimately combustible dilemma at the core of British imperial ideology." *The Ideological Origins of the British Empire* (Cambridge: Cambridge University Press, 2000), 94 (see also 93–4, 96–8, and 122–4).

[9] I will have much more to say about divisible sovereignty later. A valuable starting place for considering its role in European empires is Edward Keene, *Beyond the Anarchical Society: Grotius, Colonialism and Order in World Politics* (Cambridge: Cambridge University Press, 2002).

emergence, in the long nineteenth century, of a concept of international order based on law formed through the agreements of separate sovereign polities.[10] Exploring the complexities of imperial sovereignty challenges this narrative at many levels. First, the irregular thrust of imperial jurisdiction into extra-European space can be viewed as giving rise to an interimperial legal politics in which participants, even while invoking natural law principles, imagined a broader regulatory order shaped by legal practices and institutions replicated across empires.[11] Put differently, a modified positivism, deriving not from legislation or from agreements among polities but from proliferating practices and shared expectations about legal processes, stretched across the centuries of European imperial expansion and rule. Patterns of legal variation, including "anomalous legal zones," formed a pervasive and persistent element of this global legal order.[12] Second, the continued existence of empires into the long

[10] My efforts to complicate this narrative build on the work of other scholars who have identified problems in the standard account and offered other corrections. See Antony Anghie, *Imperialism, Sovereignty, and the Making of International Law* (Cambridge: Cambridge University Press, 2007); Keene, *Beyond the Anarchical Society*; David Armitage, *The Declaration of Independence: A Global History* (Cambridge, MA: Harvard University Press, 2007); Casper Sylvest, "The Foundations of Victorian International Law," in *Victorian Visions of Global Order: Empire and International Relations in Nineteenth-Century Political Thought*, ed. Duncan Bell (Cambridge: Cambridge University Press, 2007), 47–66.

[11] For an argument about the simultaneous invocation of natural law principles and positive law in international law of the late eighteenth century, see Armitage, *The Declaration of Independence*, chap. 2. Most accounts emphasize treaties as the central element of interimperial legal ordering; I do not ignore treaties but wish to give more prominence to other, more decentralized ways in which mutual recognition of imperial legal authority developed.

[12] I adapt this phrase from Gerald Neuman, "Anomalous Zones," *Stanford Law Review* 48, no. 5 (1996), 1197–1234. Neuman treats "anomalous zones" as areas in which fundamental norms of law have been suspended, and this condition is expanded to create additional legal deviations. His examples span from the anomalous voting regime of Washington, D.C., to Guantánamo Bay as a place of suspended rights for prisoners. I explore similar examples, in particular penal colonies, in Chapter 4, but I use the term more capaciously throughout this book to refer to areas within empires that present a range of legal variations, not always connected to the suspension of norms. See Chapter 6 in this volume and also Lauren Benton, "Constitutions and Empires," *Law & Social Inquiry* 31 (2006), 177–98. Note that Radhika Singha employs "anomalies" and "legal anomaly" to characterize the results of British attempts in colonial India to appeal to religious norms and traditional authority while implementing legal policies designed to affirm their subordination to imperial law. *A Despotism of Law: Crime and Justice in Early Colonial India* (New York: Oxford University Press, 1998), 82, 85. I investigate the interrelation of colonial legal anomalies and understandings of global order.

nineteenth century disturbs the narrative of a forming international legal regime. We can learn about how to analyze global legal norms and their transformation in the nineteenth century and after by analyzing earlier interimperial engagements and cross-imperial discourses. This history leads us to pay attention to elements of a shared legal repertoire rather than search for early signs of differentiated, national styles of rule. And by tracing the origins of and changes in conventions for referring to areas of partial, contested, or shared sovereignty, we become better able to identify variants of those conventions in later periods.

Geographic tropes featured prominently as a shorthand way to describe some of the spatial variations of imperial law. In somewhat haphazard and decentralized ways, a fluid discourse about geography urged associations between physical properties and qualities of law and sovereignty. Descriptions of geographic elements such as rivers, oceans, islands, and highlands were creatively combined with discourses about law and with reports about patterns of legal practice. Through repetition, the process formed widely circulating conventions – ways of communicating, often indirectly, odd and enduring links between landscapes (or seascapes) and law. In response to a range of influences, particular geographic tropes became symbolically more central to imperial pursuits in certain periods. Both metropolitan observers and agents in empire meanwhile sought to characterize the singular geographic features and anomalous legal qualities of parts of empire. Charles Maier has argued that the "overarching spatial imagination" of the long twentieth century was a strong "territorial imperative."[13] Five centuries of earlier European imperial projects seem to betray no single overarching spatial imagination – unless we understand territorial variation itself as an organizing

[13] Maier perhaps exaggerates the power of territoriality as an organizing principle of the century, particularly if one considers the continued creation of spaces of uneven sovereignty such as the quasi-sovereign enclaves of the late nineteenth century analyzed in Chapter 5 of this volume and discussed by Frederick Cooper in "Globalization" in *Colonialism in Question: Theory, Knowledge, History* (Berkeley: University of California Press, 2005), 91–112. But Maier should be credited for his efforts to identify an imperative within a historical period "to keep its political institutions and its images of the physical world in some sort of congruence." "Consigning the Twentieth Century to History: Alternative Narratives for the Modern Era," *American Historical Review* 105 (2000), 807–31. Saskia Sassen's attempt to incorporate territoriality in a narrative of global change is less successful; she represents medieval territorial "assemblages" and imperial geographies as mainly precursors to the emergence of national political economies. *Territory, Authority, Rights: From Medieval to Global Assemblages* (Princeton, NJ: Princeton University Press, 2006).

rubric and recognize the inherent lumpiness of imperial formations as its animating feature.[14]

As European imperial projects in successive periods tended to invoke particular geographic tropes to describe patterns of partial and uneven sovereignty, multiple contexts influenced these trends. Interimperial relations appear to have been especially influential. From the fifteenth through the seventeenth centuries, as European powers jockeyed over claims to commercial influence in undefined regions, they drew on a shared repertoire of Roman law and emphasized the strategic location of settlements, trading posts, garrisons, and other symbols marking occupation or supporting claims to possession. Riverine regions formed the spine of passageways to imagined rich, interior realms, and sea lanes threaded together commercial networks. The middle decades of the eighteenth century brought an intensification of interimperial competition over global spheres of influence and new regional markets, a conjuncture that stimulated greater attention not only to territorial boundaries but also to strategic points, especially islands, along maritime corridors of control. In the middle and late nineteenth century, as the turn toward territorial empire coincided with the rise of a concept of state sovereignty linked to the exercise of control over bounded space, global rivalries focused more closely on the consolidation of rule and the construction of ordered, if complex, imperial bureaucracies. One result was to bring into sharper relief the theoretical and practical problems posed by mountainous enclaves of supposedly primitive and semiseparate legal administration set within more closely controlled colonial territories. Another was to call into question the project of imagining international law as a force capable of eclipsing empire as a unit of global governance.

An active legal politics of agents in empire also motivated particular strategies for referencing geography. We can observe a peculiar homology between the lived experience of individual Europeans and their descriptions of law and geography. Representations of travel as a sequence of scenes, impressions, and encounters corresponded with the legal imagination of imperial corridors. Residence in enclaves colored understandings of the exercise and reach of delegated legal authority, while also corresponding to understandings of empire as an assemblage of discrete and

[14] This insight might be extended chronologically and expanded methodologically as the basis for rewriting global history, as Cooper proposes in advocating "coming to grips with the lumpiness of power and economic realtions and the way such asymmetries shifted over time." "Globalization," 101.

often widely separated locations. Sojourners and settlers tended to describe landscapes they encountered in ways that affirmed or enhanced their own interests and prerogatives.[15] Reconciling "odd" colonial and "normative" metropolitan law was one aspect of this project, but this distinction was one among many ways of differentiating legal zones.[16] Encounters with locals were clearly very important influences on ideas about nature and assessments of the constraints on the extension of authority. European jurists responded directly to particular problems in interimperial relations and in the process struggled to make sense of legal and territorial variations within and across empires. Anomalous legal spaces of empire emerged from the combination of such processes and presented new challenges to the project of defining imperial sovereignty and establishing its relation to emerging global law.

This chapter lays the groundwork for chronologically ordered case studies of the interrelation of geographic discourse, colonial legal politics, and international law in the production of imperial space between the years 1400 and 1900. It does so by exploring some similarities in the ways that epistemology and experience converged within European geographic and legal imagination, particularly in the early phases of overseas expansion. The first step is to reexamine a prominent and seductive narrative about the progressive rationalization of space in an increasingly interconnected world. European empires were both experienced and imagined as a congeries of repeating but irregular places, and modes of gathering geographic knowledge contributed to this effect. In addition to sponsoring programs of mapping, Europeans accumulated geographic knowledge through itineraries or "tours" and through the collection of thick descriptions of discrete locations, often filtering both kinds of information through legal reports or in connection with legal cases. Law formed an important epistemological framework for the production and dissemination of geographic knowledge, while geographic descriptions encoded ideas about law and sovereignty.

[15] In using the term *sojourners* here and throughout this chapter, I am drawing on Alan Karras's discussion of Scots in the Atlantic world. Karras notes that many Europeans considered themselves transients in empire; they moved frequently and planned ultimately to return. *Sojourners in the Sun: Scottish Migrants in Jamaica and the Chesapeake, 1740–1800* (Ithaca, NY: Cornell University Press, 1992), chap. 1.

[16] The legal tensions between centers and peripheries have received most attention from historians as an element of spatial and legal differentiation within empire. See Jack P. Greene, *Peripheries and Center: Constitutional Development in the Extended Polities of the British Empire and the United States, 1607–1788* (Athens: University of Georgia Press, 1986).

Corridors and Enclaves

There is something logical and perhaps even comforting about a narrative of European empire as generating a slow but steady rationalization of space. Periodic advances in techniques of navigation and mapping, a persistent focus on geographic boundaries as elements of treaty making between imperial rivals, and the accumulation of geographic knowledge of conquered and colonized territories by the colonizers – these trends operate in both older and more recent imperial histories as intimately bound up with the construction of imperial power. Mapping features in this telling as both a technology in the service of empire and a metaphor for the colonial project of mastery through the accumulation and control of knowledge.[17]

This narrative has many virtues. We see that in the early centuries of European colonization, cartographic advances both permitted and were stimulated by imperial claims to vast territories that could be demarcated by lines of latitude and longitude with increasing precision. An early and often-cited example of a sharpening sense of territoriality and its related advance, a conceptual flattening of mappable space, is the 1494 Treaty of Tordesillas, which divided the world into Portuguese and Spanish spheres of influence on either side of a line running between the poles at a distance of 370 leagues from the Cape Verde Islands.[18] The Portuguese in particular have been described as European colonizers who associated the new imperial claims with heavenly markers, using astronomical references to define the scope of their dominions.[19] The Spanish empire engaged multiple bureaucracies in the collection and interpretation of geographic

[17] This section addresses one aspect of what is obviously a much broader literature merging history and geography. See Alan R. H. Baker, *Geography and History: Bridging the Divide* (Cambridge: Cambridge University Press, 2003).

[18] The line is marked on the map in Figure 3.1. Disputes over Portuguese and Spanish claims to the Molucca Islands and in the South Atlantic later focused in part on which island should be the starting place for measuring the 370 leagues to the west. See Jerry Brotton, *Trading Territories: Mapping the Early Modern World* (London: Reaktion Books, 1997), 122–159; Charles E. Nowell, "The Loaisa Expedition and the Ownership of the Moluccas," *The Pacific Historical Review*, 5:4 (1936): 325–336; and W. Rela, *Portugal en las exploraciones del Río de la Plata* (Montevideo, Uruguay: Academia Uruguaya de Historia Marítima y Fluvial, 2002), 139–68.

[19] Jorge Cañizares-Esguerra, *Nature, Empire, and Nation: Explorations of the History of Science in the Iberian World* (Stanford, CA: Stanford University Press, 2006), chap. 4; Patricia Seed, *Ceremonies of Possession in Europe's Conquest of the New World, 1492–1640* (Cambridge: Cambridge University Press, 1995), chap. 4.

information about empire.[20] The British used lines of latitude to mark the northern and southern boundaries of chartered British colonies in North America.[21] In general, maps proved to be valuable, and perhaps essential, political tools both in interimperial controversies over the extent and location of extra-European claims and in intraimperial efforts to consolidate authority and erase the presence and counterclaims of indigenous peoples.[22]

These new ways of staking claims over distant and vast territories – according to the narrative of a progressive rationalizing of space – initiated a process that continued to advance with improved mapping techniques. The association of bounded territory and empire became sharper over the course of the long eighteenth century. By the middle of the nineteenth century, geographic information was clearly established as one of an array of categories of knowledge that played a dual function of making strange landscapes subject to control and rendering them as property – one sense of *dominium*. In this account, imperial mapping functioned as a panopticon writ large, a means for constructing authority through observation. Examples offered in support of this part of the story include the massive undertaking of the Triangulation Survey of British India in the middle decades of the nineteenth century and the reproduction of techniques of land surveying elsewhere in the British Empire in support of the commodification of land along settlement frontiers.[23] By the time political tensions had begun to focus on boundary disputes between various colonial holdings, the relation between bounded territory and political control was taken for granted, so that the very definition of

[20] María M. Portuondo, "Cosmography at the *Casa*, *Consejo*, and *Corte* During the Century of Disovery," in *Science in the Spanish and Portuguese Empires: 1500–1800*, eds. Daniela Bleichmar, Paula De Vos, Kristin Huffine, and Kevin Sheehan, 57–77; and *Secret Science: Spanish Cosmography and the New World* (Chicago: University of Chicago Press, 2009).

[21] See Sack, *Human Territoriality*, chap. 2.

[22] For example, J. B. Harley, "New England Cartography and the Native Americans"; and "Rereading the Maps of the Columbian Encounter," *Annals of the Association of American Geographers* 82, no. 3 (1992), 522–36. And on the legal meanings of mapping within a discourse on possession, see Ken MacMillan, *Sovereignty and Possession in the English New World: The Legal Foundations of Empire, 1576–1640* (Cambridge: Cambridge University Press, 2006).

[23] Edney, *Mapping an Empire*; John C. Weaver, *The Great Land Rush and the Making of the Modern World, 1650–1900* (Montreal: McGill-Queen's University Press, 2006). See also Sudipta Sen, *Distant Sovereignty: National Imperialism and the Origins of British India* (New York: Routledge, 2002).

empire had come to be associated with its mappable extent. In this way, the coloring of the British empire on maps became both a tool of political discourse and an iconic representation of the empire.[24]

Taken together, these observations, and the detailed studies that underlie them, compose a story of territoriality and empire as developing in tandem, along a path that was largely linear. This story is set within a broader narrative of globalization over the same centuries. The concept of globalization has a relatively unexamined but implicit spatial dimension. One expected element is a telescoping of space as the histories of distant regions came into increasingly close relation. Some scholars associate the resulting collapse of space and time with the annihilation of barriers to capitalist expansion. Another powerful but implied spatial element of globalization is the emergence of "the global" as a new scale of human society. The emergence of the global has been variously situated in the late fifteenth century, with the first mapping of the world in the form of a globe; in the sixteenth and seventeenth centuries, with the creation and expansion of global trade networks; in the eighteenth century, with Enlightenment conceptualizations of knowledge and physical systems; in the nineteenth century, with the multiplication of truly global circuits of labor and capital; and in the twentieth century, with the potential eclipse of the nation-state by transnational cultural movements and economic institutions.[25] Such spatial renderings of globalization are

[24] See, e.g., Jeremy Black, *Maps and History: Constructing Images of the Past* (New Haven, CT: Yale University Press, 1997), 58. Edney cites by way of analogy the Borges story about the imperial mapmaker who was called on to make increasingly accurate maps until he finally rendered a map that simply reproduced the kingdom to scale. See Edney, *Mapping an Empire*, 1, 337. For studies of British representations of empire's "empty spaces," see D. Graham Burnett, *Masters of All They Surveyed: Exploration, Geography, and a British El Dorado* (Chicago: University of Chicago Press, 2000); Felix Driver, *Geography Militant: Cultures of Exploration and Empire* (Oxford, U.K.: Blackwell Publishers, 2001); and Patrick Brantlinger, *Rule of Darkness: British Literature and Imperialism, 1830–1914* (Ithaca, N.Y.: Cornell University Press, 1988).

[25] On late fifteenth-century globes and globalization, see Jerry Brotton, "Terrestrial Globalism: Mapping the Globe in Early Modern Europe," in *Mappings*, ed. Denis Cosgrove (London: Reaktion Books, 1999), 71–89; on the birth of the global in the sixteenth century, see Dennis O. Flynn and Arturo Giráldez, "Cycles of Silver: Global Economic Unity through the Mid-Eighteenth Century," *Journal of World History* 13 (2002), 391–427 and Saskia Sassen, *Territory, Authority, Rights*; on the imagination of global systems in the eighteenth-century Scottish Enlightenment, see Clifford Siskin, *Blaming the System: Enlightenment and the Forms of Modernity* (Chicago: University of Chicago Press, forthcoming); and Jonathan Sheehan and Dror Wahrman, "Matters of Scale: The Global Organization of the Eighteenth Century" (paper presented at "Geographies of the Eighteenth Century: The Question of the Global," Indiana University, May 19–22, 2004).

not dependent on the earlier historical narrative of a flattening of space through imperial and colonial expansion, but it is easy to see how the two approaches inform each other. The conceptualization of the global was made possible by representations of distant territories as knowable spaces, while the transcendence of space by market forces assumes at least a logical progression from exploration to conquest, to integration, and to exploitation.[26]

Several ways of complicating and even challenging this story of spatial rationalization in empire are already in view. Historians have noted, for example, that the precision of new coordinates for marking imperial space was matched by the uncertainties of how to recognize the boundaries on the ground and water, and by the relative ignorance of vast territories that were not yet mapped.[27] The Treaty of Tordesillas, for example, provided an awkward guide to sorting out Iberian claims on the other side of the globe, an especially difficult task without accurate measures of longitude.[28] This indeterminacy meant that instead of settling interimperial claims the treaty created new tensions. Similarly, in British North America, the northern and southern boundaries of chartered colonies trailed off into unmapped and contested country to the west. The promise of a straightforward linear extension of territorial claims was foreclosed both by Indian agency and by the impermanence

For a sophisticated account of many strands of globalization across the long nineteenth century, see C. A. Bayly, *The Birth of the Modern World, 1780–1914: Global Connections and Comparisons* (Malden, MA: Blackwell, 2004). Frederick Cooper notes the diversity of arguments about the origins of globalization in the historiography on empire. "Empire Multiplied," *Comparative Studies in Society and History* 46 (2004), 247–72.

[26] Denis Cosgrove argues that representations of the globe "have constructed and communicated the distinctive Western mentality that lies behind the universalist claims of contemporary globalism." *Apollo's Eye: A Cartographic Genealogy of the Earth in the Western Imagination* (Baltimore: Johns Hopkins University Press, 2001), x. For a monograph that argues forcefully for a strong link between geographic representation and political power, see Derek Gregory, *The Colonial Present: Afghanistan, Palestine, Iraq* (Malden, MA: Blackwell, 2004).

[27] For an especially interesting study showing the ways in which the dearth of knowledge about inland territories reinforced imperial powers' focus on the control of maritime and coastal spaces, see Dale Miquelon, "Envisioning the French Empire: Utrecht, 1711–1713," *French Historical Studies* 24, no. 4 (2001): 653–677. And for discussion of this point in a different colonial period and setting, see Nuria Valverde and Antonio Furtado, "Space Production and Spanish Imperial Geopolitics," in Bleichmar, *Science in the Spanish and Portuguese Empires*, 198–215, 209.

[28] Brotton, "Terrestrial Globalism"; Nowell, "The Loaisa Expedition and the Ownership of the Moluccas."

of demarcating a boundary along the ridge of the Appalachian Mountains to separate settler lands from Indian country – a boundary that was difficult to locate and impossible to police.[29] In general, the specificity of geometric coordinates was set against indeterminacy, so that even the most seemingly precise boundaries were contingent and open to interpretation. The importance of this condition is not that it somehow diminished the value of mapping but that it made the relation between imperial order and geographic information inherently unstable.

Also obvious and important as a response to the coupling of empire and the rationalization of space is the critique that the formulation is Eurocentric. The history of mapping global empire between 1400 and 1900 is one that privileges classical influences on European cartography and advances made possible by Western technological change. Recent research documents the rich cartographic traditions of the Muslim and Asian worlds and suggests that cartographic conventions crossed porous borders between world regions.[30] Studies of European mapping in the early colonial world have permitted a greater appreciation of the influence of indigenous representations of geography on imperial mapping.[31] Historians have also recently insisted on expanding the study of geographic knowledge beyond a focus on mapping to include a wider array of narrative elements used to collect and convey geographic knowledge, with the incorporation of information from diverse groups, including non-Europeans.[32] Closer attention to the geographic imagination of

[29] Eric Hinderaker and Peter C. Mancall, *At the Edge of Empire: The Backcountry in British North America* (Baltimore: Johns Hopkins University Press, 2003); D. W. Meinig, *The Shaping of America: A Geographical Perspective on 500 Years of History*, vol. 1 (New Haven: Yale University Press, 1986).

[30] See J. B. Harley and David Woodward, eds., *The History of Cartography*, vol. 2, bk. 1, *Cartography in the Traditional Islamic and South Asian Societies*, and vol. 2, bk. 2, *Cartography in the Traditional East and Southeast Asian Societies* (Chicago: University of Chicago Press, 1992, 1995).

[31] Harley discusses this point using examples from the colonial Americas in "Rereading the Maps of the Columbian Encounter."

[32] Ricardo Padrón perceptively notes that an emphasis on mapping in the Spanish Empire has shifted attention from cultural discourses about space and geography developing outside mapping. Oddly, such discourses took on greater importance as a result of the Spanish crown's close control over the production and dissemination of maps in empire. Ricardo Padrón, *The Spacious Word: Cartography, Literature, and Empire in Early Modern Spain* (Chicago: University of Chicago Press, 2004), 9, 21. See also Rolena Adorno, *The Polemics of Possession in Spanish American Narrative* (New Haven, CT: Yale University Press, 2007); Ralph Bauer, *The Cultural Geography of Colonial American Literatures: Empire, Travel, Modernity* (Cambridge: Cambridge University Press, 2003); Andrew Hadfield, *Literature, Travel, and Colonial Writing in the English Renaissance, 1545–1625* (Oxford: Oxford University Press, 2007).

indigenous peoples has suggested that their sense of territoriality was often not so radically different from that of European settlers.[33]

Such findings have helped to frame more nuanced assessments of the ways that Europeans invoked existing geographic categories in imagining "new" worlds. John Gillis has argued that islands were an important ingredient in the imaginary construction of the Atlantic well before regular cross-Atlantic voyaging brought knowledge of a sea of islands in the Atlantic.[34] Barry Cunliffe proposes a grammar of regional geography that Atlantic Europeans shared and that informed their engagement with the wider Atlantic world: together with islands, dangerous coasts and estuaries composed a trilogy of regional types out of which reconnaissance strategies and overseas settlement patterns were formed.[35] As these authors acknowledge, the lexicon of geographic tropes was available to Europeans from their own religious, literary, and scholarly traditions, and sojourners drew on this symbolic repertoire selectively, and in different combinations, in response to colonial conditions and encounters.[36] For example, the idea of the desert, with its biblical and classical associations, took on new meanings in the context of eighteenth- and nineteenth-century imperial expansion.[37] Changing representations of geographic elements within and outside Europe did not always match, of course. Landscape painters in Europe, for example, were beginning to portray the seacoast as a more domesticated place and a site of leisure at the same time that stories in circulation about the high seas proclaimed the peculiar dangers of escalating maritime violence.[38]

[33] For example, see Nancy Shoemaker, *A Strange Likeness: Becoming Red and White in Eighteenth-Century North America* (New York: Oxford University Press, 2004), chap. 1.

[34] John Gillis argues that islands long continued to be a central organizing category for understanding imperial space, supplanted only in the transition to land-based empires of the nineteenth century. *Islands of the Mind: How the Human Imagination Created the Atlantic World* (New York: Palgrave Macmillan, 2004).

[35] Barry Cunliffe, *Facing the Ocean: The Atlantic and Its Peoples, 8000 BC–AD 1500* (Oxford: Oxford University Press, 2001), chaps. 1–2.

[36] In his rich study of European cultural associations with landscape, Simon Schama notes the "surprising endurance through the centuries" of landscape myths and memories. *Landscape and Memory* (New York: Vintage, 1995), 15.

[37] Donald Worster sees it as the organizing trope of western U.S. imperial projects. *Rivers of Empire: Water, Aridity, and the Growth of the American West* (Oxford: Oxford University Press, 1992). See also Patricia Nelson Limerick, *Desert Passages: Encounters with the American Deserts* (Albuquerque: University of New Mexico Press, 1985).

[38] See Alain Corbin, *The Lure of the Sea: The Discovery of the Seaside in the Western World, 1750–1840* (Berkeley: University of California Press, 1994); and Philip E. Steinberg, *The Social Construction of the Ocean* (Cambridge: Cambridge University Press, 2001).

Lived experience, too, played an important role in determining when and how Europeans would invoke familiar geographic tropes. As Carter has argued in relation to the records of Captain James Cook's voyages, the perception of space as an element unfolding before the traveler's gaze merged geography and storytelling in Europeans' accounts. Points along travel routes corresponded to moments within a sequence of events. Carter describes naming as the activity that most clearly blended the ambition of geographic mastery with the production of a kind of knowledge inseparable from movement through space, producing what Carter calls a "traveling epistemology" in which names represented points of arrival and departure. Cook, for example, changed the hopeful name Endeavour Bay, given on his ship's first arrival in New Zealand, to Poverty Bay after the HMS *Endeavour*'s violent encounter with Maoris there.[39]

We can draw from these insights in noting other processes that lead us to amend the story of the rationalization of space in empire. Both in sojourners' experiences of space and in the production of knowledge about distant geographies, Europeans adapted old strategies and created new ways of describing territory as differentiated, fragmented, and uneven. The experience of travel as movement along passages to discrete locations corresponded to ways of making sense of new landscapes and conveying information about them. In contrast to the rationalization of space through progressively accurate mapping, this project emphasized a set of repeating geographic features and, within this grammar, attention to distinctive qualities, the oddities or singularities of the specific case. Rather than producing the image of blank territories that could be known and dominated, this parallel process insisted that some parts of the world, and even integral parts of empire, might resist categorization or control.

Consider the contrasts and connections between spatial perceptions of maps and tours.[40] Accounts of voyages took the form of tours, purposeful blends of individual, eyewitness testimony, political reporting,

[39] Paul Carter, *The Road to Botany Bay: An Essay in Spatial History* (London: Faber and Faber, 1987), 31, 15.

[40] Michel de Certeau discusses the contrast of maps and tours, drawing on research reported in the 1970s on New York City with respondents who were asked to describe their apartments. The research shows that while some people in describing a particular space tend to draw maps, a larger group of people convey geographic knowledge in the form of a tour. Asked about the layout of an apartment, for example, they describe the sights encountered in moving from one room to another. *The Practice of Everyday Life*, trans. Steven Rendall (Berkeley: University of California Press, 2002), 118–21. Padrón, in *Spacious Word*, explains that such perceptions of space based on sensory experience informed "itinerary maps" or "way-finding maps" (55, 58).

and cataloguing of nature. In following courses marked by coastlines, rivers, mountain ridges, ocean currents, and island chains, chronicles presented the natural landscape in the form of passageways that were also objects of potential imperial control. Just one example, all the more interesting because it appears in a relatively obscure account, is provided by the Dominican friar Gabriel Salazar in describing part of his trip in 1620 through the southeastern Maya lowlands:

> I left Guatemala and turned right onto Lake Izabal, where I took a canoe at Xocolo and, following the coast, arrived at Tzoite.... I came and entered the town of Xibun.... From here I entered Çactan, and from Çactan entered Chinamit, both being on lagoons and rivers of saltwater. From Chinamit, they took me by water to what is an inlet of an arm of the great lagoon. From there, going through the ranch of Pedro Hernández, I came to Bacalar. All this was by canoe. As you know, then I came to the city of Mérida, and from there to Campeche there was always a range of hills on my left-hand side.[41]

As with the rest of Salazar's voyage, reported in the form of an itinerary, it would be difficult even now to map this sequence of moves. Yet the geographic references were not without meaning; they supported Salazar's claims to eyewitness authority, traced a route connecting markers of Spanish presence ("the ranch of Pedro Hernández," "the city of Mérida"), and served as a guide to future travelers.[42]

Stopping places and destinations punctuated imperial corridors. The voyage chronicle, with its underlying narrative of movement along passageways, had its corollary in the descriptions and visual representations of discrete locations. Widely produced views of settlements and ports, and the plans of fortifications at strategic places along trading corridors, formed another kind of repository for knowledge about the

[41] S. Gabriel Salazar, "Brief Description of the Manché: The Roads, Towns, Lands, and Inhabitants," in *Lost Shores, Forgotten Peoples: Spanish Explorations of the South East Maya Lowlands: Chronicles of the New World Order*, ed. Lawrence H. Feldman (Durham, NC: Duke University Press, 2000), 22–54, 34.

[42] Both local guides and European travelers tended to organize geographic information around significant events along routes. In the early modern Atlantic, Indians and Europeans appeared to share understandings of the landscape as intelligible through the tracing of past events (see Shoemaker, *A Strange Likeness*, chap. 1). The geographic markers might even overlap in memorializing episodes of violence between Indians and Europeans. Consider another example from Salazar's journal summarizing the accomplishments of his voyage in relation to the murder by Indians of another Dominican friar: "I had traveled up the river to where died Friar Domingo de Vico... and those who go upstream just as those who go downstream can take their bearing and meet where Father Friar Domingo died, a three-day journey from Cobán" (53–4, in *Lost Shores*).

extra-European world. Sponsors of overseas ventures commissioned collections of town or harbor views modeled on the island books (*isolarios*) produced for Mediterranean navigation, in which individual islands appeared as "disconnected from all spatial markers except for a scale and a compass rose."[43] Elements of the tradition influenced the Spanish imperial project of *Relaciones Geográficas*, thick descriptions of Spanish imperial regions in response to questionnaires, including both sketch maps and prose accounts of landscape, governance, and settlement patterns.[44] The newly prominent subfield of descriptive geography and a related genre, chorography, provided an epistemological framework for representations of empire as a set or series of discrete locations.[45] Together with notions circulating within literary, religious, and popular cultural circuits about the properties of particular kinds of geographic sites, chroniclers could rely on an emerging lexicon of descriptive geographic categories: familiar and seemingly universal elements such as harbors, forests, rivers, mountains, hills, coasts, and islands.

[43] On chorography and city views, see Richard L. Kagan and Fernando Marías, *Urban Images of the Hispanic World, 1493–1793* (New Haven, CT: Yale University Press, 2000), chap. 1. On the development of the *isolario* in the Mediterranean region and the broader influence of representing islands as "self-contained . . . worlds," see Cosgrove, *Apollo's Eye*, 90–95; quotes from 94.

[44] Padrón, in *Spacious Word*, points out that many of these maps fit the pattern of wayfinding maps, which were often referred to not as maps but as sketch maps or drawings. He identifies a Spanish term, *croquis*, for this genre of sketch maps (55, 76–7).

[45] On the connections between descriptive geography and ideas about early English empire, see Lesley B. Cormack, *Charting an Empire: Geography at the English Universities, 1580–1620* (Chicago: University of Chicago Press, 1997), chaps. 4–5. Cormack also traces the influence of studying geography on a generation of men involved with overseas ventures; in early seventeenth-century England, many of the men involved in the promotion of empire had studied descriptive geography and chorography at Oxford and Cambridge. In the Spanish world, cartographic projects reflected an emphasis on local description and knowledge about pieces of empire. The maps produced as parts of the *Relaciones Geográficas* were of microregions, and the project was conceptually related to the long-standing interest of the Spanish crown in producing accurate views of cities in the empire. See Barbara E. Mundy, *The Mapping of New Spain: Indigenous Cartography and the Maps of the* Relaciones Geográficas (Chicago: University of Chicago Press, 1996). On the production and style of views of Spanish cities, see Kagan and Marías, *Urban Images*. On the role of descriptive geography in merging and then supplanting cosmology (as a discipline based on classical learning) with the collection of knowledge through observation, see María M. Portuondo, "Spanish Cosmography and the New World Crisis," in *Más allá de la leyenda negra: España y la revolución científica*, eds. William Eamon and Victor Navarro Brotóns (Valencia, Spain: Instituto de Historia de la Ciencia y Documentación López Piñero, Universitat de Valencia, 2007). Padrón explicitly notes in *Spacious Word* that the perception of space undergirding many descriptions of geography in the early Spanish empire involved the "representation of territory as a network of routes connecting preferred destinations of travel" (58).

As with the experience of travel as a kind of tour that could be narrated, reference to a set of geographic tropes to characterize new landscapes brought together epistemology and experience.[46] Using such categories required both forming analogies to other landscapes and identifying the ways in which the particular instance of the type was unique. The first step in defining this singularity was often a comparison or contrast with European landscapes.[47] For example, Europeans' understanding of what constituted a riverine region was modeled on the geography of river basins located in Atlantic Europe.[48] Newly encountered rivers invited references to familiar waterways, either as analogies or to point out exceptional features.[49] In part, this exercise implied a reference to Europe as the place of accumulated knowledge about, and the home of, ideal-typical geographies. But the assignment of singularity to places and regions necessarily also involved a more open-ended and multiform discourse about global variation. Singularity was defined not just in relation to ideal types associated with the metropole but also against a multiplicity of other widely distributed examples. A particular bay, for example, could be described as lacking or sharing the features of an ideal-typical bay modeled on European experience and understandings, but it also had to be distinguished from other bays around it – otherwise, the description had no practical value and did not enhance the authority of the author as eyewitness.[50]

[46] In *Road to Botany Bay*, Carter distinguishes this "traveling mode of knowledge" from the categorizing epistemology championed by and exemplified in the work of the botanist Joseph Banks (9, 18). He also views Banks's taxonomical approach to knowledge as aspatial (21). But I see colonial officials' interest in developing imperial typologies as clearly connected to a spatial discourse. See especially Chapter 5 in this volume.

[47] Eric J. Leed points out that travel in the early modern world became identified as a philosophical and scientific project precisely because it implied and required making comparisons in order to acquire knowledge. The comparison came to be regarded "as a defense against the strange and unusual." *The Mind of the Traveler: From Gilgamesh to Global Tourism* (New York: Basic Books, 1991), 68. Pimentel characterizes Baroque science as a combination of analogy-building and the search for "unusual phenomena." Juan Pimentel, "Baroque Natures: Juan E. Nieremberg, American Wonders, and Preterimperial Natural History," in Bleichmar, *Science in the Spanish and Portuguese Empires: 1500–1800*, 93–111, 107.

[48] This point is made in Cunliffe, *Facing the Ocean*. It is discussed in depth in Chapter 2 of this volume.

[49] Columbus, for example, on his first voyage, came across a river "as big as the Guadalquivir coming through Cordova" and gave it the same name. O. C. Dunn and James E. Kelley, eds., *The* Diario *of Christopher Columbus's First Voyage to America, 1492–1493* (Norman: University of Oklahoma Press, 1989), 229.

[50] Paula De Vos notes that "the search for the rare and the singular" conferred prestige well into the eighteenth century. "The Rare, the Singular, and the Extraordinary: Natural

The assignment of singularity occurred precisely at the moment when comparisons broke down. The process is easy to track in the many descriptions of landscape and geography in voyage chronicles that move from metaphor to exception. Consider just one example: Columbus's descriptions of harbors on his first voyage to the New World. Hopeful of finding estuaries and harbors where ships might lie safely and where large settlements might cluster, Columbus carefully described each bay. He often used European referents, as he did in comparing an estuary to the mouth of the Tagus River and a large harbor to the Bay of Cádiz.[51] European standards also provided the measures of a good harbor, and Columbus noted when a particular bay might "hold all the ships of Spain" or have "room for a hundred ships."[52] But comparisons faltered. In a move related to the discourse of the marvelous, Columbus found himself without referents to describe a harbor that he found to be superior to all the others he had encountered.[53] The unique harbor was so nearly perfect that it seemed an "enchanted" place that "one might not wish to leave." Columbus worried that "a thousand tongues would not suffice" to describe the place. Abandoning references to European geographies, he finally resorted to the quotidian metaphor of "a soup bowl" to describe it.[54]

Identifying singularities in nature was in some ways very similar to drawing attention to marvels and prodigies, those oddities that defined norms and appeared to multiply at the margins of the civilized world. Yet, as Lorraine Daston and Katherine Park have pointed out, a geographic feature had the qualities of "a regular anomaly." It "expressed rather than violated the created order of nature." Whereas "*individual* anomalous occurrences" might elicit alarm and even horror, patterns of geographic anomaly signaled the diversity of nature and prompted expressions of wonder.[55] In the sixteenth and seventeenth centuries, the new prominence in both European natural philosophy and European

History and the Collection of Curiosities in the Spanish Empire," in Bleichmar, *Science in the Spanish and Portuguese Empires: 1500–1800*, 271–289, 287.

[51] Dunn and Kelley, *The* Diario, 201 and 177.

[52] Dunn and Kelley, *The* Diario, 163, 173.

[53] On the discourse of the marvelous, see Lorraine Daston and Katharine Park, *Wonders and the Order of Nature, 1150–1750* (New York: Zone Books, 2001); and Stephen Jay Greenblatt, *Marvelous Possessions: The Wonder of the New World* (Chicago: University of Chicago Press, 1991).

[54] Dunn and Kelley, *The* Diario, 181–3. See, again, Carter, in *Road to Botany Bay*, on the "indescribable" (44) nature of Australia when English observers abandoned metaphors.

[55] Daston and Park, *Wonders and the Order of Nature*, 50. Emphasis in original.

travel of a science of particulars, together with the necessary emphasis on descriptions of singularity, challenged such distinctions by proposing the possibility of arriving at general truths from the investigation of the sights and sounds attached to specific examples of phenomenological types.[56] This shift meant that, increasingly, empiricism was "grainy with facts," with fragments of information or events that fit uncomfortably with theory.[57] It also meant that discerning irregularities depended on the testimony of witnesses, and on their reports of perceptions and experiences.[58]

Such epistemological shifts help to explain the growing enthusiasm for modes of representing geography through narratives or tours and through descriptions of singular examples of universal types. Imperial geographies were fragmented in patterns produced through the naturally occurring repetition of features such as rivers, bays, and mountains, and then further variegated by sometimes unexplained local irregularities. Natural philosophers sought to devise rules that would explain both regular and irregular features while at the same time increasingly championing a view of nature as stubbornly productive of anomaly – as Bacon put it, "full of... winding and intricate folds and knots."[59]

This background to an emerging imperial geographic imagination was deeply influenced in theory and in practice by law as an epistemological framework. Law has been largely left aside in recent treatments of the collection and organization of geographic information in empire, and in the analysis of European travel narratives.[60] The oversight is significant.[61]

[56] Daston and Park, *Wonders and the Order of Nature*, chap. 4. On the emergence of a "knowledge... of particulars" in Spanish writings on the New World, see Antonio Barrera-Osorio, "Nature and Experience in the New World: Spain and England in the Making of the New Science," in Eamon and Navarro Brotóns, *Más allá de la leyenda negra*, 132.

[57] Daston and Park, *Wonders and the Order of Nature*, 237.

[58] See Daston and Park, *Wonders and the Order of Nature*, 237; Barrera-Osorio, "Nature and Experience in the New World"; and Juan Pimentel, who discusses the unstable relation between travelers and verisimilitude in *Testigos del mundo: Ciencia, literature y viajes en la ilustración*. Madrid: Marcial Pons, 2003, chap. 1.

[59] Daston and Park, *Wonders and the Order of Nature*, 240.

[60] An exception is Portuondo, who notes that Spanish cosmographers and *letrados* were closely associated and occasionally positioned as scientific rivals. "Cosmography at the *Casa*, *Consejo*, and *Corte*," 69. See also *Secret Science*, chap. 3.

[61] It is an especially egregious omission if we credit Donald R. Kelley's argument that the "science of law" rather than natural philosophy shaped "the principal questions, terminology, and lines of investigation of the study of humanity" in Western history, or even the more modest claim that "ideas of law were often homologous with, if not

As we shall see, law and legal practices provided methods for the collection and organization of geographic knowledge. Law also operated as a medium for conflicts over the size and shape of imperial territories. Further, because conflicts were spatially distributed and legal stories or cases possessed a spatial dimension, associations formed with surprising ease between patterns of law and landscape. As the associations forged new categories of social space and drew attention to variations within those categories, observers struggled to define their fit within broader frameworks of spatial and legal ordering. Drawing further attention to forces of fragmentation and variation, the legal history of empire ultimately adds to the critique of narratives pairing the rationalization of space with expanding imperial control.

By way of illustrating the multifaceted relation of law and geography and before examining these qualities of legal cultures in empire more closely, we can return once more to the Treaty of Tordesillas, that exercise in line drawing often considered the quintessential example of the tightening connection between European imperial ambitions and the rationalization of global space. I have already mentioned some ways in which the difficulties in finding the lines converted the treaty into something less than a simple division of the world. A closer look at the legal meanings of the agreement reveals further layers of complexity. The treaty followed a series of papal bulls on the division of territories between the Iberian crowns but represented a peace pact rather than a ruling over Iberian powers.[62] Further, the accord opened the way to continued jockeying over

indistinguishable from, ideas of natural order or disorder." *The Human Measure: Social Thought in the Western Legal Tradition* (Cambridge, MA: Harvard University Press, 1990), 3.

[62] It specifically asked that in future the pope "order his bulls in regard to it" and incorporate within them "the tenor of this agreement." ("Treaty between Spain and Portugal concluded at Tordesillas, June 7, 1494," Document 9 in Frances Davenport and C. O. Paullin, *European Treaties bearing on the History of the United States and its Dependencies* [Washington, D.C.: Carnegie Institution of Washington, 1917], 99.) The treaty thus marked the beginning of the end of universal papal authority rather than a high point in the workings of Christendom as a transnational legal order presided over by the pope. It affirmed the importance of Catholicism as a rationale for empire and undermined papal authority by authorizing sovereigns to act on their own to oppose a threat by infidels. Portugal used this argument to justify unilateral military action in parts of North Africa nominally under Spanish control. The Spaniards for their part never sought papal approval for their conquest of the Canary Islands but relied instead on the justification of conquest over infidels. This was a "politics of facts on the ground" or of "faits accomplis" ("la política de hechos consumados") and a strategically motivated challenge to papal authority. See Santiago Olmedo Bernal, *El dominio del Atlántico en la baja Edad*

claims by awarding something short of full title to both Iberian powers in their respective spheres of influence.[63] In recognizing that ownership attached only to lands in each sphere that had been or would be discovered by a crown's agents, the treaty bestowed "the right to navigate the said sea within certain specified limits and seek out and take possession of newly discovered lands."[64] Sovereignty was not a given, in other words, but would depend on recurring proofs, including mapping, description, the founding of political communities, ceremonies recognizing new vassals, and administrative acts designed to support claims to discovery and possession. The same treaty that appears to represent the extra-European world as an object of European imperial rule instead shows the ways it stimulated a fluid geographic discourse and open-ended legal politics.

Legal Posturing and Imperial Knowledge

Often portrayed as actions preliminary to conquest and settlement, even the earliest European overseas voyages were colonial projects guided by administrative routines and by law. We tend to think of legal cultures as differing considerably across European polities, but early expeditions displayed variations of familiar legal forms, and Europeans drew elements from a widely shared legal repertoire.[65] Like colonial polities, every collection of travelers or settlers operated on the assumption of a legal relationship binding subject and sovereign, and every such group recognized a formal division of authority between lower and higher levels of legal hierarchy.

Media: Los títulos jurídicos de la expansión peninsular hasta el Tratado de Tordesillas (Valladolid, Spain: Sociedad V° Centenario del Tratado de Tordesillas, 1995), 420–2; quote on 428. For an account of the legal rationales for Iberian expansion that explains clearly the organizing tension between canon law and the thrust of secular authority, see James Muldoon, *Popes, Lawyers, and Infidels: The Church and the Non-Christian World, 1250–1550* (Philadelphia: University of Pennsylvania Press, 1979).

[63] On John Dee's lawyerly interpretation of the grant as marking a sphere of influence rather than a gift of title, see MacMillan, *Sovereignty and Possession in the English New World*, 67–74. See also Steinberg, *The Social Construction of the Ocean*, 76–77.

[64] Davenport, *European Treaties*, 99.

[65] I am not denying profound differences across empires and even within them but am choosing just to emphasize the continuities arising from referencing the same or similar legal concepts and sources, often indirectly. For an interesting study of the varieties in legal culture that could have been generated by the concentration of settlers from different microregions, see Christopher Tomlins, "The Legal Cartography of Colonization, the Legal Polyphony of Settlement: English Intrusions on the American Mainland in the 17th Century," *Law and Social Inquiry* 26, no. 2 (2001): 315–72.

These broad rubrics left most of the details of imperial legal administration undefined. Many people operating as legal officials in empire had no formal training in law, and even those with training found few clear precedents and wide discretion in interpreting, applying, and inventing procedures and rules.[66] Distance nurtured innovation. Metropolitan attempts to impose orderly administration often faltered when local officials saw enforcement as a threat to their interests. The quip that captures this dynamic for the Spanish Empire – "obedezco pero no cumplo" ("I obey but do not comply") – had its counterpart in other empires and in tactics such as failing to send requested records back to European courts or blaming divergent local practices on delays in receiving imperial directives.[67] Yet we should not represent distance and noncompliance as forming the only barriers to the creation of coherent imperial legal orders. Metropolitan efforts to construct internally consistent legal orders were desultory at best. Periods of energetic and often ineffective imperial legal planning interrupted longer spans of time when metropolitan officials mainly reacted to shifting circumstances and recognized the advantages of ad hoc solutions in loosely conforming systems of law.

The most important sources of variation derived from local legal politics. Europeans far from home reenacted legal rituals as they remembered them and imperfectly reconstructed legal practices and arguments. In early centuries this devotion to what I will call "legal posturing" can be explained partly by a system of rewards that required subjects to sustain their ties to sovereigns and seek future patronage on the basis of evidence that they had advanced crown interests. Litigiousness in Europe also urged travelers to devise and then stick to legal scripts in positioning themselves to fend off litigation or indictments.[68] The influence of law on the actions of sojourners and settlers was grounded in their knowledge

[66] On the pervasive influence of medieval canon law on the "legally trained" men who "played the central role in shaping the terms of political discourse in the early modern world as it concerned international relations," see James Muldoon, "Discovery, Grant, Charter, Conquest, or Purchase," in *The Many Legalities of Early America*, ed. Christopher L. Tomlins and Bruce H. Mann (Chapel Hill: University of North Carolina Press, 2001), 25–46, 26; and Muldoon, *Popes, Lawyers, and Infidels.*

[67] For example, Mary Sarah Bilder traces the subtle noncompliance of Rhode Island officials to requests from London to send lists of local legislation. Imperial officials could not disapprove of local laws that they did not know about. *The Transatlantic Constitution: Colonial Legal Culture and the Empire* (Cambridge, MA: Harvard University Press, 2004).

[68] On litigiousness, see Richard L. Kagan, *Lawsuits and Litigants in Castile, 1500–1700* (Chapel Hill: University of North Carolina Press, 1981).

about past legal practice as well as suppositions about possible future legal entanglements.[69] Other forms of legal posturing included the inventive referencing of various sources of law in support of often ad hoc local policies.[70] Imperial agents regularly invoked elements of Roman and canon law; cited juridical passages from the Bible; and reasoned by analogy, referring to procedures and practices from home while working with very incomplete knowledge or devising intentionally selective applications of metropolitan law.[71] Legal cultures, including an active legal imagination connecting lessons from law to everyday practices, were already diffuse and varied in Europe.[72] Imperial sojourners were not simply failing to apply law correctly; they were continuing inventive applications of law as a familiar kind of strategic cultural practice.

The importance of legal posturing is reflected in the pervasive (but often overlooked) reporting about law in early overseas ventures. Scholars have tended to regard voyage chronicles as falling within the genre of travel literature, but many accounts of early voyaging are better understood as examples of legal writing, produced by chroniclers who were also royal officials or by participants in overseas commercial ventures positioning themselves or others in relation to ongoing or anticipated cases. From an early stage in Atlantic voyaging, for example, royal interests compelled documentation of mariners' and merchants' activities by legal personnel. The Portuguese king placed *escribães* (legal officials who served both as scribes and notaries; in Spanish, *escribanos*) on crews of early expeditions to Atlantic islands and West Africa and charged them

[69] For an example of the adaptation of a legal routine in constituting political communities in Spanish America, see Tamar Herzog's study of *vecindad*, or membership in municipalities. Tamar Herzog, *Defining Nations: Immigrants and Citizens in Early Modern Spain and Spanish America* (New Haven, CT: Yale University Press, 2003).

[70] For an example of a study seeking to understand an aspect of legal history through the analysis of types of narratives, see Natalie Zemon Davis, *Fiction in the Archives: Pardon Tales and Their Tellers in Sixteenth-Century France* (Stanford, CA: Stanford University Press, 1987).

[71] One kind of legal positioning has been studied by John Philip Reid, who found that the reputation for lawlessness on the overland trail to California in the mid-nineteenth century did not match a surprising orderliness in the legal treatment of property and persons on the trail. In the absence of formal legal institutions and enforcers, people tended to act out legal practices as remembered. *Law for the Elephant: Property and Social Behavior on the Overland Trail* (San Marino, CA: Huntington Library, 1997).

[72] A rich and persuasive study of legal imagination is that of Paul Raffield, *Images and Cultures of Law in Early Modern England: Justice and Political Power, 1558–1660* (Cambridge: Cambridge University Press, 2004). See also John Barrell, *Imagining the King's Death: Figurative Treason, Fantasies of Regicide, 1793–1796* (Oxford: Oxford University Press, 2000).

with producing written records of the voyages.[73] Private investment and interest in crown patronage also motivated the production of chronicles that were based on, or overlapped with, legal documents. An early example is the fifteenth-century narrative of a voyage along the African coast, Eustache de la Fosse's *Voiaige à la Guinée*, which probably drew from a deposition recorded to inform financial backers of the reasons for the loss of the ship and its cargo.[74] Acutely aware of the need to provide proofs to the crown of their meritorious actions if they were to obtain future patronage in the empire, Spaniards recorded and collected sworn statements, or *probanzas*, about expeditions. These testimonials were more practical and prosaic than the flowery descriptions that have been used to characterize Spaniards' visions of New World landscapes and encounters as "marvelous."[75] Some letters to the crown, such as the one to the Spanish king that Orellana penned after he had abandoned Gonzalo Pizarro and his company on a doomed expedition in the Amazon region, sought to stave off charges of disloyalty or to improve the chances for future imperial postings. Letters from ship captains or merchants to sponsors or business partners at home similarly sought to present information in ways intended to bolster particular legal arguments; for example, a captain reporting a storm might be recording a routine event in the log while also adding to a narrative about his valor in the face of adversity to deflect a suit or to prepare the way for an insurance claim for his sponsor.[76]

Such pervasive engagement in legal writing reflected a deeper influence of the law. On a fundamental level, law represented an important epistemological framework for the organization and evaluation of evidence of

[73] The Spanish adopted this practice in 1476 for voyages to Guinea. The *escribanos* were regarded as an extra layer of protection of the crown's interests and were also charged with keeping an inventory of all cargo, as well as records of purchases and sales. P. E. Russell, "Castilian Documentary Sources for the History of the Portuguese Expansion in Guinea, in the Last Years of the Reign of Dom Afonso V," in *Portugal, Spain, and the African Atlantic, 1343–1490: Chivalry and Crusade from John of Gaunt to Henry the Navigator and Beyond* (Brookfield, VT: Variorum, 1995), XII, 1–23.

[74] P. E. Russell, "New Light on the Text of Eustache de la Fosse's *Voiaige à la Guinée* (1479–1480)," in Russell, *Portugal, Spain, and the African Atlantic*, XIII, 1–13, see especially 13.

[75] James Lockhart and Enrique Otte comment on the "often down-to-earth first reports on new areas" and the contrast of their tone with that of later writings. *Letters and People of the Spanish Indies: Sixteenth Century* (Cambridge: Cambridge University Press, 1976), 1. See also Greenblatt, *Marvelous Possessions*.

[76] On the influence of insurance law on reporting by slave ship captains to their sponsors, see James Oldham, "Insurance Litigation Involving the *Zong* and Other British Slave Ships, 1780–1807," *Journal of Legal History* 28 (2007): 299–318.

all kinds, and of geographic information in particular.[77] Even the most informally organized and unofficially sponsored ventures boasted some sort of legal structure, which was a precondition of internal order, the securing of profits, and the recognition of claims. Not surprisingly, this structure encouraged reliance on legal procedures for establishing truth claims, especially because law had moved in early modern Europe more quickly than science had toward an understanding of discrete events as facts supported by evidence.[78] As imperial agents gathered information from native guides and other locals, depositions and other routines for questioning witnesses served as models for the interrogation of many voyagers on their return.[79] Such gathered testimony seconded the most highly valued form of evidence, which in the Roman-canon legal tradition was eyewitness testimony.[80] So, for example, the legal training of Juan López de Velasco, who oversaw the collection of data for the *Relaciones de Indias*, together with his experience collecting notarized depositions to investigate New World governance, led him to favor signed, eyewitness statements as the basis of information about New World geographies.[81] The privileged status of first-person accounts added to

[77] Daniel Lord Smail makes the interesting argument that multiple cartographic sensibilities in late medieval Marseille gradually gave way, through the influence of property disputes, to an emphasis on a notarial template for describing space. Other similar processes may have been at work to enhance the currency of legal discourses about geography, including other practices that, like the methods for marking the perimeter of properties, merged the individual experience of space with cartographic representations and legal forms. *Imaginary Cartographies: Possession and Identity in Late Medieval Marseille* (Ithaca, NY: Cornell University Press, 1999).

[78] See Barbara J. Shapiro, *A Culture of Fact: England, 1550–1720* (Ithaca, NY: Cornell University Press, 2003).

[79] Some travelers' accounts were recorded as sworn depositions. On Hakluyt's compilation of data on Drake's circumnavigation, see E. G. R. Taylor, *Late Tudor and Early Stuart Geography, 1583–1650: A Sequel to Tudor Geography, 1485–1583* (London: Methuen, 1934), 19.

[80] The importance of eyewitnesses in establishing truth claims is discussed in Anthony Pagden, *European Encounters with the New World from Renaissance to Romanticism* (New Haven, CT: Yale University Press, 1993), chap. 2. See also Barbara J. Shapiro, *"Beyond Reasonable Doubt" and "Probable Cause": Historical Perspectives on the Anglo-American Law of Evidence* (Berkeley: University of California Press, 1993).

[81] The method had been adopted early in gathering information from pilots about navigation routes. Returning pilots were presented with questionnaires that were not unlike those administered to witnesses providing sworn statements (*probanzas*) in legal cases. Cosmographers then interpreted and consolidated this information. See Alison Sandman, "Controling Knowledge: Navigation, Cartography, and Secrecy in the Early Modern Spanish Atlantic," in *Science and Empire in the Atlantic World*, ed. James Delbourgo and Nicholas Dew (New York: Routledge, 2008), 31–52, 42; and Antonio Barrera-Osorio, "Empiricism in the Spanish Atlantic World," in *Science and Empire in the*

incentives to produce and disseminate chronicles in the form of itineraries. In England, where many of the men involved in championing North Atlantic voyages had legal training, the elder Richard Hakluyt's career as a lawyer might have accounted for the decision of the younger Richard Hakluyt to assemble first-person voyage accounts as if they constituted an array of evidence instead of composing a comprehensive narrative of English overseas travel.[82]

If it is difficult to trace with precision the influence of legal practices on approaches to the collection of knowledge about the extra-European world, it is partly because the law and geography shared a "malleable epistemological foundation."[83] That is, approaches to the production of knowledge were not pre-formed but developed in part in response to practices and conflicts in empires. As with the elaboration of geographic knowledge, understandings of law depended upon analogizing and categorization. Such approaches cut across late medieval and early modern European polities, in part because a broad Humanist project sought to identify general principles in Roman law that could accommodate new legal phenomena, conditions, and cases.[84] Also as with geographic knowledge, imperial ventures provided new stimuli to analogy-driven approaches to legal analysis. Disputes in empires were defined simultaneously as similar to other conflicts and as in some respects singular. The very qualities that made law transplantable to distant places guaranteed that legal conflicts in those places would generate phenomena resistant to analogies or categorization.

It might be said that the whole of the imperial world represented a zone of legal anomaly vis-à-vis the metropole. Certainly we can find important strands of legal discourse and administrative change focused on defining

Atlantic World, ed. James Delbourgo and Nicholas Dew (New York: Routledge, 2008), 177–202.

[82] Taylor, *Late Tudor and Early Stuart Geography*, 14. See also Peter C. Mancall, *Hakluyt's Promise: An Elizabethan's Obsession for an English America* (New Haven, CT: Yale University Press, 2007). On the legal training of men involved in early empire, see MacMillan, *Sovereignty and Possession in the English New World*, especially his comments on the influence of legal training on John Dee (67–74).

[83] This is Portuondo's phrase characterizing sixteenth-century Spanish cosmography; it is useful as a broader description of approaches to knowledge. *Secret Science*, 11.

[84] I stop short of the claim that analogizing and categorization were universal qualities of legal epistemology. On this point, see Bernard S. Jackson, "Analogy in Legal Science: Some Comparative Observations," in *Legal Knowledge and Analogy: Fragments of Legal Epistemology, Hermeneutics, and Linguistics*, ed. Patrick Nerhot (Dordrecht, The Netherlands: Kluwar, 1991), 145–64. And see also Geoffrey Samuel, *Epistemology and Method in Law* (Burlington, VT: Ashgate, 2003), chap. 1.

the extra-European world as legally different from realms closer to the seats of sovereign power. British colonial legal histories often begin with an analysis of Calvin's Case in 1608, which occasioned Sir Edward Coke's ruling that the protections of the common law did not extend beyond England to the crown's other realms, though the king's legal authority and English subjecthood were both projected beyond England's borders.[85] In the Spanish Empire, efforts by the crown to limit ecclesiastical authority and to create new institutions for Indian subjects can be viewed as marking foundational moments for divergence between metropolitan and colonial law. Yet, as with representations of extra-European geographies as variants of familiar European types, this exercise of defining colonies as legally different in relation to the metropole paralleled a more diffuse and fluid project of characterizing multiple and repeating zones of legal variation.[86] The discourse and politics about subjecthood (and, later, citizenship) and divided sovereignty provided part of the framework for describing legally uneven imperial territories. Reporting on conditions in empire meanwhile teased out subtle distinctions between ownership and jurisdiction, natural and positive law, and direct and indirect rule while recommending their recombination in new forms. As with singular geographies, legal anomalies urged new ways of arranging knowledge precisely because they appeared to defy categorization. Some colonial officials themselves used the word "anomalous" to describe places for which they could not easily define structures of law or the nature of sovereignty. Scholars in Europe, including Alberico Gentili, Hugo Grotius, Jeremy Bentham, and Henry Sumner Maine, took up this challenge in responding

[85] Recent analyses of Calvin's Case caution that it should not be read as a blueprint for subsequent imperial legal policy. Christopher Tomlins notes that although Coke offered a distinction between the legal status of colonies of conquest and inherited realms, this difference did not solidify into a contrast between conquered and settled territories until later, and it was a formula that even then left most questions about legal administration open to interpretation. "Law, Population, Labor," in *The Cambridge History of Law in America*, ed. Michael Grossberg and Christopher Tomlins (Cambridge: Cambridge University Press, 2008), 1:211–52. Daniel Hulsebosch has argued that Coke also laid the basis for viewing the protections of common law as culturally diffuse and transportable. *Constituting Empire: New York and the Transformation of Constitutionalism in the Atlantic World, 1664–1830* (Chapel Hill: University of North Carolina Press, 2005), 22–28.

[86] William Nelson argues that historians have lavished too much attention on studying the continuities and discontinuities of law in British North American colonies with law in England. He suggests that the project is flawed in part because many metropolitan legal processes remain opaque. He proposes refocusing North American colonial legal history on comparisons across colonies. *The Common Law in Colonial America* (New York: Oxford University Press, 2008).

to individual cases that revealed peculiar interimperial entanglements and intraimperial puzzles. At the same time, anomalous legal zones were so common that they came to be regarded as integral and expected elements of empire.

The value to historians of thinking about anomalies is the implied diversity of spaces of law in empire. The perspective captures a good deal more complexity than is implied by documenting the contemporary discourse about a contrast between zones of lawlessness and of law or about distinctions between metropolitan and colonial law, and it saves us from the assumption of a smooth and steady progression toward territorial sovereignty. At the same time that legal anomalies of empire posed deep puzzles for local officials and international lawyers, they formed parts of networks of imperial control and sources of interimperial regulation. Even when they operated within substantively very different legal systems, Europeans shared the understanding that legal posturing and politics in empire mattered to the theory and practice of global legal order.

Law, Geography, and the Search for Sovereignty

As we explore the connections between legal and geographic imagination, it is rather difficult to know when chroniclers and other observers were describing accurately variations in legal geography, when they were using geographic categories suggestively but without fixed meanings attached, and when they were intending only to record physical details without implying political or legal significance. (Sometimes, surely, a mountain is just a mountain.) Though we cannot always make such distinctions, legal references and geographic descriptions intersected often enough to give us some confidence that they belonged to the same world of discourse. More specifically, both law and geography produced ways of structuring understandings of empires as configurations of corridors and enclaves, objects of a disaggregated and uneven sovereignty.

We see the links between law and geography clearly in political conflicts centering on subjecthood, the definition of membership in political communities, and the scope and nature of delegated legal authority. The problem of subjecthood corresponded in interesting ways to the imagined political significance of subjects moving through space. The presence of European subjects itself implied the extension of law. Sojourners had many good reasons to assert their continued and direct ties to sovereigns. Informal and formal imperial agents positioned themselves for rewards, sought protection of their interests and property, and claimed sponsorship to secure or improve their social standing. All European empires gained advantage at some point from unofficial agents, whose activities cost governments little or nothing but promised to extend their influence and eventually produce revenue that would reach their coffers. As they moved, subjects performed legal rituals and acted as (sometimes self-appointed) representatives of European powers, tracing pathways that became conduits for law and even corridors of jurisdiction.[87]

A variety of individuals and corporate groups could carry delegated legal authority into empire in ways that helped to shape the contours of imperial territories: ship captains, leaders of reconnaissance voyages, trading companies, municipalities, colonial governors or viceroys, and garrison commanders possessed an array of often-powerful legal prerogatives. Imperial representatives presided over local legal proceedings, often on the basis of a familiar jurisdictional arrangement whereby only capital offenses needed to be referred to metropolitan courts for judgment. Relations between delegated legal authority and imperial sovereignty became the basis, in turn, for the articulation of indigenous legal and political systems with metropolitan and colonial law. The resulting "layered sovereignties" emerged as one of the defining characteristics of empire.[88] The analogy of layers is useful but also incomplete. Centers of

[87] Although not explicitly referring to law as part of this effect, Carter insightfully writes in *Road to Botany Bay* that imperial spaces were produced through "a criss-cross of routes gradually thickening and congealing into fixed seas and lands" (23).

[88] The phrase is used by Frederick Cooper in describing a late imperial variation in "Alternatives to Empire: France and Africa after World War II," Douglas Howland and Louise White, eds. *The State of Sovereignty: Territories, Laws, Populations* (Bloomington, IN: Indiana University Press), 94–123, 106. Sugata Bose notes the prevalence in the Indian Ocean world of a "shared and layered concept of sovereignty." *A Hundred Horizons: The Indian Ocean in the Age of Global Empire* (Cambridge, MA: Harvard University Press, 2006), 25. On layered sovereignty as a property of empires in general, see Jane Burbank and Frederick Cooper, *Empires in World History* (Princeton, NJ: Princeton University Press, forthcoming). And on layered sovereignties as shaping the relations of early modern polities, see Philip Stern, "'A Politie of Civill & Military Power': Political Thought and the Late Seventeenth-Century Foundations of the East Indian Company-State," *Journal of British Studies* 47 (2008): 253–83. In finding the origins of layered sovereignty in delegated legal authority, we should note one element of discontinuity. Though Rome was a model that participants at all levels of European imperial projects routinely referenced, magistrates under Roman law were not, strictly speaking, delegated legal authorities but instead actually possessed imperium. See J. S. Richardson, "Imperium Romanum: Empire and the Language of Power," *Journal of Roman Studies* 81 (1991), 1–9; and Susan Reynolds, "Empires: A Program of Comparative History," *Historical Research* 79, no. 204 (2006), 151–65. European overseas empires often blurred the distinction between sovereign and delegated authority, as they did, for example, in defining the legal authority of viceroys, who were supposed to serve as stand-ins for the king (see Alejandro Cañeque, *The King's Living Image: The Culture and Politics of Viceregal Power in Colonial Mexico*, New York: Routledge, 2004). As we shall see, though, conflicts in overseas empire repeatedly raised questions about the prerogatives

delegated legal authority produced irregular and only roughly concentric zones of control around them. The layers of authority thickened and thinned as one traveled between enclaves and through the territories at their margins.[89] Geographic categories at times became a convenient shorthand for describing these variations.

Studying patterns of law and geographic discourse leads us to challenge the emphasis in many accounts of the legal geography of empire on sharp distinctions between European and extra-European spaces. Some legal theorists have tended to represent Europe as a zone of law contrasting with an extra-European world imagined as a zone of lawlessness.[90] Often lost in this framing is the difference between an historically occurring European discourse about extra-European lawlessness and historically occurring patterns of law and legal practice. There is no doubt that a discourse about lawlessness became more prominent in particular periods.[91] It was related to ideas about wildness and barbarism, categories contrasted to civility as a property of Christendom or of particular European political communities.[92] Yet the supposedly empty box of

of delegated legal authority and underscored for various European scholars the strains of defining sovereignty as indivisible and the continued necessity of recognizing divided sovereignty. On this point, see Keene, *Beyond the Anarchical Society.*

89 Henri Lefebvre describes this effect as the interpenetration or superimposition of social spaces. They produce "a structure far more reminiscent of flaky *mille-feuille* pastry than of the homogeneous and isotropic space of classical (Euclidean/Cartesian) mathematics." *The Production of Space* (Malden, MA: Blackwell, 2004), 86. I have described early modern legal orders as "multicentric," a term intended in part to avoid any implicit assumption that layered systems of law and sovereignty corresponded to neat hierarchies of authority. Lauren A. Benton, *Law and Colonial Cultures: Legal Regimes in World History, 1400–1900* (Cambridge: Cambridge University Press, 2002), 102.

90 Carl Schmitt, whose approach to global law will be discussed in Chapter 6, has argued that the "bracketing" of violence outside Europe permitted the founding of an international legal community within Europe. *The Nomos of the Earth in the International Law of the Jus Publicum Europeaum* (New York: Telos Press, 2003).

91 Eliga Gould traces the shifts within an Atlantic legal regime from the period when the "lines of amity" marked a division between a zone of negotiated peace and a zone of war to a brief period around the time of the Seven Years' War, when European discourse highlighted the savagery of Indian warfare, to a period after the war when the distinction between European and outer-Atlantic legal practices became less sharp. "Zones of Law, Zones of Violence: The Legal Geography of the British Atlantic, circa 1772," *William and Mary Quarterly* 60, no. 3 (2003), 471–510. On the discourse of Indian savagery during the Seven Years' War, see also Peter Silver, *Our Savage Neighbors: How Indian War Transformed Early America* (New York: W.W. Norton, 2007).

92 On evolving ideas about Christendom and their relation to the conceptualization of empire, see James Muldoon, *Empire and Order: The Concept of Empire, 800–1800* (New York: Macmillan, 1999). I discuss barbarism and wildness in more detail in Chapter 5.

lawlessness, a legal void, was in fact full of law. Imperial agents actively promoted the thrust of jurisdiction "beyond the line," and no goal of empire could be achieved without the legitimization of subordinate legal authorities in distant locations. Complex plural legal orders included and even depended on indigenous sources and forums of law.[93] As we find in declarations of martial law in colonial settings and in other moments of apparent legal rupture, even the suspension of law did not create legal voids, or spaces of lawlessness, but instead generated arenas for novel procedural and doctrinal experiments that continued to reference imperial law.[94]

In its unorthodox telling of the history of variegated legal spaces in empire, this book examines the intersection between geographic and legal imagination in four chronologically arranged periods. Each chapter combines attention to a geographic trope, discussion of an aspect of jurisprudence, and analysis of a case study or set of case studies of conflicts in empire. Europeans' efforts to structure and understand forms of partial or attenuated sovereignty drew from and led them to highlight discourses about particular geographic tropes. Rivers, ocean passages, islands, and hills – these elements sometimes symbolized remoteness and wildness, categories with their own legal and political valence. Geographic elements also developed more specific legal associations in particular periods. Shifting conditions of interimperial rivalry encouraged the selective emphasis on geographic tropes and peculiar interpretations of their legal significance.

Chapter 2 investigates legal practices in play in European reconnaissance along Atlantic rivers in the long sixteenth century. In riverine reconnaissance, Europeans emphasized the authority of expedition leaders as sovereign representatives extending law into yet unclaimed territory. For participants, the stakes of positioning for resources and patronage were high. The combination of these conditions produced charges of mutiny and treason, set against the imagined dangers of rogue polities led by imperial agents usurping royal authority. Geographic imagination and political danger overlapped as the conflicts drew attention to distant and difficult-to-reach places – the upper Paraguay River, the middle reaches

93 See Benton, *Law and Colonial Cultures.*

94 On martial law in empire, see Nasser Hussain, *The Jurisprudence of Emergency: Colonialism and the Rule of Law* (Ann Arbor: University of Michigan Press, 2003); and R. W. Kostal, *A Jurisprudence of Power: Victorian Empire and the Rule of Law* (Oxford: Oxford University Press, 2005). More detailed discussion of these themes appears in Chapters 4 and 6.

of the Amazon –where the temptations of self-rule might not be resisted. Possession of river regions meanwhile developed into a complex affair linking signs of settlement and legal acts designed to affirm the composition of political communities. Representations of upriver country as potentially politically rebellious arenas continued through the seventeenth and early eighteenth centuries, but the relation between coastal and backwater communities shifted as some colonial polities began to assert authority beyond river corridors. This legal politics began to shape imperial zones defined by territorial jurisdictions and loosely bounded by geographic features.

Images of rivers as corridors of elusive but essential imperial control paralleled emerging understandings of ocean law. Chapter 3 examines the legal geography of oceans, with special emphasis on the origins of the Atlantic and Indian oceans as separate regulatory spheres at the turn of the eighteenth century. Pirates, often viewed romantically as purveyors of lawlessness or of alternative legal orders, participated actively in the construction of imperial ocean space by insisting on their ties to distant sovereigns. Even in the midst of open raiding, mariners engaged in legal posturing, scripting cover stories that they might present in prize proceedings or criminal courts. In doing so, they affirmed the view also held by Gentili, Grotius, and other founding figures of international law that the sea could not be owned but could be subject to control and to the jurisdiction of imperial powers. Even as freedom of the seas developed as a legal doctrine, Europeans recognized that ocean space was crisscrossed by corridors of imperial control. The high seas were not a lawless zone but a legal space constructed by interimperial tensions. The emerging regulatory order of the Atlantic world depended as much on the parallel elaboration of imperial prize courts as on shared understandings of the law of nations. A thickening network of imagined corridors produced distinctive regional regulatory spheres.

The second part of the book turns to analysis of some examples of imperial enclaves of particular kinds. Military law was especially important in early modern colonizing, providing the structures for establishing authority over discrete and often fortified enclaves. This form of "garrison government" varied in its operation but was similar in structure across European empires.[95] Chapter 4 traces the renewed emphasis

[95] The phrase is from Stephen Saunders Webb, *The Governors-General: The English Army and the Definition of the Empire, 1569–1681* (Chapel Hill: University of North Carolina Press, 1987 [1979]). J. H. Elliott discusses the limitations of the model in the English

on military governance within the period of intensified, fully global inter-imperial rivalry from the late eighteenth century to the first decades of the nineteenth century. Islands figured prominently in imperial planning and in European political imagination as places essential to the protection of expanding global empires and as sites whose natural boundaries supposedly made the scope of jurisdiction transparent and claims of sovereignty straightforward. But even the most seemingly uncontested colonial island ventures came to be characterized by unresolved tensions between local authority and imperial oversight. The history of colonial island penal colonies shows this ambiguity and helps to explain the timing of an energetic application of martial law in empire. Early European criminal law eschewed imprisonment, so that experiments with isolating penal labor were conducted mainly under military authority, as in Spanish presidios or on French galleys. Banishment was nevertheless a part of the legal repertoire, and as transportation of convicts to the colonial world developed into a routine practice, colonial polities also began to isolate convicts in penal settlements. Such phenomena built on popular images of marooning mutineers on remote islands and raised new legal questions about whether penal settlements were garrisons, places of transition, or the legal equivalents of slave plantations. I explore these parallels in examining late eighteenth-century Spanish experiments with colonial transportation, a trend that directly linked garrison administration with penal practice in a range of island settings, from Puerto Rico to the Juan Fernández Islands off the coast of Chile, to the Philippines. I also analyze debates over the administration of a forced labor system on the penal colony of Norfolk Island, in the South Pacific. Drawing on this case, the chapter explores the links between debates about island penal colonies and the constitutional meanings of declarations of martial law. Understanding this connection allows us to reframe discourses about slavery, servitude, abolition, and militarism as variants of a broader debate about the scope of legal control over colonial enclaves rather than as, principally, elements of a discourse about rights.

The mirror images of European-administered enclaves were the reserves of territory sited within European empires yet remaining under non-European control. The difficulties of defining the nature of sovereignty in these colonial enclaves became increasingly acute as Europeans began to

and Spanish empires in *Empires of the Atlantic World: Britain and Spain in America, 1492–1830* (New Haven, CT: Yale University Press, 2006). See also the discussion of militarism and empire in the late eighteenth century in Chapter 4.

highlight territorial sovereignty as a key attribute of statehood. Chapter 5 turns to the legal politics of colonial enclaves and their place within international law. Geographic representations are again central to the story. Colonial officials' ideas about the nature of sovereignty in hill regions of India framed a set of complex and intractable legal conflicts involving Indian princely states. Colonial officials ultimately recognized that the project of systematizing legal politics was impossible while also insisting that the suspension or partial application of law in certain territories formed a routine product of imperial law and indirectly flowed from international law. In the same decades that international lawyers were emphasizing territorial sovereignty as a property of sovereign states in the international order, they were forced to recognize that imperial sovereignties preserved and created highly variegated legal geographies.

Recognition of a shared repertoire of law helps to make sense of the processes through which legal conflicts on the margins of European spheres of influence, and in places that were widely defined as remote or anomalous, generated broad patterns and often similar assessments and actions. Without understanding European assumptions that crown subjects could carry jurisdiction into distant places, for example, we would not be able to revise fully the image of a world divided into European and non-European legal spheres. I will pay particular attention in this study to legal practices and concepts available to Europeans across different empire-states. Particularly in early centuries, this shared legal repertoire consisted mainly, though not exclusively, of Roman and canon law, combined with the familiarity across Europe with jurisdictional complexity in multiple forms. The book's detailed case studies draw mainly from the Spanish and English empires and include some French, Portuguese, and Dutch examples and materials. A different set of scholarly objectives might lead one to emphasize the differences rather than similarities across these legal orders; the goals of this book call for attention mainly to continuities and parallels.[96]

[96] The category "European" as it is used here thus refers to the European polities of the Atlantic world and the term "empire" to overseas activities and colonies. I do not discuss land-based imperial polities of Europe and Asia, but recent work by legal historians suggests both some continuities and contrasts. Jane Burbank, for example, has argued that the Russian empire propagated a distinctive structure, definition, and culture of rights. She has also suggested that the full participation of peasants in Russian imperial law is similar to the engagement of commoners in other imperial legal systems. *Russian Peasants Go to Court: Legal Culture in the Countryside, 1905–1917* (Bloomington: Indiana University Press, 2004); and "Thinking Like an Empire: Estate, Law, and Rights in the Early Twentieth Century" in *Russian Empire: Space, People, Power, 1700–1930*,

One benefit of the analysis of the formation of corridors and enclaves within imperial spheres of influence is that it moves us beyond a reliance on the concept of borderlands to describe spaces in which imperial sovereignty was contested.[97] The term itself implies the clash of imperial powers over territorial control, and describes the spatial pattern that emerged when imperial zones bumped up against one another. But indeterminacy of sovereignty sometimes resulted from conditions other than competing claims, and from politics not centered on territorial mastery. Precisely because effective imperial control was defined by sets of narrow corridors and clusters of enclaves, multiple imperial powers could operate in the same region without producing abutting or conflicting spheres of control. The reach of jurisdiction could follow a snaking pattern of travel and trade routes that might cross or parallel other passages without entanglement. In fact, officials, merchants, and settlers sometimes angled to avoid borderland conflicts, and, as we will see, this goal influenced arguments about the nature of legal claims in vast areas. Interimperial politics often centered not on territory but on the policing of travel routes, rights to trade, definitions of subjecthood, or the fruits of imperial patronage. In some enclaves, control shifted from one imperial power to another many times over several decades with a regularity that itself rendered sovereign ties tenuous.[98] And everywhere, imperial agents failed to dictate colonial conditions on their own; locals maneuvered politically in ways that altered territorial claims and legal institutions. The resulting

ed. Jane Burbank, Mark Von Hagen, and A. V. Remnev (Bloomington: Indiana University Press, 2007), 196–217. In emphasizing Spanish and English empires, I intend to contribute both to the project of studying the empires' entanglements and to the scholarship on comparisons between them. For a recommendation to study "entanglements," see Eliga Gould, "Entangled Atlantic Histories: A Response from the Anglo-American Periphery," *American Historical Review* 112 (2007), 764–86. A broad comparative study of the Spanish and English empires is provided in J. H. Elliott, *Empires of the Atlantic World*.

[97] For overviews of borderlands that emphasize their relation to the formation of borders, see Jeremy Adelman and Stephen Aron, "From Borderlands to Borders: Empires, Nation-States, and the Peoples in Between in North American History," *American Historical Review* 104, no. 3 (1999), 814–40; Michiel Baud and Willem van Schendel, "Toward a Comparative History of Borderlands," *Journal of World History* 8, no. 2 (1997), 211–42.

[98] This pattern occurred with special regularity in the period of intensified interimperial rivalry in the decades at the end of the eighteenth century and into the first decades of the nineteenth century. Consider just two notable examples: Colonia del Sacramento in the Río de la Plata estuary, which changed hands multiple times between the Spanish and Portuguese empires, and the Cape Colony's transfer between Dutch and English rule.

variegated legal zones were not lawless but legally complex – places where political authority was widely understood as a work in progress.[99]

The book returns at the end to some of the theoretical problems raised in this chapter. In recent decades, theorists such as Henri Lefebvre, Anthony Giddens, David Harvey, and Edward Soja have extolled the importance of bringing space back in to social theory, while other scholars have defined a cross-disciplinary field labeled "spatial history."[100] It is easy enough to appreciate the importance of space, both in theoretical terms and in the context of particular histories. It has proved to be more difficult to move beyond the exhortations to attend to space and the examples of its importance to arrive at concepts that migrate out of monographs, terms that become established parts of the social theory lexicon, or insights that catch the imagination of scholars across fields and become the starting point for waves of new research. We have to look to Michel Foucault's analysis of the panopticon, David Harvey's spatial fix, or Immanuel Wallerstein's three-tiered world system for examples of influential concepts with a strong spatial component. Even in these cases, the result has not been to put space in a prominent place in social theory or in the research agendas of colonial history. This book does not

[99] The problems of using a borderlands approach in understanding imperial sovereignty and interimperial legal politics are evident in Jeremy Adelman's description of the historical process whereby the uneven spread of sovereignty produced "gray zones that would eventually evolve into borderlands" in Latin America. Adelman agrees with me and other historians who argue that imperial sovereignty is best understood "as a bundle of claims, images, and assertions of authority that can be aggregated at more than one juridical level." But he views the uneven reach of sovereignty as especially characterizing the "outer boundaries of the governable hinterlands." In this view, the contingent character of sovereignty in the hinterlands is seen as preparing the way for its tenuous hold later in borderlands zones. "An Age of Imperial Revolutions," *American Historical Review* 113, no. 2 (2008), 319–40. Yet sovereignty was not simply weaker in such regions but in fact geographically uneven – more like complex puzzles of negative and positive space than gray zones. And the zones were not lawless but, as Adelman argues elsewhere, encompassed within a state legal order purposely constructed as incomplete. *Republic of Capital: Buenos Aires and the Legal Transformation of the Atlantic World* (Stanford, CA: Stanford University Press, 1999), 117–20. In rural areas, caudillos held relatively strong but geographically limited control through spatially irregular networks of patron-client relations. These were not entirely separate from but did intersect with networks of state authority. A focus on complex patterns of legal pluralism is more likely to reveal such patterns than adoption of even a modified borderlands approach.

[100] For a set of compelling essays exploring the development of various approaches to spatial history, see Baker, *Geography and History*, especially 62–71. Baker favors a variant closely related to historical geography and distinguishes the approach from Paul Carter's emphasis on discourses about place in *The Road to Botany Bay*.

propose a new way of incorporating space in social theory writ large, but it does take seriously the challenge of evaluating the larger significance of understanding the relation between geography and law in European empire. A spatial rendering of exception as imagined by Giorgio Agamben provides a promising but ultimately flawed way of capturing the complexities of European imperial geographies, and Chapter 6 analyzes Agamben's approach and suggests some possibilities for moving beyond his distinction between norm and exception, and for avoiding the stark contrast between European and extra-European legal spheres. The aim is to capture the complexities of a world of spatially and legally uneven empires.

2

Treacherous Places

Atlantic Riverine Regions and the Law of Treason

The big trees were kings.

– Joseph Conrad, *Heart of Darkness*

It is hard to avoid beginning with Conrad. In *Heart of Darkness*, Marlow's journey up the Congo conjures every sort of metaphor for quests and conquests, and the river has been famously transposed to other settings of colonial encounter. A certain timelessness attaches to the novel's associations of upriver isolation, loss of bearings, violence, and cultural dislocation. Simply raising the topic of rivers and their place in colonizing calls up surreal images of a slow ascent into a zone where all norms become distorted.

Assigning the novel such historical transcendence gives Conrad too much credit, of course. The romance with darkness and barbarity, and the portrayal of Africans as merely parts of an ominous natural landscape – these tropes are not universal but products of Conrad's century, and of Europe's bright ideas about its own civility. His version of the dangers and allure of passing into a psychological and physical state of no restraints seems also to depend on a purely secular and perhaps even republican understanding of sociability. Conrad was more concerned, after all, with Kurtz's abandonment of "the Intended" than with his spiritual malaise or betrayal of King Leopold, a figure well offstage throughout the novel. Kingship, for Kurtz, was very much beside the point.

A purely private betrayal would have mattered less three centuries before, just as madness itself would have been defined differently. Upriver dangers in early European colonizing included the temptation to set up rogue polities, but the operative tensions were not between individual appetite and civilized restraints. The wilderness threatened to lure men into the usurpation of sovereign authority, into delusions of kingliness that might have borne some superficial similarity to Kurtz's interior empire but were very different in other ways. Whereas Conrad worried about the dark places upriver where nature ruled and "the trees were kings," sixteenth-century Europeans wondered whether the upper reaches of distant rivers might be places for men to think of replacing the king's two bodies with one of their own. Subjecthood, not sanity, was at stake.

The political dangers of distant riverine regions were set against their almost mythical promise. European Atlantic geography taught that estuaries would lead to interior riches, trading opportunities, or bodies of fresh water where colonizers might find, or settle, prosperous and stable communities. Yet estuaries themselves offered notoriously difficult conditions for sustained settlement: bad water, poor soil, exposure to severe storms. And once parties traveled beyond the points where deep water could accommodate oceangoing vessels, rivers began to signal not so much opportunity as trouble. They were difficult to navigate safely and to cross. Travelers foraged for provisions along uncultivated banks, ported arduously around dangerous rapids, lost their bearings in the confusion of channels and tributaries, and saw men and animals drown at crossings. Heavy reliance on locals for information about river regions presented new problems, as guides who held the keys to upriver safety also sometimes led travelers into ambushes and swamps, and away from shortcuts, shelter, and food. Despite these dangers, rivers had a persistent allure. In addition to expectations that they led to cross-continental passages or interior riches, rivers played an important symbolic role in Europeans' attempts to signal possession and occupation of Atlantic regions. Formulas for staging claims to river regions were not fixed, and contenders included not just other European powers and their agents but also local polities and peoples. To forge political communities in remote places, Europeans could rely on an array of established legal routines and sources, including charters, procedures for incorporating towns, and military regulations for governing garrisons.

They also had to improvise. The difficult conditions of estuary and upriver travel and settlement drew a surprising number of reconnaissance expeditions into tense and dramatic confrontations featuring accusations of treason. Like rituals of possession drawn from Roman law, treason was understood in broadly similar ways across European legal orders, but it was also open to interpretation. Accusations of treason might succeed in damaging rivals' reputations while also laying the groundwork for formal charges, and for harsh punishments: public execution and the forfeiture of property and estates. At home, treason was invoked for crimes such as aiding enemies or usurping crown jurisdiction, as well as for an array of other acts defined as disruptive of the peace of the realm. Both its flexibility and its symbolic power recommended treason as a legal and political tool in nascent political communities far from home. Pardoning apparent acts of treason could enhance an official's legitimacy, a useful function in the conditions of political uncertainty of remote and tenuous settlements. Charges of treason could be – and sometimes were – applied after the fact as rationales for violence against other Europeans or locals. European monarchs approved invoking a legal device that referenced royal authority and, they hoped, sidestepped questions about the degree of autonomy and power of local officials or colonial polities.

It was not rivers, of course, that inspired men to question one another's loyalty. Treason charges surfaced in all sorts of geographic settings, including on the seas. But an association between political danger and riverine landscapes did emerge as Europeans' attachment to a geographic imaginary centered on rivers overlapped with the peculiar challenges of constituting political communities and establishing imperial claims in distant regions of unsettled sovereignty. The special dangers of river reconnaissance seemed to multiply opportunities for insubordination and betrayal, while the promise of riches in upriver regions enhanced the stakes of political rivalries. Dangers of reconnaissance in river regions and dependence on locals urged their political incorporation and, at the same time, intensified anxieties about the loyalties of both European and indigenous subjects. Like other legal acts, treason trials could be used to leave a spatial imprint; executing a man for treason at a critical bend in the river, as the French would do at Quebec on the St. Lawrence River, was a more dramatic way of marking possession than building palisades or reading proclamations. And, as settlements became better established and could exert their own claims to allegiance, treason charges reinforced campaigns for the regional dominance of colonial polities over hinterlands. This tension between the designation of rivers as corridors of imperial expansion and their imagination as places of special political danger turned river regions into distinctive legal spaces of empire.

This chapter begins by exploring the central place of rivers in European Atlantic reconnaissance and settlement, including the significance of settlement on rivers within campaigns to establish imperial claims. I then turn to a discussion of the law of treason and its attractions for Europeans far from home. The middle section of the chapter analyzes a set of sharp conflicts in Spanish expeditions along the upper reaches of the Paraguay River. This case sets up an examination of how Spanish narratives of betrayal and treason influenced English and French accounts and actions at the beginning of the seventeenth century. Finally, I consider the shifting role of treason in the intraregional politics of colonies from the late seventeenth to the early eighteenth centuries. Across all these settings and periods, and well before Conrad ever reached the Congo, geographic imagination and crises of belonging were closely intertwined.

Atlantic Riverine Geographies

The workings of the European coastal trade from Iceland to Portugal promoted shared expectations about rivers and estuaries. Key trading ports located just inside harbors connected agrarian interior regions with coastal and long-distance markets. London on the Thames, Bordeaux on the Gironde, Nantes on the Loire, Lisbon on the Tagus, and Seville on the Guadalquivir – these cities were estuary ports, as were an array of lesser towns such as Southampton, Bristol, Vannes, Bayonne, and Huelva. Mariners knew well that the estuaries were not always easy to navigate, and entry into some required the services of local pilots. Yet, while the physical geography of river harbors varied, the human ecology, even as port settlements shifted gradually to areas of deeper anchorage, remained remarkably stable: outports, or minor settlements on the outer rim of estuaries, served as initial contact points for most larger entrepôts, which were often located at places where bridges could span the rivers and at points reachable by barges or boats from upriver regions. Sometimes outports replaced inner estuary towns as the main harbors as larger ships and silting made the inner ports less viable (consider Seville in relation to Cádiz and Sanlúcar de Barrameda, for example). Some outports failed in their bids to supplant upriver ports as centers for trade (think of Middelburg in relation to Antwerp), and some important trading cities, such as Bordeaux and even London, developed without these appendages.[1]

Europeans' experiences in West Africa mainly reinforced the expectation that estuaries were the logical entry points for regional trade. By the 1440s, Portuguese and Italian traders had given up coastal slave raiding and shifted to a strategy of traveling up navigable rivers in order to get

[1] On ports and outports, see Michel Mollat, *Europe and the Sea* (Oxford, U.K.: Blackwell, 1993), 74–6, 184–6. On other prominent geographic elements in the European Atlantic, see Cunliffe, *Facing the Ocean*, chaps. 1–2; Gillis, *Islands of the Mind*.

closer to interior towns and fairs. The traders knew about the important entrepôts located at the southern edge of the Sahara, and they conjectured that traveling upriver would facilitate their access to trade goods that flowed overland to Mediterranean ports.[2] Larger West African rivers were navigable beyond the tidal inlets. Portuguese ships could sail up the Senegal River about 120 miles to Tucurol, and traders continued in small boats some 500 miles to Felu Falls, though they had to maneuver around dangerous shallows and rocks, and found they could not reach the Saharan trading centers by this route.[3] The Gambia River was navigable by oceangoing vessels as far as two hundred miles inland. South of the Gambia, a series of deep tidal estuaries reminded Portuguese mariners of the fjordlike waterways, or *rias*, of northern Portugal and Galicia, and early coastal reconnaissance traced the many inlets and small rivers from Sierra Leone through the Niger Delta. Further south, after finding the Congo River on his first voyage in 1483, Diogo Cão returned the following year to sail up the Congo as far as the falls at Yellala.

The purpose of these forays was explicitly to engage in, and locate sources for, trade. We tend to think of the founding of Arguim in 1445 as the initiation of a Portuguese plan to extend a string of factories down the coast. But these nodes were part of a wider web that extended up West African rivers. Before founding the coastal factory of Elmina in 1481, the Portuguese had set up a trading post at Cantor on the Gambia River and another fifteen miles up a tidal estuary off the coast of Sierra Leone.[4] As Portuguese traders entered and described not just the great waterways but also the smaller inlets and rivers they encountered, they reported both riverine routes and trading possibilities.[5]

[2] Some coastal peoples were avid traders, but others, like groups encountered at the mouth of the Gambia River, were hostile; Ca' da Mosto wrote of "hoping that in the country farther upstream we might find more civilized people than those we had seen" in the estuary. "The Voyages of Alvise Cadamosto and Pero de Sintra," in Alvise Ca' da Mosto et al., *The Voyages of Cadamosto and Other Documents on Western Africa in the Second Half of the Fifteenth Century*, trans. G. R. Crone (London: Hakluyt Society, 1937), 1-84, 58.

[3] Inquiries about the origins of the Senegal River produced descriptions of summer flooding in the interior that seemed to affirm classical conjectures that the Senegal and Nile rivers flowed from a broad lake in the interior and encouraged the Portuguese to imagine Timbuktu as a lake city. Duarte Pacheco Pereira, *Esmeraldo de situ orbis*, trans. George H. T. Kimble (London: Hakluyt Society, 1937), 80. And see *infra* note 20.

[4] M. D. D. Newitt, *A History of Portuguese Overseas Expansion, 1400–1668* (New York: Routledge, 2005), 45.

[5] Duarte Pacheco Pereira's description in *Esmeraldo de situ orbis* of one of the channels of the Niger Delta is typical in its combination of information about river navigation and commerce. He records a detailed guide to entering the river, provides instructions about how to reach "a place of barter," and lists goods that can be traded there (128–9).

Despite the collection of such intelligence and extensive reconnaissance efforts, West African river trade was increasingly in the hands of intermediaries. In some places, nature seemed to block riverine travel, as on the Congo, where an abrupt fall line made upriver navigation impossible. A more imposing obstacle was the disease environment, which converted lengthy expeditions along rivers into death watches. Disease outbreaks pushed upriver expeditions back on many occasions, as they did when Alvise Ca' da Mosto retreated "suddenly" to the mouth of the Gambia River when "men began to suffer from a high fever, sharp and continuous."[6] The first attempt by the Portuguese to build a fortress on the Senegal River, imagined by John II as "a door" through which "he might be able to penetrate the interior of that great country," was abandoned when the crew began to die off.[7] In some places, Africans prevented voyaging inland; Mandinka, Banyun, and other trade diasporas in West Africa prohibited Portuguese entry into markets they controlled. Luso-African intermediaries were operating along most major river routes by the end of the sixteenth century.[8]

Despite the evident constraints on upriver travel and trade in West Africa, in many ways European expectations about the promise of rivers as routes to wealthier interior communities were borne out. Limited upriver travel did not prevent access to markets or the flow of goods to coastal ports. For Iberians, such patterns shaped a familiar human ecology, one that encouraged a strategy of founding and protecting coastal trading posts and the licensing of traders in those enclaves.

New World rivers suggested the same promise but produced more confounding results. With the notable exceptions of the St. Lawrence and the Hudson, New World rivers disappointed early voyagers in their search for trading centers that might connect to more profitable interior networks. One could sail ocean-going vessels only short distances on the Connecticut, Delaware, Susquehanna, Potomac, and James, and the minor rivers north of the Connecticut and south of the James offered

6 Ca' da Mosto et al., "The Voyages of Alvise Cadamosto and Pero de Sintra," *Voyages of Cadamosto*, 1–85, 69.

7 The ostensible reason for abandoning the fort was the discovery of a plot of treason by the converted local king. On the treason case, see section in this chapter titled "Treason Far from Kings." The report of the high incidence of disease is from "Extracts from the Decades of João de Barros," in Ca' da Mosto et al., *Voyages of Cadamosto*, 103–47, 141.

8 See George E. Brooks, *Eurafricans in Western Africa* (Athens: Ohio University Press, 2003); and Peter Mark, *"Portuguese" Style and Luso-African Identity: Precolonial Senegambia, Sixteenth-Nineteenth Centuries* (Bloomington: Indiana University Press, 2002).

sheltered harbors but not much more.[9] For Spanish America, historians have tended to tell the story of conquest and colonization as one that centered on the Mexican and Peruvian highlands. But highland expeditions followed or paralleled important campaigns to travel along and settle the rivers of Florida and Atlantic South America.[10] When rumors reached Spain about the existence of rich Incan mines, the strategy of choice was not to approach the region by sending free lances south from New Spain but to try to penetrate the continent through Atlantic waterways. Pedro de Mendoza was dispatched in 1535 with a force of more than two thousand men and thirteen ships – a huge expedition by the standards of the day – to found settlements along the Río de la Plata and open a path to interior mines. Through the first decades of the seventeenth century, English, Irish, German, Dutch, Spanish, and Portuguese mariners and settlers competed for footholds in the estuary of the Amazon and its distributaries in an effort to position themselves to control what they imagined to be a rich upriver country.

New World rivers did not just disappoint; they often posed formidable obstacles. The early French and Spanish experiences in Florida illustrate the difficulties. The eloquent Laudonnière describes the first French trip up the Florida coast as a series of providential discoveries of rivers, each one "beautiful" and most named for rivers in France: the May, Seine, Somme, Loire, Charente, Garonne, Gironde, Belle, Grande, Jordan, Belle a Veoir, Port Royal, and Basse (see Figure 2.1). The travelers regarded the rivers as possible avenues to rumored mines, wealthier Indians, and valuable trade, and the French settlers adopted the use of Indian canoes on inland passages revealed by local guides. As food ran out for the second French settlement, rhapsody about the beauty of the rivers gave way to Laudonnière's suspicion that "the land and water fought against us."[11] On the doomed Narváez expedition to Florida, the Spaniards had

[9] Meinig, *Shaping of America*, 42–43.

[10] Expectations about the promise of rivers were apparent on Columbus's first voyage, when he poked into harbor after harbor, hoping to find great cities or kingdoms. *The* Diario records his bafflement when he finds no large settlements near a good harbor with many rivers where "there ought to be" big towns (189). Near another "extremely large river which must come from very far... there should be large settlements [*grandes poblaciones*]" (199), but none were found. Dunn and Kelley, *The* Diario. From one "remarkable harbor" Columbus "sent two men inland to discover whether there was a king or any great cities." They returned disappointed. Christopher Columbus, *The Four Voyages of Columbus: A History in Eight Documents Including Five by Christopher Columbus, in the Original Spanish, with English Translations*, ed. Lionel Cecil Jane (New York: Dover Publications, 1988), 4.

[11] René Laudonnière, *Three Voyages* (Tuscaloosa: University of Alabama Press, 2001), 131.

FIGURE 2.1. "The Discovery of Six Other Rivers" (1591). Theodore de Bry worked from the paintings of Jacques Le Moyne, who accompanied Laudonnière to Florida in 1564, to create a series of engravings showing French forays into rivers discovered while sailing along the Florida coast. Le Moyne's caption was preserved by de Bry: "Sailing on, the French discovered six miles farther another river, which they called the Loire, and after this five more, naming them the Charente, the Garonne, the Girdone, the Belle, and the Grande. After they had explored these nine rivers carefully and found many singular things, all within the space of less than sixty miles, they were not yet satisfied. They went still farther north, until they reached the River Jordan, one of the most beautiful rivers of the whole northern region." Stefan Lorant, Jacques Le Moyne de Morgues, and John White, *The New World: The First Pictures of America* (New York: Duell, Sloan & Pearce, 1946), 43.

arrived at this conclusion much more quickly. Just days after beginning the march into the interior, the expedition encountered a river with a swift current. The party needed a day to cross, by swimming and riding on rafts.[12] At the next river crossing, a rider and his horse drowned in

[12] Álvar Núñez Cabeza de Vaca, *Chronicle of the Narváez Expedition* (New York: Penguin Books, 2002), 14. The technique of using makeshift rafts was one that Indians taught to the Spaniards. Acarate de Biscay recounts the way this was done in the Río de la Plata: "The way was this, my Indian kill'd a Wild Bull, flead the hide off, stuffed it with straw, and ty'd it up in a breat bundle with throns of the same Hide, upon which I plac'd my

the current. The Spaniards worried that river and lake crossings made them more vulnerable to attack. Struggling in chest-deep water to cross a lake – a tree-filled swamp, we can infer – the Spaniards were ambushed by Indians who apparently had as their goal the recapture of an Indian guide.[13] Even streams and bays posed obstacles. Traveling along the coast, the group suffered setbacks and hardships in trying to march around or cross a series of intricate inlets.[14] Such dangers, together with the Spaniards' failure to find sufficient food, led Álvar Núñez Cabeza de Vaca finally to describe the landscape as "foreign and evil and . . . utterly without resources of any kind either to stay or to leave."[15]

Other voyagers reported deep confusion about the geography of estuaries. In West Africa, Portuguese traders had at first entirely missed the mouth of the Niger, distracted by the multiple channels and islands where it met the sea.[16] Mariners had similar problems identifying the main channel at the mouth of the Amazon and, when traveling downstream, in distinguishing the Orinoco and the Marañón rivers.[17] On the gulf coast

self with my Baggage; he swam over hauling me after him by a Cord ty'd to the bundle, and then he repass'd and swam my Horses and Mules over to me." "An Account of A Voyage up the River de la Plata, and Thence over Land to Peru," in Cristóbal de Acuña, et al., *Voyages and Discoveries in South-America, the First up the River of Amazons to Quito in Peru, and Back Again to Brazil, Perform'd at the Command of the King of Spain by Christopher D'acugna: The Second up the River of Plata, and Thence by Land to the Mines of Potosi by Mons. Acarete: The Third from Cayenne into Guiana, in Search of the Lake of Parima, Reputed the Richest Place in the World by M. Grillet and Bechamel: Done into English from the Originals, Being the Only Accounts of Those Parts Hitherto Extant: The Whole Illustrated with Notes and Maps* (London: Printed for S. Buckley, 1698), 1–79, 26.

[13] Núñez Cabeza de Vaca, *Chronicle of the Narváez Expedition*, 19.

[14] According to Núñez Cabeza de Vaca in *Chronicle of the Narváez Expedition*, neither task was easy: "From time to time we would enter some inlet or cove that reached very far inland, but we found them all to be shallow and dangerous" (25).

[15] Núñez Cabeza de Vaca, *Chronicle of the Narváez Expedition*, 22.

[16] I am grateful to Joseph Miller for pointing out this fact to me in conversation.

[17] For example, the chronicler of the Lope de Aguirre mutiny was uncertain about the river route taken by the mutineers in 1560, whether down the Orinoco or the Marañón River. See Pedro Simón, *The Expedition of Pedro De Ursua and Lope De Aguirre in Search of El Dorado and Omagua in 1560–1*, trans. William Bollaert (Boston: Adamant Media, 2001). The anonymous editor of the first publication in England of Padre Cristóbal de Acuña's account of his 1638 voyage on the Amazon observed: "The many Difficulties of entering [in] the Mouth, and getting into the true Channel of the River of Amazons, have often discouraged the Spaniards, English and Dutch from attempting to trade in it, whereas upon Practice and Experience it might prove as navigable as most of the great Rivers of the World, whose Mouths are generally encumred either with Sands, Flats, Isles, or impetuous Currents, which after a few Trials become familiar." "Introduction," in *Voyages and Discoveries in South-America*, iii-viii, vi. The vast Amazon Basin was not

of Florida, pilots struggled to locate known bays, even when they possessed correct coordinates. On Luna's voyage in 1559, though the site for settlement had been selected in advance, pilots missed the opening to both Mobile Bay and Pensacola Bay on the trip east and again sailed past Pensacola Bay on the trip west, forcing an overland march from Mobile Bay. The coastal openings were disguised by islands and difficult even for trained eyes to spot.[18]

Europeans could not rely on a well-developed body of knowledge about hydrology at home and in fact were often misled by widely circulating ideas about riverine systems.[19] Rivers were thought to originate either in mountains or in large interior bodies of water, and the latter, it was assumed, could collect at watershed points so that they might give rise to rivers draining in opposite directions. This expectation is reflected in early European maps of Africa, which often depicted an interior sea as the headwaters of both the Niger and the Senegal rivers.[20] The idea

the only place where navigators had difficulty distinguishing the mouth of a river from a bay. C. R. Boxer claims that the Portuguese often used the terms interchangeably. *The Tragic History of the Sea, 1589–1622* (Cambridge: Cambridge University Press, 1959), 73n1.

[18] Jerald T. Milanich, *Florida Indians and the Invasion from Europe* (Gainesville: University Press of Florida, 1995), 139.

[19] Despite the surge of interest in geography that was fueled by Dutch, French, and English challenges to Iberian overseas empires, geography had not yet emerged as a distinctive field of inquiry. Information on physical geography was avidly collected, but until the second half of the seventeenth century, there were few attempts to systematize the data or generalize about physical features from information gathered in the field. Taylor, in *Late Tudor and Early Stuart Geography*, characterizes the English as especially "indifferent geographers" (133). Yet, as Portuondo argues in describing the tensions between cosmography and descriptive geography in Spain, we should resist the temptation to characterize the lack of more scientifically based comprehensive works on geography before the late seventeenth century as an intellectual failure. The critique of classically based cosmography required a period of privileging observation and the accumulation of information about particular events and places. See Portuondo, "Spanish Cosmography." In *Charting an Empire*. Cormack notes that the study of geography at Oxford and Cambridge for many colonial promoters involved mainly descriptive geography and chorography rather than mathematical geography.

[20] The idea that there was a western branch of the Nile followed the writings of medieval cosmographers, including the description in Leo Africanus's *The History of Africa*. This conjectural geography embraced the Niger River, whose westward bend was thought by some geographers, and some Portuguese travelers, to flow from the same source as that of the Nile. One version of Ca' da Mosto's account of the Senegal River makes this connection explicit: "This river, according to what learned men say, is a branch of the river Gihon, which flows from the terrestrial paradise. This branch was called by the ancients, Niger, which waters all Ethiopia; and drawing near to the Ocean Sea towards the west where it debouches, it forms many other branches and rivers, as well as this Senega.

carried over to the New World; early maps often represented an interior sea as the shared source of the Amazon, San Francisco, and Paraná river systems.[21] In the north, English optimism about finding the Northwest Passage also drew inspiration from this notion.[22] The *Instructions for the Intended Voyage to Virginia* advised:

> You must observe, if you can, whether the river on which you plant doth spring out of mountains or out of lakes. If it be out of any lake, the passage to the other sea will be more easy, and [it] is like enough that out of the same lake you shall find some spring which runs the contrary way towards the East India Sea: for the great and famous rivers of Volga, Tanais and Dwina have three heads near joyn'd: and yet one falleth into the Caspian Sea, the other into the Euxine Sea, and the third into the Pallonian Sea.[23]

Another branch of the Gihon is the Nile, which flows through Egypt, and falls into our Mediterranean Sea. And this is the opinion of those who have known the world." "The Voyages of Alvise Cadamosto and Pero de Sintra," in Ca' da Mosto et al., *Voyages of Cadamosto*, 1–84, 28n2. Not all the information gathered was consistent with this interior geography. Diogo Cão heard reports on his second voyage of a watershed in the interior and a separate waterway, probably the Niger, beyond. See "Introduction," in Ca' da Mosto et al., *Voyages of Cadamosto*, xi–xlii, xxv. Similar alternative theories began to appear by around 1600. See Pacheco Pereira, *Esmeraldo de situ orbis*, appendix 1.

[21] Some other earlier maps were more accurate. Cortesão suggests that a 1534 map by Gaspar Viegas, which provides at least a correct schematic of the relation of the major headwaters, was probably based on information provided by the Indians because European voyagers had not yet recorded traveling so far upriver. Cortesão and Mota, *Portugaliae Monumenta Cartographica*, 116 (map is Figure 44). Other Portuguese maps, including one as late as 1640, showed a lake with outlets to the Amazon, San Francisco, and Río de la Plata systems. See Júnia Ferreira Furtado, "The Indies of Knowledge, or the Imaginary Geography of the Discoveries of Gold in Brazil," in Bleichmar, *Science in the Spanish and Portuguese Empires*, 178–215, especially 193–6. This convention was picked up and repeated by cartographers elsewhere in Europe as, for example, in world maps by Jean Guérard (1634) and Joan Blaeu (1665). See Figure 2.2 for a 1599 map showing the Paraná and Amazon river systems connected by a lake.

[22] This was one of several competing ideas about the hydrology of the Northwest Passage. The other, based on classical cosmography and its interpretation by medieval and Renaissance scholars, imagined that northern lands were interspersed with channels or water emptying into, or flowing from, an ocean at the pole. The vision was of a symmetrical world, leading geographers to reason that the Northwest Passage had to exist to balance the globe. In this version, the passage would be a sea-level corridor or strait leading from the North Atlantic to the "South Sea." See John Allen, "The Indrawing Seas: Imagination and Experience in the Search for the Northwest Passage, 1597–1632," in Baker, *American Beginnings*, 7–35.

[23] Virginia Company of London, "Instructions Given by Way of Advice by Us Whom It Hath Pleased the King's Majesty to Appoint of the Counsel for the Intended Voyage to Virginia, to Be Observed by Those Captains and Company Which Are Sent at This Present to Plant There [1606]," Thomas Jefferson Papers, Virginia Records Manuscripts,

Like many ideas about river hydrology in circulation at the time, this one was generously aided by rumor. News of the French reconnaissance of the St. Lawrence River – which, after all, did lead to a region of interconnected lakes as large as imagined interior seas – circulated widely in Europe and among mariners.[24] In South America, Indians ported from one major river system to another in the interior, and reports by locals gave credence to the early Portuguese notion that Brazil might be an island. Information provided to John Smith about an interior waterway leading south to the sea (probably the Mississippi) was accurate at the same time that it was misleading.[25] Many more reports of navigable inland waterways were fueled by miscommunication, conjectural geographies, and, as in the case of persistent rumors about the location of the rich city of El Dorado on a wide lake of the South American interior, transpositions of classical and medieval literary tropes or utopian visions.

The difficulties of crossing and navigating rivers pushed voyagers and settlers to rely heavily on local guides. The violent seizure of captives was a routine occurrence on Atlantic river voyages – more ubiquitous, perhaps, than many other practices that have received greater attention from historians, including ceremonies of possession and proselytizing. Captives were seized and pressed into service as guides on the first Portuguese forays along the West African coast, and the practice continued in New World voyages, from Baffin Island to Patagonia.[26] The strategy often

1606–1737, Virginia, 1606–92, Charters of the Virginia Company of London, Library of Congress, Manuscript Division, http://memory.loc.gov/cgi-bin/ampage?collId=mtj8&fileName=mtj8page062.db&recNum=0017 (accessed 13 July 2008).

[24] Chronicles of Cartier's voyages were among the first collected by the younger Hakluyt.

[25] Smith actively solicited this information because he was searching for a water passage through to the so-called South Sea, and his eagerness might have caused him to interpret the information he was given expansively. He reported that when he was being held captive by Opechancanough, the Indian leader told him "that within 4 or 5 daies journey of the falles, was a great turning of salt water." Smith, "A True Relation," in *Narratives of Early Virginia, 1606–1625*, ed. Lyon Gardiner Tyler (New York: Charles Scribner's Sons, 1907), 25–71, 45. Later, Powhatan confirmed this information to Smith, adding that beyond the fall line there was also "a mightie River issuing from mightie Mountaines betwixt the two Seas" (49). Karen Kupperman notes that Powhatan clarified that there was no "salt water beyond the mountains," but the settlers continued to believe that they were not far from the South Sea. Karen Ordahl Kupperman, *The Jamestown Project* (Cambridge, MA: Belknap Press, 2007), 152–3.

[26] The reliance on captive guides began early in Atlantic voyages. Written instructions to Portuguese captains sailing to Guinea in the fifteenth century included "a routine instruction directing the explorers, whenever they reached a linguistically unfamiliar region, to kidnap, as a first priority, at least one native and bring him or her back with them to Portugal" to be trained as interpreters and guides for future voyages. P. E. Russell, "Some

backfired as captives fled, whole bands and settlements of coastal peoples avoided contact after early violent encounters with European mariners, and guides purposely led groups in wrong or dangerous directions. Language barriers made misinterpretation of information practically routine. In the first weeks of the Narváez expedition, after the Spaniards captured two Indians to act as guides, the party marched for six or seven weeks "without finding an Indian who would dare to wait for us."[27] Sometimes guides were clearly eager to move the travelers along or even to place them in danger.[28] Cabeza de Vaca noted that distrust of the North American Indian guides was matched by nearly total dependence on intelligence collected from them. Several Indians captured to serve as guides led the party "into a terrain that was difficult to cross and strange in appearance" and where the exhausted travelers had to make long detours.[29] The Soto expedition of 1539 did reach the largest settlements in the region, though

Socio-Linguistic Problems Concerning the Fifteenth-Century Portuguese Discoveries in the African Atlantic," in Russell, *Portugal, Spain, and the African Atlantic*, XIV, 1–15, 5. Even very early examples of captives used as guides are documented; a Portuguese crew at the Isla das Garças off the coast of Guinea in the 1430s, after assembling a small raiding party, seized 165 captives, including men, women, and children, and pressed two of the men into service as guides for a subsequent raid on a village on the neighboring Island of Tiger. See "The Beginnings of the Portuguese-African Slave Trade in the Fifteenth Century, as Described by the Chronicler Gomes Eannes de Azurara," in *Children of God's Fire: A Documentary History of Black Slavery in Brazil*, ed. Robert Edgar Conrad (Princeton, NJ: Princeton University Press, 1983), 5–11. This sort of seizure of captives to serve as local guides continued in European voyages along the African coast and in Asia. Magellan, for example, employed captive guides periodically throughout his circumnavigation. He was sometimes unsuccessful in seizing guides, as he was at the mouth of the Río de la Plata, but elsewhere, as occurred on the approach to the Moluccas, captive guides played key roles. Antonio Pigafetta, *The Voyage of Magellan: The Journal of Antonio Pigafetta*, trans. Paula Spurlin Paige (Englewood Cliffs, NJ: Prentice Hall, 1969), 10, 106. Information was not always extracted from captives, of course, but was instead purchased, as when local pilots were hired to navigate unfamiliar waters.

[27] Núñez Cabeza de Vaca, *Chronicle of the Narváez Expedition*, 15. At the mouth of the Gambia River, the Englishman Richard Jobson reported that the Mandingo settled there were "very fearefull to speake with any shipping, except they have perfect knowledge of them, in regard they have beene many times, by severall nations, surprised, taken and carried away." Richard Jobson, *The Discovery of River Gambra (1623) by Richard Jobson* (London: Hakluyt Society, 1999), 96.

[28] Columbus suspected as much of his captives from San Salvador, who told him there was plenty of gold on the small cay of Santa María de la Concepción. This was "probably a lie," Columbus acknowledged, "told in the hopes of getting away." Columbus was himself practiced at this sort of lying; on the transatlantic voyage, he had routinely recorded one figure for distance traveled and quoted a shorter distance to his crew. Columbus, *Four Voyages of Columbus*, 60.

[29] Núñez Cabeza de Vaca, *Chronicle of the Narváez Expedition*, 16.

native guides apparently tried to foil Spaniards' plans by taking them on a circuitous route through the area's roughest terrain.[30]

The fear of betrayal by guides was never far beneath the surface. Charting the course of rivers in a region of Central America where Indians had attacked and murdered two Dominican friars, Gabriel Salazar worried that his guides had been complicit in the attack and were withholding information about the course of the river used by Indians to escape the Spaniards' vengeance.[31] Salazar adapted forms of legal questioning to interrogate guides and corroborate their stories. At one point in order to interview an "old wise man" about "the manner in which ran the waters," the friar gave the man cacao beans to mark rivers and towns. Salazar copied the map and had the man repeat the version three times to see if there were any changes; there were none. "For further proof," Salazar then "asked two other oldsters, who provided the same marks for the rivers and in the same order with the same names. In all [things] they agreed with what he said."[32] Here and elsewhere, there was anxiety about trusting non-Christian guides and uncertainty about whether and how to punish them for giving false intelligence. Lost on the upper Amazon, Gonzalo Pizarro ordered his Indian guides to be tortured and eaten by dogs but did not record whether he intended the violence as an an act of terror or a display of his legal authority; torture could be legally applied to extract testimony and confessions from subjects.[33] On occasion, officials enacted ceremonies specifically designed to end this ambiguity by declaring Indian guides vassals of the king.[34]

The many obstacles of river travel and settlement did not seem to dampen Europeans' enthusiasm for rivers as portals to the New World. Several decades after a series of failed Spanish forays along Florida

[30] Milanich, *Florida Indians*, 123, 135.

[31] Salazar, "Brief Description of the Manché," in Feldman, *Lost Shores, Forgotten Peoples*, 41.

[32] Feldman, *Lost Shores, Forgotten Peoples*, 36, 25, 41. Paradoxically, one of the characteristics that helped to determine whether a guide was credible was whether he was offering information voluntarily or as a captive. Salazar assured readers that his information was "based on actual eyewitnesses, and when from hearsay, from persons worthy of trust *who have volunteered information without having been asked for it*." Salazar, in Feldman, *Lost Shores, Forgotten Peoples*, 22–54, 34 (emphasis added).

[33] Pizarro held authority to act as judge through his formal post as governor of Quito, La Culata, and Puerto Viejo – a position that had been bestowed on him by his brother, who was adelantado (the crown-appointed military and judicial commander).

[34] See the next section for a description of how this was done for an Indian of suspect loyalties near Asunción, before he was ordered executed as a traitor.

waterways, Pedro Menéndez de Avilés dreamed of a water route across the peninsula to accommodate shipping to and from New Spain. He continued to promote this vision even after a trip up the St. Johns River ended abruptly where Indians had placed spikes in the river to block Spaniards' progress.[35] Father Acuña, who traveled with Pedro Teixeira on his voyage down the Amazon in 1638 from Peru to the Atlantic, envisioned the Amazon as "the only channel" connecting the Atlantic and Pacific oceans, a "great highway" leading through a vast and rich region that was "a paradise of fertility" – images that did not square with decades of failed attempts to master the river.[36] Despite mainly disappointing returns, English and Dutch settlers vied for position in Guiana, on the distributaries of the Amazon, for two decades in the early seventeenth century, producing in the process the first detailed charts of rivers in the region.[37] The English, meanwhile, followed the loss of the Roanoke colony with the selection of an estuary site for Jamestown that had poor soil and brackish water, and they then centered their reconnaissance of the region on voyages throughout the network of waterways.[38] Further north, from Cape Cod to the St. Lawrence, settlements were tried on glacially formed inlets that lacked arable land behind them.

Why this persistent attachment to riverine settlement? One factor was the important role of rivers in efforts to establish imperial claims.[39] Reports of proofs of possession or occupation were both directed toward

[35] Menéndez's failed efforts to secure a riverine empire led directly to his collection of a detailed geography of coastal waters, arrived at through a combination of reconnaissance and reliance on Indian intelligence. Milanich, *Florida Indians*, 155–93.

[36] Padre Cristóbal de Acuña, *A New Discovery of the Great River of the Amazons*, in *Expeditions into the Valley of the Amazons, 1539, 1540, 1639*, ed. and trans. Clements R. Markham (London: Hakluyt Society, 1859), 47, 62.

[37] Joyce Lorimer, *English and Irish Settlement on the River Amazon, 1550–1646* (London: Hakluyt Society, 1989). On English river charts in the region, see Sarah Tyacke, "English Charting of the River Amazon c. 1595–1630," *Imago Mundi* 32 (1980), 73–89.

[38] See James Horn, "The Conquest of Eden: Possession and Dominion in Early Virginia," in *Envisioning an English Empire: Jamestown and the Making of the North Atlantic World*, ed. Robert Appelbaum and John Wood Sweet, 25–48 (Philadelphia: University of Pennsylvania Press, 2005); Lisa Blansett, "John Smith Maps Virginia: Knowledge, Rhetoric, and Politics," in Appelbaum and Sweet, *Envisioning an English Empire*, 68–91.

[39] Schama notes that in Europe, "lines of imperial power ... always flowed along rivers." He notes, too, the symbolic ties between rivers and political, even sacred, power, and the legacy of the Roman view of rivers "as roads: highways that could be made straight; that would carry traffic and, if necessary, armed men; that defined entrances and stations." Schama, *Landscape and Memory* (New York: Vintage, 1995), 5, 261.

an interimperial audience and designed to affirm that prominent actors were advancing the interests of their sovereigns. The legal repertoire employed in making and defending claims derived mainly from Roman law and was therefore available, and legible, across Atlantic European empires.[40]

From the late middle ages, European glossators had relied on Roman property law in defining the legal status of territories subject to claims advanced by European powers.[41] They also depended on Justinian's *Institutes* in applying, by analogy, forms of acquiring property to claims for sovereign control over territory.[42] Early modern writers began to draw on a wider range of Roman sources, preserving the earlier focus on Roman property law but shifting the emphasis of analyses of possession to discussions of the natural law foundations for rights to dominium.[43] Historians still have incomplete knowledge about the connections between the writings of early modern jurists on such questions and the knowledge of law carried and applied by imperial agents.[44] But even without being able to

[40] Patricia Seed (*Ceremonies of Possession*) has argued that Europeans adopted different "national" approaches to "ceremonies of possession," with, for example, the English favoring a "turf and twig" ceremony in which a piece of the land was the central prop, the Spaniards enacting rituals to claim suzerainty over people, and the Portuguese preferring stone markers coordinated with astronomical projections. Seed's claims of widely different imperial approaches to possession do not hold up; we find instead a common repertoire of ceremonies of possession drawn on strategically with the explicit purpose of making and communicating claims to other Europeans. Spaniards engaged in early reconnaissance and in New World conquest enacted a varied array of ceremonies, sometimes in combination or quick succession. They even used chunks of earth at times in ways that resembled the turf and twig ceremonies said to be the exclusive preserve of the English in empire. (I am grateful to Thomas Abercrombie for pointing this out to me in conversation.). For their part, English settlers often followed what seemed to be – absent Catholic rituals – a script very similar to that of the Iberians. For an older treatment of acts of possession that shows the variety and flexibility of ceremonies and their shared symbols, see Arthur Schopenhauer Keller, Oliver James Lissitzyn, and Frederick Justin Mann, *Creation of Rights of Sovereignty through Symbolic Acts, 1400–1800* (New York: Columbia University Press, 1938). On Spanish ceremonies involving soil, see, e.g., Elliott, *Empires of the Atlantic World*, 31.

[41] See Richard Perruso, "The Development of the Doctrine of *Res Communes* in Medieval and Early Modern Europe," *Tijdschrift voor Rechtsgeschiedenis* 70 (2002), 69–94.

[42] MacMillan, *Sovereignty and Possession in the English New World*; and Lauren Benton and Benjamin Straumann, "Acquiring Empire by Law: From Roman Doctrine to Early Modern European Practice," *Law and History Review* (forthcoming).

[43] Ibid.; Benjamin Straumann, "'Ancient Caesarian Lawyers' in a State of Nature: Roman Tradition and Natural Rights in Hugo Grotius' *De Iure Praedae*," *Political Theory* 34, no. 3 (2006) 328–50.

[44] We do know that a significant proportion of New World projectors had legal training. We also know that legal ideas were in wide circulation. For example, in the 1580s, the

trace all direct influences, we can see clearly that sojourners and settlers in the early centuries of European overseas ventures were aware of crown interests in defending claims before other imperial powers. Sponsors often provided detailed instructions about acts to perform to mark claims on behalf of sovereigns. Imperial agents also improvised, advancing claims through an often disorderly combination of rituals and interpretive statements about them. Their invocations of Roman law were frequently implied and indirect, referencing somewhat haphazardly a set of actions widely regarded as constitutive of possession under Roman law. As Benjamin Straumann and I have argued elsewhere, the paramount interest of actors in empire and of their sponsors was not to establish absolute title to territory, or to assert the moral legitimacy of empire as debated by jurists in Europe, but to present evidence of rights to possession superior to that which other contenders could muster.[45] This objective encouraged a flexible and inclusive approach to legal proofs.

The resulting preoccupation with the siting of forts, mapping, and other ways of marking claims composed a symbolic language of possession that was widely shared across European empires – not surprisingly so, since agents and their sponsors sought to adopt ceremonies and actions intelligible across cultural and political boundaries within Europe.[46] The stock in trade for early voyages of the English, French, Portuguese, Spaniards, and Dutch was to plant markers – stone columns, wooden pillars, and especially crosses – at strategic spots, undoubtedly to signify inchoate claims to areas of undetermined dimensions. Mapping was another technique for demonstrating possession.[47] Settlements, including forts, were equally important symbols, both demonstrating an intent to occupy and serving as evidence of actual possession. The Spanish considered towns as positive proof of civility. Towns were also legal entities, in which the presence of officials exercising legal authority affirmed a

English were translating and consuming works by writers of the Salamancan school. See Andrew Fitzmaurice, *Humanism and America: An Intellectual History of English Colonisation, 1500–1625* (Cambridge: Cambridge University Press, 2003), 141–2.

[45] Benton and Straumann, "Acquiring Empire by Law."

[46] Ibid., and see *supra* note 40.

[47] MacMillan, *Sovereignty and Possession in the English New World.* The literature on mapping as an element of a discourse of possession is vast. See the seminal article by J. B. Harley, "New England Cartography and the Native Americans," in Laxton, *New Nature of Maps*, 169–97, and two essays that make this point for Virginia: James Horn, "The Conquest of Eden: Possession and Dominion in Early Virginia," and Lisa Blansett, "John Smith Maps Virginia," in Appelbaum and Sweet, *Envisioning an English Empire*, 25–48 and 68–91.

direct connection to sovereigns.[48] Even in the absence of settlements, the trappings of legal institutions could be used to show the presence of royal authority. Leading an expedition of reconnaissance and settlement in the Río de la Plata region in the early sixteenth century, Juan de Solís carried instructions to take possession of new lands by making a show of legal authority: "[Y]ou shall make a gallows there, and have somebody bring a complaint before you, and as our captain and judge you shall pronounce upon and determine it, so that, in all you shall take the said possession."[49] Particularly if we recognize the flexible and inclusive strategies used routinely by European agents to demonstrate possession, we begin to understand a wide range of staged legal acts – from the simple registration by a notary of testimony or events to elaborate trials and public executions – as part of a broader campaign to show the active and enduring presence of institutions and practices clearly sanctioned by sovereigns.

Rivers held a privileged place in these strategies of claims making. The markers and settlements used by early modern Europeans to indicate possession in the Atlantic world were not set just anywhere in the landscape. They were most often placed in estuaries, or at the joining of two rivers near the sea, precisely in order to indicate the intention to travel and settle vast, unbounded riverine regions. This strategy cut across empires. Diogo Cão erected a *padrão*, or stone column, for the Portuguese crown at the mouth of the Congo River on his first voyage in 1483; three years later on a return journey, he traveled to the fall line and had his men make carvings in the cliff face to mark their progress.[50] Cartier's thirty-foot-high cross erected in Gaspé Harbour in the Gulf of St. Lawrence in 1534, and Ribault's column in Florida "in a high place of the entrie of a great river" marked intended French claims.[51] At Jamestown, Newport had a cross put up at Cape Henry near the entrance to the Chesapeake Bay; another cross upriver at the falls bore the inscription "Jacobus Rex.

[48] For this reason, the founding of municipal councils sometimes offered a means for bypassing intermediate authorities and communicating directly with royal officials. This was the strategy famously employed by Cortés in founding a municipal council or cabildo at Veracruz, despite the absence of any substantial Spanish settlement, to enable him to avoid reporting to officials at Havana.

[49] The instructions for Solís began by ordering him to make a clearing and erect "some small building" in the presence of an *escribano* and "the greatest possible number of witnesses." Keller, Lissitzyn, and Mann, *Creation of Rights*, 3–4.

[50] Diogo Cão appears to have been the first Portuguese captain to erect stone pillars rather than wooden crosses. Pacheco Pereira and, *Esmeraldo de situ orbis*, 142n1.

[51] Keller, Lissitzyn, and Mann, *Creation of Rights*, 109.

1607."[52] Traveling down the Mississippi and near the river's mouth in 1682, La Salle paused to erect a column and a cross, and to claim possession for France of the region "from its source... as far as its mouth to the sea" and everything in between.[53] Fortifications, rudimentary settlements, and simple garrisons were likewise seated at river mouths and narrows. The symbolic link between markers or settlements at key places along rivers and claims to vast interior regions explains, for example, Spanish anxiety about the fledgling settlements and simple fortifications erected by the English and Dutch at the mouth of the Amazon in the first decades of the seventeenth century; the Spanish noted the danger of allowing such footholds, since "this river and its branches cross the whole mainland including Peru." Estuary settlements announced the intention to extend dominion inland.[54]

The objective of possessing river regions provided an additional incentive for Europeans to focus attention on the formation of recognizable political communities. Even as the conditions in riverine regions often militated against political stability, the search for sovereignty necessarily involved a search for legitimacy. Recognizing this connection provides us with a clearer understanding of an association long noted by intellectual historians between European rationales for conquest and European ideas about civility. The usual account of this pairing often begins not with its classical roots or with the politics of conquest and settlement but instead with the writings of John Locke. Yet Locke wrote after the early colonial pronouncements that are said to reflect his blending of rights to property with the capacity for civility.[55] The error is compounded in the repetition of the generalization that the English and French responded to Spanish claims based on papal donations by applying Roman doctrines of *vacuum domicilium* and/or *terra nullius*.[56] This statement represents the Roman

[52] Horn, in Appelbaum and Sweet, *Envisioning an English Empire*, 31, 33.

[53] The document was drawn up on the spot and was signed by a notary and eleven witnesses. Keller, Lissitzyn, and Mann, *Creation of Rights*, 129.

[54] Tyacke, "English Charting of the River Amazon," 75.

[55] Paul Corcoran, "John Locke on the Possession of Land: Native Title vs. the 'Principle' of *Vacuum Domicilium*" (paper presented at the Australasian Political Studies Association Annual Conference, Melbourne, Monash University, 2007), APSA refereed papers, political theory: http://arts.monash.edu.au/psi/news-and-events/apsa/refereed-papers/index.php.

[56] The concepts are sometimes used interchangeably, though it is interesting to note that neither is explicitly referenced in Roman legal sources. See Corcoran's discussion of *vacuum domicilium* (ibid.) and, on confusion about the origins and applications of *terra nullius* and *res nullius*, see Benton and Straumann, "Acquiring Empire by Law." The statement about the influential role of a doctrine of *res nullius* is so commonplace that it is impossible to list all its appearances. A particularly influential statement is by

concept of *res nullius* as implying a finite series of steps leading in a fixed order to ownership of previously unowned things. A closer reading of the Roman sources and their use by imperial agents reveals that often-indirect references to *res nullius* appeared as part of an array of available, and sometimes even conflicting, arguments for the superiority of claims over those of rivals.[57] This process allowed evidence of the constitution of political community to share legal significance with mundane physical markers and mere utterances as signaling possession. In short, it was more than a cultural attachment to notions of civility or commonwealth that linked political solidarity on the ground to the search for sovereignty. Law endowed political communities with a symbolic power legible across Atlantic European cultures.

We are now in sight of a potent connection between riverine expeditions and the legal politics of treason. Urgent fears about betrayals by locals and anxieties about the political loyalties of European participants connected to broader imperial goals. Crown and merchant sponsors stood to lose everything if renegades spiraled beyond the reach of patronage and punishment. Elite rivals meanwhile understood the rewards of unseating leaders and taking command if their actions could be subsequently defended as necessary to the maintenance of recognizable forms of political order, which in turn might support their sovereigns' claims before an audience of other sovereigns. In this charged atmosphere, and along rivers where voyagers were often disoriented, hungry, and at war with others and among themselves, the logic of charges and countercharges of treason seemed irresistable.

Treason Far from Kings

In the same way that Europeans referenced Roman law indirectly and creatively in a widely shared legal discourse about possession, they invoked

Anthony Pagden, *Lords of All the World: Ideologies of Empire in Spain, Britain and France c. 1500–c. 1800* (New Haven, CT: Yale University Press, 1995), 76–7. For a more recent summary of this view that draws heavily on Pagden, see Elliott, *Empires of the Atlantic World*, 12, 30–2. Pagden revised his view of the doctrine in "The Struggle for Legitimacy and the Image of Empire in the Atlantic, to c. 1700," in Nicholas Canny, ed., *The Origins of Empire* (Oxford: Oxford University Press, 1998), 34–54, but he returned in a later essay to using the term *terra nullius* as a broad concept covering a range of practices, while at the same time noting that the term itself was not in use until the nineteenth century. See "Law, Colonization, Legitimation, and the European Background," in Michael Grossberg and Christopher Tomlins, *The Cambridge History of Law in America, Vol. I, Early America 1580–1815* (Cambridge: Cambridge University Press, 2008), 1–31.

[57] Benton and Straumann, "Acquiring Empire by Law."

elements of the Roman law of treason in jockeying for political authority and royal favor far from home. The law of treason intersected with claims-making practices as Europeans sought to establish sovereignty over old and new subjects in empire. Treason was sometimes tricky, though. The Roman approach to treason centered on the idea of *maiestas*, insult to the honor of the sovereign, while the Germanic law evolved from the notion of betrayal of trust by a subject against his lord.[58] Across late medieval and early modern Europe, Roman ideas about treason grew in influence as rulers sought ways to bolster their political power and control. A law of treason based solely on the idea of a breach of trust was a clumsy tool in the service of royal power because it implied mutual obligation and raised the possibility that subjects might justify their withdrawal of loyalty to a particular ruler by asserting that the sovereign had not met his own obligations.[59]

Roman definitions of *maiestas* were capacious and included waging war against the state, taking up arms without the sovereign's authorization, aiding an enemy, and abandoning or betraying an army. Words as well as actions were punishable. Under the Republic, treason sometimes encompassed sedition or forms of political violence, and, while any citizen could commit treason, the nature of offenses implied that officials such as governors or military commanders would have more opportunity to be traitors than common citizens or foot soldiers.[60] Partly for this reason, treason blended with political crimes, so the usual punishment of death might be replaced by exile, the sentence of choice for high-status citizens

[58] The Romans also called treason *perduelli*, which seems to have carried the connotation of collaboration with an outside enemy. The term *maiestas* became more common, and its meaning sometimes blended with that of *vis*, "violence" – in particular, sedition or other political violence. O. F. Robinson, *The Criminal Law of Ancient Rome* (Baltimore: Johns Hopkins University Press, 1995), 74–5. And see John G. Bellamy, *The Law of Treason in England in the Later Middle Ages* (Cambridge: Cambridge University Press, 1970).

[59] Germanic influences did not disappear, however, and in some places continued to be strong. Numerous Spanish *fueros*, or local law codes, for example, drew from Germanic constructions of treason in labeling as traitors a wide variety of perpetrators of crimes involving betrayal of trust, such as murdering someone with whom one had agreed to a truce or, even, committing adultery. Many Spanish codes also used the term *alevosía*, from the Germanic word for treason, which was mainly synonymous though sometimes more capacious, encompassing, for example, the crime of merely injuring the party to a truce. See Juan García González, "Traición y alevosía en la Alta Edad Media," *Anuario de Historia del Derecho Español* (1962), 323–46. The notion of betrayal was also fundamental to definitions of petty treason across European legal orders, a crime usually involving rising against or injuring a master.

[60] For a good overview of Roman treason, see Robinson, *The Criminal Law of Ancient Rome*, 74–7.

who crossed the emperor.[61] Crimes of *laesa maiestas* (lèse-majesté), or acts against the honor of the sovereign or his family, were also punished as treason.

As did the Romans, Europeans in the late medieval and early modern periods interpreted treason flexibly according to shifting political conditions. In both France and England, conspiracy to commit treason was as serious an offense as aiding the king's enemies. Usurping the royal power and "treason against the realm" were late additions to the roster of crimes of treason, coming into use only in the fourteenth century in England, not without controversy, and gaining importance in fifteenth-century France.[62] From the end of the fourteenth century and for most of the fifteenth century, historians have traced an increasingly supple use of the charge for political purposes.[63] Lèse-majesté expanded to encompass crimes against royal officials, as well as acts of insurrection against men loyal to the crown, crimes against their property, and aid to others in revolt.[64] Even as multiplying crimes of treason fit under the categories of compassing the king's death and levying war against the king, treason gradually moved away from an emphasis on crimes against the person of the king toward a definition highlighting acts against the public order.[65] Across European legal orders, punishments for high treason often followed a similar pattern: traitors were dragged to execution sites, their bodies were quartered (or their severed heads displayed), and their estates and possessions were confiscated by the crown.[66]

[61] On punishment regimes for high-status persons in European history, see James Q. Whitman, *Harsh Justice: Criminal Punishment and the Widening Divide between America and Europe* (New York: Oxford University Press, 2003).

[62] The crimes were rarely if ever the sole justification for the prosecution of treason and arose mainly as a way of rendering accusations more serious. Robinson, *The Criminal Law of Ancient Rome*, 71–2. French magnates were executed for usurpation of royal power in the fifteenth century. S. H. Cuttler, *The Law of Treason and Treason Trials in Later Medieval France* (Cambridge: Cambridge University Press, 1981), 45. There were many other substantive and procedural differences between French and English definitions and prosecutions of treason – too many, in fact, to summarize here. In emphasizing commonalities, I do not mean to suggest that the law of treason in these polities was the same. For the differences, compare Bellamy, *The Law of Treason in England*, and Cuttler, *Law of Treason and Treason Trials*.

[63] Bellamy, *The Law of Treason in England*, 103. Cuttler, in *Law of Treason and Treason Trials*, argues that the vagueness "was no doubt deliberate" and provided more flexibility for bringing cases (18).

[64] Eventually insurrection came to be interpreted as a form of lèse-majesté. An important addition was the creation in 1450 of a procedure of outlawry that allowed men accused of treason to be convicted in absentia.

[65] Cuttler, *Law of Treason and Treason Trials*, 15.

[66] There were variations on this theme. In the early Tudor period, traitors might be ordered hanged, or partially hanged before being cut down and disemboweled. Women were

The widening scope of treason provided useful ammunition in jurisdictional disputes between the crown and municipal, ecclesiastical, and seigneurial authorities.[67] A peculiar variation on this broad pattern was made possible after the thirteenth century, when in response to church anxieties about heresy, evaluating orthodoxy became a juridical and penal matter, and heresy became closely linked to treason.[68] The tribunal of the Inquisition drew on Roman legal culture and procedures, filtered through canon law, and the view that monarchical sovereignty was in the service of divine authority meant that a traitor acted against both king and God. The association seems to have aided the Spanish monarchy in pressing treason charges in ways that avoided controversy or bypassed jurisdictional tangles. After the *comuneros* uprising in 1520, Inquisitors aided royal authorities by bringing charges against members of the clergy who had supported the rebels; the crown had no jurisdiction over clerics. Phillip II later used the Inquisition to try to extradite his ex-secretary Antonio Pérez, who had been accused of high treason and was claiming the protection of the *fueros*, or local laws, of his native Aragon.[69] On at least two occasions, Phillip II did not use the Inquisition but ordered secret treason trials to avoid controversy over the execution of public figures: Florys de Montemorcency, an emissary from Flanders at the time of the outbreak of revolt there; and Martín de Acuña, who had played a role in negotiating a truce with the Ottomans but was suspected of being in their service.[70] In both cases, the crown called on trusted friars to prepare the traitors for death; Acuña's Jesuit confessor reported that the prisoner declared before witnesses that he had never intended "to commit treason

burned at the stake. See K. J. Kesselring, *Mercy and Authority in the Tudor State* (Cambridge: Cambridge University Press, 2003).

[67] On this point, see especially Cuttler, *Law of Treason and Treason Trials*, 54 and chap. 3.

[68] Diego Blázquez Martín, *Herejía y traición: Las doctrinas de la persecución religiosa en el siglo XVI* (Madrid: Dykinson, 2001), 26.

[69] The Pérez case also illustrates the limits of treason as a legal weapon of the crown. When Pérez fled to France, the only recourse was to convict him in absentia. Joseph Pérez, *The Spanish Inquisition: A History* (New Haven, CT: Yale University Press, 2005), 206. And see Víctor Fairén Guillén, *Los procesos penales de Antonio Pérez* (Zaragoza, Spain: El Justicia de Aragón, 2003); Gregorio Marañón, *Antonio Pérez* (Madrid: Espasa Calpe, 2006).

[70] Adela Repetto Álvarez, "Traición y justicia en los tiempos de Felipe II, 1565–1570," *Fundación para la Historia de España* III (2000), 37–56; Javier Marcos Rivas and Carlos J. Carnicer García, *Espionaje y traición en el reinado de Felipe II: La historia del vallisoletano Martín de Acuña* (Valladolid, Spain: Diputación Provincial de Valladolid, 2001).

against God nor against his Church nor against the King" – a phrase that captures the purposeful confusion of divine and secular authority in both the royal and popular understandings of treason.[71]

Just as the Spanish crown utilized religious law against political enemies, the English monarchy prosecuted religious dissenters, especially Catholics, as traitors. After 1570, legislation was passed to define certain kinds of religious dissent as treason, and many prominent Catholics were charged as traitors, tortured to extract names of accomplices, and executed.[72] An idea was also emerging that not all acts of treason were enumerated by statute and that common law treasons might be invoked. This notion helped to support expanding treason to encompass acts of usurping royal power, as well as mere statements challenging the king's authority.[73] By the middle of the seventeenth century, treason came to be defined as a crime not just against the person of the king but also against the corporate body of the state, an understanding succinctly affirmed by the trial and execution of Charles I for high treason in 1649.[74]

Yet it would be misleading to represent the history of the law of treason in Europe as one that developed in parallel or predictable ways or led inexorably to a construction of sovereignty as a quality of the state rather than of the ruler. A widening definition of treason emerged against contradictory currents.[75] The common thread of these accounts is instead that the law of treason was everywhere flexible, and in transition. The shared categories of the Roman law of treason could be interpreted in new ways, and the law provided long-standing routines for linking treason discursively to everyday forms of betrayal, new religious controversies, and unanticipated political dangers. Surveying these qualities, we should be surprised not to find treason charges surfacing in empire.

[71] Marcos Rivas and Carnicer García, *Espionaje y traición*, 77.

[72] Edward Peters, *Inquisition* (Berkeley: University of California Press, 1989), 140. Also see Peter Lake and Michael Questier, "Agency, Appropriation and Rhetoric under the Gallows: Puritans, Romanists and the State in Early Modern England," *Past and Present*, 153 (1996), 64–107.

[73] See Conrad Russell, "The Theory of Treason in the Trial of Strafford," *English Historical Review* 80 (1965), 30–50.

[74] See D. Alan Orr, *Treason and the State: Law, Politics and Ideology in the English Civil War* (Cambridge: Cambridge University Press, 2002); Lisa Steffen, *Defining a British State: Treason and National Identity, 1608–1820* (New York: Palgrave, 2001).

[75] The doctrine of the king's two bodies accommodated many of the changes. See Ernst Hartwig Kantorowicz, *The King's Two Bodies: A Study in Medieval Political Theology* (Princeton, NJ: Princeton University Press, 1957).

Yet some qualities of treason law also made it a peculiar tool for participants in extra-European ventures. To begin with, in most situations only a subject could commit treason.[76] Even the strongest versions of New World claims making did not assume that projections of territorial control converted the inhabitants automatically into subjects. Though this nicety was not always observed, treason charges against "rebellious" Indians, or against Africans, seemed to require some preliminary recognition of subjecthood. The delegated nature of legal authority in imperial settings also posed puzzles. To what extent were local authorities stand-ins for the king? To what degree did they command allegiance? The physical absence of the king created a novel layer of complexity. Spaniards would prove more willing to lodge accusations of treason when the wronged officials were viceroys, clearly intended proxies of the king.[77] Yet other officials proclaiming their closeness to the king were themselves in danger of being accused of usurping royal authority if they asserted their rights to subjects' allegiance too strongly. In Ireland, extending English sovereignty without even a visit to the realm by an English monarch before 1689 depended on arguments that the king's majesty, power, and authority spread throughout his realms.[78] A further complication of treason charges lodged far from home was the doubt that they could be made to stick, rather than drawing legal actors into protracted, costly struggles that exacted their own punishments.[79] Finally, treason was a charge brought most often, though not exclusively, against members of the elite. Lowly vassals could be accused of rebellion and dealt with in less ceremonial, more summary ways. But the line between rebellion and treason was a thin one, and, particularly in early empire, officials of middling status – nonnoble conquistadores are the prime example – could rise to prominence quickly.

[76] This was not consistently true in Rome, and there continued to be exceptions. Megan Williams shows that in the early sixteenth century, diplomats passing through some royal territories were threatened with prosecution for lèse-majesté if they had not secured the proper safe conducts. Though they were not subjects of the realm, their unauthorized presence was construed as an affront to the majesty of the king. "Dangerous Diplomacy and Dependable Kin: Transformations in Central European Statecraft, 1526–1540" (Ph.D. diss., Columbia University, 2008).

[77] That viceroys stood in for the king is one of the central themes of Cañeque, *King's Living Image*.

[78] This was an adaptation of the doctrine of the king's two bodies. See Kantorowicz, *King's Two Bodies*. On Ireland, see Orr, *Treason and the State*, 48.

[79] Ernst Pfining notes that criminal prosecutions of smugglers in the Portuguese empire were so protracted that the ordeal itself constituted a kind of punishment. Ernst Pfining, "Contrabando, ilegalidade e medidas políticas no Rio De Janeiro de século XVIII," *Revista Brasileira de História* 21, no. 42 (2001), 397–414.

Accusations of treason sometimes indicated officials' ascendance before it received formal recognition.

The complexities of developing accusations of treason did not deter rivals from nurturing rumors of betrayal or from helping them grow into something more promising. Treason was too useful and powerful a charge – and too deeply ingrained in political and legal culture – to be left behind on European shores. The crown's sensitivity to challenges to its authority in remote settings sometimes allowed for a certain laxness about summary punishments, and about the requirement of subjecthood for traitors. These possibilities are illustrated by an early Portuguese case in 1488, when a Wolof king (called Bemoim by the Portuguese) was carried to Lisbon to appeal directly to John II for support in an ongoing war in the region of the Senegal River. While in Lisbon, Bemoim converted, and he traveled as a Christian ally of the king back to the Senegal estuary with three hundred caravels under Pero Vaz da Cunha, who had instructions to build a fort in the estuary to support upriver trade. The site chosen for the fortress was "an ill-chosen place on account of the floods of the river" and "very unhealthy."[80] As men began to sicken and die, Pero Vaz accused Bemoim of plotting treason, killed him on board one of the ships, and sailed back to Lisbon. Charging Bemoim with treason might have been a strategy to allow the beleaguered force to sail home, as one of the chroniclers later speculated.[81] It might also have been concocted after the fact as a rationale for Bemoim's murder. Both because a charge of treason should have been referred to the king for judgment and because Bemoim had been prized as one of a few high-ranking converts from Islam in the region, "the King was very displeased with the event."[82] But the crown brought no charges against Pero Vaz. P. E. Russell has suggested that executing "a white Portuguese of noble rank for killing a black African, king or not" would have been politically unwise. As a Christian convert and vassal of the king, Bemoim was capable of treason, but his legal status was not to be equated with that of Portuguese nobles.

[80] This is from one of two accounts of the voyage. "Extracts from the Decades of Joâo de Barros," in Ca' da Mosto et al., *Voyages of Cadamosto*, 103–48, 141. P. E. Russell analyzes both accounts thoroughly in "White Kings on Black Kings," in *Portugal, Spain, and the African* Atlantic, XVI, 153–63.

[81] Russell, "White Kings on Black Kings," in Russell, *Portugal, Spain, and the African Atlantic*, XVI, 153–63, 141.

[82] Russell, "White Kings on Black Kings," in Russell, *Portugal, Spain, and the African Atlantic*, XVI, 153–63, 141. The other chronicler of the event, Rui de Pina, acknowledged that it was the duty of Pero Vazto bring someone suspected of treason back to Lisbon for the king's justice. See Russell, "White Kings on Black Kings," 161.

If treason charges could be used to legitimize summary executions of new vassals in empire, they might also be employed against crews on ships and the inhabitants of early settlements. It is possible that Pero Vaz was exploiting this ambiguity in killing Bemoim aboard a ship rather than on land. Under the laws of Oléron, the merchant law code relied on across European polities as one source for maritime law, the relationship between crew members and their captain was characterized as a feudal tie, and acts against the captain could be defined as treasonous – though they were sometimes viewed more as the petty treason of a breach of trust to a lord than as high treason committed against a sovereign. In England, the first statute designed to set up a regular system for trying shipboard offenses was enacted in 1535 and amended the following year to make clear that not just serious crimes were covered but also acts labeled "treasons" and "confederacies." Decades later, Coke was still trying to clarify the difference between petty treason and high treason at sea.[83] The tendency of ship captains to abandon North Atlantic expeditions to engage in piracy provided a link between shipboard law and the founding laws of settlements. This connection might have accounted for Sir Humphrey Gilbert's proclamation at St. John's Harbour in 1583 of a provision for punishing anyone committing treason or speaking against the honor of the queen; Gilbert had seen his first voyage dissolve in the face of mutinies and desertions before he had even crossed the ocean. The authority of commanders over their small fleets blended with their legitimacy as political leaders on land.[84]

This connection is also apparent in the use of treason during Champlain's 1609 voyage up the St. Lawrence River. Champlain was a veteran of failed colonies in Arcadia on the island of St. Croix and at the mouth of the Annapolis River when he chose a site for settlement further upriver at Quebec, in 1609, at a point where "begins the fine, good country of the great river, distant one hundred and twenty leagues from its

[83] The statute, 28 Hen. VIII c. 15 (1536), created commissions to try these crimes under common law, though there continued to be uncertainty, addressed later by Coke, over the issue of whether piracy was a form of petty treason or of high treason. Coke argued that only English subjects could be guilty of the latter. See Alfred P. Rubin, *The Law of Piracy* (Newport, RI: Naval War College Press, 1988), 51, 65–7. This argument had implications for understandings of the application of English jurisdiction to the sea, as discussed in Chapter 3 in this volume.

[84] On an earlier voyage, Gilbert had seen several of his ships desert the expedition to engage in piracy. The emphasis on discipline on the second voyage did not prevent the ships on the second from being separated in a storm at sea, in which Gilbert's ship went down.

mouth."[85] French anxiety about imperial rivals in the region was running high both because of awareness of English designs on New World settlement and because of the nearby presence of Basque fishermen. According to Champlain's account, some of his men hatched a plot several days after the party arrived at Quebec to kill Champlain and give the site to the Basques. A locksmith named Jean Duval and several accomplices "imagined that by handing over the place to the Basques or Spaniards they would become very rich."[86] When Champlain learned of the plot from one of the conspirators, he took action in a way that recalls the Spaniards' penchant for enacting legal rituals in remote places. He isolated the conspirators' followers aboard one of the ships in the river and told them he would pardon them all if they provided sworn statements about the plot and professed their remorse.[87] Duval and the ringleaders were held in irons until Champlain could arrange a formal hearing. He rendered the verdict in concert with "the Captain of the ship, the surgeon, master, mate and other seamen," after taking many "depositions and cross-examinations" aboard the ship.[88] Duval was to be put to death to "serve as an example" and "in order that the Spaniards and Basques who were numerous in the region might not rejoice over the affair."[89] His conspirators were sent back to France, presumably to be tried and hanged there. Duval was strangled, and his head was placed on a pike at a high point in the fort.

This case hints at the peculiar power of treason charges in remote stretches of territory, where physical dangers, fears of mutiny, and Indian threats combined to promote political anxieties. Champlain's execution of Duval at Quebec reinforced his own authority and affirmed French claims before a Basque and Indian audience. Like political actors at home, Europeans in empire were drawing creatively on an element of European law that was both widely recognized and open to interpretation. Treason was part of an available legal repertoire. It was also a legal concept linked closely to the extension of royal authority. Not surprisingly, treason

[85] Henry Percival Biggar, ed., *The Works of Samuel de Champlain*, 6 vols. (Toronto: Champlain Society, 1922), 2:23. I am grateful to Alan Greer for calling my attention to the treason case on this voyage.

[86] Biggar, *Works of Samuel de Champlain*, 2:30.

[87] Champlain recounts: "On the following day I received all their depositions, one after the other, in the presence of the pilot and of the sailors of the ship, and had them committed to writing." Biggar, *Works of Samuel de Champlain*, 2:31.

[88] Biggar, *Works of Samuel de Champlain*, 2:33.

[89] Biggar, *Works of Samuel De Champlain*, 2:33.

charges tended to surface in remote parts of empire, including and perhaps especially in upriver regions, where lines of political authority blurred, imagined fortunes and sovereign claims were at stake, and legions of new vassals exhibited uncertain political loyalties.

"[H]e called himself King"

The treason case resulting from early Spanish reconnaissance and settlement on the Río de la Plata unites many of the factors at play in the legal politics of allegiance in riverine regions. The central actor, Cabeza de Vaca, has been studied most often as the author of a chronicle about his desperate eight-year trek from Florida to New Spain after the Narváez expedition was lost.[90] Appointed after the Florida debacle as adelantado of the Río de la Plata, Cabeza de Vaca ended this journey in chains, transported back to Spain by a group led by Spanish treasury officials and a rival official, Domingo Martínez de Irala, who then succeeded in establishing himself as adelantado.[91] The conflict between these factions

[90] On scholars' misrepresentations of Cabeza de Vaca, see Bauer, *Cultural Geography of Colonial American Literatures*, chap. 2.

[91] Cabeza de Vaca's appointment followed his tenacious campaign for patronage on his return from North America, a plea made mainly on the basis of his grandfather's prominent role in the conquest of the Canary Islands and his own earlier service in Italy. Legal histories of the Spanish empire tend to center on the operation of the audiencias, or high courts. The audiencias were fixed relatively early, and recent studies have affirmed their power and appeal. For example, Sergio Serulnikov provides detailed examples of Andes Indians traveling great distances to present cases to the audiencia in Buenos Aires. *Subverting Colonial Authority: Challenges to Spanish Rule in Eighteenth-Century Southern Andes* (Durham, NC: Duke University Press, 2003). Yet before and after the audiencias were established, the Spanish crown also used the appointment of adelantados as a means of extending legal authority. These appointments featured agreements about the proportion of proceeds of raiding, trade, and tribute that would fall to the adelantados, who in turn often contributed to the costs of expeditions, at times making a heavier financial investment than the crown. The adelantados were also crown legal officials, and their performance in this role was crucial to their success. The crown appointed adelantados to govern in particular geographic areas, and they usually moved quickly to found towns, with councils that also took on important legal functions, including regulating membership in the local community (this membership was called *vecindad*; see Tamar Herzog, *Defining Nations*, on the adaptations to *vecindad* when Spaniards carried the institution to the Americas). But it was also understood that legal authority traveled with adelantados. They could conduct hearings, pass judgment on misfits or criminals, and record legal acts as representatives of the crown at any point once expeditions were under way and at any place within the loosely defined territory that corresponded to their jurisdictions. These functions reflected the origins of the post, created in the thirteenth century under Alfonso X as an exclusively judicial post. Adelantados were appointed to assume judicial oversight of coreligionists on expeditions of

and the legal contests that followed centered on accusations of treason on both sides. The charges grew directly out of the conditions of reconnaissance and settlement in the estuary: a landscape marked by past massacres, Spaniards' murky understanding of the riverine environment, their desperate reliance on Indian intelligence, and Indians' efforts to use the invaders to shift the balance of power in the region. The resulting legal case in Spain lasted almost as long as Cabeza de Vaca's earlier ordeal of wandering in the New World, and longer if we consider his lifelong attempts to clear his name.

The Spaniards' knowledge of the river system and its human ecology form an important part of this story. The estuary is the widest in the world, with a breadth of 136 miles at the opening into the Atlantic and tidal conditions extending 120 miles up the Uruguay and Paraná rivers, and it was a tantalizing target for settlement and reconnaissance, especially after early visits to the region gave rise to rumors of rich interior mines. But the semisedentary Indians on both sides of the estuary did not meet Spanish demands to supply them with food or labor; the Indians either fled or, once provoked, attacked. The Spanish decision to found a settlement on the future site of Buenos Aires can be understood only by recalling European fixed ideas about patterns of estuary settlement. The site itself was dreadful – exposed to coastal storms; nearly unreachable in winter because of currents and winds; devoid of firewood and game; stifling in summer; far from fishing grounds; and in a border region, it turned out, of territories visited by different groups of Indians on a seasonal basis only. Upriver, agricultural Indian communities were more promising targets of Spanish aggression, but the rivers gave way to a perplexing landscape unlike any headwaters the Spanish had experienced. Instead of a large lake – depicted on many maps into the eighteenth century as forming the source of both the Paraná and Amazon river systems (see Figure 2.2) – the Spaniards found a vast alluvial plain with confusing and impassable river channels bordered by thick brush. The

raiding and settlement under the Reconquista. See Robert MacDonald, "Introduction: Part II," *Leyes de los adelantados mayores: Regulations, Attributed to Alfonso X of Castile, Concerning the King's Vicar in the Judiciary and in Territorial Administration*, ed. Robert A. MacDonald (New York: Hispanic Seminary of Medieval Studies, 2000), 5–29. This judicial aspect of the position was never lost and continued to operate on the other side of the Atlantic, though the office fell out of use toward the end of the sixteenth century. Adelantados were the highest legal authority on expeditions and had the right to appoint and replace military, legal, and treasury officials; to form militias; and to found new districts.

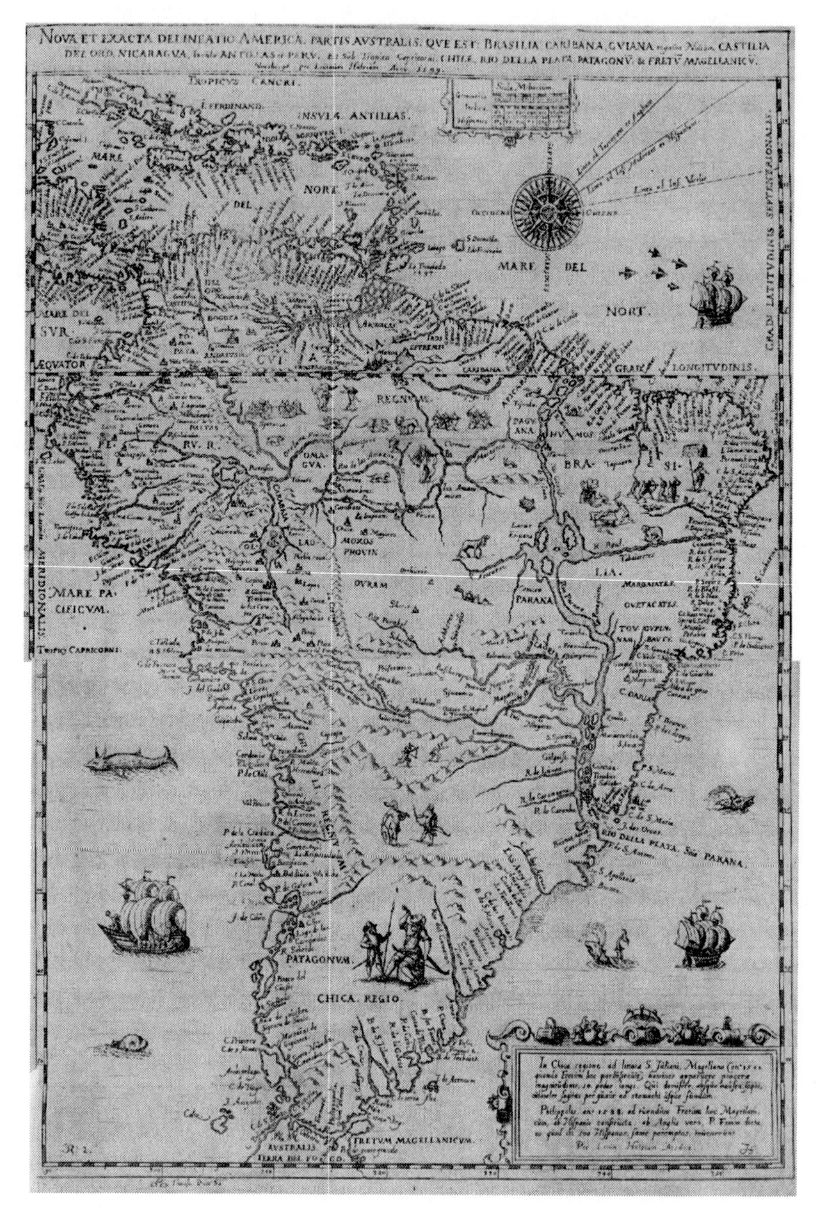

FIGURE 2.2. Map of South America (1599). This map was made by Levinus Hulsius and Jodocus Hondius and accompanied the first edition of Ulrich Schmidel's account of the Mendoza expedition. It shows the continent's large river systems as connected, with the Paraná River flowing from a large lake, Lake Eupana, and a tributary of the Amazon flowing north from the same lake. Ulrich Schmidel, *Warhafftige Historien einer wunderbaren Schiffart... von Anno, biss 1554 in Americam* (Nuremberg: Imensis Levini Hulsii, 1599), two foldout maps following p. 1. Courtesy of the John Carter Brown Library at Brown University.

whole region flooded for several months out of the year, a fact that the Spaniards learned from Indians but chose at several critical moments to ignore. Swamps were familiar enough to some of these men – the lower Guadalquivir Valley merges into wetlands – but they had no experience with an inland swamp of such dimensions and certainly did not expect to find one forming the headwaters of a large river system.

Proficient parasites that they were, the Spaniards founded a more permanent settlement in the only part of this environment that could sustain them.[92] At Asunción, on the Paraguay River, they were able to coerce a community of Guaraní Indians to provide them with agricultural supplies and with hundreds of women to serve them. By the time Cabeza de Vaca arrived, this post was all that was left of the grand expedition under Pedro de Mendoza to settle the estuary; Buenos Aires had been abandoned, and a reconnaissance march into the interior led by Mendoza's replacement, Juan de Ayolas, had met the same fate as earlier voyagers, with Ayolas and his men massacred by semisedentary Indians on the banks of the upper Paraguay.

Cabeza de Vaca heard these and other stories of calamity as he trekked to Asunción from the Brazilian coast.[93] One circulating ghost story was about a Portuguese crew member from Juan de Solís's 1518 expedition, Aleixo Garcia, who was said by the Indians to have reached the mines of Charcas with four or five Guaraní guides before being killed on the banks of the Paraguay River. Ayolas's death was eerily similar – he was said to be traveling with one of "Garcia's Indians" as a guide, and the lone Indian survivor of the trip claimed that the Spaniards had been returning laden with silver and gold.[94] Then there was the added twist of rumors

92 I use "Spaniards" to refer to the Europeans in the Río de la Plata, but not all would have embraced the term. At least one soldier, Ulrich Schmidel, was from a German principality, and those from Spain routinely referred to themselves and one another by their regional origins. Domingo de Irala was Vizcayan, and the men from Vizcaya and Córdoba seem to have been particularly active in the rebellion he led.

93 Cabeza de Vaca's decision to reach the settlement by trekking overland from the coast rather than traveling upriver was the first indication of the Spaniards' realization that the estuary was not conforming to expectations. It was difficult even to reach the site of Buenos Aires by sea in winter, battling against the strong southerlies. A relief ship sent by Cabeza de Vaca returned to the island of Santa Catalina, where he was preparing to stage his entry to the continent.

94 Later Cabeza de Vaca would send men in search of "Garcia's Indians" ("los indios de Garcia") to guide them. Manuel Serrano y Sanz, ed., *Relación de los naufragios y comentarios de Álvar Núñez Cabeza de Vaca (ilustrados con varios documentos inéditos)* (Madrid: Liberería General de Victoriano Suárez, 1906), 1:293. All translations from this source are mine.

of Ayolas's betrayal by his lieutenant Domingo de Irala, who had been ordered to stay and wait for him on the river. By some accounts, Irala had been forced to leave the post because he had enraged the local Indians by seizing the cacique's daughter. All reports agreed that Irala had left the rendezvous point on the river, had traveled downriver to Buenos Aires, where he let the desperate soldiers abandon the place and move to Asunción, and then officially had taken charge after learning from Indians of Ayolas's death. Irala was firmly in command when Cabeza de Vaca arrived at the settlement with orders that he be received as the new adelantado.[95]

The story of conflict between the two men and their followers seems clear in its outlines.[96] Irala was a capable military leader and had designs on leading his own upriver expedition to find silver, and he resented the imposition of Cabeza de Vaca's authority. Cabeza de Vaca was appalled at the settlers' pattern of essentially enslaving Indian women, and his attempts to rein in the practice, in Cabeza de Vaca's own words, led Irala's men to develop "a great hate" for the new governor.[97] Sensing Irala's popularity, Cabeza de Vaca sent him to lead an upriver scouting trip, refrained from pressing charges against him when twice presented with the opportunity, and made Irala field commander for Cabeza de Vaca's own upriver voyage of reconnaissance. But the tensions finally boiled over, and Irala had the adelantado and some of his followers sent back to Spain, with a file of depositions sworn against him. After an eight-year battle against the resulting array of charges lodged by the

[95] Irala seemed to grasp the potential for trouble to result from these decisions. Even before the arrival of Cabeza de Vaca, he dictated an affidavit defending his decision to leave the upriver post, reporting Indian accounts of Ayolas's murder, and explaining the logic of ordering the abandonment of Buenos Aires. "La relación que dejó Domingo Martinez de Yrala en el puerto de Buenos Aires quando la despobló a instancias del requerimineto que le hizo Alonso del requerimiento que le hizo Alonso de Cabrera," in Serrano y Sanz, *Relación de los naufragios y comentarios*, 2:361–77 (Madrid: Liberería General de Victoriano Suárez, 1906) 2:361–77.

[96] See David A. Howard, *Conquistador in Chains: Cabeza de Vaca and the Indians of the Americas* (Tuscaloosa: University of Alabama Press, 1997). Much of the scholarship has focused on debating whether Cabeza de Vaca or Irala was right in these disputes. Serrano y Sanz defends Cabeza de Vaca (see "Advertencia," in Serrano y Sanz, *Relación de los naufragios*, 1:v–xxx, especially xxiii–xxvii). Others fault Cabeza de Vaca's arrogance (e.g., Julián María Rubio, *Exploración y conquista del Río de la Plata, siglos XVI y XVII*, Barcelona and Buenos Aires: Salvat Editores, 1942), chap. 4. For a very useful biography of Cabeza de Vaca, see Rolena Adorno and Patrick Charles Pautz, *Álvar Núñez Cabeza de Vaca: His Account, His Life, and the Expedition of Pánfilo de Narváez*, 3 vols. (Lincoln: University of Nebraska Press, 1999), 1:295–413.

[97] "Relación General," in Serrano y Sanz, *Relación de los naufragios*, 2:1–98, 29.

Consejo de Indias (Council of the Indies) against him, Cabeza de Vaca was found guilty, though his sentence was later reduced from misrule to mismanagement, and probably never enforced.

Historians have wondered why the case against him ever succeeded.[98] Particularly because the most detailed surviving records are the accounts written by or for Cabeza de Vaca in his defense, together with a series of sworn statements solicited from sympathetic witnesses, the case seems to be one of clear insubordination, even rebellion. Irala and his men had seized a royally appointed adelantado and his legal officials, and had placed themselves in power. Cabeza de Vaca labeled the rebel party *comuneros*, after the leaders of the revolt against the crown in Castille in 1520–1521.[99]

Part of the reason for Irala's success was certainly his effort, from the first moments of the insurrection, to maintain some form of legal cover for his actions, and to affirm his loyalty to the king. His followers

[98] For example, Rubio describes the outcome as a mystery. Rubio, *Exploración y conquista*, chap. 4. Much of the historiography on the expedition has focused on the unpromising question of whether Domingo de Irala or Cabeza de Vaca was the better leader (see *supra* note 96). Adorno and Pautz's recent biographical essay goes beyond this question but does not place the case against him in a larger legal context that would help explain either the nature of the charges or the outcome of the case. The work is very clear, though, in situating Cabeza de Vaca himself within Spanish legal culture. Adorno and Pautz show that Cabeza de Vaca was typical of men of his class and aspirations in sixteenth-century Spain in the degree to which his life and career were molded by entanglements with the law. Before reaching the age of majority, he had testified before a judge and arranged for legal representation in connection with his parents' estates. His campaign for a post in the New World after the Florida expedition involved the preparation of a series of *probanzas*, witnesses' sworn statements recorded by notaries in response to a series of prepared questions. Cabeza de Vaca also learned on his return that, without being present, he had played a key role in a celebrated case, the divorce proceedings of his old employer, the Duke of Medina Sidonia. Four witnesses, no doubt confident that he was dead, had quoted Cabeza de Vaca as the source of information that the duke's marriage had never been consummated. In the four suits brought in connection with his governorship in the Río de la Plata, Cabeza de Vaca had dozens more *probanzas* prepared in at least eighteen Spanish towns: in "Córdoba, Écifa, Jaén, Seville, Antequera, Beza, Cádiz, Arjonilla, Linares, Toledo, Málaga, La Rambla, El Coronil, Vélez Málaga, Utrera, Jerez, Sanlúcar de Barrameda, Andújar, and 'other places in these kingdoms.'" Cabeza de Vaca became sufficiently knowledgeable about legal matters – and about maneuvering at court – to be retained to handle the legal affairs of his cousin in the last years of his own appeal. Adorno and Pautz, *Álvar Núñez Cabeza de Vaca*, 1:398. Even after the charges against him had been settled, he persisted with a legal campaign to have his financial rights as adelantado restored.

[99] Cabeza de Vaca had fought against the *comuneros* for the crown before his first voyage to the New World. Adorno and Pautz, *Álvar Núñez Cabeza de Vaca*, 1:362. On the revolt, see Stephen Haliczer, *The* Comuneros *of Castile: The Forging of a Revolution, 1475–1521* (Madison: University of Wisconsin Press, 1981).

shouted "¡Libertad! ¡Libertad!" as they seized Cabeza de Vaca and his officers, but they also quickly added, "¡Viva el rey!" Irala was careful to preserve favorable records, create a new paper trail, and selectively purge damaging documents. One of the first acts after the governor's arrest was to find and destroy a cache of legal records, including statements and charges prepared against Irala and his men. When Cabeza de Vaca was sent back to Spain, Irala shipped with him a file of new depositions taken to support charges listing the governor's crimes. Though Irala seems to have been tempted to kill Cabeza de Vaca by staging an accident, he apparently recognized that an order to execute the governor would have been very difficult to defend. For his part, Cabeza de Vaca responded to his arrest not by inciting his followers to fight Irala but by lining up his own witnesses. The two sides were locked in a battle of affidavits.

The insistence on legal positioning does not explain the content of the charges and countercharges, nor does it entirely account for the case's outcome. The remoteness of the region, the peculiar conditions of riverine reconnaissance, and the role of Indians as legal subjects were other important forces shaping the legal contest. These pieces of the story help to explain both the decision to make treason the main charge against the governor and the willingness of the Council of the Indies to condone the rebellion.

The Guaraní Indians were bearing the burden of supporting the Spaniards at Asunción, and Indian women had been, for all intents and purposes, pressed into slavery by the hundreds. But the Indians were not mere victims. The Guaraní were clearly using the Spaniards to defend against and attack enemies in the region. Here the Spaniards' interest in navigating on the upper Paraguay to find a route to the silver mines was especially helpful because several of the semisedentary Indian groups residing along the river had been raiding agricultural Guaraní communities. Indians in and near Asunción drew Cabeza de Vaca into military campaigns against some of these groups soon after he arrived. At the same time, Cabeza de Vaca was enraging Irala's followers by pressing charges against Spaniards for abuses against Indians. The governor's reliance on Indian testimony in such cases must have been especially provocative to Spaniards. Bernardo de Castañeda was found guilty and given one hundred lashes after an Indian from a settlement near Asunción came to Cabeza de Vaca to complain that the Spaniard had entered the Indian's house "at midnight, and by force, in front of the Indian man, grabbed her in order to lie with her."[100] Before Cabeza de Vaca's tenure, such behavior would probably not have been punished at all, and never so harshly.

The battles against other Indian groups and the cases brought as a result of Indian complaints helped to sharpen the distinction between Indians who were considered vassals of the king and those who were still outside the scope of Spanish authority. Once Indians had submitted to Spanish rule and were labeled as vassals, they had legal standing to complain of abuses, and future acts of aggression by them against Spaniards could be considered acts of treason.[101] Well before Irala was agitating openly against him, Cabeza de Vaca introduced the subject of betrayal into the strained legal politics of the place by bringing charges of treason against several Indians. Both cases involved Irala indirectly, and it seems possible, even likely, that Cabeza de Vaca was flexing his muscles against Indian subjects to send a message to potentially mutinous Spaniards.

One case of petty treason involved a Christian Indian woman who had poisoned her Spanish master some time before Cabeza de Vaca arrived. The woman was arrested and confessed to the crime, but then the victim's cousin came forward to say that the Indian was his fiancée – though it is difficult to know what this term meant when each Spaniard had multiple Indian women in his household – and pleaded for her life. The woman was freed without punishment. On learning of the crime, Cabeza de Vaca had her arrested again. Domingo de Irala tried to intervene, but this time the magistrate appointed by Cabeza de Vaca found the woman guilty on the basis of her confession in the earlier trial. She was executed and quartered – a traitor's death. Cabeza de Vaca insisted that the punishment was a necessary deterrent to other Indians who might rise against their masters, and perhaps he hoped it would also serve as notice to others contemplating petty treason or rebellion.

A case of an Indian charged with high treason figures more prominently in accounts of the tensions leading up to political rupture. Cabeza de Vaca

[100] "Relación general," in Serrano y Sanz, *Relación de los naufragios*, tomo 2:1–98, 37.

[101] Amy Turner Bushnell notes that the Spanish practice of summoning locals and asking them to promise obedience to the king was very common and also signified an affirmation of Spanish claims. Bushnell notes, too, that once the ceremony took place, even nonviolent resistance by a cacique and his followers could be styled as rebellion. The only way to withdraw obedience involved physical isolation: "walking away and not coming back." Situado *and* Sabana*: Spain's Support System for the Presidio and Mission Provinces of Florida* (New York: American Museum of Natural History, 1994), 35.

sent Irala on an important reconnaissance mission up the Paraguay River, beyond the place Ayolas's party had been attacked, to find a suitable spot to begin another march inland. A splinter party had trouble with their guide, Aracaré, an Indian leader who had already fought against the Spaniards but had made peace with them and was now considered a vassal. The Spaniards reported that Aracaré had set fires to attract the attention of hostile Indian groups, a tactic he had tried on a previous trip leading Spaniards to search for Ayolas. Aracaré had also exhorted other Indians not to show the Spaniards their villages or to guide them through the country. Cabeza de Vaca held a trial and condemned Aracaré in absentia to death as a traitor. He sent word to Irala, who was returning from his own scouting trip, to find and hang Aracaré. Cabeza de Vaca explicitly noted that the killing was not an act of war but the execution of a rebellious subject of the king, punishment for "the mutiny he led and for impeding discovery of the land."[102] A charge of treason based on "impeding discovery" required at least minor contortions of legal logic. It seemed to rely on the notion that the act was one committed against the king's army. For a governor with shaky legitimacy planning a major expedition upriver, the execution of Aracaré for this crime must have seemed pedagogically useful; the same charge might be raised against Spaniards.

The opportunity soon presented itself. Cabeza de Vaca's entrada, his own march inland to find silver from a point on the upper Paraguay River, began at the start of the rainy season, against Indian advice. Desperate to find guides, Cabeza de Vaca searched for the elusive "Indians of Garcia" who had made the trip before. Rumors placed them here and there, but the party turned up guides with only vague notions of the route. Finally seizing on one who seemed more certain but said it would be sixteen days of hard travel to the silver, the exhausted men fell back to the camp by the Paraguay River.[103] Cabeza de Vaca proposed to wait for the waters

[102] "Relación general," in Serrano y Sanz, *Relación de los naufragios*, tomo segundo, 2:1–98, 37.

[103] The first guide said he had been part of a western migration when very young and remembered details of the trip to a land where his relatives had plundered gold and silver. Cabeza de Vaca did his best to confirm the story; in this case, all he could do was impress on the man that there would be serious consequences if he was not telling the truth. After five hard days of bushwhacking, the guide admitted he could not find the old paths, and the party was once again lost. The Spaniards searched desperately for a new guide, finally encountering one who said that a populated, rich land lay far inland. They had perhaps five days of supplies left and, by then, a deep distrust of the Indians and of the landscape's ability to sustain them. All were aware that the

to recede and try again. A scouting party confirmed that the interior was now a vast "lagoon" that "covered more than two leagues of land."[104] Travel in this season meant days of miserable slogging through water that could reach chest high, with supplies balanced on platforms between canoes. Waiting out the flood, the Spaniards missed signs from the Indians that this was a lean time on the river and found themselves starving and sick, drinking dirty water, and surrounded by the foul-smelling mud flats left by the receding waters.

It was here, at the miserable port on the upper Paraguay, where Cabeza de Vaca asked his *escribano* to begin taking testimony on Irala's actions "to impede and disturb my voyage of reconnaissance."[105] It was probably at the same spot that Irala and his men resolved to move against the governor, though they delayed in arresting him until after the party returned to Asunción. They probably did not know how they were going to explain their coup. As the adelantado's imprisonment in Asunción dragged on over seven months, Irala destroyed the governor's legal papers; replaced the *escribano* and the other legal officers with hand-picked allies; and hoped, we can imagine, that Cabeza de Vaca might die from his illness or from some unfortunate, possibly staged, accident.[106] Irala warned anyone still supporting the governor that if Cabeza de Vaca were freed, he would accuse them all of treason "and cut off our heads."[107] At some point, Irala and his followers fixed on the idea of turning the tables and accusing Cabeza de Vaca of treason. Unless he conveniently died, the adelantado would have to be accused of something, after all. Perhaps the idea took more definite form as Cabeza de Vaca pronounced accusations of treason against Irala and his men. Cabeza de Vaca, by his own account,

decision to continue rested entirely on the credibility of an Indian guide – just days after one had led them astray. Cabeza de Vaca claimed he was warned by his officials that "the Indians never tell the truth; it could be 16 days traveling the way shown by the guide or it could be many more." See "Comentarios de Álvar Núñez Cabeza de Vaca, adelantado y gobernador del Rio de la Plata, escritos por Pero Hernández, escribano y secretario de la provincia, y dirigido al serenisimo, muy alto y muy poderoso señor el Infante Don Carlos N.S.," in Álvar Núñez Cabeza de Vaca, *Naufragios y comentarios* (Mexico City: Porrúa, 1988), 168. Passages quoted from the "Comentarios" are my translation.

[104] "Relación de las cosas sucedidas en el Rio de la Plata, por Pero Hernández," in Serrano y Sanz, *Relación de los naufragios*, 2:307–58, 333.

[105] "Relación general," in Serrano y Sanz, *Relación de los naufragios*, 2:1–98, 56.

[106] A fire broke out one night in Cabeza de Vaca's house, where he was chained and could not escape. He claimed it was an attempt on his life.

[107] "Relación de las cosas sucedidas," in Serrano y Sanz, *Relación de los naufragios*, 2:307–58, 346.

lashed out after hearing about acts of violence against Indians being carried out under Irala: "Does it seem just to you that each one of you wants to be king of this land? Well, I want you to know that there is no other king, nor should there be, nor other lord, than His Majesty and I in his name."[108] After this outburst, we are told, the magistrate appointed by Irala began to take sworn statements "that the governor had said he was king."[109]

Whatever the precise timing, the charge of treason took root. The formal charge later filed against Cabeza de Vaca in Spain, based on depositions taken in Asunción – Cabeza de Vaca claimed that the witnesses had been bribed or intimidated – asserted that the adelantado "called himself King and [declared], 'I am the prince and lord of this land.'"[110] Evidence of his intent to usurp royal authority included his naming of the region on the coast of Brazil after his famous grandfather, a conquistador of the Canary Islands.[111] A more serious charge was that, when leading expeditions, Cabeza de Vaca had used his own family's coat of arms in place of the king's. Irala portrayed Cabeza de Vaca's insistence on control over Indians as an arrogant attempt to concentrate all authority in his own hands and accused him of stirring up Indians in the region. The broadest charge was a version of the one that had been brought against the Indian Aracaré. In his letter to the king, Irala explained that Cabeza de Vaca "had not accomplished what Your Majesty had ordered," the discovery of a route across the continent to find silver.[112] Failing at reconnaissance – by leading his men into the quagmire of the upper Paraguay – was itself construed as an act of treason.

Cabeza de Vaca's arrest and subsequent legal struggles belonged to a series of episodes shaping the association of remote spaces of empire and treason. Cabeza de Vaca's legal chances were probably hurt and then ultimately helped by the outbreak around the same time of open rebellion elsewhere in the Indies in response to the New Laws of 1542. In Peru, Gonzalo Pizarro refused not only to accept the laws restricting Spanish control of Indian labor but also to recognize the viceroy sent from Spain.

[108] "Relación de las cosas sucedidas," Serrano y Sanz, *Relación de los naufragios*, 2:346.

[109] "Relación de las cosas sucedidas," Serrano y Sanz, *Relación de los naufragios*, 2:347.

[110] Quoted in Adorno and Pautz, *Álvar Núñez Cabeza de Vaca*, 1:337.

[111] He called the province Vera, after Pedro de Vera.

[112] "Carta de Domingo de Yrala a S.M. dando extensa cuenta del estado de las provincias del Río de la Plata, prisión de Cabeza de Vaca, etc. 1545," in Serrano y Sanz, *Relación de los naufragios*, 2:379–5, 394.

While failing to comply with the laws fit a widespread pattern of passive resistance, dismissing the authority of the viceroy was unquestionably the act of a rebel. Pizarro's revolt, and the series of minor rebellions that followed in a climate of generalized political upheaval, made the dangers of disloyalty plain to the Council of the Indies. The turn of events might have contributed to the crown's reluctance to act quickly to clear Cabeza de Vaca of the charges against him, even though his alleged crimes paled by comparison to those of the rebels in Peru. It is worth noting that Pizarro's execution for treason marked the end of a career that was already intertwined with stories of betrayal. Until the time of his rebellion, Gonzalo Pizarro was mainly known for his unsuccessful expedition in the upper Amazon, the voyage that produced Orellana's "treachery" in leaving the main force to wander and starve in the upper reaches of the river.[113] Tales of treason traveled throughout Spanish America, especially along rivers, and they would eventually migrate into other imperial spheres.

Telling Treason Tales

Writing about treason in remote places was an emerging genre. Spanish chroniclers produced detailed accounts of the rebellions in Peru, as well as narratives about mutinies that occurred on a series of expeditions in search of riches in the Amazon. The familiar plotlines included betrayal of stranded armies and forgiveness of treasonous acts by practical and merciful officials.[114] These stories of upriver betrayal were reworked in English sources in ways that popularized associations of particular geographies with potential political crises.

One story provided both the culmination and the exception to this body of narratives: the chronicle of Lope de Aguirre's rebellion against the commander of a reconnaissance expedition sent to the upper Amazon in 1559. Aguirre's actions in many ways fit the pattern; he induced his men to revolt against Pedro de Ursúa, the expedition commander, at a

[113] In Oviedo's sixteenth-century history of the Indies, treason appears as only a very minor theme in detailed descriptions of various expeditions through nearly five volumes, until Oviedo begins to recount the rebellions in Peru. See Gonzalo Fernández de Oviedo y Valdés, *Historia general y natural de las Indias*, vol. 5 (Madrid: Ediciones Atlas, 1992).

[114] Oviedo's account (Oviedo y Valdés, *Historia general*) of the activities of the viceroy in Peru at the time of Pizarro's rebellion features numerous instances when he accused followers of treason and then pardoned them.

time when the army was desperately searching for food and lost on an unknown branch of the river system. But Aguirre was exceptional not because he conspired in the death of Ursúa but because he refused to join the effort to take legal cover after the murder by endorsing a document drawn up by other mutineers declaring that their act had been a necessary response to Ursúa's tyrannical rule. The other leaders of the mutiny, including a nobleman recruited by Aguirre to serve as Ursúa's replacement, reasoned that the men could regain the favor of the Spanish king by continuing their reconnaissance; if they found and settled a wealthy new province, the Spanish king would forgive their violence. The logic recalls the successful legal strategies of Irala and his men, or of Orellana after his separation from Pizarro. But Aguirre was a thoroughly uncommon subject. Asked to approve the statement, Aguirre took the pen and signed, "Lope de Aguirre, Traitor." He exhorted the men to give up any hope of reestablishing their loyalty. They would eventually be held accountable for Ursúa's murder, he told them; even if they found wealthy new lands, they would be cast aside in favor of new royal appointees, who would have an interest in displacing and punishing the first group. Through a combination of terror and persuasion, Aguirre prevailed and led his men in repudiating their ties to the Spanish king and in electing their own "King of Tierra Firme."[115]

Aguirre renounced his loyalty to the crown, cursed the king, and railed against royal appointees, especially legal officials. Going further than Shakespeare's character Dick the Butcher, Aguirre would have killed not only the lawyers but also, "with cruel torments, all bishops, viceroys, presidents, judges, governors, lawyers, and law clerks" who were destroying the Indies.[116] Yet Aguirre never gave up many of the trappings of Spanish authority, and he reaffirmed his deeply felt Catholic faith. His letters to the king expressed open defiance but also continued to offer advice, exhorting Phillip II, for example, not to mount any more upriver expeditions in so dangerous a region ("I advise thee not to send any Spanish fleet up this ill-omened river; for, on the faith of a Christian, I swear to thee, king and lord, that if a hundred thousand men should go up, not

[115] Aguirre sailed to the mouth of the Orinoco River and attacked and held the island of Margarita off the coast before falling on the mainland to a force of loyalists sent out from Mérida to meet him. Along the way, he murdered scores of his own followers, some for attempted desertion and some for minor infractions or imagined plots. The main chronicle is by a contemporary, Pedro Simón (*The Expedition of Pedro de Ursua and Lope de Aguirre*).

[116] Simón, *The Expedition of Pedro de Ursua and Lope de Aguirre*, 129.

one would escape").[117] While plundering Indian and Spanish settlements, Aguirre continued to hand out and redistribute scores of minor posts to subordinates as rewards for their loyalty to him, appending salaries to be paid from the proceeds of future conquests. Even as he embraced the role of rebel, Aguirre gave his reasons, and they were also legal arguments, mainly drawn from a Germanic legal understanding of the bonds of loyalty between subject and king.[118] In one of his letters to Phillip II, Aguirre explained that he had been driven to rebel because the king was a "breaker of thy faith and word" for failing to reward his subjects for their participation in the conquest and allowing royal officials and friars to seize and squander the wealth of the Indies. In a final passage indicating that his break with the king was forced by a rupture of obligations rather than lapsed allegiance, Aguirre offered his prayers that Phillip II would succeed in defeating the Turks.

The Spanish chronicler saw Aguirre's treason as a political lesson, and speculated that the story's circulation had contributed to the quieting of rebellions in the Indies. While repeating familiar tropes of treason in remote places, the story was shocking because the traitor, unlike Cabeza de Vaca and many others, had openly rejected the possibilities of legal and political maneuvering to regain royal favor. Aguirre and his men had even been offered pardons, which only some had accepted. To be caught in a web of charges and countercharges that required appeals to the king's mercy was one thing; to declare oneself a traitor and refuse mercy turned mere literary allusion to the political dangers of remote places into a bloody prospect, the equivalent of a riverine horror story.

The Spaniards, it turned out, were not the only Europeans consuming such stories. In *The Discovery of the Large, Rich, and Beautiful Empire of Guiana*, Walter Raleigh relied heavily on Spanish sources to make his case that some six hundred leagues up the Orinoco River, Incas pushed east by the invading Spaniards had founded a city rich in gold on a wide salt lake.[119] Raleigh recounted in some detail the failures of successive Spanish

[117] Simón, *The Expedition of Pedro de Ursua and Lope de Aguirre*, 194.

[118] See *supra* note 59 on the prevalence of Germanic legal approaches to treason in the Spanish *fueros*. The influence of local legal traditions was important in all Spanish expeditions, where participants identified themselves and others according to regional origins (see *supra* note 92).

[119] This work is an account of Walter Raleigh's first voyage to the Orinoco River, in 1596. *The Discoverie of the Large, Rich, and Bevvtiful Empire of Gviana with a Relation of the Great and Golden Citie of Manoa (Which the Spanyards Call El Dorado) and the Prouinces of Emeria, Arromaia, Amapaia, and Other Countries, with Their Riuers, Adioyning*. (London: By Robert Robinson, 1596). Ralph Bauer analyzes this work as

expeditions cut short by mutinies, including the rebellion of Aguirre, who had set out "not onely to make himselfe Emperour of *Guiana*, but also of *Peru* and of all that side of the *West Indies.*" Raleigh in part cited the Spaniards' many "tragedies" as evidence that the region had "never been conquered or possessed by anie Christian prince" and could therefore be claimed by the English. His vision relied on familiar images of an interior empire with a singular river gateway; he promised that "by keeping one good fort, or building one towne of strength, the whole Empyre is guarded."[120] In addition to bolstering English claims, the emphasis on Spanish betrayal and treason in the region was probably also intended to contrast with Raleigh's fidelity.

This implied contrast between Spaniards' frequent betrayals and Raleigh's loyalty framed his first work but became explicit and vitally important to him later. No longer protected at court after James I came to the throne, Raleigh was convicted of treason in 1603, in an unlikely plot to back a rival successor. Confined to the Tower of London until 1616, Raleigh persuaded the king to allow his release to undertake another voyage to the Orinoco to find the gold mines of which he now claimed certain knowledge. James was hostile to Raleigh's anti-Spanish imperial vision, and, on the advice of Gondomar, the influential Spanish ambassador, made it clear that any military action against the Spaniards in the region was forbidden. The voyage would have been doomed to failure anyway – there was no mine – but when Raleigh's men took a small Spanish fort at the mouth of the Orinoco and then failed to search for the mine, any chance of redemption was ruined. On Raleigh's return, the crown's

an example of an "imperial mysticism" in which European occult philosophy became a vehicle for appropriating hybridized Indian-European geographic knowledge. See "A New World of Secrets: Occult Philosophy and Local Knowledge in the Sixteenth-Century Atlantic," in *Science and Empire in the Atlantic World*, ed. James Delbourgo and Nicholas Dew (New York: Routledge, 2008), 99–126, 116.

[120] Raleigh, "The Discoverie of the Large, Rich, and Bevvtiful Empire of Gviana," 17–18, 19, 98. Raleigh had found the region as difficult to traverse as the Spaniards, even with the help of coerced local guides: "I know all the earth doth not yeelde the like confluence of streames and branches, the one crossing the other so many times, and all so faire & large, and so like one to another, as no man can tell which to take: and if we went by the Sun or compasse hoping thereby to go directly one way or other, yet that way we were also caried in a circle amongst multitudes of Ilands, and euery Iland so bordered with high trees, as no man coulde see any further than the bredth of the riuer, or length of the breach." (39) Yet his enthusiasm for establishing an English empire to rival that of the Spaniards led him to believe accounts that beyond the "broken Ilands & drowned lands" (41) of the estuary and the few easily navigable stretches of the Orinoco River lay a region with "more abundance of Golde then any part of Peru." (10)

advisers could not find a new charge that would both fit Raleigh's actions and allow James to satisfy the Spanish demand for his punishment. The attack on the Spanish settlement had contravened the king's orders, and several witnesses accused Raleigh of undermining the voyage through delays and of intending to go over to the side of "some Forraigne Prince."[121] But there was little evidence that Raleigh had committed any acts of disloyalty, and even the attack on the Spanish fort had been carried out by his subordinates and against his instructions. The only solution was to execute Raleigh on the strength of his earlier conviction for treason.

Raleigh's attempt to win a pardon for treason by discovering riches along a New World river entailed an elegant narrative inversion of Spanish stories of upriver betrayal told about men like Cabeza de Vaca and Aguirre.[122] Raleigh was working with familiar legal themes and narrative conventions when he turned the possibility of political danger far from home into a story of political redemption through acts of allegiance in a riverine region; his argument for pardon depended on an implicit understanding by his audience that he had placed himself in the ideal setting for the corruption of loyalties, yet had kept his attention fixed on service to the king. At the same time, Raleigh's arguments also fit within the flexible set of strategies for claiming possession of territory in the New World. In his pursuit of control of a mine near the mouth of the Orinoco, Raleigh imagined a claim to the Orinoco region as a whole, and he cited the tenuousness of Spanish settlements as a sign that no effective occupation had yet secured a Spanish claim. Stories of Spanish mutiny fit within a discourse about the inadequacy of Spanish proofs of possession.

Raleigh was certainly not the only English captain influenced by Spanish narratives of upriver betrayal. A last, brief example will help to support the view that the circulation of these and similar narratives linked geographic and political-legal imaginaries. Settlers' strenuous reconnaissance from Jamestown to chart the rivers flowing into the Chesapeake Bay both reflected and shaped a vision of the region as a network of rivers. John Smith's map based on these voyages gave form to this vision; it blended European and indigenous geographic knowledge by showing crosses at

[121] Walter Raleigh, *Sir Walter Rawleigh His Apologie for His Voyage to Guiana* (London: Printed by T.W. for Hum. Moseley, 1650). Raleigh defended himself by pointing out that he his return to England was proof that he had never contemplated treason.

[122] Cañizares-Esguerra also describes accounts of Raleigh's exploits as comprising an inversion of Spanish chronicles, though his emphasis is not on narratives of danger. See Cañizares-Esguerra, *Nature, Empire, and Nation.*

upriver locations to note the places where reliance on experience ended and dependence on information from Indian informants began.[123]

As a central figure of the reconnaissance efforts and their main chronicler, John Smith, like Cabeza de Vaca, played up his singular expertise in reading both native intentions and the environment. He was more reticent in describing several episodes of serious political jeopardy. When the expedition first reached Jamestown, Smith was under arrest. He had spent nearly three months in chains aboard ship, accused of having "intended to usurpe the government, murder the Councell, and make himselfe king" and of plotting with confederates spread across three ships.[124] Given a reprieve and admitted to the council after the small fleet's arrival at Jamestown, Smith began to position himself as a uniquely skilled interlocutor in dealing with the Indians. On one of several upriver reconnaissance trips, and the first for any Jamestown settlers beyond the fall line, Smith was held captive by Indians and brought before Powhatan. He was probably initiated as a subject of the Indian leader in a ceremony he later presented as a narrative of salvation, with Pocahontas's intercession to prevent his execution; he was certainly offered political protection in exchange for recognizing Powhatan's authority.[125] On the same trip, Smith had left several men in a barge to travel further upriver by canoe – pushed forward, he contended, by the "idle exceptions being muttered" about his failure on an earlier scouting trip to locate the head of the Chickahominy River. Three men were killed by Indians – one downstream, where the men from the barge had gone ashore, and two upstream, where they waited by the canoes. When Smith returned to Jamestown, he was greeted with "the truest signs of joy" by most settlers but also threatened by the new members of the council, who blamed Smith "for the losse of our two men" upriver.[126] Given the earlier charges

[123] Smith's own description of the map presents it in precisely these terms, emphasizing the primacy of rivers and explaining the dual sources of information: "[T]his annexed Mappe... will present to the eye, the way of the mountains and current of the rivers, with their severall turnings, bays, shoules, Isles, Inlets, and creekes, the breadth of the waters, the distances of places and such like. In which Mappe observe this, that as far as you see the little Crosses on rivers, mountains, or other places, have been discovered; the rest was had by information of the Savages, and are set downe according to their instructions." John Smith, "Description of Virginia," in Tyler, ed., *Narratives*, 76–118, 89. And see Blansett, "John Smith Maps Virginia," in Appelbaum and Sweet, eds., *Envisioning an English Empire*, 68–91.

[124] "Proceedings of the English Colony," in Tyler, ed., *Narratives*, 119–204, 124.

[125] "A True Relation," in Tyler, ed., *Narratives*, 25–71, 50. And see Horn, "The Conquest of Eden," in Appelbaum and Sweet, eds., *Envisioning an English Empire*, 25–48.

[126] "A True Relation," in Tyler, ed., *Narratives*, 52.

and perhaps the influence of circulating tales about betrayals of men in eerie upriver regions, Smith might have been facing the revival of the earlier treason charges.[127] The fate of his men upriver would have supported a charge of abandoning or betraying the king's army very similar to the accusation lodged against Cabeza de Vaca.

It is possible, too, that Smith's enemies were uneasy about his understanding with Powhatan, and were prepared to allege that Smith had shifted his loyalties as a result of his close contact with the Indians. This possibility is not so far-fetched as it might seem. The European practice of seizing Indians to serve as guides and interpreters was matched in Jamestown by the routine placement of young men and boys among the Indians. In 1619, the Virginia Assembly would try one of these boys, Henry Spelman, for treason, accusing him of serving Powhatan's successor, Opechancanough.[128] Europeans like Smith who championed their own abilities to negotiate with Indians risked being tainted by these associations, and by their access to the dangerous backcountry. Indeed, the year after being accused of endangering his men upriver, Smith's enemies were again preparing charges against him, this time with the support of testimony from men stationed at the falls who "complained he caused the Savages assalt them." This new campaign by Smith's enemies developed against the background of rumors that Smith "had the Salvages in such subjection, hee would have made himselfe a king, by marrying Pocahontas."[129]

[127] The Jamestown settlers were well acquainted with the Spanish chronicles circulating in England and contrasted their own difficulties with "the histories of the Spanish discoveries and plantations" and their accounts of "mutinies, discords, and dissentions." In Chapter II of the "Proceedings of the English Colony," this contrast is presented just after the account of Smith's upriver reconnaissance trip. Tyler, ed., *Narratives*, 131.

[128] As Karen Kupperman has argued, English suspicions of Indians' penchant for "treachery" was an early product of Indian-English encounters. Karen Ordahl Kupperman, "English Perceptions of Treachery, 1583–1640: The Case of the American 'Savages,'" *Historical Journal* 20, no. 2 (1977): 263–87. I would like to thank Karen Kupperman for bringing the case of Henry Spelman to my attention. On this case, see Virginia Company of London and Susan M. Kingsbury, *The Records of the Virginia Company of London: The Court Book, from the Manuscript in the Library of Congress*, 4 vols. (Washington, D. C.: Government Printing Office, 1906), 3:174–75. And see Kupperman, *Jamestown Project*, 289–90.

[129] In "Proceedings of the English Colony," surely composed either for or by Smith, the description is of charges and counter-charges of usurping the government. The claim is that Smith's enemies, Martin, Ratcliffe, and Archer, first plotted to kill Smith, and then "joined together to usurp the governement... and excuse themselves by accusing him." See "Proceedings," in Tyler, ed., *Narratives*, 196.

The extent to which the structural similarities of these accounts of betrayal and treason along rivers resulted from their circulation across empires and regions is something we will probably never be able to measure – though the English preoccupation with Spanish chronicles is well documented in general, and both Raleigh and Smith explicitly cite Spanish accounts to provide a contrast to their own claimed loyalty. The referencing of past rebellions, as in Cabeza de Vaca's (and Aguirre's) labeling of mutineers as *comuneros*, also hints at a wider political role for these stories. Still, if a handful of treason charges in riverine settings were all we had to go on, the case that sojourners and settlers rendered these corridors as peculiar places of physical and political danger would be suggestive but incomplete. It helps to know that stories of treason in Europe were beginning to take shape within a wider literary project of imagining the state as sovereign, and portraying, through narrative, mere thoughts of violence as acts of rebellion.[130] The key, though, is our placement of the legal contests of reconnaissance and settlement in the larger context of ambitions attached to river regions: the pursuit of wealth, including mines; the wider political and legal routines for making claims; and the related and ubiquitous politics of defining legal authority and fixing the boundaries of political communities in empire. These conditions raised the stakes and provided the dramatic mise-en-scène for tales about treason along rivers. As settlement cultures and economic interests changed, the geographic and political imaginary of rivers also shifted.

Treason's Second Atlantic Career

When tenuous settlements developed into more stable settler communities, the politics of treason did not subside but came to be linked in new ways to definitions of the nature and scope of colonial polities. In the Río de la Plata, mestizo elites battling over the control of Asunción, its regional trade, and Indian labor nearly two hundred years after Cabeza de Vaca's expedition adopted the mantle of *comuneros* and invited charges of treason by disobeying or ignoring orders from the viceroy in Lima. In North America, especially in the conflicts of the mid-1670s in New England and Virginia, treason was invoked in triangulated struggles involving established colonies, new and remote settlements, and Indian communities. In

[130] See Rebecca Lemon, *Treason by Words: Literature, Law, and Rebellion in Shakespeare's England* (Ithaca: Cornell University Press, 2006); Raffield, *Images and Cultures of Law in Early Modern England*. For eighteenth-century discursive shifts, Barrell, *Imagining the King's Death*.

all these settings, treason still referred to crimes against the sovereign, and political rivals still sought to form mutual accusations of treason. But colonial entities now also asserted claims to settlers' and Indians' allegiance and more often punished rebels directly rather than sending the accused to Europe.

The geography of legal politics also shifted. The emphasis on riverine claims as part of an interimperial politics over New World possession began to fade, while tensions between estuary and upriver settlements increasingly centered on intraimperial politics over the control of Indians and trade, and the rivalries of colonial authorities. These late seventeenth-century and early eighteenth-century conflicts have often been viewed as turning points in settler-Indian relations; they also mark subtle changes in the geographic imagination of regions in areas of established European settlement, away from the integration of regions centered on river basins and toward a politics of tensions between riverine subregions defined by jurisdiction.

Consider first changes in the nature of colonial rebellions in Asunción. In the decades after Cabeza de Vaca's arrest, bitter conflicts over the governorship continued.[131] For example, when Felipe Cáceres, one of the leaders of the revolt against Cabeza de Vaca, was named acting governor in 1567, he immediately became embroiled in a political battle with the bishop, Pedro Fernando de la Torre, in a struggle between secular and ecclesiastic authorities that was common in Spanish America, especially in remote settlements.[132] After having a rival tried and executed for treason, Cáceres was imprisoned for a year and then sent, like Cabeza de Vaca, back to Spain, with de la Torre along to represent the case against him.[133] This sort of deadly squabbling over the governorship began to take new forms under changing political and economic conditions. By the beginning

[131] Participants often referred back to the events following the city's founding. Asunción elites recalled later that in the aftermath of Mendoza's failed expedition in the early sixteenth century, Charles V had signed a *cédula* (order) in 1537 allowing the members of the expedition to gather and elect a new governor for the province. Though the *cédula* was superseded when Cabeza de Vaca was sent as adelantado, the document became a resource for locals in subsequent struggles over the governorship. Various factions claimed that the *cédula* demonstrated the crown's willingness to have governors appointed locally. Adalberto López, *The Colonial History of Paraguay: The Revolt of the Comuneros, 1721–1735* (New Brunswick, NJ: Transaction Publishers, 2005), 6–7.

[132] See Benton, *Law and Colonial Cultures*, chap. 3, on disputes over jurisdiction between secular and religious authorities.

[133] In addition to de la Torre, Cáceres had enemies among the rising mestizo elite, and when he was seized in church in 1569, the town leaders cited the 1537 *cédula* when they met to elect a replacement.

of the seventeenth century, the Río de la Plata region had been split into two administrative parts, with Buenos Aires as one center and Asunción the other. Asunción was increasingly operating as a hinterland capital, with its main source of income the export of yerba mate, the plant used to make a tealike infusion. Tensions were meanwhile mounting between city elites and the Jesuits, whose missions to the south were becoming the main centers of production for yerba mate. The Jesuits had strongly opposed the encomienda system in Paraguay and had managed to attain royal approval for exempting mission Indians from encomienda labor at a time when the population of nonmission Indian towns was fast declining.[134] The Tebicuary River, a tributary of the Paraná River, was coming to signify not a corridor of imperial expansion but a dividing line between two intraimperial zones, the missions and the area around Asunción. The city was developing a reputation for insisting on local autonomy and governing through its cabildo instead of deferring to governors appointed by royal officials in Peru or to the rulings of the audiencia at Charcas.

Treason continued to be the legal weapon of choice in struggles over leadership. The most celebrated case was that of José de Antequera at the beginning of the eighteenth century. The conflicts connected with the case deserve a closer look because they illustrate clearly both the continuities of political discourse about loyalty and the new meanings of accusations of betrayal in a changed political and economic landscape. In Charcas, Antequera had been a popular member of the elite, an official on the audiencia, and the *protector de indios*.[135] He was sent as *juez pesquisidor* (investigative judge) to assess treason charges being lodged by political rivals in Asunción. Shortly after he arrived, the Asunción cabildo recognized Antequera as the interim governor, and he set about interviewing scores of witnesses about the alleged actions of disloyalty by a former governor. Guided by Antequera, a faction of the Asunción elite embraced a series of measures against the Jesuits, including their removal from the town. The actions made Antequera into a local hero, but they also pitted the viceroy in Peru, who saw Antequera's appointment as interim governor as a challenge to his authority, against the Charcas audiencia,

[134] López, *Colonial History of Paraguay*, 51; see also Barbara Anne Ganson, *The Guaraní under Spanish Rule in the Río de la Plata* (Stanford, CA: Stanford University Press, 2003). My account of the Antequera affair draws mainly from López.

[135] The *protector de indios* was an official appointed by the crown to represent Indians in Spanish courts.

which sought to define the case as a judicial and not an administrative affair.

While the dynamics of the case were guided by the rivalry of powerful colonial authorities, they were also shaped by new conditions in the political economy of the river region. To dodge his investigation, Antequera's enemies simply moved downriver, an action made possible by the support of the Jesuits and the merchants at Corrientes, where the cabildo agreed to seize goods coming down the river from Asunción. Eventually, a force authorized by the viceroy and composed mainly of mission Indians with leadership from Buenos Aires engaged a larger army under Antequera's command. Though Antequera won the battle near the border formed by the Tebicuary River, he and a group of supporters retreated in a position of weakness to Charcas. Here the viceroy's authority trumped the protections that the audiencia could offer. After a five-year trial, begun in 1726, Antequera and his associate Mena were beheaded in Lima as traitors.

In some respects, the trial itself and the rhetoric employed on both sides echoed the conflicts of a century before. Antequera and Mena argued that the Jesuits were guilty of usurping sovereign authority in the region while Antequera had been legitimately installed as interim governor by order of the audiencia of Charcas. All his actions had been in the service of the king, Antequera argued, for the purpose of maintaining order. The defense also insisted that Antequera had been unable to control the angry Paraguayan populace. This line of defense built on the reputation of Asunción's inhabitants as semirebellious and seemed to be supported by news during the trial of yet another revolt in Asunción – by men calling themselves *comuneros,* after Irala's supporters in the sixteenth century.

In many ways, though, the conditions and context of Antequera's treason trial were very different from those of Cabeza de Vaca's time. Antequera had to maneuver in relation to an array of powerful imperial institutions: the Charcas audiencia, the office of the viceroy in Peru, cabildos in Corrientes and Buenos Aires, and the Jesuit missions. Antequera's rivals did not have to invoke the king; disobeying the viceroy was itself interpreted as an act of treason. Further, the conditions that had created an atmosphere of suspicion about allegiances in Cabeza de Vaca's time – the remoteness of Asunción and its upriver isolation – were now working against Antequera. Yerba mate had to be traded through towns down the river, and the cabildos of those towns were positioned to exploit their favorable geographic positions in further isolating Asunción economically and politically. It was a climate well suited to stories about the innate rebelliousness of Asunción – not of the people, but of the place, which seemed to turn outsiders like Antequera into insurgents.

Antequera's treason trial prompted various participants to paint themselves as defenders against rival empires and Indians. This discourse also repeated themes from early conflicts in the region while reflecting new conditions. Anxieties about Indian aggression focused on the consolidation of rule over upriver regions; fear of incursions by the English and other powers plagued mainly coastal areas. An official writing in defense of Antequera hailed the loyalty of the inhabitants of Asunción, citing their service in manning thirteen garrisons that protected Spanish settlements from "continual invasions... by diverse infidel enemies."[136] He represented upriver inhabitants as the true defenders of the Spanish imperial frontier. The Jesuits, the report noted, talked up their role as "the nearest striking force... to oppose the Europeans, especially the English, who could penetrate Peru by the Uruguay and the Paraná," but portrayed the danger that the English or Dutch would take Buenos Aires and move to attack upriver settlements ("tierra adentro") as insignificant.[137]

Colonial institutions making claims on the loyalty of colonial subjects, the increasing power of port merchants, and a geographic imaginary featuring upriver regions as colonial frontiers – these factors also shaped the politics of treason in late seventeenth-century British North America. Daniel Richter has argued that the English displacement of the Dutch at New Netherland in 1663 set in motion changes that contributed to both Bacon's Rebellion and King Philip's War.[138] The English occupation disrupted the Dutch-Indian trade network in the Hudson River Valley and led to the removal of the Swedish settlement at the mouth of the Delaware, so that Indians in two major river-trading systems were forced to look laterally for trading partners and new European and Indian allies. The

[136] "Copia del informe que hizo el General D. Mathias de Angles y Gortari, corregidor del Potosí, sobre los puntos, que han sido causa de las discordias sucedidas en la ciudad de la Asunción de la provincia del Paraguay, y motivaron la persecución de D. Josef de Antequera de parte de los regulares de la Compañia," in José de Antequera y Castro, *Colección general de documentos, que contiene los sucesos tocantes a la segunda época de las conmociones de los regulares de la Compañía en el Paraguay, y señaladamente la persecucion, que hicieron a Don Josef de Antequera y Castro* (Madrid: Imprenta Real de la Gaceta, 1769), 3:2.

[137] "Copia del informe que hizo el General D. Mathias de Angles y Gortari," in Castro, *Colección general de documentos*, 3: 53, 54.

[138] Daniel Richter, "Dutch Dominos: The Defeat of the West India Company and the Reshaping of Eastern North America" (paper presented at "Transformations: The Atlantic World in the Late Seventeenth Century," Harvard University, March 30–April 1, 2006).

riverine geographies of New England and Virginia were meanwhile shaping intraregional tensions of their own. The Massachusetts Bay Colony found itself in possession of an excellent harbor but in secure control of two disappointing rivers, the Charles and, to the north, the Merrimack. Claiming control over the region extending south of the headwaters of the Merrimack River, Massachusetts colonists both maneuvered to gain access to the Connecticut River Valley – through aggression against the Pequots on the eastern bank of the river and through settlement on the upper Connecticut River to the west of Boston – and represented the size and position of the Merrimack River in ways that bolstered their claim to portions of Maine and New Hampshire under their charter (see Figure 2.3).[139] In Virginia, fall lines along a series of rivers marked a divide between coastal areas controlled by well-connected planters and upcountry regions of more tenuous settlement. In both places, colonists distinguished between Indians living within the jurisdiction of the colonies and those living in regions still sparsely settled by Europeans. The former were considered subjects while the latter were still referred to as belonging to nations. Among Indian subjects, further distinctions were made depending on whether Indians were Christianized, lived among English settlers, were members of groups nominally subordinate to the English, or identified themselves as relatively independent of and allied with the colonies.[140] Indians in the last two groups sought to offset the encroaching power of the colonies by insisting that they were loyal subjects of the English sovereign with a direct relationship to the crown that might bypass colonial authorities.

[139] The colonial charter of Massachusetts awarded the Massachusetts Bay Company control over all territory between a line running east-west three miles north of any part of the Merrimack River and three miles south of any part of the Charles River. Massachusetts and New Hampshire disputed the meaning of this clause, with New Hampshire claiming that the intent had been to mark a territory three miles north of the mouth of the river (as early colonists had thought that the river's course ran west to east). Massachusetts leaders insisted on an interpretation that would extend their territory much further north and provided maps that rendered the Merrimack as rather grand. See Figure 2.3 and Jenny Hale Pulsipher, *Subjects unto the Same King: Indians, English, and the Contest for Authority in Colonial New England* (Philadelphia: University of Pennsylvania Press, 2005), 200. In 1741, the line was established three miles north of Pawtucket Falls. Samuel A. Green, *The Boundary Line between Massachusetts and New Hampshire: From the Merrimack River to the Connecticut: A Paper Read before the Old Residents' Historical Association of Lowell, on December 21, 1893, the Twenty-Fifth Anniversary of the Formation of the Society* (Lowell, MA: Lowell Courier, 1894).

[140] James David Drake, *King Philip's War: Civil War in New England, 1675–1676* (Amherst: University of Massachusetts Press, 1999), 38.

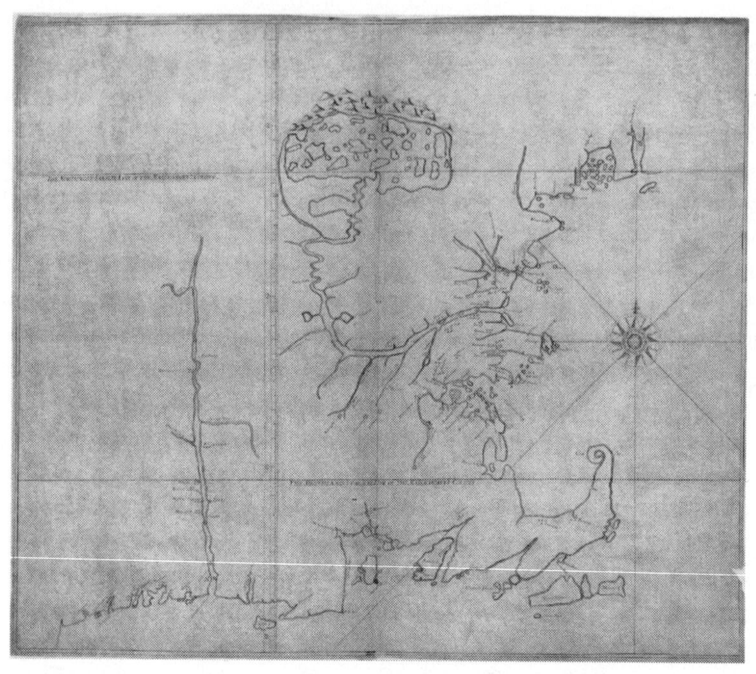

FIGURE 2.3. Map of Massachusetts and Merrimack Rivers (1678). Colonists created this map to bolster claims to the northern extent of Massachusetts. The colony's charter had fixed its northern boundary in relation to the Merrimack River (see Chapter 2, note 139). The map depicts Massachusetts as a riverine region, with towns to the west of Boston, such as Concord, Groton, and Lancaster, sited along tributaries of the Merrimack and forming part of a region centered on its basin. Note the depiction of the Connecticut River as a less significant waterway. Courtesy of the John Carter Brown Library at Brown University.

This tendency was established early in New England as the Narragansetts petitioned the king directly in the 1640s in search of relief from Massachusetts controls. It was a strategy that resembled, and perhaps imitated, the actions of settlers in outlying areas or weaker colonies who also insisted repeatedly on their direct connection to the king. In the 1660s, royal commissioners reinforced this strategy in visits to Indian groups as well as to settlements in New Hampshire and Maine, promising to take grievances to the crown. A central element in the struggle to define authority in the region was controversy over the demand by the Massachusetts Bay Colony that subjects swear an oath of fidelity to the commonwealth. From the 1660s, the oath was cited in England as a justification for revoking the Massachusetts charter and placing the colony under more direct royal control. Settlers in outlying regions where

Massachusetts control was disputed also resisted the oath. Nonroyalist Massachusetts leaders did not hesitate to insist on loyalty to the commonwealth, arguing that allegiance to the colony also signaled allegiance to the crown.[141] In 1664, the Massachusetts General Court went further and issued a new law defining crimes of sedition and treason "against our commonwealth," unleashing a period in which "competing interests freely launched accusations of treason."[142]

While the surprising intensity and scope of Indian attacks during King Philip's War temporarily united white settlers against the Indians, the conflict also provided further foundation for grievances in outlying communities that were especially hard hit by Indian attacks. Inhabitants of western Massachusetts towns showed little stomach for enforcement of edicts against disloyal speech, for example, and Maine residents, feeling that they had suffered disproportionately during the war, maneuvered to avoid taxation.[143] The more radical break, however, occurred in the withdrawal of loyalty of Indians allied with Philip. Precisely because Philip, as leader of the Wampanoags, in the past had followed a political strategy of defining himself as an equal subject of the English king, the outbreak of violence was interpreted not as an act of war between nations but as an insurrection.[144] The different status of Indian groups at the start of the war influenced the way they were characterized as combatants. Philip and the Wampanoags were rebels who had committed "high treason," while Indians in the north country who had not formally submitted to colonial rule were "enemies."[145] An intermediate category of Indians who at first either remained neutral or even aided in suppressing the Indian rebellion was eroded after Indians of the upper Connecticut River Valley joined in alliance with Philip and conducted a series of attacks on western towns. These raids marked a turning point in the conflict precisely because the Nipmucks and other upriver Indians had been viewed as subjects whose loyalties were secure.[146] The attacks led directly to English confinement of praying Indians and a broadening of the war to encompass the Narragansetts.

[141] Pulsipher, *Subjects unto the Same King*, 61.

[142] Pulsipher, *Subjects unto the Same King*, 66, 67.

[143] See the case described in Pulsipher, *Subjects unto the Same King*, 173. On Maine-Massachusetts relations during King Philip's War, see Pulsipher, *Subjects unto the Same King*, chap. 9.

[144] Drake, *King Philip's War.*

[145] Drake, *King Philip's War*, 44.

[146] Drake, *King Philip's War*, 87.

When English settlers acted against Indian subjects as traitors, they did not draw narrowly on the English law of treason but invoked a broad and flexible legal culture defining treason and its punishment. Legislation on treason in the colonies encompassed language from the English Statute of Edward III (listing the main categories of treasonous acts, including compassing the death of the sovereign, levying war, and aiding the king's enemies) as well as the terms in charters and proprietary grants establishing the authority to impose martial law to punish sedition or rebellion.[147] Historians have noted that formal charges of treason appear to have been rare before the American Revolution, occurring most notably at critical moments prompted by royal succession, as with the trial of Jacob Leisler for treason in New York.[148] Yet the use of treason both as a label for the actions of Indian "rebels" and as a flexible legal tool against them during and after King Philip's War reminds us that it was symbolically central to colonial polities' authority, combining definitions of subjecthood with affirmation of the power and scope of colonial governance.[149] Both the geographic reach of the colonies and their ability to command loyalty were at stake. As in Spanish expeditions in South America, labeling and punishing Indians as traitors could serve as a warning to non-Indians who might also be tempted by sedition.

The insistent yet flexible uses of treason law are illustrated by the trial of a group of Indians at Newport, Rhode Island, in August 1676, at the end of King Philip's War. The trial was conducted as a court martial, under the Rhode Island charter's provision to exercise martial law in actions against Indians "and other Enemies" of the colony. The trial singled out a handful of Indians for possible execution; the more usual punishments for Indian captives were to assign them to fixed terms of servitude or to sell them as slaves. The charges brought in this case

[147] James Willard Hurst, *The Law of Treason in the United States: Collected Essays* (Westport, CT: Greenwood, 1971), chap. 3. In Maryland and Pennsylvania, it was briefly made a crime to compass the death of the proprietor; the queen in council overturned Pennsylvania's act, and Maryland's act was only in effect for three years.

[148] Hurst, *Law of Treason*. See also Bradley Chapin, *The American Law of Treason: Revolutionary and Early National Origins* (Seattle: University of Washington Press, 1964). On the context of Dutch-Anglo tensions leading up to and continuing after Jacob Leisler was executed for treason, see Adrian Howe, "The Bayard Treason Trial: Dramatizing Anglo-Dutch Politics in Early Eighteenth-Century New York City," *William and Mary Quarterly* 47, no. 1 (1990), 57–89. See also Peter Charles Hoffer, *The Treason Trials of Aaron Burr* (Lawrence: University Press of Kansas, 2008).

[149] Treason law was also related to a broader discourse about Indian treachery. See Karen Ordahl Kupperman, "English Perceptions of Treachery."

included failure to follow "the Government established in this said Colony by his said Majesty" and adherence instead "to Indians of another Colony called Plymoth, namely, Philip chiefe Sachem of the Indians in that said Colony." The "trayterous" and "rebellious" acts committed "didst doe great Damage to our soveraigne Lord the King, by killing his Subjects, burning their Houses, killing and driving away their Cattell, and many more Outrages of that Nature."[150]

Several of the Indians on trial, like the defendant Quanopen, admitted to having been "in Armes against the English Nation" and were condemned to death by execution, but others were delivered into the hands of settlers, presumably to use or sell as slaves.[151] Several of the Indians appeared to attempt to mount a defense, mainly by claiming to have played a minor role in attacks on settlers. But few denied a part in the violence. John Wecopeak testified that "he was never out against the English" but admitted to being present when "Georg Crafts Wife was shott with a Sluff, and chopt in some Parts of her Body with a Hatchett." Wecopeak was condemned to death; the violence of men who had Christian names and had worked for English settlers or lived near them prompted the harshest punishment. Earlier in the same month, Philip's body had been pulled from a swamp to be beheaded and quartered – treated, in other words, as the body of a traitor. His head was taken to Plymouth to be mounted on a pole.[152]

As in the Río de la Plata, trying and executing Indians as traitors were acts that figured in political tensions among settlers, who routinely used the label of "traitor" to taint political enemies. Sometimes this connection was more than rhetorical. A Rhode Island farmer named Joshua Tift was also tried for treason in the wake of King Philip's War. Tift claimed he had been seized by the Narragansetts and made their captive, but there was little evidence that he had been tortured or even coerced, and he was found living among the Narragansetts and suspected of having

[150] Rhode Island (Colony), *A Court Martial Held at Newport, Rhode Island, in August and September, 1676, for the Trial of Indians, Charged with Being Engaged in King Philip's War* (Albany, NY: Printed by J. Munsell, 1858).

[151] As Jill Lepore notes, enslavement was not the usual punishment for treason. Its substitution for death was cited by colonial officials as evidence of their leniency. Use of the punishment also shows the still-ambiguous status of Indians on the edges of the colonial polity who were not yet formally made subjects to the English crown or colony. See Lepore, *The Name of War: King Philip's War and the Origins of American Identity* (New York: Vintage Books, 1999), 164.

[152] Rhode Island (Colony), *A Court Martial.* On the treatment of Philip's body, see Drake, *King Philip's War*, 162.

been among Narragansett warriors as they battled the English in the Great Swamp Fight.[153] The suspicion was that he had gone to live with the Indians voluntarily. A poorly educated farmer with little property, Tift was culturally close to the Christian Indian Captain Tom, who was tried for treason for living with the Nipmucks though he claimed he had "never ingaged against the English."[154] Anxieties similar to those about Indian loyalty attached to settlers who were perceived as socially marginal – especially those living in remote regions, including towns along the Connecticut River and the poor farmland of coastal Rhode Island. Ironically, as one response to the Indian attacks, colonial officials in Boston drew the circle of their control more tightly, so that at one point in the conflict they were ready to abandon active defense of a ring of outlying towns from Groton to Concord. The polity to which settlers owed loyalty, and swore oaths, was simultaneously expanding its geographic range and insisting on a well-defined center of power.

The association of political and geographic fault lines is even more apparent in Virginia in the same period. Participants in Bacon's Rebellion followed a legal script about Indian and settler loyalties that was very similar to the rhetoric in King Philip's War. As in New England, legal politics highlighted geographical distinctions between coastal regions and upriver country. Nathaniel Bacon was one of a group of settlers with farms above the fall line, a place of transition from the coastal plains to the plateau before the mountains and bisecting the region's rivers, the Rappahannock, the York, and the James rivers and their tributaries. Settlers in the regions at the heads of the rivers were especially vulnerable to a new wave of Indian attacks.[155] The government's policy of stationing forts at the fall line had proven ineffective; Indians simply avoided the forts and pillaged nearby farms. The dispute between Bacon and Governor Berkeley

[153] Lepore, *The Name of War*, 131–4.

[154] Lepore, *The Name of War*, 143.

[155] One of the participant-chroniclers of Bacon's Rebellion, Thomas Matthew, described the Indian attacks as the result of the movement of hostile Indians over the whole upland region: "These escap'd Indians (forsaking Maryland) took their rout over the head of that river, and thence over the heads of Rapahanock and York rivers, killing whom they found of th' upmost plantations untill they came to the head of James river, where (with Bacon and others) they slew Mr. Bacon's overseer, whom he much loved, and one of his servants, whose bloud hee vowed to revenge if possible." "The Beginning, Progress, and Conclusion of Bacon's Rebellion in Virginia, in the Years 1675 and 1767," in *Tracts and Other Papers, Relating Principally to the Origin, Settlement, and Progress of the Colonies in North America, from the Discovery of the Country to the Year 1776*, ed. Peter Force (Washington, D.C.: Printed by P. Force, 1836), 1, no. 8, 10.

began with Bacon's decision to lead a group of settlers against the Indians without a commission from the governor in 1676.

In the series of political maneuvers and military skirmishes that followed, Bacon and Berkeley were attentive to legal arguments that might bolster their positions. Both claimed to be acting in concert with the crown's wishes by defending the commonwealth.[156] Bacon argued that he was protecting the colony from invasion by Indians because he knew that acting against invaders was allowed in law even without approval of the governor; Berkeley – who declared Bacon a rebel, then publicly pardoned him, then again labeled him a rebel – represented himself as fighting against disorder and rebellion, and pointed out that even though English law did allow government officials to "rayse what forces they could to protect his majesties subjects," such actions were not considered legal if taken against the "Kings prohibition."[157] Both men sought to affirm their positions by insisting on the loyalty of their followers and by labeling their opponents as traitors. Bacon demanded that his supporters sign an oath of allegiance that included a pledge to repel the king's forces until word could be gotten to the king to explain the rebels' actions. Some coastal landowners who were sympathetic with Bacon's anti-Indian posture balked at signing an oath that would commit them to levying war against the king's forces. Bacon urged his followers to oppose Berkeley and loyal government officials by labeling them "Traytors to the King, and Countrie."[158] Berkeley, for his part, lost no opportunity to characterize Bacon as a traitor and to warn his followers of the consequences of treason. This message was most effectively delivered in the form of the summary trials and executions of fourteen of Bacon's followers during the course of the campaign against him, including four convictions in court-martial proceedings aboard a ship near the mouth of the York River in January 1767, and six more later in January, as Berkeley's forces secured the area around Jamestown.[159] Berkeley also awarded some

[156] James Horn notes that historians have tended to neglect "the degree to which Bacon and his followers initially tried to cast their opposition to the governor's authority in legitimate constitutional forms." *Adapting to a New World: English Society in the Seventeenth-Century Chesapeake* (Chapel Hill: University of North Carolina Press, 1994), 376.

[157] Quoted in Alexander B. Haskell, "'The Affections of the People': Ideology and the Politics of State Building in Colonial Virginia, 1607–1754" (Ph.D. diss, Johns Hopkins University, 2004), 239.

[158] Quoted in Haskell, "The Affections of the People," 268.

[159] According to one account, Berkeley insisted that the manner of execution clearly reflect that the men had been convicted of treason. Hansford, executed in Accomack, asked

pardons, and he ordered Henry West, one of the men convicted of treason and rebellion against the king, banished from the colony because he was not "so notorious as the rest."[160]

Accusations of treason against the rebels generated new legal and political entanglements once Berkeley was again in control. Royal commissioners sent to aid in establishing order arrived in the colony and almost immediately clashed with Berkeley over a set of interconnected issues involving who would be pardoned and how the property from the forfeited estates of convicted rebels would be handled and distributed. The commissioners wanted to publish a proclamation they carried from the king pardoning the rebels without exception. Berkeley and his followers, reeling from the financial burdens of the war and its destruction, insisted that dozens of men identified as leaders of the rebellion ought to be exempted. Each side invoked English legal precedent. Berkeley reminded the commissioners of property seizures carried out during the English Civil War. The commissioners, for their part, cited Sir Edward Coke on the inadmissibility of property seizures without a trial (for felonies, however, not for treason) and argued that it was one thing to proceed against rebels under court-martial in time of war but "that the Lawes might returne to their owne proper Channell, and that all future proceedings of this might bee by a Jury."[161] Defining the rebels as traitors was of signal importance to Berkeley, who persuaded the Virginia assembly to exempt fifty-five people from a pardon and specifically stated that the men, together with Bacon (now dead from disease), were attainted of high treason.[162] In insisting on defining Bacon and his followers as traitors, Berkeley was protecting the economic interests of loyalists; he had planned to distribute property from

"that he might be shot like a soulder, and not to be hanged like a Dog. But it was tould him, that what he so passionately petitioned for could not be granted, in that he was not condemned as he was merely a soldier, but as a Rebell, taken in Arms, against the king, whose laws had ordained him that death." He insisted in his speech on the gallows "that he dyed a loyal subject, and a lover of his countrey; and that he had never taken up arms, but for the destruction of the Indians, who had murthered so many Christians." "Ingrams Proseedings," in Force, ed., *Tracts and Other Papers*, 1, no. 11, 33.

160 Wilcomb E. Washburn, *The Governor and the Rebel: A History of Bacon's Rebellion in Virginia* (New York: W. W. Norton, 1972), 91, also 89–91.

161 Washburn, *Governor and the Rebel*, 110–11. The commissioners' position was at odds with their own actions. They had, after their arrival in Virginia, participated in trials of some of the rebels. Washburn counts nine additional executions after the rebellion had been put down. Washburn, *Governor and the Rebel*, 119, 146. Matthew in his account suggests that members of the assembly, not the commissioners, pleaded for an end to the executions, one member expressing the feat that "the govern'r would have hang'd half the countrey, if they had let him alone." "The Beginning, Progress, and Conclusion," in Force, ed., *Tracts and Other Papers*, 1, no. 8, 24.

162 Washburn, *Governor and the Rebel*, 118.

the estates seized. He was also reminding the commissioners that he was still the highest-ranked representative of the king in Virginia and head of the commonwealth. Disloyalty to him amounted, in Berkeley's mind, to strong evidence of treason.[163] This view, ironically, was the corollary of Bacon's argument that Berkeley acted against the crown by abandoning his obligations to the settlers to keep them safe. Both men constructed stories about betrayal by pointing to the disruption of reciprocal obligations between the governor and the colonists.

Also at stake, as in New England, was the status of Indians as legal subjects. Several Indian groups in the region were considered subjects of the crown and were afforded, according the Berkeley's government, the "benefit and Protection of the law."[164] Yet it was precisely their inability to be held accountable under the law that rankled Bacon, who called the Indians "wholly unqualified" to participate in the colony's legal system and suggested they would not be punished under its laws.[165] Bacon was advocating precisely the shift in Indian legal status that would emerge in New England as a direct result of King Philip's War. As in New England, this view originated in remote settlements of the colony and in response to Indian attacks. Bacon, having never accepted the status of Indians as subjects in the upriver territories of Virginia, saw these attacks not as signs of rebellion, punishable by death, but as the acts of enemy invaders. Though both rationales meant deathly hostility toward Indians, Bacon's position removed from settlers the responsibility of determining the loyalty of Indians before killing them. Bacon's expeditions against Indians beyond the fall line produced many more deaths of Indians who had lived in amity with settlers than of those responsible for the recent attacks against them.

In some respects, the examples surveyed here of treason charges resulting from war and rebellion in the late seventeenth- and early eighteenth-century colonies recall the practices of reconnaissance and very early settlement. Settlers and officials drew on a repertoire of legal concepts and forms in attacking and establishing authority and in protecting settlers'

[163] The blending of personal and political loyalties is made especially clear in Berkeley's comments before the execution of Thomas Hall during the rebellion. He reported that Hall had "dyed very penitent confessing his rebellion against the King and his ingratitude to me." Washburn, *Governor and the Rebel*, 89. See also Haskell, "The Affections of the People," 275–6.

[164] Quoted in Haskell, "The Affections of the People," 233.

[165] Quoted in Haskell, "The Affections of the People," 234. Ann Cotton observed that one of Bacon's complaints against the governor was his refusal "to admit an English mans oath against an Indian, when that Indians bare word should be accepted of against an Englishman." In "An account of our late troubles in Virginia, written in 1676, by Mrs. An. Cotton of Q. Creeke," in Force, ed., *Tracts and Other Papers*, 1, no. 9, 6.

interests. The law of treason was creatively invoked – often as a simple slur against political opponents but always as a charge that held the special, awful possibility of the consequences of death and the forfeiture of estates. The instability of remote regions and the ambiguities of Indians' subjecthood, so important in the politics of reconnaissance expeditions, also figured prominently in the political crises of settlements.

The key difference in the later period was the intermediate position of established colonial polities. Allegiance to the crown was now defined in part in terms of loyalty to colonies as instruments of the sovereign. Colonial officials claimed the authority to try, convict, and execute rebels and traitors, and to impose lesser sanctions and administer pardons. Metropolitan authorities recognized this power as both essential to imperial control and occasionally corrosive of crown authority. The layers of intraimperial legal authority added to the unpredictability of events on the ground. Antequera's conviction and execution for treason, the suspicion and trial of Christian Indians in New England, and the political consequences for Berkeley of insisting that rebels be attainted as traitors – these legal turns were contingent, not necessary, outcomes of applications of the law in multisided political and military conflicts.

Finally, while past usage influenced representations of particular subregions as remote and politically unstable – Virginia above the fall line, the upper Connecticut River Valley, the Paraguay River beyond Asunción – changes in the strength and stature of colonial polities also urged subtle shifts in colonial geographic imagination. The model of colonial regions formed around river systems was undergoing change. Upriver regions were still on the edges of settlement, but they were now in relation to more powerful and ambitious coastal polities whose elites wanted to define the economic potential of remote regions in their own terms. Asunción was recast as a hinterland in a divided Río de la Plata region, no longer considered a starting point for potentially lucrative forays to find mines or a critical point along a unified corridor of imperial control. In jockeying not just to expand the colony's jurisdiction but also to establish their city at the center of a regional economy, Boston elites sought control over fragments of the Connecticut and Hudson river valleys.[166] In Virginia,

[166] On English designs on the upper Hudson Valley, even during periods of Dutch rule of New Amsterdam, see Donna Merwick, *Possessing Albany, 1630–1710: The Dutch and English Experiences* (Cambridge: Cambridge University Press, 2003). Merwick, however, assumes that the contrast between the Dutch emphasis on water routes and the English ambitions to control land stemmed largely from different national conceptions of space. I would suggest that the English understood and even favored a model of colonial expansion along rivers.

Bacon's Rebellion marked the zenith of a stark division in the political geography of the colony into coastal and plateau regions, with a border at the fall line.[167] Violent conflicts and accompanying political contests helped to shape these transitions, just as expectations about colonial geographies influenced the rise of rebels who defined themselves as loyal subjects of the king.

Conclusion

When rivers that seemed like clear paths across unknown terrain and gateways to new worlds of trade turned out to lead nowhere, the resulting crises threatened not only survival but also political reputations, future patronage, and political order. In the critical moments when expeditions foundered, other ruptures occurred: leadership changed hands, groups splintered, factions formed, and mutinies simmered. These were times for invoking royal, religious, and personal authority; for mustering rhetorical resources; and for standing on, or judiciously abandoning, procedure. At remote points along strange rivers, often at places no European could yet place on a map, hungry and lost travelers called for notaries and rehearsed legal stories. The voyagers plotted actions and recorded statements in the service of narratives intended for legal proceedings in distant courts.

The resulting jurisdictional net was long and thin, spread along river corridors. Holes and tangles made it possible for legal actors to be inside the net one moment and outside the next. This was true for people of ambiguous status, such as captive guides, as it was for Christians whose subjecthood was settled. Men suspected of treason were implicitly accused of having placed themselves outside the political community by renouncing loyalty, a condition of membership. Ironically, the capacity for treason itself depended on that membership. Many Indians, most Africans, and even some descendants of Europeans and locals, such as Luso-Africans, could not be easily defined or prosecuted as traitors.[168]

[167] The geographical distinction between coastal and hill country continued to have importance, but settlement beyond the fall line changed the nature of this dividing line and reduced its importance as a marker between politically unstable and administratively central regions. Horn, *Adapting to a New World*, 163.

[168] The question of whether a slave could be charged as a traitor surfaced explicitly in a 1781 case in Virginia in which a slave named Billy was tried for treason. Two judges wrote a dissenting opinion stating that a slave "Cannot Commit Treason against the State not being Admitted to the Privileges of a Citizen." Malick W. Ghachem, "Introduction: Slavery and Citizenship in the Age of the Atlantic Revolutions," *Historical Reflections* 29, no. 1 (2003): 13. I am grateful to Malick Ghachem for bringing this example to my attention.

It is tempting to try to match the legal politics of subjecthood and treason with the formation of discrete zones in empire existing outside the legal order – areas under the command of heathens, rogues, or rebels. Yet zones of lawlessness and experiments in countersovereignty were in fact rare. Even Aguirre, the self-declared traitor, penned letters to the king and kept in place the hierarchy of the crown's military-bureaucratic order. We are not observing the intentional dilution or distortion, in Conradesque fashion, of European law in remote places. Instead, in conflicts about the boundaries of political community that were geographically dispersed, Europeans in empire insisted on referencing metropolitan law and precedent. Cabeza de Vaca had not tried to set up a kingdom of his own near the Río de la Plata but was accused of usurping crown authority, with added charges related to his conduct on the march to Asunción and during the entrada from the upper Paraguay. The possibility for treason moved with travelers; it was even enhanced by the conditions of river reconnaissance, with its mobilization of law as a framework for gathering and storing geographic information, and the use of legal acts to support contested imperial claims.

Travelers reaching into a repertoire of legal concepts and procedures in order to advance their interests were responding to specific political contexts at home – think of Cabeza de Vaca's labeling his political adversaries in Asunción as *comuneros* – and searching for legal rhetoric that would appeal to particular sponsors, and to jurists. At the same time, legal routines and rituals were chosen for their promise in defending and solidifying political positions out in empire. The law of treason changed as it was applied in these circumstances. Whereas trials for treason were relatively rare in sixteenth-century Spain, the New World created opportunities for rivals to lodge charges against each other, and the crown found new interest in treason as a mechanism for controlling distant subjects. Cabeza de Vaca's definition of impeding discovery as a crime of treason was probably an informed innovation. English voyagers, usually imagined as more sparing in applying treason law in the colonies before the American Revolution, invoked it as part of an Atlantic legal politics shaping new colonial enterprises. Raleigh and Smith drew on Spanish narratives to frame accounts of their own exploits, while an interimperial discourse about possession added to the pressures on the English and the French to place political loyalties at the center of many early New World conflicts. Indians were not automatically defined as imperial subjects but were brought under crown authority through acts and declarations affirming their subjecthood. Among other fluid boundaries, this distinction created legally differentiated intraimperial zones and, within them, anomalous enclaves such as Christian Indian towns and Indian missions.

Together, these connections shaped a distinctive legal geography for riverine regions. In an environment experienced as unruly and unpredictable, where both subjecthood and loyalty were in doubt, asserting European sovereignty was not enough to ensure orderly imperial expansion and rule. Sovereignty did not have an even territorial or juridical dimension. Instead, sovereign spaces followed corridors of control, from estuary enclaves through river networks, and they depended on reinforcement through the formal incorporation of subjects in political communities, while sheer distance strained ties between subjects and sovereigns.

Even as territorial sovereignty solidified as a model in the nineteenth century, the representation of upriver country as conducive to treason continued to have an active political valence.[169] Perhaps some echoes of this discourse reached Conrad after all. For an extended period, from the mid-fifteenth century to the beginning of the long eighteenth century, geographic imagination and legal practice blended in rendering riverine regions as treacherous places.

[169] In the first decades of the nineteenth century, the upriver regions of the Mississippi River Valley spawned inter imperial intrigues and more treason cases than any other region in the new United States. See Andrew R. L. Cayton, "'When Shall We Cease to Have Judases?' The Blount Conspiracy and the Limits of the 'Extended Republic,'" in *Launching the "Extended Republic": The Federalist Era*, ed. Ronald Hoffman and Peter J. Albert (Charlottesville: University Press of Virginia, 1996), 156–89.

3

Sovereignty at Sea

Jurisdiction, Piracy, and the Origins of Ocean Regionalism

Reflect how close by now we were,
to defeat, emaciated by hunger,
exhausted by storms, by climates
And seas beyond all our experience,
So weary of promises dashed,
So often driven to despair beneath
Heavens with scarcely one familiar star
And hostile to the kind of men we are!
Our provisions were thoroughly rancid;
To consume them made our bodies worse
While nothing brought any comfort,
In pursuing such fleeting hopes!
Would you believe that had our company
Of soldiers not been Portuguese,
They would have remained so long obedient
To their king and to me, their king's agent?

– Luís de Camões, *The Lusíads*[1]

Oceans have become the quintessential metaphor for globalization. People, ideas, germs, plants, and capital move in transnational and cross-regional currents, while global trends and migrants arrive on shore in waves. Behind this choice of language is the image of the sea as a conduit for exchange but not a place of significance independent of those flows. The idea of the ocean as a backdrop for movement informs a narrative of globalization as a story of increasing interconnectedness. It

[1] Luís de Camões, translated by Landeg White, *The Lusíads* (Oxford: Oxford University Press, 1997), 112.

begins with European transoceanic trade and moves through successive transportation revolutions, each enhancing the supposedly frictionless, undifferentiated nature of ocean space.

A narrative about the law of the sea has run parallel to this story. From Grotius on, the law of the sea has featured prominently in the history of international law. Maritime regulation has appeared as a privileged arena for implementing international agreements, a condition arising from the peculiar qualities of the sea as a place that cannot be occupied. By its very nature, the ocean has seemed to demand the mutual recognition of legal norms derived from natural law or other law standing outside the control of polities. At the same time, the historical weakness of such legal regimes has given the oceans an enduring association with lawlessness – a legal void to accompany its emptiness as a medium of travel and communications.

These related themes are implicit in many treatments of early modern European representations of oceans in cartography, literature, and voyage narratives. Cluttered with compasses and rhumb lines, the portolan charts of the Mediterranean gave way to world maps that styled the oceans as a blank expanse. In this account, sea monsters and ships began to function as mere decorative conventions used to populate an increasingly undifferentiated space, dreamed up by mapmakers drawing more on literary visions of the terrors of the unknown than on mariners' observations.[2] Voyage chronicles typically offer only brief descriptions of the sea, and land sightings and interactions with locals figure as the dramatic turning points of these narratives, and as contrast to the monotony of ocean travel. The only real action on the high seas, it seems, comes in the form of marauding or mutiny – twin symbols of that other quality of the open sea, its apparent lawlessness.

These readings – of law, cartography, and storytelling – leave out an important dimension of the experience of and discourse about ocean space. Alongside interconnected representations of oceans as empty, vast, and lawless, Europeans held and developed understandings of oceans as variegated spaces transected by law. As Camões boasts about Portuguese sailors, mariners understood that authority flowed through captains from sovereigns. The ships dotting world maps often indicated well-traveled

[2] Philip Steinberg, in *The Social Construction of the Ocean*, describes a "shift from the ocean's representation as a terrifying wild wherein societies and nature interact to its representation as an empty space to be crossed by atomistic ships" in the seventeenth century (105).

regions of the sea and routes plied by representatives of particular sovereigns instead of mere fillers decorating the oceanic equivalent of terrae incognitae (see Figure 3.1).[3] In developing trade routes, merchants promoted the idea of sea space as divided into sea lanes.[4] Polities meanwhile could and did claim jurisdiction in ocean corridors, and the strategies of mariners often reinforced such claims by emphasizing the ties of ships to sovereigns. Even while developing new arguments about the natural law basis for regarding the sea as the common property of all mankind, European jurists and statesmen continued to provide legal justifications for claims to specific rights over limited ranges within the sea, defending not ownership but the control of commerce and navigation along vaguely defined ocean corridors.[5]

Understanding early modern visions of the sea as a space crossed in many directions by jurisdictional corridors helps us to make sense of imperial visions organized around the discovery and militarization of maritime passages. Spaniards thought of their maritime voyages as marking *derrotas* (routes) or *caminos* (roads) within the sea and understood the value of keeping secret any precise knowledge about such tracks.[6] The

[3] The imagination of sea routes was also very clearly influenced by knowledge of water currents and wind patterns. Padrón makes this point in *Spacious Word* in arguing that Spaniards did not imagine the oceans as "trackless expanses" but as "a network of routes of sail" (83).

[4] Jan Glete defines warfare at sea between 1500 and 1650 as principally over the control of these "maritime lines of communication" generated by trade. *Warfare at Sea, 1500–1650: Maritime Conflicts and the Transformation of Europe* (New York: Routledge, 2000), 1.

[5] Steinberg, in *The Social Construction of the Ocean*, notes that early modern jurists were more concerned with control than possession. Yet he defines this as a distinctive legal regime because it contrasted with the world order of "territorial states that comprised its paradigmatic spatial structure" (109). I argue throughout this book that the spatial order of territorial state sovereignty was less well established than the layered sovereignty and uneven spatial patterns associated with empires.

[6] A notable example of this perspective comes from the record of Columbus's first voyage. On his return, Columbus "presented to have gone a greater distance to confuse the pilots and sailors who were charting their course so that he would remain the master of the route [*derrota*] to the Indies, as in fact he does, since none of them showed on their charts his true route [*camino*], because of which no one could be sure of his route to the Indies." Dunn and Kelley, *The* Diario, 375. More generally, the Spanish crown went to great lengths to keep navigation information secret from imperial rivals. A tension existed, however, between the desire for secrecy to protect access to resources and the need to make such information public in order to secure claims. See Alison Sandman, "Controlling Knowledge: Navigation, Cartography, and Secrecy in the Early Modern Spanish Atlantic," in *Science and Empire in the Atlantic World*, ed. James Delbourgo and Nicholas Dew (New York: Routledge, 2008), 31–52. And see María M. Portuondo, *Secret Science: Spanish Cosmography and the New World* (Chicago: University of Chicago Press, 2009).

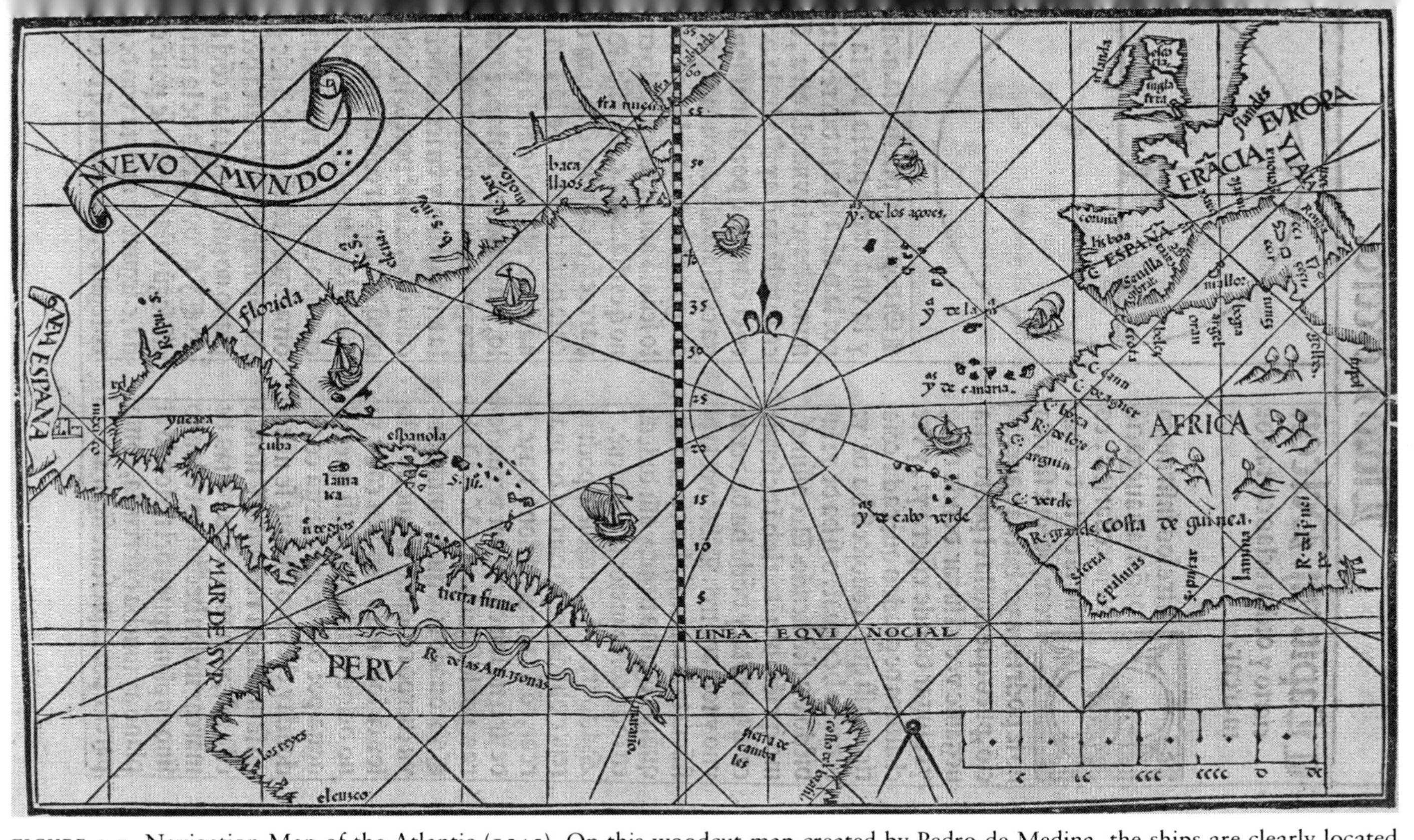

FIGURE 3.1. Navigation Map of the Atlantic (1545). On this woodcut map created by Pedro de Medina, the ships are clearly located to mark Atlantic routes, with their sails positioned accordingly. The convention extended to a wide range of other maps of the period. *Arte de navegar en que se contienen todas las reglas, declaraciones, secretos, y avisos, q a la buena navegacio[n]* (Valladolid: En casa de Francisco Fernandez de Cordoua). Courtesy of the John Carter Brown Library at Brown University.

Dutch entered Asian trade in part by constructing a corridor of control that occasionally crossed but largely avoided Portuguese sea lanes. The English sought the Northwest Passage, a corridor to China that they might claim and protect as distinct from Spanish routes. Such constructions were not just the work of men in imperial centers. Even the most freewheeling European mariners carried law to distant seas as they insisted on their legal ties to sovereign sponsors at key points along ocean paths. Land-based empires manipulated European claims to the control of sea lanes to their own advantage. The interimperial maritime conflicts in the eighteenth century represented less struggles over principles such as free trade and neutral shipping than contests over the tracks of sea lanes and the nature of legal control within them. The vision that united these projects was one of the ocean as an uneven legal space divided into long, thin zones of imperfect control connecting port towns, coasts, garrisons, and islands.

Hydrographers concurred. Through the nineteenth century, the oceans as we now know them were labeled inconsistently, often with many separate seas within them.[7] European scholars, mariners, and a small cadre of early oceanographers focused their attention on understanding the variations within and across oceans: the patterns of tides, the movement of currents, and the flow of water through connecting straits.[8] An enduring idea with ancient roots explained these phenomena with reference to an imagined network of subterranean passageways connecting seas and oceans, sometimes envisioned as flowing to a giant reservoir at the earth's core (see Figure 3.2). While known sea passages marked corridors for travel and trade, imaginary water channels traced peculiar transregional connections, much like the wormholes of space in modern astronomy. Athanasius Kircher pictured invisible tunnels leading from vast subterranean lakes in South America, southern Africa, northern India, and elsewhere, sometimes with outlets in the middle of oceans or seas.[9] As the English scientist John Greaves put it in 1646, the earth

[7] Martin W. Lewis, "Dividing the Ocean Sea," *Geographical Review* 89:2 (1999), 188–214. On the Atlantic, see Joyce Chaplin, "Knowing the Ocean: Benjamin Franklin and the Circulation of Atlantic Knowledge," in *Science and Empire in the Atlantic World*, ed. James Delbourgo and Nicholas Dew. New York: Routledge, 2008, 73–96.

[8] Margaret Deacon, *Scientists and the Sea, 1650–1900: A Study of Marine Science* (London: Academic Press, 1971).

[9] Imperfect knowledge about currents was related to conjectures about subterranean waterways. Mariners had observed strong surface currents flowing from the Atlantic into the Mediterranean, and out of the Baltic and into the Atlantic. Imagined underground corridors helped to explain why such flows could be perpetual without creating different water levels in separate seas. Athanasius Kircher's *Mundus subterraneus*, which appeared in

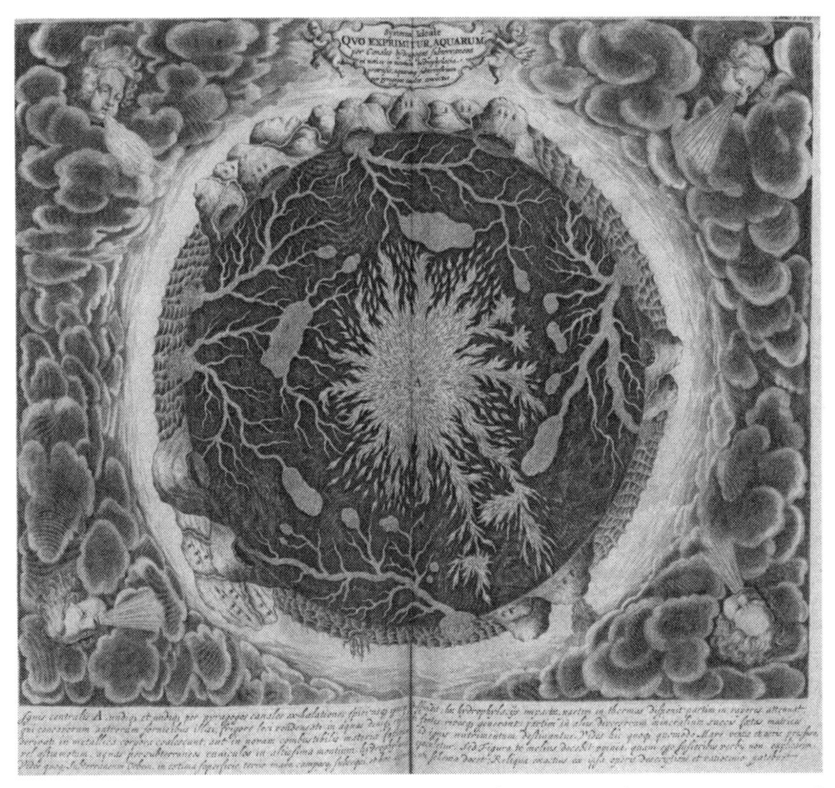

FIGURE 3.2. The World's Subterraneous Canals (1665). This image appeared in Athanasius Kircher's *Mundus subterraneus* (Subterranean World) and shows Kircher's vision of a world of underground canals linking oceans and interior seas. Athanasius Kircher, *Mundus subterraneus*, vol. 1, folio I, 186. Courtesy of the New York Public Library.

was "tubulous."[10] Even the increasingly sophisticated art of navigation, with its movement toward the precise placement of landfalls and

1665, stated that all ocean water cycled through the earth's core. See Deacon, *Scientists and the Sea*, 53–5, 132–5. On the circulation of Kircher's works in the Americas, see Paula Findlen, "A Jesuit's Books in the New World: Athanasius Kircher and his American Readers," in *Athanasius Kircher: The Last Man Who Knew Everything* (New York: Routledge, 2004), 316–50. On the importance of an understanding of currents to the imagination of the Atlantic Ocean, see Philip L. Richardson, "The Benjamin Franklin and Timothy Folger Charts of the Gulf Stream," in *Oceanography: The Past*, ed. Mary Sears and Daniel Merriman (New York: Springer-Verlag, 1980), 703–17. Joyce E. Chaplin shows that sailors knew about Atlantic currents well before nonsailors recognized and mapped them. See "Knowing the Ocean." And on Franklin's contributions to the study of currents, see Joyce E. Chaplin, *The First Scientific American: Benjamin Franklin and the Pursuit of Genius* (New York: Basic Books, 2006).

[10] Deacon, *Scientists and the Sea*, 71.

landmarks on a grid, directed its advances toward tracing the movements of voyagers and defining ocean passages.[11]

Such renderings must be taken into account in characterizing the maritime regulatory order that emerged between the fifteenth and nineteenth centuries. As with voyages of reconnaissance on distant rivers, Europeans imagined law as traveling with them along sea routes composing their "tubulous" world. Individuals – including seemingly legally marginalized rogues and pirates – did not imagine themselves as cut off from legal authority even when very far from home and on the open seas. European sovereigns, for their part, had a clear interest in maintaining such ties, and they acted on the expectation that others would do the same. From the resulting interimperial legal politics, regional regulatory orders took shape in ocean basins. The high seas, meanwhile, came to be understood as a peculiar legal region in which multiple powers exerted influence but not control.

Viewing the sea as a space of intersecting corridors helps us to revise several prominent narratives about the nature and timing of key transformations in the maritime regulatory order. On the one hand, some historians have highlighted the turning point of the early seventeenth century, when prominent European jurists analyzed maritime disputes to articulate the origins of international law. On the other hand, some historians have emphasized the significance of changes in the long nineteenth century. The domestication of the sea in European geographic imagination altered associations of oceans and coasts with death and danger, and gave way to representations of the shore as a place of pleasing prospects and of leisure.[12] Also, the definitive rise of British naval hegemony and the emergence of an interstate order in the nineteenth century permitted the first coordinated, global campaigns to contain piracy and prepared the way for a global maritime treaty regime.[13]

We need not discard such findings in order to emphasize the importance of the first half of the long eighteenth century, a period from about

[11] For example, when William Bourne made corrections to his navigation manual, *A Regiment for the Sea*, for a third edition in 1580, he added a "Hydrographicall Discourse" describing five passages to Cathay, "two of them knowen and the other three supposed." William Bourne and E. G. R. Taylor, *A Regiment for the Sea, and Other Writings on Navigation* (Cambridge: Published for the Hakluyt Society at the University Press, 1963), 301.

[12] Corbin, *Lure of the Sea.*

[13] Janice E. Thomson, *Mercenaries, Pirates, and Sovereigns: State-Building and Extraterritorial Violence in Early Modern Europe* (Princeton, NJ: Princeton University Press, 1994).

1680 to 1750, and its place in a slightly different narrative. Several trends of the maritime history of the period are well documented, including the geographic extension of European-sponsored piracy and privateering and a general intensification of naval violence as an integral feature of global warfare. Important institutional shifts framed these trends and have received less attention from historians. European maritime empires adapted legal institutions to deal with prize adjudication and piracy in places far from Europe. Rather than building on the Grotian notion of maritime affairs guided by natural law, imperial agents operated in ways consistent with other widely circulating ideas about the law of the sea, in particular emphasizing the legal ties between ships and sovereigns, and promoting routines for extending jurisdictional claims into ocean space. The replication of such strategies produced a tangle of sea corridors and a thickening of maritime networks. One result was to reinforce emerging understandings of ocean basins as comprising separate regulatory regions.[14] The period also marked the beginning of new ways of referencing the law of nations in maritime disputes – again, not so much as a means of championing the idea of an overarching legal regime but in the service of attempts to equate the law of powerful empires with supposedly universal principles.

This chapter develops these points in four parts. It begins with the strategies of mariners, including pirates, in promoting a particular understanding of sovereignty at sea. It then backtracks chronologically to consider the continuities between the arguments of jurists at the turn of the seventeenth century, especially Gentili and Grotius, and the legal framework for expanding maritime violence in the next centuries. I then turn to patterns of legal institutional change between 1680 and 1750, tracing first the relation between regulatory practices and the emergence of ocean regionalism. I consider also some of the ways in which diplomatic pressures brought to bear in conflicts over sea raiding helped to promote a discourse about the authority of the law of nations. In different ways and across the period, specific and resilient sovereign claims to ocean space brought the ocean, or parts of it, within an interimperial regulatory order.

[14] For a discussion of ocean regionalism as a product of thickening trade networks, see Hancock, *Oceans of Wine*, "Introduction," i–xviii; see also Lauren Benton, "The British Atlantic in Global Context," in *The British Atlantic World, 1500–1800*, ed. David Armitage and Michael Braddick, 2nd ed. (New York: Palgrave Macmillan, 2009), 271–89.

Pirates as Lawyers

European sovereigns and mariners imagined in broadly similar ways the relation of ship's law to crown rule. The legal authority of ship captains was one variety of a wider array of subordinate and semiautonomous legal authorities.[15] Early Iberian overseas missions awarded ship captains and the military commanders of overseas fortresses judicial authority over their crews and factories, with the duties and powers of, essentially, petty magistrates. English and French ship captains also had wide-ranging authority to conduct inquiries and inflict punishments on their crews. Capital cases, in all these systems, were routinely transferred to metropolitan, nonmilitary courts. This semiautonomy in judicial matters formed the basis for the harsh shipboard disciplinary order shared across the European maritime world.[16] The arrangement also presupposed the right of state legal officials to oversee and intervene in regulating maritime affairs. Ships played a dual role as sources of order in the oceans: they were islands of law with their own regulations and judicial personnel, and they were representatives of municipal legal authorities – vectors of law thrusting into ocean space.

The history of piracy has often focused on the challenge posed by mariners to these elements of maritime order. Mutinies attacked the legitimacy of captains, and piracy turned ships into vectors not of law but of lawlessness.[17] Piracy was not merely a challenge to order, however. In the arena of international law, as we shall see, defining piracy became related to the question of legitimate sponsorship – indirectly important to understandings of sovereignty. Maritime practice meanwhile focused

[15] For a broader discussion of the influence of this model, see Benton, *Law and Colonial Cultures*, chap. 2; and Lauren A. Benton, "The Legal Regime of the South Atlantic World: Jurisdictional Complexity as Institutional Order," *Journal of World History* 11, no. 1 (2000), 27–56.

[16] On shipboard discipline, see especially Marcus Rediker, *Between the Devil and the Deep Blue Sea: Merchant Seamen, Pirates, and the Anglo-American Maritime World, 1700–1750* (Cambridge: Cambridge University Press, 1987). See also Pablo E. Pérez-Mallaína, *Spain's Men of the Sea: Daily Life on the Indies Fleets in the Sixteenth Century*, trans. Carla Rahn Phillips (Baltimore: Johns Hopkins University Press, 1998).

[17] See, e.g., Peter Linebaugh and Marcus Rediker, *The Many-Headed Hydra: Sailors, Slaves, Commoners, and the Hidden History of the Revolutionary Atlantic* (Boston: Beacon Press, 2000). A contrasting treatment of piracy that notes its close relation with claims to the monopoly of trade routes is Anne Pérotin-Dumon, "The Pirate and the Emperor: Power and Law on the Seas, 1450–1850," in *The Political Economy of Merchant Empires*, ed. James D. Tracy (Cambridge: Cambridge University Press, 1991).

attention on the nature of legal ties between mariners and their sponsors. The approaches had in common the notion that the extension of jurisdiction into the international space of the seas was a function of the extension of municipal law through the presence of legal actors with ties to particular sovereigns.[18] This construction was supportive of the legal underpinnings of ships' law and captains' authority, and added an opening to international law through the requirement of ascertaining sponsors' legitimacy or intentions.

Even pirates participated in and reinforced this legal order. The term *piracy* in the seventeenth century could be applied to an array of actions, including mutiny, shipboard felonies, and unlicensed raiding of various kinds. The line between privateering and piracy was thin, and the distinction was blurred by cycles of interimperial war and peace: in times of war, the demand for privateers surged, and in periods of peace, experienced and decommissioned sea raiders found themselves without sponsors and sometimes continued to engage in raiding, especially in places where lucrative shipping was poorly protected.[19] The legality of their actions depended on open and conflicting interpretations of whether the timing, location, and targets of raids fell within the terms of often-dubious commissions. Not surprisingly, both captains and common sailors cultivated a certain expertise in representing their commissions as legitimate and the assets they seized as legal prizes. Mariners had one eye always on return and on the possibility, however remote, of being brought to trial or being forced to defend the legitimacy of captures in prize courts. As a consequence, they actively engaged in imaginative legal posturing, rehearsing stories that might serve to establish actions as legal in judicial forums. Certainly there was some shared knowledge of defense arguments that might be effective; even when very far from home, mariners gave considerable thought to strategies for preserving the pretense of legality.

Pirates went out of their way to obtain flawed commissions and to represent fraudulent commissions as valid. In the Atlantic, letters of marque and letters of reprisal could be broadly interpreted to permit attacks on a wide range of targets; nationality could be changed or disguised to render illegal seizures quasi-legal; and the disciplinary order of ships themselves

[18] *Municipal law* in this context means the law of a sovereign entity.

[19] For an overview of long and short waves of early modern piracy and an analysis of the impact of cycles of warfare, see David Starkey, "Pirates and Markets," in *Bandits at Sea: A Pirates Reader*, ed. C. R. Pennell (New York: New York University Press, 2001), 107–24.

could be cited to blame acts of piracy on captains' orders or on the intimidation of mutinous crews. Added to these conditions was the simple fact of distance from metropolitan courts, which could be cited by privateers, pirates, and their backers to justify attacks on shipping because of the slow pace of news travel and the ambiguities of diplomacy and war making in regions regarded as lying "beyond the line."[20] The privateering commission had neither uniform standing nor consistent terms; in many cases, it was little more than sham.

Mariners coveted commissions. Examples abound of privateers and pirates going out of their way to obtain or create commissions that they might present in defense of raiding. At his trial for piracy in the English Channel (a capture that followed a longer stretch of piracy in the Atlantic), George Cusack presented a commission in someone else's name; the court rejected his explanation that his own valid commission had been accidentally exchanged for the invalid one he carried and pointed out that even a commission in his own name would not have entitled him to capture an English ship.[21] William Dampier reports on the enthusiasm for forged or flawed commissions in describing a pirate voyage to raid Spanish ports on the Pacific in the 1680s. The ships in Dampier's party, captained by Edward Davis and Charles Swan, met up with a large group of French and English freebooters off the coast of Panama. In exchange for provisions, the French offered the English captains blank commissions issued at Petit Goâve. Davis accepted one to replace his expired commission, but Swan chose to keep his commission from the Duke of York. Though it

[20] Which line was meant when Europeans invoked the phrase "no peace beyond the line" underwent change from the more precise delineations of fifteenth- and early sixteenth-century treaties to the simple designation of the Tropic of Cancer, and to the more informal reference to the equator as the dividing line. As Ian Kenneth Steele has shown, these differences paralleled emerging definitions of zones of peace. Treaties routinely came to recognize phases in treaty enforcement in several zones of increasing distance in the wider world. However, as Steele also notes, these zones were not precisely bounded and, for all intents and purposes, North America was included in the southern Atlantic zone. This geography of diplomacy provided yet another dimension to the legal structuring of piracy since the interpretation of these boundaries had important and concrete implications for the characterization of seizures as legal or illegal. See *The English Atlantic, 1675–1740: An Exploration of Communication and Community* (New York: Oxford University Press, 1986). On changes in the eighteenth century in the discourse in England about Europe as a zone of law and the outer Atalntic as lawless and barbarous, see Gould, "Zones of Law."

[21] *The Grand Pyrate, or, the Life and Death of Capt. George Cusack, the Great Sea-Robber with an Accompt of All His Notorious Robberies Both at Sea and Land: Together with His Tryal, Condemnation, and Execution/Taken by an Impartial Hand* (London: Printed for Jonathan Edwin, 1676).

explicitly ordered him not to attack Spaniards, he reasoned that a skirmish at Valdivia, where some of his crew had been killed, could be used to argue that subsequent raids on Spanish ports were justified and that "he had a lawful Commission of his own to right himself."[22] One English captain rested his defense against charges of piracy on a commission supposedly issued by a Central American Indian leader.[23] And when Edward Mansfield seized Santa Catalina from the English in 1666, at the end of an unprofitable six-month voyage around the Caribbean, he could be relatively sure that he would not be punished by British officials even though he had only carried a letter of marque approving attacks on the Dutch. Mansfield had earlier justified raids in Cuba by producing a commission permitting attacks against the Portuguese issued by the French governor at Tortuga. Taking hostages in a raid on a Cuban port in violation of the peace with Spain and with the use of a dubious French commission to attack the Portuguese stretched interpretations of legality. Yet when the Spanish townspeople requested the paperwork, Mansfield cared enough to produce the commissions. Both parties seemed to be preparing their reports on the incident, with Mansfield betting that a flimsy legal cover would be enough to protect him on his return to Jamaica, given the island's insecurity and local interests in sustaining privateering.[24]

The terms of valid commissions were also open to creative interpretation. Henry Morgan, for example, carefully analyzed the scope of his commission of 1667. The document did not authorize attacks on Spanish targets, but it did allow Morgan to stop Spanish ships to determine whether the Spaniards were plotting against Jamaica. Morgan was certainly aware that if he concocted a story about a discovered plot against the English, it would provide a rationale for aggression. And the commission's failure to regulate land attacks made them all the more attractive. The crew would be able to divide the booty from such raids among themselves without worrying about shares for the shipowners or the crown. Morgan clearly understood this opportunity and formed a contract with

[22] This is from Dampier, quoted in Peter T. Bradley, *The Lure of Peru: A Study of Maritime Intrusion into the South Sea, 1598–1701* (New York: St. Martin's Press, 1989), 136.

[23] Ignacio Gallup-Diaz, *The Door of the Seas and Key to the Universe: Indian Politics and Imperial Rivalry in the Darién, 1640–1750* (New York: Columbia University Press, 2004), 73.

[24] Several days before Mansfield took Santa Catalina, the Jamaican Governor Modyford had actually declared war on the Spaniards – though Mansfield did not know this until later – making his expedition against the Spaniards legitimate.

his crew that distinguished "free plunder" taken on land from goods of captured ships; the latter would have to be taken to a prize court for distribution according to a predetermined formula.[25]

We find an especially clear example of mariners' legal strategies in the trial of William Kidd, whose career connected Atlantic freebooting, elite politics in England, colonial tolerance for piracy, and an increasingly valuable Indian Ocean trade.[26] Kidd became a mariner in the Caribbean, settled in and sailed from New York, obtained sponsorship from the highest reaches of London society, traveled through the South Atlantic and into the Indian Ocean, returned to New England via the Caribbean, and was tried and hanged in London in 1701. His prosecution coincided with newly vigorous attempts to suppress piracy in the British empire and political discord over the management of the East India trade. Like his peers, Kidd fashioned out of his experience in the Atlantic an imperfect framework for understanding Indian Ocean maritime politics. Even as he misjudged the larger forces of imperial politics that would lead to his being turned into an example, he operated on the more or less accurate assumption that the Atlantic system of letters of marque and the Indian Ocean pass system both rewarded the exploitation of legal ambiguity. Like most other seventeenth-century pirates, Kidd never perceived his actions as entirely outside the regulatory order and fashioned a narrative of his voyage that he hoped would protect him at trial.

Kidd sailed from London with a commission permitting him to capture pirates and French merchant ships and with the financial backing of several powerful sponsors, including the king. On the trip down the Atlantic coast, Kidd threatened to seize a Portuguese ship and refused the request of a British navy ship to provide it with healthy crew members. These actions would not have won friends for Kidd, but they were hardly piratical. Once in the Indian Ocean, though, Kidd's status changed quickly. After friendly exchanges with pirates at Madagascar, Kidd sailed to the mouth of the Red Sea in search of ships returning from Mocha to Surat. Often laden with valuable goods and wealthy pilgrims returning

[25] Peter Earle, *The Sack of Panamá: Sir Henry Morgan's Adventures on the Spanish Main* (New York: Viking Press, 1981), 60–1.

[26] For analysis of the broader connections between Atlantic and Indian Ocean maritime activity in the period, see Kevin P. McDonald, "Pirates, Merchants, Settlers, and Slaves: making an Indo-Atlantic Trade World, 1640–1730," Ph.D. diss., University of California-Santa Cruz, 2008; and Philip J. Stern, "British Asia and British Atlantic: Comparisons and Connections," *William and Mary Quarterly* LXIII: 4 (2006), 693–712.

from Mecca, such ships were attractive – and, given Kidd's commission, illegal – targets. Kidd captured two merchant ships in the Indian Ocean, one of which, the *Quedah Merchant*, was leased by a high official of the Mughal court. Kidd sailed the larger ship back to the Caribbean, where he scuttled and hid it before returning to New England.

After a careful approach and attempts to negotiate his safety, Kidd was arrested on the orders of Lord Bellomont, Governor of New York and Massachusetts and ironically one of Kidd's London sponsors, and was transferred to London to stand trial for piracy and murder (both capital crimes) in consecutive trials. Although he did not have a particularly sophisticated legal strategy and did not use all the legal arguments available to him, Kidd defended himself vigorously at both trials. The evidence against him for murder was strong; while in the Indian Ocean, Kidd had smashed a heavy bucket over the head of a member of his crew, who died several days later. Ship captains' authority on board was vast, but it did not encompass murder. Evidence to support the piracy charges was weaker, but in a political climate that had turned against both piracy and the irregular practices of privateers as forces disruptive to trade, conviction was inevitable. Even more clearly than the antipiracy legislation with which it nearly coincided, Kidd's trial and execution signaled a shift in official policies toward piracy at the beginning of the eighteenth century. It is this significance that has largely fueled the interest of historians in the case.[27]

We can also mine Kidd's case for clues to aspects of maritime legal culture. When arrested, Kidd defended his capture of the two merchant ships in the Indian Ocean by citing his possession of French passes seized from the ships. That the ships were carrying such passes was itself an indication of the legal ambiguity of global shipping. Like other trading ships, the prizes carried multiple flags and passes, and the captains had been tricked by Kidd into presenting the French documents that he hoped would provide legal cover for his actions. Conveniently for English authorities, the French passes were misplaced after Kidd's arrival in London, and he was never able to present them at trial. He was reluctant to abandon this

[27] The best account of William Kidd's voyage and trial focuses on the political context of his prosecution. See Robert C. Ritchie, *Captain Kidd and the War against the Pirates* (Cambridge, MA: Harvard University Press, 1986). I rely throughout this section both on Ritchie's account and on the documents in the Kidd case contained in J. Franklin Jameson, ed., *Privateering and Piracy in the Colonial Period: Illustrated Documents* (New York: Augustus M. Kelley, 1970).

strategy, though, and persistently pleaded with authorities to recover the lost passes.

His only remaining strategy was to plead coercion. He tried arguing that a mutinous crew had forced him into taking the prizes in the Indian Ocean. Claiming that he had dissuaded his men from taking another unlawful prize, Kidd informed the court that "with all the arguments and menaces he could use [he] could scarce restraine them from their unlawful Designe, but at last prevailed."[28] He also reported that he had told Governor Bellomont's envoy, who had met with Kidd off the coast of Rhode Island, that he had discovered soon after its capture that his largest prize in the Indian Ocean was in fact not French, though it traveled with a French pass, but that it "belonged to the Moors." He then "would have delivered her up again, but his men violently fell upon him, and thrust him into his Cabbin, saying the said Ship was a fair Prize, and then carryed her into Madigascar and rifled her of what they pleased."[29]

Kidd was not wrong to think that such arguments might carry some weight in pirate trials; he was only wrong to suppose they might prove useful at his own trial. Given the political vulnerability of his former sponsors, the strong interest in London in protecting Indian Ocean trade, the embarrassing ability of the notorious pirate Henry Avery to escape capture, and the fact that the trial was being watched by Mughal observers, conviction was a foregone conclusion (and a moot point, given that Kidd had already been convicted of murder and could not be hanged twice). Kidd at no point gave up trying to defend himself. He did fail to present other arguments available to him, in particular that his return with the booty to the Caribbean was necessary because of the absence in the Indian Ocean of a functioning prize court. Instead, his choice of defense strategies relied on familiar interpretations of legal ambiguities at sea – the permissible range of a captain's authority, the definition and threat of mutiny, and the liberties taken in interpreting both letters of marque and the sponsorship of other ships.

The defense of having been forced into raiding against one's will failed for Kidd, but the strategy was not always unsuccessful.[30] Three members

[28] "Narrative of William Kidd. July 7, 1699," in Jameson, *Privateering and Piracy*, 208.

[29] "Memorial of Duncan Campbell," in Jameson, *Privateering and Piracy*, 203.

[30] This defense continued to be common – and sometimes effective – at pirate trials into the eighteenth century. The project of sorting out unrepentant offenders from forced participants came to be a routine function of court proceedings and invited testimony from pirates about how they came to serve, whether they participated willingly, and even whether they fought with gusto or appeared unhappy with their lot. In the trial

of Kidd's crew were acquitted on the strength of their defense that they were servants and had no choice but to follow their masters into piracy. One crew member, a Jewish jeweler named Benjamin Franks, provided a deposition in India describing the voyage in detail but protesting that his information came "of the Seamen" as he lay below decks, too ill to participate in sailing the ship or in any of the raids.[31] Another member of the crew, Edward Buckmaster, who joined another pirate ship after leaving Kidd's, reported that "he had been often in the hold" during the voyage and "saw nothing but water Casks."[32] Other privateers turned pirates tried similar tactics to position themselves for a safe return. In a letter sent across the Central American isthmus home, Swan implored his wife to assure his employers that he had been forced to abandon trade in favor of plundering: "So desire them to do all they can with the King for me, for as soon as I can I shall deliver myself to the King's justice, and I had rather die than live skulking like a vagabond for fear of death."[33] Protests of ignorance and innocence occasionally had an element of truth. On several ships that turned from trade to freebooting in the South Seas, the crew were not told even of their destination until they were in the south Atlantic. Leaving the Caribbean with a pirate ship under the command of John Cook in 1683, the pilot William Cowley recorded in his journal that he had been told the ship was heading only to Tortuga and that he had not learned it was a freebooter until they were at sea.[34] Kidd was not the only one for whom the strategy proved unsuccessful. When six men of Henry Avery's crew were tried for taking part in the mutiny that gave Avery command of the English ship *The Charles the Second* in the waters off La Coruña, and for the acts of piracy committed under Avery afterward, several of the men pleaded that they had been ignorant of the mutiny until it was too late, and then they were forced to go along. William May even claimed he had intended to report the mutiny to authorities. Asked why he had missed opportunities to do so, even at Bristol after his return to England, May replied – no doubt

of 168 men from Bartholomew Roberts's crew at Cape Coast Castle in 1722, 77 were acquitted on such grounds while 39 were punished and 52 were hanged. See Peter Earle, *The Pirate Wars* (London: Methuen, 2003), 207.

[31] "Deposition of Benjamin Franks. October 20, 1697," in Jameson, *Privateering and Piracy*, 194.

[32] "Examination of Edward Buckmaster. June 6, 1699," in Jameson, *Privateering and Piracy*, 199.

[33] Anton Gill, *The Devil's Mariner: A Life of William Dampier, Pirate and Explorer, 1651–1715* (London: Michael Joseph, 1997), 165.

[34] Gill, *Devil's Mariner*, 144.

hoping to ingratiate himself with the court – that he had "intended to declare to none but the Lords of the Admiralty."[35]

Pleas of coercion might best be understood as a common and cheap form of insurance. With the success of Exquemelin's and Dampier's published journals and the popularity of pamphlets reporting on the trials of Avery's men and of Kidd, they were also an emerging literary device: good men went to sea and fell into bad company. The story was one that seemed curiously to reinforce the legitimacy of shipboard discipline, as well as the larger legal framework of competing jurisdictions. Though sailors' work was notoriously grueling and dangerous, and the punishments inflicted on crew members were often arbitrary and cruel, voyage narratives typically faulted particular captains without criticizing their prerogatives in a general way. And mariners positioned themselves to be able to present a variety of stories before the bar. In many pirate trials, including that of Kidd, defense strategies joined in vilifying mutineers and upholding captains' authority, and they reinforced rather than challenged norms of legitimate sponsorship.

Oceans of Law

As piracy expanded and mariners carried legal strategies around the globe, disputes from distant seas entered metropolitan politics and prompted early modern jurists to begin to define the law of the sea as a particular strand within the *ius gentium*, the Roman term for the law of nations. They did so by drawing from a wider range of ancient texts in arguing that the sea could not be owned and that the right to navigate freely within it was based on natural law. This innovation marked the sea as a privileged arena within the global order. Historical narratives have sought to explain these contrasting and parallel trends by pointing to a gap between theory and practice. In one version of this story, maritime practice took time to catch up to theories of international legal ordering

[35] Unfortunately for May and the other defendants, the king's witnesses included crew members who testified that all had been free to leave the captured ship; all six defendants were hanged. High Court of Admiralty, England and Wales, *The Tryals of Joseph Dawson, Edward Forseith, William May, [Brace] William Bishop, James Lewis, and John Sparkes for Several Piracies and Robberies by Them Committed in the Company of Every the Grand Pirate, Near the Coasts of the East-Indies, and Several Other Places on the Seas: Giving an Account of Their Villainous Robberies and Barbarities: At the Admiralty Sessions, Begun at the Old-Baily on the 29th of October, 1696, and Ended on the 6th of November* (London: Printed by John Everingham, 1696).

circulating in the early seventeenth century. The supposed triumph of international cooperation occurred only in the nineteenth century, when the interstate order finally became sufficiently powerful to restrain non-state violence.[36] Alternatively, others posit this gap between theory and practice and then dismiss it, arguing that international law was consistently an empty rhetorical device – a form of "cheap talk" – used strategically by state actors and their advocates.[37] In this version of a story about the gap between theory and practice, international law writing in the early modern period was important mainly because it expanded the repertoire of rationales from which colliding maritime powers could draw to support self-interested positions.

But what if the gap between theory and practice is itself a fiction? What if Gentili, Grotius, and others could be read as supporting rather than challenging a maritime legal order consistent with the expansion of maritime violence, and of emphasizing not just natural law but also interimperial relations as sources of international law? This view would not deny the innovations of applying new sources and concepts derived from natural law (through Roman law) to maritime affairs, but it would highlight other ways in which these authors represented sea space as subject to the control of sovereigns, in the process both directly responding to maritime legal conflicts around them and supporting a framework for sea raiding throughout European and extra-European waters.

The key to this rereading of the work of founding figures in international law is their distinction between ownership of the sea and jurisdiction over sea space.[38] In outlining scenarios and conditions under which sovereign authority might extend into seas owned by all, these writers represented the sea both as a privileged zone governed by natural law and as a sphere of conflicting thrusts of sovereign law. Competing sovereign claims over intersecting corridors of sea space underlay a system of maritime regulation featuring the persistent militarization of ocean space. I consider these insights first by describing the Roman legal arguments employed by late medieval commentators to characterize the

[36] Thomson, *Mercenaries, Pirates, and Sovereigns.*

[37] Jack L. Goldsmith and Eric A. Posner discuss "cheap talk" as an element of international law in arguing that nation-states declared their submission to international legal principles while opportunistically determining when to comply and when to ignore international norms. *The Limits of International Law* (Oxford: Oxford University Press, 2005), especially 177–180.

[38] This argument builds on the observation of this distinction in Grotius's work in Keene, *Beyond the Anarchical Society.*

sea as a legal space. I then turn to a discussion of Alberico Gentili, whose writings about maritime cases in the first decade of the seventeenth century recognized the natural law basis for shared access to the sea while also envisioning conditions under which jurisdiction might be expanded – in some cases almost without limits – by sovereigns over sea space. Gentili provides a lens through which Grotius can be reexamined. While usually represented as the key figure responsible for asserting the natural law basis of the freedom to navigate, Grotius also presented arguments both directly and indirectly in support of the recognition of jurisdictional claims over sea space. Contemporary interimperial politics and pervasive practices of privateering and piracy influenced both writers directly.

Late medieval commentators and early modern writers before the mid-sixteenth century followed Justinian's *Institutes* in characterizing property as falling into four main categories: *res publicae* (public things, the property of the state), *res communes* (common things, the property of all men), *res universitatis* (things owned by a community but not the state), and *res nullius* (things without owners). Faced with numerous "ambiguities and inconsistencies" in the system of categorization, glossators and commentators sought to develop clear ways of determining the implications of these different categories of property for the way rights to property might be acquired.[39] The sea posed a particular problem. It was classified as common property and thus could not be acquired through forms of acquisition delineated in the *Institutes*, for example, through *occupatio* (occupation).

Fourteenth- and fifteenth-century commentators' solutions to this problem were influenced by notions favored by Ovid that all property had once been held in common and that other categories of property derived later. The commentators could thus view *jurisdictio* as a form of property. That is, the right to collect taxes or other revenue, or even to hold court proceedings, could be attained by a state or individual in the same way that the state or the individual could acquire dominion under Roman law.[40] Even if the sea could not be occupied, states could hold jurisdiction over it (established mainly through prescription or custom), and they could grant jurisdiction over it to others. Thus it was possible

[39] Perruso, "Development of the Doctrine of *Res Communes*," 75.

[40] Perruso, "Development of the Doctrine of *Res Communes*," 81. See also Lauren Benton and Benjamin Straumann, "Acquiring Empire by Law: From Roman Doctrine to Early Modern European Practice," *Law and History Review* (forthcoming).

for Baldus to argue that the Holy Roman Empire held jurisdiction over the sea and that the Genoese and the Venetians, who claimed jurisdiction over their proximate seas, could obtain it from the emperor by grant or prescription. As common property, the sea could not be owned, but it could be controlled. What the Venetians and Genoese claimed was not the right to navigate, which they held with everyone, but "the right to exclude others from navigating." This amounted to a kind of property right that was nominally different from dominion.[41]

Even if based on a fine legal distinction between functionally equivalent forms of control, this approach to the seas reflected the realities of a world in which maritime polities sought to collect fees of various kinds – famously labeled "protection money" by Frederic Lane – from ships navigating in sea lanes under their control.[42] The imagined legal structure was one of layered sovereignty, in which rights to patrol and control sea space did not diminish the rights of either overarching powers or of all Christendom. Of course, the commentators had not truly solved the problem of determining how jurisdiction over sea space could be acquired – the lines dividing prescription and custom in particular were blurred, and the inability to assert occupation was a nagging problem – but the possibility of layered and defensible claims to sea space was well established.

This was the maritime legal world that sixteenth- and seventeenth-century writers observed.[43] They addressed its problems with a new set of tools, drawing in particular on classical literary and philosophical texts that had been largely ignored by late medieval glossators and commentators. Cicero especially provided the basis for arguing that the natural law prohibition on ownership of the sea meant that it was unlawful to place restrictions on navigation. This view would receive its fullest elaboration by Grotius, though Vazquez and Gentili also pointed to some natural law protections over access to ocean space.[44]

If the new emphasis on natural law reflected an innovative turn in the use of Roman sources, it also responded to rapidly changing conditions of

[41] Perruso, "Development of the Doctrine of *Res Communes*," 83.

[42] Frederic Chapin Lane, *Venice, a Maritime Republic* (Baltimore: Johns Hopkins University Press, 1973).

[43] And on debates about imperium and dominium at sea in early modern England, see Armitage, *Ideological Origins*, chap. 4.

[44] Perruso, "Development of the Doctrine of *Res Communes*," 86–90; and on Grotius's use of Cicero, see Straumann, "Ancient Caesarian Lawyers." And see also, on Grotius's concept of a natural right to punish, Benjamin Straumann, "The Right to Punish as a Just Cause of War in Hugo Grotius' Natural Law," *Studies in the History of Ethics* 2 (2006), 1–20.

maritime competition. The two key writers elaborating new approaches to the law of the sea, Gentili and Grotius, were responding to maritime conflicts in the first decade of the seventeenth century. Gentili is usually seen as a precursor of Grotius because his main works on the law of war were published in the late sixteenth century, while Grotius's principal writing on the law of war, *De iure belli ac pacis*, appeared in 1625.[45] Yet both theorists produced important writings on the law of the sea in the first decade of the seventeenth century, when they had in sight overlapping patterns of maritime violence in the Atlantic, Mediterranean, and Indian Ocean worlds. Gentili spent the last three years of his life (from 1605 until 1608) working mainly as an advocate for the Spanish crown before the admiralty court in London. A volume of his writings about admiralty cases was published posthumously, in 1613, as *Hispanica advocatio.* Grotius was retained by the Dutch East India Company (the Verenigde Oost-Indische Compagnie, VOC) in 1604 to write a tract in defense of the seizure in the East Indies of a Portuguese ship, the *Santa Catarina*, by a Dutch ship sponsored by a forerunner of the VOC. The full tract was not published until the nineteenth century, but Grotius reworked one chapter for publication in 1609 as *Mare liberum* (The Free Sea), and he later drew on other chapters – and on Gentili's writings – in preparing his *De iure belli ac pacis.*[46] While directly involved in arguments about prize law, Gentili and Grotius were positioned on opposite sides of the rift between Spain and the rebellious United Provinces. As an advocate for the Spanish crown, Spanish merchants, and English merchants who were stand-ins for Spanish clients, Gentili was directly involved in two arenas of maritime conflict. Dutch attacks on Spanish ships in the seas near England were showing up in English admiralty court cases, and this raiding occurred in the context of increasing prize court business related to seizures by English and other mariners in these waters, now being only lightly patrolled by the English navy. A second important context for Gentili was the raiding by ships sponsored by the Barbary states. English merchants were purchasing goods from Barbary corsairs, and the original owners sometimes appeared in the London admiralty court

[45] Gentili's *De jure belli commentatio prima* (First Commentary on the Law of War) was published in 1588, followed by the completed series in 1598, *De jure belli libri tres* (The Three Books on the Law of War).

[46] On Grotius's reworking of Chapter 12 of *De iure praedae*, see Martine van Ittersum, "Preparing *Mare liberum* for the Press: Hugo Grotius' Rewriting of Chapter 12 of *De iure praedae* in November-December 1608," in Blom, *Property, Piracy and Punishment*, 246–80.

seeking compensation for their losses. Grotius was well aware of these disputes, which he observed from a different angle, the perspective of Dutch sponsors. But he was much more closely involved, at the time of his writing of *De iure praedae*, in the more distant arena of Dutch-Iberian competition in the East Indies in his work for the VOC. As we shall see, for different reasons both writers retained the distinction between dominion and jurisdiction.[47] Both imagined circumstances under which jurisdiction in its former sense – the right to restrict navigation by others – continued to be possible. And both drew information for the basis of their arguments from ship captains and sponsors who were reporting on actions and views common to an increasingly global maritime legal culture.

The outlines of Gentili's approach to the law of the sea are readily apparent in his writings on the law of war.[48] He argued clearly that restrictions by a sovereign on others' rights to navigate could serve as a cause of just war. But Gentili also proposed a series of ways in which sovereigns might lawfully exercise the equivalent of jurisdiction over the sea. One way was through the control of pirates. Gentili's definition of pirates was straightforward; they were "the common enemies of all mankind," brigands who stole on water instead of on land.[49] Because pirates operated in violation of natural law, a sovereign could take action – in effect asserting jurisdiction – on the sea for the purpose of punishing them. Sovereigns were also released from the obligation to share the sea with enemies. Seizing ships as an act of war was perfectly legal.

These qualifications opened more questions than they settled. Because defining a state of war or amity flowed more from policy than from law, relations between polities formed a poor guide to prize adjudication. The difficulty of pinning down Barbary sea raiders would serve as illustration of a larger problem. The North African city-states engaged in Mediterranean sea raiding had all the trappings of sovereign states but were embedded, at least formally, in the Ottoman empire and its net of alliances and enmities. When did the Barbary states act as sovereigns, and when was their status colored by the broader imperial politics of the Mediterranean? Meanwhile, creating a special prerogative to chase pirates anywhere did little to settle other questions about jurisdiction at sea. To what extent did the subjecthood of captains or crew members

[47] And so did others writing in the same period, as Armitage discusses in *Ideological Origins*, chap. 4.

[48] Alberico Gentili, *De iure belli libri tres*, trans. John Carew Rolfe (Oxford: Clarendon Press, 1933).

[49] Gentili, *De iure belli*, chap. 4.

determine the ties of ships to sovereigns? How far did territorial waters extend? What roles could neutral powers play in raids between enemies at sea? Gentili's answers to such questions were often inconclusive and at times suggested that naval power would create its own jurisdictional order.

Gentili's attempts to grapple with the complexities of his approach to the law of the sea are mainly contained in *Hispanica advocatio.*[50] This work is sometimes dismissed because it shows Gentili at his most facile in switching arguments when necessary to represent his clients' commercial interests. But the cases prove useful in allowing us to see the possibilities for the flexible application of notions of jurisdiction. Consider two cases involving the legal disposition of captured goods that had been purchased by third parties. Gentili was acting to protect the interests of Spanish traders whose goods had been seized by Barbary corsairs and then purchased by English merchants. Arguing in one such case that the purchasers had not obtained title because they were buying stolen goods, Gentili conceded that the oversight of Barbary officials gave the sale an air of legality. But Gentili asserted that the intermediary role of Berber officials amounted only to a legal fiction and that "the substance of the contract was with the pirates."[51] This position was consistent with his approach to a similar case in which he questioned whether the law of Barbary states could be regarded as legitimate when the states were subordinated to the "Turkish Empire," though Gentili also at times asserted that their law was superior to the law of the emperor. If the English were permitted to buy captured Spanish goods in Barbary ports, Gentili argued, the North African officials would have succeeded in setting up a haven "quite close to Spanish lines of trade and occupied by English merchants, where they may distribute their booty."[52]

In a third, celebrated case, Gentili defended precisely the opposite position. The dispute involved several English ships that had carried back to London goods purchased in Tunis. Venetian merchants claimed that the

[50] Alberico Gentili, *Hispanica advocatio*, in *Hispanicae advocationis, libri dvo [1613]*, trans. Frank Frost Abbott, vol. 2, bk. 1 (New York: Oxford University Press, 1921).

[51] Gentili, *Hispanica advocatio*, 55. Gentili further points out that England and Spain were at peace and so *post liminium*, the Roman concept applied to the legal disposition of goods seized in wartime, did not apply, though he takes this argument to its strained limits in suggesting that Spain could not even be represented as "foreign" to England because the Spaniards "retain their freedom and ownership of their property in our country exactly as they do at home, and the same is true of us in their country" (56).

[52] Gentili, *Hispanica advocatio*, chap. 15, 71–2.

goods had been seized from them at sea by an English pirate, John Ward, who had taken them to Tunis. The vice admiral in Dartmouth seized the goods, and a four-year case ensued, with actions in common law and admiralty courts, and the intercession at various moments by the Venetian ambassador, an array of merchants, and a distinguished cast of leading jurists.[53] Gentili argued that because the English merchants had bought the goods from "the highest Tunisian officer" acting as "the Turkish fiscus," the transaction had been legitimate. Noting the apparent contradiction of his earlier arguments, Gentili explained that the Venetians had treaty relations with the Ottomans and therefore possessed legal recourse in the place where the transaction occurred.[54] The Venetians, he asserted, would need to prove that the goods had been obtained by plunder. But they would never be able to do so, Gentili continued; those who seized the goods could not be pirates because they were enemies. The passage is worth quoting at length:

> [T]here is no difficulty raised by the fact that the Turk has a treaty with Venice and is a friend, as the Venetians likewise assert; for it is certain that in spite of their friendly relations this treaty and this friendship do not embrace pirates. They are left outside. They are left beyond the reach of any public complaint. Accordingly, they are left in the general law which deals with infidelity and hostility. Then, too, no difficulty is presented by the fact that goods seized by pirates do not become their property: because this is true only of pirates who are not enemies, and not of pirates who are likewise enemies. These pirates are enemies, as I say, and the Turk along with them is an enemy of the Venetians since he protects those pirates openly everywhere and always.[55]

By this logic, Venice could not win: the treaty regime created law that did not apply to pirates, and sponsorship of sea raiding by the Ottomans rendered the treaty regime irrelevant because it showed that the two polities were at war.[56]

[53] Alain Wijffels, "Sir Julius Caesar and the Merchants of Venice," in *Geschichte Der Zentraljustiz in Mitteleuropa: Festschrift für Bernhard Diestelkamp zum 65. Geburtstag*, ed. Friedrich Battenberg and Filippo Ranieri (Weimar: Böhlau, 1994), 195–219. Christopher Warren establishes the influence of the case in tracing literary allusions to the dispute, especially in Shakespeare's *Pericles*, and explores the epistemological connections between comedy and legal reasoning. Christopher Warren, "Literature and the law of nations in England, 1585–1673" (D. Phil. thesis, University of Oxford, 2007).

[54] "Those who are safe in accordance with the law of the place where the transaction occurred, are safe in England also." Gentili, *Hispanica advocatio*, 109.

[55] Gentili, *Hispanica advocatio*, 112–13.

[56] Of course, Venice could win, and did. The diplomatic pressure brought to bear by the Venetian ambassador, combined with James I's eagerness to preserve recently established good relations with Venice, moved the case to extrajudicial channels, where Venetian

Particularly when viewed in the context of Gentili's earlier pronouncements in disputes about the legality of trading in goods seized by pirates, the Venetian merchants' case illustrates more pervasive tensions generated in representations of the "common sea" as a place transected by private claims.[57] In other admiralty cases, Gentili struggled to define when and under what conditions legal authority extended to transactions on the sea. Arguing cases involving Spanish opposition to the transport of Dutch goods to or through English territory, Gentili repeatedly asserted that captures at sea did not confer ownership of captured goods because "property taken, but not brought within fortified lines, is regarded as not taken" and a ship did not count as the captors' "confines."[58] The view rested in part on the notion that transport through the sea represented a state of potential or incomplete action. Thus the Dutch had to transport captive Spaniards along enemy shores where people "were on the watch to prevent the taking of booty and were prepared to checkmate it" and where even the weather continued to pose a threat.[59] In a similar vein, Gentili argued that an English ship carrying arms toward Turkish ports in the Mediterranean should not be assumed to be transporting weapons to the enemy because while the English were in transit, the possibility still existed that they might "return and repent" or simply refuse to sell their merchandise at Constantinople.[60]

Such arguments were consistent with (and in part depended on) the understanding that English law extended into sea space in two ways: through the ties of English subjects to their sovereign and through the exercise of a version of jurisdiction over territory (stretches of sea near England or waters controlled by English ships). Gentili used this territorial proposition to support his argument that the English had a right to seize goods first captured and then transported by the Dutch near English

interests found favor. The English merchants retaliated with delaying tactics, a common strategy in prize cases. See Wijffels, "Sir Julius Caesar and the Merchants of Venice," for a full account of the case. Note that with regard to the question of the legality of seizures as determined by the treaty regime, Gentili's logic developed differently in commentary on a case about Tuscan goods, in which he argued that mere raiding between Tuscany and Turkey did not constitute war, or "a lawful struggle." Gentili, *Hispanica advocatio*, 17.

[57] On this tension as a legal and literary trope, see Warren, "Literature and the Law of Nations."

[58] Gentili, *Hispanica advocatio*, 17. And on the ship as "a moveable thing" rather than a fortified line, see Gentili, *Hispanica advocatio*, 5, and bk. 1, chaps. 6 and 11.

[59] Gentili, *Hispanica advocatio*, 5.

[60] Gentili, *Hispanica advocatio*, 91.

coasts. He argued that "the English sea" represented "a new jurisdiction" when entered by the Dutch so that they could retain captured goods only by exercising unlawful force: "It is of importance that no captives whatever be taken, held, or dragged off except by order of the ruler of the territory, for these acts derive from jurisdiction, and jurisdiction in the territory of our king does not belong to any foreigner.... This is the claim in the case before us, in which sovereignty and jurisdiction are being asserted."[61] Gentili himself characterized this view as amounting to the argument that "the word territory... applied equally to land and to water" and nullifying the Dutch claim that they had been operating on the high seas.[62] He also recognized that subjecthood could determine the legal status of men and ships at sea. In the case of an English ship sailing as part of a Dutch convoy, Gentili argued that the crew could not act under cover of the Dutch flag.[63] And he insisted in another case that a man who resided in England was a British subject and could not pass his Dutch commission, obtained by virtue of his birth in Holland, to his sons.

The tensions inherent in simultaneously recognizing the extension of some sovereign rights on the sea and highlighting the qualities of the sea as common to all (e.g., the shared legal right to intercept pirates anywhere) surface in the ways in which Gentili cited natural law and the law of nations. For Gentili, the origins of the law in "natural reason" dictated that it would hold "everywhere." In a case regarding the Spanish attempt to recover goods seized by the Dutch and sold in Brazil, Gentili argued that the fact that "the natural law... [was] in force everywhere" underlay the principle that every jurisdiction had an obligation to enforce the law.[64] At the same time, Gentili viewed the coexistence of different jurisdictions as a condition inherent in the law of nations and derived from natural law. The Dutch could not rely either on assertions of general principle

[61] Gentili, *Hispanica advocatio*, 27.

[62] Gentili, *Hispanica advocatio*, 35. To be clear, we cannot conclude that Gentili is arguing for English jurisdiction or for restrictions on Dutch navigation on the high seas. His arguments seem to be based on the view that sovereign jurisdiction extends to proximate seas. Yet his lack of attention to the limits of such claims also suggests that he was not arguing for a narrow interpretation of territorial waters. A more expansive vision of claims over proximate seas was of course championed by Selden later. I do not take up Selden's views here in part because my reading of Grotius suggests that the antipathy of the authors' positions has been somewhat overstated.

[63] Gentili, *Hispanica advocatio*, chap. 10.

[64] More specifically, in this case Gentili was arguing that the Spanish merchants be recognized as having standing to bring the case in England rather than in Brazil. See Gentili, *Hispanica advocatio*, 62.

or on ignorance in flouting English jurisdiction, for "under the law of nations, which is well known to everybody, domains are distinct, and everybody knows that it is not lawful to commit [certain] acts in foreign territory."[65] Most broadly, the Dutch should not be permitted to claim the simple right to navigate freely in the sea: "Let the Dutch, let everyone enjoy the use of the sea, but without violating the jurisdiction of another nation. Let everyone remember too that there are limits to a journey by sea as well as to every other journey. Let them remember that other things, once undefined, are defined today, and that the distinction made by the law of nations, of eminent domains and jurisdictions, should be most scrupulously observed."[66] In seeking to base restrictions on the freedom of the seas on the plurality of polities implied by the law of nations, Gentili produced what might best be described as one version of a modified positivism. That is, he recognized the authority of agreements among polities while also noting that the very conditions creating a plurality of states to form agreements derived from natural law.

We see the same blended approach in Gentili's approach to piracy. On one level, the definition of pirates as "the common enemies of all mankind" was simplifying. The actions of pirates were different from the actions of sea raiders acting for a legitimate sponsor who was in turn responding to a state of war.[67] The simplicity of this distinction disappeared quickly in practice because it depended on the recognition of the sovereignty of a sponsoring polity by other states.[68] Treaties were useful in settling whether states were in friendship or at war but only went so far in establishing sovereignty for signers. Distinguishing between piracy and privateering ultimately required a political act of choosing to recognize or to question the legitimacy of the polity sponsoring maritime violence.

Taken together, these views corresponded to a maritime legal regime in which a polity both possessed a modicum of jurisdiction and could effectively extend jurisdiction anywhere into ocean space to punish offenders after declaring their sponsors illegitimate. Allowing jurisdiction

[65] Here the act in question is to bar Spaniards from traveling in safety from a besieged port in the Dutch states to Flanders. Gentili, *Hispanica advocatio*, 66.

[66] Gentili, *Hispanica advocatio*, 38.

[67] Rubin, *Law of Piracy*, 29.

[68] Rubin, *Law of Piracy*, 30. Not surprisingly, this was a position the Spanish favored in their struggle with the Dutch, and it would be revived implicitly in early nineteenth-century debates about the legality of privateering sponsored by new Latin American states and by Haiti. On this point, see Armitage, *The Declaration of Independence.*

over ocean space in order to pursue pirates was a very large loophole. Vagueness about the boundaries of proximate seas over which polities alongshore could extend jurisdiction opened the door still wider. Natural law could be seen as forming the basis for freedom of navigation while also explaining a world of multiple, competing jurisdictions. For Gentili, the key to interpreting the legalities of the ocean lay only partly in the nature of the sea as a special kind of thing. Actual legal order was generated in two dimensions: through the treaty regime of sovereigns and through obligations created by the relation between sovereign sponsors and their agents – or others traveling through the ocean. This background helps us to place Grotius's writings on the law of the sea in a different light. It is true that Grotius went further than Gentili and others in outlining arguments in favor of the freedom to navigate the seas in *Mare liberum* (1609). This book was drawn from the twelfth chapter of the manuscript by Grotius that came to be known after it was found and published in the late nineteenth century as *De iure praedae* (The Law of Prizes).[69] Many of the ideas in *De iure praedae* were reworked by Grotius and incorporated in *De iure belli ac pacis* (1625). Grotius not only argued that natural law generated rights to free navigation but also proposed that, in holding such rights, private actors obtained the prerogative to punish those who infringed on them.[70] In chapters 11 and 12 of *De iure praedae*, Grotius catalogued the ways the Portuguese had violated natural law in forcefully preventing the Dutch from conducting peaceful trade in the East Indies and by capturing and killing Dutch subjects in East Indies ports. This background allowed him to argue that the Dutch capture of the Portuguese ship *Santa Catarina* in the Strait of Singapore was lawful because the agents of a forerunner of the VOC were punishing the Portuguese for these infractions. Yet while staunchly defending the right of free navigation as derived from natural law in order to support Dutch rights to enter the Indies trade alongside the Iberians,

[69] Martine van Ittersum has attempted to date the manuscript and argues that Grotius made major revisions to the text between the years 1604 and 1609. The purpose of both the revisions and the publication of *Mare liberum* in 1609 was to support the expansion of the Dutch empire and the activities of the VOC in the East Indies. See "Dating the manuscript of De Jure Praedae (1604–1608)," *History of European Ideas*, 35:2 (2009), 125–193.

[70] See Richard Tuck's introduction in Hugo Grotius, *The Rights of War and Peace*, 3 vols, ed. Richard Tuck (Indianapolis: Liberty Fund, 2005), 1:ix-xxxiv, especially xx, xxvii. And see Straumann, "Ancient Caesarian Lawyers." See also, on Grotius' concept of a natural right to punish, Straumann, "Right to Punish."

Grotius also explored the ways in which Dutch-Roman law regulated sea voyages. Grotius was not following Gentili, but he was responding to the same legal maritime culture and would surely have recognized the impulse to define, as Gentili had put it, the "limits to a journey by sea."

If these aspects of Grotius's writings have been hard to appreciate, it is partly because a number of factors converged to produce an interpretation of Grotius's writings that emphasized the innovations by which his work elevated natural law as a source of international law. One factor was the publication of *Mare liberum* in 1609, with its singular focus on freedom of navigation, rather than the publication of the full manuscript *De iure praedae*, which presented more varied arguments in support of the Dutch seizure of the *Santa Catarina.* Another was Grotius's own explicit claims, notably in the very first passage of *De iure belli ac pacis*, that he was staking out a new field of analysis in examining law that derived not from civil or Roman law but from "that Law, which is common to many Nations or Rulers of Nations, whether derived from Nature, or instituted by Divine Commands, or introduced by Custom and tacit Consent."[71] The work of English jurists advocating an expansive view of the extension of sovereign territory into proximate seas further drew attention to Grotius's emphasis in *Mare liberum* on the natural law basis of the freedom to navigate.

Certainly recognizing the centrality of natural law as a source of international law in Grotius's writings is preferable to interpreting him narrowly as an exponent of a European state system in which states agree to be constrained in their actions by a shared set of norms.[72] Yet either reading of Grotius simplifies the implications of his approach for an understanding of state sovereignty and, especially, imperial sovereignty. In treating sovereignty and ownership as separate categories – a distinction that is important to his conception of the legal regime of the sea – Grotius in fact suggested that degrees of sovereignty and multiple spatial relations of sovereignty were integral to empire.[73] We can explore further the

[71] Grotius, *Rights of War and Peace*, 1:75. As Richard Tuck notes in the introduction, this phrasing was found in a later edition (1631) of *De iure belli ac pacis*. Grotius used the phrase with an eye toward calming his critics in the United Provinces, who found the subordinatation of divine to natural law in the first edition troubling. Grotius's earlier works "had restricted the derivation of natural law to what all men agreed on as the basic physical principles governing all beings" (xxiv–xxv).

[72] See Keene's critique of Headley Bull in Keene, *Beyond the Anarchical Society*, 34–7.

[73] Keene, *Beyond the Anarchical Society*, 44–5. Keene views these approaches in Grotius as exceptions to his agreement with Bodin in representing sovereignty as indivisible. But

implications of this reading of Grotius for the law of the sea by examining three aspects of his writings: his consideration of the extension of public authority into sea space, his emphasis on the right to use military force under certain circumstances at sea, and his reliance on private Roman law doctrines to limit claims of ownership over the sea.[74] Through these three analytical moves, Grotius added to his natural law platform to construct a legal framework for maritime encounters that would have been very familiar to Gentili and, indeed, to late medieval commentators.

In the thirteenth chapter of *De iure praedae*, Grotius turned to a consideration of the basis in public law for the Dutch actions in the East Indies. Although omitted from *Mare liberum*, the arguments Grotius presented were not intended as merely supplemental rationales for Dutch aggression. Grotius noted that it was "more accurate to say that in actual fact it is a public war and that the prize in question was acquired in accordance with public law."[75] Grotius was aware that this view depended on recognition of the legitimacy, as a response to tyranny, of the revolt of the United Provinces against Spain. The state of war – a just war, as he defined it – between the Dutch and the Portuguese (then under the crown of Castile) necessarily determined the legality of actions by Dutch or Iberian subjects in the East Indies. And this was true, Grotius argued, quite apart from whether one accepted the arguments already presented about the unjustness of the Portuguese claims, for "whenever a prince is an enemy, his subjects are also enemies."[76]

In discussing the implications of the existence of a state of war between the United Provinces and Portugal, Grotius raised in new ways themes

it is worth noting that their views are closer under a different reading of Bodin. While affirming the absolute power of the sovereign, Bodin also understood sovereignty to be constituted through the relations of subjects to sovereign. This construction created the possibility of tighter and looser (and nearer and more distant) ties that would in turn promote different registers of sovereign power. It is possible, in other words, to glimpse some overlap between Bodin's and Grotius's use of the term *marks* of sovereignty. See Chapter 6 in this volume. Compare Peter Borschberg, *Hugo Grotius' "Commentarius in Theses XI": An Early Treatise on Sovereignty, the Just War, and the Legitimacy of the Dutch Revolt* (Berne: Peter Lang, 1994).

[74] These points relate to the broader challenge to Grotius scholars of understanding the "connection between prize and just war, and between just war and the European state system," but my focus is narrower and concerns the integration in Grotius's writings of widely recognized conventions for the extension of state authority into ocean space. For an overview of recent scholarship on *De iure praedae*, see Hans W. Blom, "Introduction," in Blom, *Property, Piracy and Punishment*, 1–15, quote on 8.

[75] Hugo Grotius, *Commentary on the Law of Prize and Booty*, trans. Gwladys L. Williams, ed. Martine Julia van Ittersum (Indianapolis: Liberty Fund, 2006), 392.

[76] Grotius, *Commentary on the Law of Prize and Booty*, 402, quote from 418.

that would have been familiar to other lawyers in maritime disputes, including Gentili. For example, Grotius noted that although the States-General permitted "Portuguese persons" to move goods from territory of the United Provinces to other lands, the guarantee of protection did not extend to or from "hostile localities," a category that would include Portugal or Portuguese colonies.[77] In developing this point, Grotius moved far from the view that the legality of the seizure lay in the Dutch enforcement of navigation rights and toward a view that the Dutch held different legal prerogatives along particular sea routes. Grotius also argued that the bonds of subjecthood were even tighter for Dutchmen (and for Portuguese) far from home, so that there could be no question that the state of war between the countries determined the legality of acts of war in the Indies.[78] In a final argument for the public law basis for the legal capture, Grotius proposed that the Dutch ship was acting on behalf of the king of Johore, ruler of a "sovereign principality" who "asked for help in warfare" against Portuguese agents interfering with his ability to trade.[79]

Grotius went still further and explicitly linked these points to consideration of jurisdiction over the capture of the *Santa Catarina*. He noted the failure of the Portuguese "in that particular part of the world" to punish those who had committed crimes against the Dutch.[80] The Dutch assumption of the prerogative to punish filled a void left by the lack of Portuguese judicial oversight. Meanwhile, jurisdiction flowed from Dutch authorities to the admiral and captains who, even without a specific order to capture the prize, "had been granted jurisdiction by the state" and "empowered – in the absence of other judges, and in defence of the rights of subjects as well as their own authority – to impose punishment on Portuguese offenders against that authority, and to seize the property of those offenders."[81] Implied in this authority was the right to take any captured goods to the United Provinces for adjudication in a prize court. These prerogatives, Grotius argues, were precisely "the powers proper to *captains*."[82]

[77] Grotius, *Commentary on the Law of Prize and Booty*, 421.
[78] Grotius, *Commentary on the Law of Prize and Booty*, 425.
[79] Grotius, *Commentary on the Law of Prize and Booty*, 432–5. And see Peter Borschberg, *Hugo Grotius, the Portuguese, and Free Trade in the East Indies* (Honolulu: University of Hawaii Press, 2009), chap. 2.
[80] Grotius, *Commentary on the Law of Prize and Booty*, 428.
[81] Grotius, *Commentary on the Law of Prize and Booty*, 429.
[82] Grotius, *Commentary on the Law of Prize and Booty*, 423. Emphasis in original.

This recognition of jurisdiction over acts at sea may seem to contradict the argument in *Mare liberum* that the sea cannot be possessed by any power. But Grotius was also careful to note the difference between the right of ownership over the sea, which no country could claim because it was impossible to complete title through occupation, and the "right over the sea to functions of protection and jurisdiction."[83] Full sovereignty would imply both jurisdiction and ownership, and would be impossible because "a ship sailing over the sea no more leaves behind itself a legal right than it leaves a permanent track."[84] But jurisdiction could travel with ships over the sea so long as the authority holding such jurisdiction did not "diminish its common usefulness."[85] Grotius recognized, finally, that the sea might be divided into different legal spheres, as under Roman law: "We admit that it was possible for agreements to be drawn up between specific nations, stipulating that persons captured upon the sea in this or that particular region should be subject to judgement by this or that particular state; and we furthermore admit that, in this sense, the boundaries upon the seas were indeed defined, for convenience in distinguishing the different areas of jurisdiction."[86] Such arrangements bound only the nations agreeing to them, and they did not convert the sea into the property of anyone. In *De iure belli ac pacis*, Grotius even more explicitly recognized the ability "to take Possession of the Jurisdiction only over some Part of the Sea, without any Right of Property."[87] And he was both more precise and more expansive about the way jurisdiction might be established and maintained: "Now the Jurisdiction or Sovereignty over a Part of the Sea is acquired, in my Opinion, as all other Sorts of Jurisdiction; that is, as we said before, in Regard to Persons, and in Regard to Territory. In Regard to Persons, as when a Fleet, which is a Sea-Army, is kept in any Part of the Sea: In Regard to Territory, as when those

[83] Grotius, *Commentary on the Law of Prize and Booty*, 329. Following further the analogy between Roman private law of property and public law of possession, Grotius notes that "some tiny part" of the sea might "prove susceptible to such occupancy" and so "conceded to the occupant" (325). Grotius further distinguishes between the Mediterranean Sea and "the Ocean" or between "a mere gulf" and "a vast maritime tract." The Portuguese claim differed from the claims of Venetians and the Genoese, too, because the former were not "possessors of uninterrupted coast-lines along the waters in question" (352). In other words, some tracts of the sea could be possessed if sufficient nearby markers of occupation could be sustained.

[84] Grotius, *Commentary on the Law of Prize and Booty*, 334.

[85] Grotius, *Commentary on the Law of Prize and Booty*, 337.

[86] Grotius, *Commentary on the Law of Prize and Booty*, 329.

[87] Grotius, *Rights of War and Peace*, 1:466.

that sail on the Coasts of a Country may be compelled from the Land, for then it is just the same as if they were actually upon the Land."[88] A ship (or a fleet) could not mark possession, in other words, but its presence could signal jurisdiction and control, or the right to protect subjects and their goods.

The distinction between ownership and jurisdiction allowed Grotius to reconcile his reasoning about why the capture of the *Santa Catarina* was lawful as an act of both private and public war, and to combine the natural and positive law approaches behind these rationales. Exercise of the right to punish transgressors of natural law implied clearly that the enforcer possessed jurisdiction. That is, the different legal rationales supported the same actions: the capture of the Portuguese ship and its conveyance to the prize court in the United Provinces. Grotius explicitly blended the two rationales when he suggested that "whatever acts could have been committed by private individuals under the law of nations . . . those individuals shall now be held to have committed with retroactive public authorization and in circumstances equivalent to a decree of war."[89] One can read this statement as establishing an extraordinarily permissive atmosphere for private acts of war. But it also signaled an attempt to call attention to the ways in which private acts of punishment effectively mimicked, and in fact conjured up, jurisdictional prerogatives.

We are not very far, in some respects, from Gentili's approach to the law of the sea. Gentili imagined an unrestricted right to punish on the sea – specifically, to act against pirates as "common enemies of all mankind" whose raids were not sponsored by recognized sovereigns.[90] This position permitted sovereigns to determine which sponsoring parties would be recognized as legitimate and to extend the reach of municipal law to the high seas and even to coastal waters near foreign territories.[91] Grotius began from different premises, including recognizing the legitimacy of rebels asserting sovereignty – a position important to the defense of Dutch actions against the Spanish. He relied on the same logic to defend the rights of ship captains to act judicially as delegates of sovereign legal authority, even when they did not possess specific instructions. Reinforced by public law arguments, this approach ultimately implied highlighting

[88] Grotius, *Rights of War and Peace*, 1:470.
[89] Grotius, *Commentary on the Law of Prize and Booty*, 424.
[90] Rubin, *Law of Piracy*, 29.
[91] Rubin, *Law of Piracy*, 35.

the ties between ships and sovereigns in structuring the legal framework for maritime violence. In hinting at the functional equivalence between private acts of punishment of those who breached natural law and public acts of war against enemies, Grotius echoed earlier views of the law of the sea, especially the distinction between dominion and jurisdiction.[92]

The Indian and Atlantic Oceans as Legal Regions

Recognizing European representations of sea space as a place of intersecting corridors of control helps us to understand better the emergence of regional regulatory spheres at the beginning of the long eighteenth century. Mariners' practices, which we began to survey in the first section, the legal discourse about sovereignty at sea, and imperial administrative reforms – these forces worked together to shape the origins of oceanic basins as distinct legal regions. Like Kidd's seizure of the *Merchant Quedah*, distant captures were reported to Europe, where they prompted legal debates and litigation by crown agents, merchants, and investors. In response to shifting patterns of conflicts at sea, European imperial powers devised and began to implement legal policies and institutional adjustments, and these were unevenly distributed across regions. Despite and in part because of the global circulation of maritime practices, regional legal patterns diverged, and the Indian and Atlantic Oceans emerged as separate regulatory spheres.

They were in some respects very different already. European powers had long recognized the Indian Ocean as a distinctive sort of ocean space – one of crowded sea lanes dominated by coastal polities and ethnic traders. The idea matched the Ptolemaic image of the Indian Ocean as a separate sea encircled by land.[93] In contrast to the Mediterranean and the Atlantic, the Indian Ocean world prior to the incursions of the Portuguese had operated without the militarization of ocean space. Land polities could exert control over the ocean only through actions against traders and ships in ports. A ship at sea operated "as a piece of quasi-territory sailing in the legally undefined vastness of the sea."[94]

[92] For a different argument about the relation between rationales for punishment in *De iure praedae*, see Gustaaf van Nifterik, "Grotius and the Origin of the Ruler's Right to Punish," in Blom, *Property, Piracy and Punishment*, 396–416.

[93] On the legacy of Ptolemy for cartographic representations of ocean space by Europeans, see Lewis, "Dividing the Ocean Sea."

[94] Alexandrowicz quoted in Steinberg, *The Social Construction of the Ocean*, 51; and see 47, 50–1.

Some historians have suggested that early seventeenth-century writers, especially Grotius, were importing East Indies notions of the sea when they emphasized the natural law basis of the freedom of navigation.[95] The argument is difficult to sustain given the absence of evidence that Grotius was somehow informed about the maritime practices of Asian traders in the Indian Ocean in an era before Dutch, Portuguese, and Ottoman incursions.[96] But we need not discard entirely the idea that Indian Ocean maritime affairs had an influence on European lawyers and jurists. We know that they received information about the Indian Ocean through reports by mariners, captains, and company agents, as well as in the course of continuing legal conflicts originating in the Indian Ocean. We know that Grotius drew on a mass of information conveyed to the VOC by Dutch agents in the East Indies, including interpretations advancing "inchoate notions of freedom of trade and navigation" and letters asserting a broad right on the part of Dutch captains to take acts of reprisal against the Portuguese for past violence against other Dutch subjects in the region.[97] At the same time that Grotius was relying on and developing natural law discourse from Roman authorities, he was deeply immersed in Dutch politics and well informed about VOC actions in the east.[98] It is accurate to say that he was responding to Indian Ocean legal norms, in other words, so long as we stipulate that the maritime order of the east was not one of practices antedating the arrival of Europeans in the Indian Ocean but consisted of already hybridized practices that European agents were interpreting through available understandings of maritime

[95] For example, Ram Anand, *Origins and Development of the Law of the Sea* (The Hague: Martinus Nijhoff, 1983). And see Charles Henry Alexandrowicz, *An Introduction to the History of the Law of Nations in the East Indies (16th, 17th and 18th Centuries)* (Oxford: Clarendon, 1967).

[96] On the Ottomans in the Indian Ocean, see Giancarlo Casale, "The Ottoman 'Discovery' of the Indian Ocean in the 16th Century," in *Seascapes: Maritime Histories, Littoral Cultures, and Transoceanic Exchanges*, ed. Jerry Bentley, Renate Bridenthal, and Kären Wigen (Honolulu: University of Hawaii Press, 2007), 87–104. Peter Borschberg shows that Grotius had access to few sources that would have provided information about pre-European practices in the Indian Ocean and, for that matter, few sources on Portuguese practices or Portuguese interactions with Asian states and traders. "Grotius, Maritime Intra-Asian Trade and the Portuguese Estado da Índia: Problems, Perspectives and Insights from *De iure praedae*," in Blom, *Property, Piracy and Punishment*, 31–60.

[97] Martine Julia van Ittersum, *Profit and Principle: Hugo Grotius, Natural Rights Theories and the Rise of Dutch Power in the East Indies, 1595–1615* (Leiden: Brill, 2006), 190.

[98] On the Roman sources of Grotius's natural rights theories, see Straumann, "Ancient Caesarian Lawyers."

law.[99] The conditions they encountered often led those agents to emphasize the importance of ties between captains and sovereign sponsors, as well as to justify maritime violence on the basis of infractions committed by victims or the need to protect the rights of allies.[100] Indian Ocean actors had meanwhile adjusted quickly to European maritime strategies, recognizing and even strategically affirming European claims to military and legal hegemony at sea.[101] Although there is no denying the originality of Grotius's argument for a natural law-based right to freedom of navigation, the power of his writings in defense of Dutch actions in the east derived only partly from the novelty of Grotius's thinking. In defending Dutch maritime violence, he was careful to integrate well-established legal rationales and did so in terms that would have been familiar both to Dutch captains and to other Indian Ocean legal actors.

Martine van Ittersum has shown that along with glimpses of a sea space in which arguments for freedom of navigation would favor Dutch interests, Grotius took from the East Indies reports support for his strikingly "backward looking" view of privateering.[102] The *Santa Catarina* case furnishes the best example. The Dutch captain in that case, Van Heemskerck, had traveled under a commission from the admiralty in Holland that approved violent acts of self-defense as well as acts of reprisal for specific injuries. Just as the verdict of the admiralty court had insisted that Van Heemskerck's actions had been consistent with the terms

[99] In a different context, Ralph Bauer makes the point that European sojourners were often encountering "the product of several decades of intercultural hybridization." The observation is relevant to evaluating Dutch captains' reports on events in the Indian Ocean. Simply by describing those events, even while continuing to use familiar categories and arguments, Dutch agents were responding to Indian Ocean maritime practices that cannot be labeled as either Portuguese or Asian. "A New World of Secrets: Occult Philosophy and Local Knowledge in the Sixteenth-Century Atlantic," in *Science and Empire in the Atlantic World*, ed. James Delbourgo and Nicholas Dew (New York: Routledge, 2008), 99–126, 117.

[100] On this point, see Michael Kempe, "Beyond the Law: The Image of Piracy in the Legal Writings of Hugo Grotius," in Blom, *Property, Piracy and Punishment*, 379–96.

[101] In his efforts in *Hugo Grotius, the Portuguese, and Free Trade in the East Indies* to refute the notion that Grotius knew about, and was influenced by, Asian maritime practices, Borschberg goes too far in emphasizing a sharp contrast between European views of law as rigid and pre-modern Southeast Asian legal cultures of customary law regarded as fluid (chap. 4). Both before and after the arrival of the Dutch, Europeans and Asians in Indian Ocean trade found existing structural similarities and adopted substantive changes in law to facilitate trade. See Benton, *Law and Colonial Cultures*, chap. 2, and discussions of Mughal responses to European traders later in this section.

[102] That is, gazing at past practices. Van Ittersum, *Profit and Principle*, 188.

of his commission, Grotius argued that the commission itself represented the functional equivalent of a letter of marque.[103] This assertion placed the seizure of the *Santa Catarina* comfortably within the context of a system of maritime regulation featuring letters of marque and reprisal that named specific injuries and authorized recipients to take reparations in roughly equivalent form from any shipper of the same nation as those who had inflicted the injury. The terms of commissions were often intentionally capacious, authorizing privateers to make captures of enemy ships and pirates, to strike in self-defense, and sometimes to intercept shipping in particular sea lanes. Grotius went further than the Dutch admiralty court had gone in representing Van Heemskerck's commission as a letter of marque and reprisal that approved the seizure of the *Santa Catarina*, but the creative interpretation of the terms of these documents was not itself unusual.

As we have seen, mariners made captures at sea, then concocted legal stories to enhance their chances of converting the captured goods and ships into good prizes. Van Heemskerck was behaving like other captains in laying the groundwork for prize proceedings in the first reports of the capture, explaining away inconsistencies between the capture and the commission or letter of marque, and pointing to injuries sustained on the voyage that painted an act of aggression as one of self-defense. What Van Ittersum calls the "strange, hybrid nature" of Grotius's arguments – the same composite quality that we have described in noting his juxtaposition of natural law and privateering rationales – arose partly from the fact that he was "aiming at a moving target."[104] That is, an emphasis on the right to navigate freely supported Dutch efforts to penetrate Portuguese spheres of influence in the East Indies without paying protection money, but the creative reading of commissions was better suited to a world in which the Dutch were beginning to take the upper hand and seeking to exclude other traders from their own spheres of influence, in particular in disputes with England over the control of fishing rights in the North Atlantic.[105] News about maritime conflicts in the Indian Ocean featured competing story lines, in other words, and traveled in odd and unpredictable ways.

[103] Van Ittersum, *Profit and Principle*, 46–7.

[104] Van Ittersum, *Profit and Principle*, 108–9.

[105] For discussion of Grotius's shifting positions in the context of peace negotiations with England, see Van Ittersum, *Profit and Principle*. See also Armitage, "Introduction," in Hugo Grotius, *The Free Sea*, trans. Richard Hakluyt (Indianapolis: Liberty Fund, 2004), 3–16.

European agents were not the only people in the Indian Ocean holding multiple understandings of the law of the sea. Even as powerful land-based polities like the Mughal empire conceded control of the sea to Europeans, they adapted quickly in using the control of ports to exert considerable influence over maritime affairs.[106] There can be little doubt that they understood clearly the legal structures and rationales that supported the militarization of ocean space. Historians may have occasionally exaggerated Mughal inability to control maritime trade, and studying Indian and Atlantic Ocean activities separately may have led them to miss continuities in global maritime practice that then diverged, influencing peculiar regional trajectories.

Consider the Indian Ocean pass system. It had developed out of an innovation of the Portuguese, in turn based on eastern Mediterranean models, requiring every Asian merchant within Portuguese purview to purchase a pass or license called a *cartaz*. The passes were obtained at the beginning of journeys and required stopovers in Portuguese-controlled ports where customs duties were paid.[107] The Dutch, English, and French adopted the pass system in modified form in the seventeenth century. Though Lane argued famously that this system stood for little more than the collection of protection money, it rested not just on the superior strength of European ships and armaments but also on a delicate balance between Europeans' maritime superiority and "their almost total vulnerability on land for a long time."[108] The pass system was profitable only if diplomatic relations with Asian land-based powers permitted trade. To secure this cooperation, rival European merchants often found themselves in informal alliance across national lines. Thus we find records of close Portuguese cooperation with Dutch traders on the Coromandel coast in the early seventeenth century and later in the century with the English. Dampier noted in 1684 that English ships were traveling with English passes but Portuguese pilots; a decade later they were even flying

[106] Om Prakash notes that when the king of the Maldive Islands appealed to Aurangzeb to prevent English and Dutch shipping from reaching the islands, he was told that the emperor could do nothing because he was "master only of land and not of the sea." "European Corporate Enterprises and the Politics of Trade in India, 1600–1800," in *Politics and Trade in the Indian Ocean World: Essays in Honour of Ashin Das Gupta*, ed. Lakshmi Subramanian and Rudrangshu Mukherjee (Delhi: Oxford University Press, 1998), 174.

[107] On early Portuguese-Indian interactions, see M. N. Pearson, *Port Cities and Intruders: The Swahili Coast, India, and Portugal in the Early Modern Era* (Baltimore: Johns Hopkins University Press, 1998).

[108] Prakash, "European Corporate Enterprises," 174.

Portuguese colors.[109] There were many other examples of a pragmatic intermingling of European interests. English trade in particular interpenetrated with Asian trade so that the ownership of goods on board a given ship was often mixed. Any experienced trader in the East knew that the pass system provided only a loose set of rules for much more complex and layered arrangements. Ships sailed with multiple passes and multiple flags, and they chose to display the colors and present the passes selectively and according to the ports, ships, or courts with which they were engaged.

If such ambiguity was familiar to Atlantic mariners, an important and growing difference with Atlantic conditions lay in the political impact of Mughal authority. Kidd's undoing was not, after all, the coordination of British legal authority but the protests of the Mughal emperor. Though Indian Ocean traders before 1500 did not militarily enforce their right to trade at sea, they were accustomed to using diplomacy and viewed their control of select ports as key to the protection of trade interests. Certainly Mughal officials quickly grasped the possibilities of turning European maritime claims in the region to their advantage. Doing so required, after all, only an extension of existing Mughal land-based jurisdictional arrangements and of controls on other, subordinate trading groups. The Mughal emperor rehearsed this policy a few decades before clashes with the English when Maratha insurgents attempted to construct independent maritime trading networks in the Indian Ocean. In the 1660s and again after a brief hiatus in the 1670s, the Maratha leader Shivaji, who had developed a network of inland, fortified posts, began to seize coastal towns and conducted two raids on the key port of Surat. His forces established fortresses on islands off the coast, engaged in Indian Ocean trade, and disrupted Mughal ocean trading. The Mughal response was to put pressure on other powers, including European traders, to intercept the Maratha fleet whenever possible.

The approach continued and culminated in the Mughal response to the taking of the *Ganj-I Sawai*, the largest ship of the Surat merchant fleet. Captured by Henry Avery on its return trip from Mocha in 1695, the ship was laden with trade goods and was carrying wealthy, well-connected passengers returning from the pilgrimage to Mecca. The Mughal court stopped trade out of the European factories and demanded that the English and Dutch send armed ships in convoys to protect shipping from

[109] Kenneth McPherson, "Trade and Traders in the Bay of Bengal: Fifteenth to Nineteenth Centuries," in Subramanian and Mukherjee, *Politics and Trade*, 196.

Mocha. English traders were imprisoned – fifty-three at Surat and eighteen at Swalley – and more than a dozen died. Two years later, an English ship bound for Madras was also seized in response to pirate attacks by "three Saile of Arabs" and "after having Cruized up and down the Gulf five or six day[s]" was plundered and all its crew imprisoned on shore after first having been forced to assist in fighting off an attack by a Portuguese ship.[110]

The East India Company (EIC) officials involved in such acts of reprisal characterized them as piracy. But their complaints about the lack of procedural formality surrounding these seizures also underscored the understanding that the reprisals were part of a more elaborate legal politics. The senior EIC official at Surat wrote to the Company about the "barbarous usage we have met with from these unreasonable oppressive Moors on no real and only Base affirmacions of the rabble without somuch as the Least Shadow or pretence of proof."[111] The same complaint about the lack of attention to procedure was sounded by the captain of the Madras-bound ship, who noted the "absence of any official proceeding" as the crew and passengers were taken into custody.[112] At the same time that British actors complained about the illegality of the seizures, they signaled their expectation that such acts should follow formal procedures as part of a diplomatic relationship and in accordance with broader maritime norms.[113] But the traders faced a serious imbalance of power on land and were subject to easy Mughal retaliation for raids at sea. When Kidd seized the *Quedah Merchant*, acts of reprisal against traders at Surat were immediate, and the Company, struggling in the midst of a downturn in trade, urged Kidd's capture and punishment to prove that there was no official support for this sort of raiding.[114]

The taking of English ships was an example of Mughal action in coastal waters to complement the pressures it exerted on land. To insist that Europeans collaborate to pacify the pirate-ridden Indian Ocean was, in effect, to hold these powers to their jurisdictional claims over

[110] The British Library, India Office Records (hereafter IOR) E/3/53, 6404.
[111] IOR, E/3/52, 6205.
[112] IOR, E/3/53, 6404.
[113] Philip Stern points out that this expectation flowed in large part from the East India Company's qualities as a sovereign entity empowered to engage in diplomacy and warmaking. "'A Politie of Civill & Military Power': Political Thought and the Late Seventeenth-Century Foundations of the East Indian Company-State," *Journal of British Studies* 47 (2008): 253–83.
[114] On the changing fortunes of the East India Company during this period, see Ritchie, *Captain Kidd*, 128–31.

ocean passages. And while Mughal officials protected their rights by paradoxically reaffirming English sovereignty at sea, EIC officials reinforced Mughal legal authority on land and on the coasts as a way of protecting English enclaves and European-Mughal arrangements for trade.[115] English traders extended this strategy to agreements with coastal principalities. One example is an episode reported by an EIC official in April of 1696. Writing from the Malabar Coast to the head of the Company at Fort St. George, the official was responding to a complaint he knew was being lodged by a pair of traders who had been denied permission to trade along the coast, in the small principality of Signaty. Interlopers in the trade were a familiar problem for the Company, and this dispute was in many ways typical, though in making his case, the EIC official provided an unusually elaborate rationale. After pointing out that the English in the area had "conquered the whole Malabar Coast by the Right of the Sword, from the Portuguese," the official went on to make it clear that he was not claiming English possession of the region, only asserting the right to control trade. He was careful to point out that the Company had claimed only very limited jurisdiction in the area controlled by the prince of Signaty. That jurisdiction, he insisted, extended only "500 Rods from the Walls within and 60 outwards" and did not in any way compromise the sovereignty of the prince of Signaty, who continued to be "the lawfull possessor of the said Kingdom" and to enjoy undisturbed sovereignty over the area, "Especially on the Sea Shore of Signaty."[116] The English readily recognized Indian sovereignty on land; it made English trade possible and even enhanced the legitimacy of English sea power.

European maritime power implicitly recognized Mughal regional dominance. The arrangement neatly merged Atlantic and Indian Ocean patterns and power: an Atlantic-style convoy system was to be staffed by Europeans operating as clients of Mughal authority and representatives of European sovereigns while in the service of trading companies. The Indian Ocean was not a Mughal lake, but it was not a European one, either. English traders crafted their claims to the control of sea lanes

[115] Stern quotes the East India Company's president at Surat, Samuel Annesley, as noting approvingly that the convoys would render "our Ships... in the Nature of Castles and those under our Command as in our harbours the Lawes of Nature and hospitality obliges us to defend." Stern complicates the picture I draw here even more by pointing out that Annesley was describing not English but company sovereignty of the seas. Stern, "A Politie of Civill & Military Power," 253.

[116] IOR, E/3/52, 6198.

in response to the demands of Indian Ocean polities. At the same time, Mughal pressures reverberated as far as the Atlantic, where Kidd's arrest and, more generally, attempts to construct an imperial legal system capable of containing piracy directly responded to maritime politics thousands of miles away.

In the Atlantic, the most significant institutional change in the same period was the beginning of the proliferation of prize courts. The shift was not the product of the growing importance of maritime law but rather a result of its absorption into other jurisdictions – the common law in England and its colonies and nonspecialized mercantile law in the Spanish, Dutch, and French empires. In Spain, for example, a separate jurisdiction for maritime law had its origins in the fusion of Mediterranean and Atlantic traditions of self-regulating maritime merchant communities and in the proliferation, after the end of the fifteenth century, of *consulados* that brought commercial disputes under the ambit of maritime judges and created a separate procedural regime emphasizing arbitration. While the impulse to regulate new long-distance trade at first gave rise to a greater prominence for Spanish maritime law, this trend was followed by its gradual merging with other jurisdictions, in particular with undifferentiated merchant law courts. As in England, imperial expansion unsettled the system of regulating privateering and adjudicating prize cases in local, specialized forums with appeals to the Consejo de Guerra. In 1674, the crown made it possible for the first time for prizes to be taken to the nearest audiencia, or high court, and for pirates to be tried by local justice. The earlier system was flawed, from the crown's perspective, because it provided local communities with the incentive and means of using prize cases as a cover for contraband trade. Prizes could be brought to port, condemned, and distributed as a way of avoiding duties.[117]

In England, by a gradual process culminating in the second half of the seventeenth century, common law courts effectively stripped from admiralty law its authority over nontidal waters and maritime disputes

[117] One measure of the importance of maritime law in the early Spanish empire is that maritime laws made up by far the largest category of laws listed in the *Recopilación de las leyes de los Reynos de las Indias* (1680). See Patrick S. Werner, "El régimen legal de actividad marítima del imperio hispánico: El libro nuevo de la Recopilación," *Nicaraguan Academic Journal* 3 (2002), 39–62. On the *consulados*, see Marta Milagros del Vas Mingo, *Los consulados en el tráfico indiano* (Madrid: Fundación Histórica Tavera, 2000). On corsairs, Enrique Otero Lana, *Los corsarios españoles durante la decadencia de los Austrias: El corso español del Atlántico peninsular en el siglo XVII (1621–1697)* (Madrid: Editorial Naval, 1992).

arising on land.[118] In defense of the admiralty jurisdiction, prominent civil lawyers argued that the forum and its law were peculiarly suited for handling matters involving commercial activities of shipping, in ports, and on navigable rivers, having incorporated the customary law of the sea, which in turn constituted simply the sea-based portion of ancient *lex mercatoria*.[119] The civilians insisted that the admiralty court should have purview over all affairs of the regions "within the flowing and ebbing of the Sea" or on adjoining banks, and involving all personnel connected with maritime affairs.[120] Admiralty judges affirmed this view when they routinely read in pirate trials a statement about the commission, and about the court's jurisdiction, before charging grand juries. The court's claims in such cases were not controversial. The curtailment of admiralty jurisdiction was most concentrated in the area of commercial law; criminal jurisdiction, which increasingly focused on piracy, went relatively unchallenged, and the right to try prize cases was also preserved. These prerogatives were consistent with a substantially reduced jurisdiction over commercial maritime disputes and affairs not arising on the high seas – a victory for advocates of the common law.[121]

The tensions played out in complex ways in the colonial sphere. The various admiralty courts of the British Atlantic colonies developed with highly localized concerns at their core – fishing in Newfoundland, sea wrecks in Bermuda, piracy in Jamaica.[122] Authority radiated out unevenly from these points. The courts were in their operation driven by local interests, resulting, for example, in the unwillingness in Jamaica and New

[118] This process is traced in the introduction to M. J. Prichard and D. E. C. Yale, eds., *Hale and Fleetwood on Admiralty Jurisdiction* (London: Selden Society, 1993).

[119] This argument was most forcefully put forward by Richard Zouch (or Zouche), a prominent civilian and judge of the High Court of Admiralty from 1641 to 1649. He wrote the eight-volume *Jurisdiction of the Courts*, which is included as chapter 22 in Richard Zouch and Edward Coke, *The Jurisdiction of the Admiralty of England Asserted against Sr. Edward Coke's Articuli Admiralitatis, in XXII Chapter of His Jurisdiction of Courts*, (London: Printed for Francis Tyton and Thomas Dring, 1663).

[120] The words are from Zouch, quoted in Joanne Mathiasen, "Some Problems of Admiralty Jurisdiction in the 17th Century," *American Journal of Legal History* 2, no. 3 (1958): 223, 223–4.

[121] The most outspoken and effective opponent of preserving or extending civil law jurisdiction was Sir Edward Coke, who defended a narrow definition of admiralty jurisdiction, particularly on the grounds that the court did not use juries. See Mathiasen, "Some Problems of Admiralty Jurisdiction"; see also Brian P. Levack, *The Civil Lawyers in England, 1603–1641: A Political Study* (Oxford: Clarendon Press, 1973).

[122] On the origins of various admiralty jurisdictions in the Atlantic, see Helen Josephine Crump, *Colonial Admiralty Jurisdiction in the Seventeenth Century* (London: Published for the Royal Empire Society by Longmans, Green, 1931).

York to prosecute pirates who were active clients of local merchants. Mariners contributed to and benefited from local legal differences by engaging actively in forum shopping. With multiple prize courts operating, it became possible to secure a letter of marque in one port and take prizes to another forum, where captures and shares might be awarded more favorably or certain legal requirements overlooked.[123] While colonial admiralty courts extended English legal authority through the empire, jurisdictional tangles made them a clumsy instrument of imperial legal authority. The system not only opened new avenues for avoiding courts in England and in particular colonies but also gave rise to a long-unresolved question about the procedures to follow in trying pirates.

The impulse to streamline colonial legal procedure often conflicted with the trend toward reining in admiralty jurisdiction. If civil lawyers were under attack in England in the seventeenth century, they were nonexistent as a professional body in the colonies, where, also, the jurisdictional complexities of English law were shunned. Seventeenth-century colonial officials could try pirates only in common law forums, where juries were often openly sympathetic to defendants. Local officials, many of whom derived direct profit from privateering and piracy, often had little interest in sending defendants to England, where they could be tried by a court of oyer and terminer, the only legal procedure recognized by statute. In 1673, an English reform required that all pirates be tried in admiralty courts, a move partly intended to allow their trial in colonial forums so that these could be made more effective in combating piracy. Attempts to shift the prosecution of pirates to colonial forums were repeatedly reversed until the 1700 Act for the More Effectual Suppression of Piracy created a special procedure for staffing a seven-person commission to try pirates anywhere.[124]

It might be assumed that this new flexibility promoted legal continuities across maritime zones. Instead, there is evidence of sharpening legal

[123] For example, the Newcastle Lieutenant Governor Usher complained in 1696 that he had issued a letter of marque to a privateer named Captain Mould, who took his prizes into Boston rather than returning to Newcastle and his sponsors. Crump, *Colonial Admiralty Jurisdiction*, 127.

[124] The 1673 Order of Council required the creation of special commissions in the colonies. It took another eight years for Jamaica to establish a conforming statute, so that royal officials could oversee the trial of pirates. But this hardly ended the legal difficulties. In 1683, a ruling by the Lords of Trade and Plantations effectively nullified the Jamaican statute by insisting that colonial admiralty courts had no jurisdiction to try capital cases but only property disputes. On this "muddled legal situation" see Ritchie, *Captain Kidd*, 143.

distinctions between the Atlantic and the Indian oceans. The assertion of maritime jurisdiction in the Indian Ocean was complicated by the fact that the crown did not claim jurisdiction in English factories; the limited legal administration that existed was in the hands of the East India Company. In 1683, the Company was awarded the right to suppress interloping and establish courts to try and contain it where necessary. These courts operated, in effect, as admiralty courts, though they lacked some qualities of such courts. They were staffed by "one Person learned in the Civil Laws, and two Merchants" and were established at Surat (though originally intended for, and later moved to, Bombay), Fort St. George, and the Bay of Bengal.[125] The three courts developed differently, in response to distinct political strategies of Company officials and the kinds of cases generated locally. Only in the court at Fort St. George, where officials were inexplicably encouraged to merge common and civil law jurisdictions, did the courts operate with some efficiency. In general, they proved relatively powerless in the face of the growing threat of piracy in the Arabian Sea at the end of the century. Operating under the aegis of the Company, the courts had no direct connection to the navy to enforce sanctions, little attraction for privateers as a place to bring prizes, and no appellate relation to the High Court of Admiralty in England. In fact, there was some confusion about whether the courts in India were official prize courts. This ambiguity was not cleared up until 1739, when the EIC legal adviser, in response to a query from the Company principals for clarification on precisely this issue, ruled that the Indian courts were not prize courts and formally requested that they be given authority to issue letters of marque and to adjudicate prize cases.[126] This long period of uncertainty about the jurisdiction of the courts over prize cases no doubt contributed to emerging mariners' perceptions that the Indian Ocean was a separate regulatory space.[127]

[125] Quoted in Crump, *Colonial Admiralty Jurisdiction*, 167.

[126] IOR, L/L/6/1, case 14. The Legal Adviser's Department wrote: "Upon Inquiry we find that there is no Court of Admiralty in any part of the East Indies belonging to the East India Company, which we are humbly of opinion is necessary [and] should be erected before any Letters of Marque and Reprisal can be granted."

[127] William May, one of Avery's men who was tried for piracy, apparently benefited, if only temporarily, from the relative weakness of Indian Ocean forums. May was left at Joanna in the Indian Ocean; he was sick and on shore trying to recover when Avery's ship sailed off to avoid three incoming English ships. Fearing "to be left to the mercy of these Negroes," May agreed to be taken to a court in Bombay, where he would be tried for piracy. But Bombay was a long way off. May perhaps changed his mind, or the leader of the small convoy could not be bothered to chase and deliver a solitary pirate; the

Sea Corridors and the Law of Nations

Patterns of enforcement would make regional distinctions even sharper in the middle decades of the eighteenth century. A new wave of piracy following the 1713 Peace of Utrecht prompted English colonial admiralty courts to prosecute piracy vigorously, leading to the widespread public executions of pirates in the 1720s that signaled a new era of rising British naval hegemony. The public hangings of pirates in Atlantic ports and the chase and capture of celebrated pirates in this decade have sometimes been characterized by historians as an episode of terror and counter-terror, with, on one side, state terror in the form of mass hangings of pirates, and, on the other, the terror of increasingly desperate and openly criminal pirates.[128] But the coordination of official attacks on piracy and the abandonment by some mariners of the usual defensive legal strategies should be placed within the longer framework of Atlantic history – and the larger framework of global maritime affairs. Lines of legality and illegality were sharply drawn for a brief period only; enforcement was regionally uneven; and, even at the height of the extermination campaign, many mariners continued to angle for legal reprieves.[129]

When hundreds of pirates accepted the king's pardon in 1718 and then took up raiding again, they were following familiar patterns of accommodation and selective law breaking. A glimpse of the persistence of such strategies is provided by the actions of the pirate Edward Teach, also known as Blackbeard. Represented as a singularly menacing pirate by Captain Charles Johnson and romanticized by some historians as the

ships sailed on without him. It was here that May met up with an African who had lived at Bethnal-Green "and spoke English very well," a minor but interesting encounter in the annals of early modern globalization. High Court of Admiralty, England and Wales, *The Tryals of Joseph Dawson, Edward Forseith, William May, [Brace] William Bishop, James Lewis, and John Sparkes for Several Piracies and Robberies by Them Committed in the Company of Every the Grand Pirate, near the Coasts of the East-Indies, and Several Other Places on the Seas: Giving an Account of Their Villainous Robberies and Barbarities: At the Admiralty Sessions, Begun at the Old-Baily on the 29th of October, 1696, and Ended on the 6th of November* (London: Printed by John Everingham, 1696).

[128] This is the premise of the account of the campaign against the pirates in Marcus Rediker, *Villains of All Nations: Atlantic Pirates in the Golden Age* (Boston: Beacon Press, 2004), chap. 1.

[129] As Rediker acknowledges in *Villains of All Nations*, it was mainly during the brief period from 1722 to 1726 that pirates gave up on legitimacy and "became more desperate and more violent and killed more of their captives" (37). Yet even as the campaign against them turned brutal, men with the pirate Thomas Anstis on the coast of Cuba hoped to receive a pardon from King George II (155).

epitome of the hardened criminal pirates of the 1720s, Teach had hardly given up on the prospect of legitimacy.[130] He and his crew had accepted the king's pardon from the North Carolina governor in 1718 and settled briefly in Bath Town, in North Carolina. Teach obtained title to his ship from the vice admiralty court in Bath Town and secured clearance papers for a trading trip to St. Thomas. Instead of trading, Teach captured two French ships on the open sea, and he appeared in the vice admiralty court at Bath Town to have one of the ships declared a legal prize, claiming, with the support of four crew members' affidavits, that the ship had been found adrift. Teach split the salvage rights with local officials.[131] Just two months later, in an Ocracoke Inlet attack organized by Virginia's Governor Spotswood, Teach was killed and his surviving crew arrested. Though there is no doubt that Teach was still raiding, his actions leading up to the attack suggest a plan to settle in Bath Town and to protect his position by creating a paper trail. Like Kidd, Teach was typical in his enthusiasm for legal posturing; like Kidd, he found that the strategy did not work in certain political climates.

The early eighteenth-century campaign against piracy was global in its ambitions but regionally varied in its effects. Of the twenty-six pirate captains hanged in the 1720s, all but one were tried in Atlantic ports.[132] This distribution did not reflect legal policy – by this time, English commissions could be formed anywhere to try pirates – but responded to a new wave of raiding in the Atlantic, pressures by merchants engaged in the West African slave trade, and naval resources. Navy patrols increased along American and Caribbean coasts, and pirate hunting was attempted in West African waters. Rarer expeditions to the Indian Ocean were less effective. The campaign did curtail European raiding in the Indian Ocean, but mainly by suppressing Atlantic sponsors and outlets.

The British campaign against pirates in the 1720s was closely followed by the intensification of sea raiding by the Spanish *guardacostas* (coast

[130] Captain Charles Johnson, *A General History of the Robberies and Murders of the Most Notorious Pyrates, and Also Their Policies, Discipline and Government, from Their First Rise and Settlement in the Island of Providence,... With the Remarkable Actions and Adventures of the Two Female Pyrates, Mary Read and Anne Bonny. To Which Is Prefix'd an Account of the Famous Captain Avery... By Captain Charles Johnson* (London: Printed for Ch. Rivington, J. Lacy, and J. Stone, 1724), 55–77.

[131] See Robert E. Lee, *Blackbeard the Pirate: A Reappraisal of His Life and Times* (Winston-Salem, NC: John F. Blair, 2002 [1974]), 80.

[132] The figure includes pirate captains hanged by the English, Dutch, French, Portuguese, and Spanish. Earle, *Pirate Wars*, 206.

guards) operating out of Caribbean and Atlantic ports.[133] The ships were supposed to control contraband trade into and out of Spanish harbors, but English merchants accused them of routinely exceeding their commissions and seizing ships merely passing near Spanish coasts, including some with permission to trade under the *asiento*. If this practice was not consistently labeled as piracy, it was partly because the term had come to refer more commonly to acts by English subjects against Englishmen or by mariners assumed to be hostile to ships of any nationality – pirates as the "enemies of all mankind."[134] But English diplomats, merchants, and mariners did use the label "pirates" pejoratively in referring to Spanish *guardacostas*, even as the politics of privateering engaged different legal issues.[135]

Spanish officials had erected their own imperial system for adjudicating prize cases, offering privateers the possibility of condemning prizes in virtually any Spanish port. This had not always been the policy. Philip II had outlawed privateering in the New World, and crown officials in subsequent years continued to worry that easy access to prize courts offered subjects a way around paying royal levies by condemning cargos that would otherwise be registered as trade goods.[136] The general statute on privateering issued in 1621 applied to the empire as a whole, but it provided few specific procedural guidelines or incentives. In contrast, a 1674 general statute on privateering was written specifically for regulation of privateering in the Indies. Whereas the earlier policy had required captured ships to be brought to the port from which privateers had sailed, the new statute directed privateers to take the ships to the closest Spanish port, with appeals to go through the nearest audiencia.[137] This change

[133] Histories of the 1720s campaign against the pirates – both traditional, triumphalist accounts and Linebaugh and Rediker's romanticized pirate-centered narrative of the repression of mariner republicanism – erroneously proclaim the end of piracy in this period. For a critique, see Lauren A. Benton, "Legal Spaces of Empire: Piracy and the Origins of Ocean Regionalism," *Comparative Studies in Society and History* 47, no. 4 (2005).

[134] See Rubin, *Law of Piracy*.

[135] A 1739 pamphlet on Spanish "depredations" refers specifically to the "Pyracies of the Guarda Costas," for example. Benjamin Robins, *An Address to the Electors, and Other Free Subjects of Great Britain; Occasion'd by the Late Secession. In Which Is Contain'd a Particular Account of All Our Negotiations with Spain*, 3rd ed. (London: Printed for H. Goreham, 1739), 9.

[136] See Otero Lana, *Los corsarios españoles*.

[137] For an account of the general statutes on privateering that also includes the text of the statutes affecting the Indies, see Oscar Cruz Barney, *El régimen jurídico del corso marítimo: El mundo indiano y el México del siglo XIX* (Mexico City: Universidad Nacional Autónoma de México, 1997).

multiplied the number of active forums for prize adjudication and inserted a level for appeal in courts located outside Spain.

The effects of this change took on greater importance when the crown began actively to encourage raiding by *guardacostas* in the early eighteenth century. Privateers from St. Augustine, Havana, Santo Domingo, Puerto Rico, Cartagena, Portobello, and other ports became more active in seizing English, Dutch, Danish, and French ships, which could be taken to any of these ports to be declared lawful prizes. The captains of the *guardacostas* searched vessels and confiscated ships and their cargos if these contained even miniscule amounts of contraband goods – a category given wide interpretation. England's 1667 treaty with Spain recognized Spaniards' right to examine ships' documents but not to search cargos; the treaty of 1670 implied recognition of English rights to navigation in some parts of the American seas but made no reference to limits on Spanish methods of suppressing smuggling. Presumably, this control was to be exercised according to the laws of Spain. In other words, international treaties recognized Spain's right to adjudicate prize cases internally and left no remedy for any overreaching by Spanish authorities other than through appeals in Spanish courts or through extrajudicial diplomatic pressures.

Claims and counterclaims therefore came to turn on the definition of the territorial scope of Spain's sovereignty in the New World. In the wrangling in Madrid in the 1730s, Spanish officials cited, and English diplomats loudly lamented, Spain's claims of possession of the Indies as a whole. The Spanish crown represented English settlements in Jamaica, Barbados, and the North American colonies as exceptions resulting from Spanish concessions of an underlying right. It is important to look beyond Spanish assertions to regional dominion and English complaints about this "imaginary Sovereignty," however.[138] Diplomatic exchanges and disputes over individual prize cases centered on interpretations of a different sort of part sovereignty by both powers: control over particular sea lanes. The Spanish government was willing to recognize English rights to sail freely in the sea lanes connecting their colonies to England. But any deviation from these routes placed English ships in "suspected latitudes," where they were fully under the jurisdiction of Spain and could be stopped, searched, released, or condemned according to Spanish law.

Geography and sailing routes guaranteed that this claim was expansive. *Guardacostas* seized ships sailing anywhere near Spanish coasts, but the

[138] Robins, *Address to the Electors*, 21.

trip to Jamaica from England took ships along the southern coasts of Puerto Rico and Santo Domingo, and ships making the return voyage had to choose between the Windward Passage between Cuba and Hispaniola or the Gulf of Florida (see Figure 3.3). Led by Sir Benjamin Keene in Madrid, the English were forced to argue that their ships should be left alone if the routes they traveled had some logical relation to the places of departure and destination listed in the papers they carried. The Spanish never conceded this point, and it became moot after the outbreak of war in 1739.

English representatives invoked the law of nations in arguing for a right to navigate on the open seas without being subject to search. The Spanish claimed that products from Spain and its colonies remained contraband no matter how many times the goods changed hands; the English questioned this doctrine of continuous voyage, a position picked up by the Dutch later in the century to argue for their rights as neutrals to carry enemy goods if these had been obtained in a neutral port. For the most part, English responses to Spanish privateering took the form of legal and extralegal interventions in particular cases. Diplomatic appeals to Madrid often met with the response that the cases were following their required path through the Spanish court system and that any judgment about the cases had to wait until proceedings were complete. Irresolution of disputes favored Spanish interests, and irregularities in procedure and poor documentation were often purposefully embraced. One English observer complained:

> If We gave the most authentick Proofs of our Vessels being illegally taken by their *Guarda Costas*, They told Us that they could only be determin'd by their own Condemnations in the *Ports*, where the Prizes happen'd to be carry'd; an Account of which They always promis'd to send for; and yet so little were even these Accounts to their Mind, though drawn up for the most Part by the very *Pyrates themselves*, that after near a Year's Delay, They deny'd their having been able, even in all that Interval, to procure any one Account from their *own People*.[139]

In addition to relying on the slowness of legal proceedings, the Spaniards were sometimes able to report that English captains had neglected to file appeals as required. The English also charged that Spanish governors entered sham defenses in order to be able to claim later that their procedures had been properly followed. Even when the Spanish system appeared to work in favor of English claimants, restitution might require multiple trips to the place of condemnation, where often the seized ship

[139] Robins, *Address to the Electors*, 16.

FIGURE 3.3. A Map of the West Indies or the Islands of America (1709). Created by Herman Moll and printed in London, this map marks the main sea lanes of the West Indies with dotted lines, including the Windward Passage to the east of Cuba. The map labels the sea routes traveled by the Spanish fleet and galleons, including the passage along the coast of Florida, which is identified mainly as a Spanish route but described in a way that indicates its utility for all mariners in the region: "The best Passage of all the Islands." Printed in London by Tho. Bowles in St. Pauls Church Yard and John Bowles at the Black Horse in Cornhill. Courtesy of the John Carter Brown Library at Brown University.

and cargo had already been sold.[140] These complications encouraged English captains to skip Spanish court appearances and apply to their government for relief. By filing claims on their behalf, English diplomats succeeded only rarely in winning redress. But their actions had the effect of exerting pressure on Spanish authorities to clarify their own legal procedures. The 1738 Spanish plan for a new general statute on privateering in the Indies outlined detailed instructions on procedures for approaching, seizing, and condemning prizes and seemed to aim at bringing Spanish procedures in line with those recognized by other European nations – especially England.

English protests settled on a formula that combined vague charges of violations of the law of nations with more specific complaints that Spanish law itself was being corrupted. In 1758 an English privateer, the *Antigallican*, captured a French ship off the coast of Galicia and took the ship into Cádiz, where the captain initiated proceedings that led to condemnation of the capture as a lawful prize by the vice admiralty judge in Gibraltar. Spanish officials at first raised no objections, but after the French interceded (and perhaps offered financial inducements), the captured ship was seized in Cádiz and returned to the French. In response to British protests, the Spaniards claimed that the legal basis of this action was that the ship had initially been taken at a distance from the coast that could not be considered the high seas and therefore placed the case squarely within Spanish, not English, jurisdiction. English protests again cited the law of nations but highlighted faulty Spanish proceedings that had "denied the British subjects the benefit of the known and established laws of Spain."[141]

English arguments in prize cases were also sometimes directly served by upholding Spanish legal jurisdiction and encouraging greater regularity and reporting in Spanish proceedings. Consider the case brought to the Rhode Island vice admiralty court in 1745 (*Revenge and Success v. Welhelm Gally*). Two Rhode Island privateers had seized a ship near Cuba that was under command of Spaniards after it was first taken from its Dutch crew by privateers out of Havana. The Dutch owners appeared in court to argue that they had been conducting a legal trading voyage

[140] Richard Pares, *War and Trade in the West Indies, 1739–1763* (Oxford: Clarendon Press, 1936), 26–7.

[141] Antigallican, *A Series of Letters Relating to the Antigallican Private Ship of War, and Her Lawful Prize the Penthievre... The Whole Containing an Unparalleled Scene of Cruelty, Perjury, and Injustice. With Proper Observations. By an Antigallican* (London: Sold by W. Owen, 1758).

from Curaçao to Amsterdam when they were captured by Spaniards, an act that they declared as "contrary to the Law of Nations."[142] The case turned on the legality of the first seizure by the Spaniards; if the ship was under command of Spain, it was fair game at a time of war, whereas the peace with the Dutch would have made a Dutch seizure unlawful. Spanish procedures appeared to be lax or, at best, incomplete. The Spanish boarding party might have intended to report the seizure to a prize court later – they were on their way to Havana when they were captured – but they testified instead that they had already ruled the ship a lawful prize. Witnesses reported that the judgment occurred on the deck of the Spanish man-of-war, where the Spanish officials "agreed... that she was a good Prize and the whole Crew rejoised."[143] The Dutch captain testified that the Spaniards had never shown a commission, that they had not asked for the ship's papers, and that he "never knew or heard that She was so tried or declared Prize neither was there any oath Administerd or Offer'd to me."[144] The irregular procedures did not prevent the Rhode Island court from ruling that the Spanish seizure and, therefore, the subsequent capture by Rhode Island privateers had been legal. The cargo was "by the Laws of Spain liable to confiscation," the Spanish crew had authority "by virtue of their Commissions" to seize the ship and declare it a lawful prize, and its seizure on its way to Havana was also lawful "by the rights of war."[145] In this case, the law of nations was invoked by the Dutch, now in the position of English merchants before the outbreak of the war with Spain, to condemn overreaching by Spanish privateers. The winning side upheld the law of nations in a different way, by reinforcing Spanish jurisdiction even in the absence of procedures conforming to international, or even merely English, norms.

The international regulation of privateering was emerging more out of a replication of administrative legal orders than as a result of adherence to a settled understanding of the law of nations. At the same time, invoking the law of nations did not run counter to this understanding of the

[142] "Revenge and Success vs. Welhelm Gally, 1745," in *Records of the Vice-Admiralty Court of Rhode Island, 1716–1752*, ed. Dorothy S. Towle (Washington, D.C.: American Historical Association, 1936), 307.

[143] Towle, *Records of the Vice-Admiralty*, 309. The Spanish crew, who must have stood to benefit from a ruling for the Rhode Island privateers, also testified that the ship was flying Spanish colors when it was taken and that the defense they mounted "should not have been made had not the Ship been the King of Spains Property." Towle, *Records of the Vice-Admiralty*, 304.

[144] Towle, *Records of the Vice-Admiralty*, 312.

[145] Towle, *Records of the Vice-Admiralty*, 303, 320.

institutional foundations for prize law. Implied in the arguments of English jurists was the notion that English civil law might be substituted for the law of nations as a standard that other jurisdictions could be enjoined to meet. This purposeful confusion of English law and the law of nations would later inform English ambitions to deterritorialize maritime jurisdiction in piracy and prize cases, that is, to award universal jurisdiction to English courts over maritime crimes or seizures committed anywhere.[146] In this sense, fighting over the definition and control of particular sea lanes in the mid-eighteenth-century Atlantic would help to construct the basis for broader claims to legal hegemony, for example in the British attempts to patrol sea lanes to inhibit Atlantic slave trading and to combat piracy in the Persian Gulf and Indian Ocean. Widely circulating understandings of the Atlantic maritime legal order in the eighteenth century encompassed both recognition of multiple, parallel jurisdictions of municipal law and the possibility of English (or European) legal ascendancy based in its identity with the law of nations. The new institutional nexus of the long eighteenth century – an Atlantic web of imperial prize courts – constituted not a new kind of law but a new field of legal politics. Talk about the law of nations entered into this politics. Mariners and merchants invoked the law of nations to publicize and enact legal rationales for various forms of sea raiding and contraband trade. Jurists and diplomats referred to the law of nations in exerting pressure on the maritime legal procedures and practices of other empires. In these and other ways, utterances about the law of nations influenced institutional forms, and vice versa.

Observing this connection between talk about the law of nations and the regulatory framework of courts helps us resolve the tension between representing discourse about the law of nations as empty rhetoric and imagining international norms as powerful constraints on states' and individuals' actions. A range of legal actors, from state officials to privateers, had incentives to reinforce the authority of prize courts and to affirm their place as one of an array of imperial administrative tools. Yet this strategy did not signify indifference to global norms. The law of nations operated in the translatability and internal consistency of discrete national and imperial prize courts. The content of English law could be represented as not just consistent with but actually an embodiment of

[146] See Rubin, *Law of Piracy*, on British claims to universal jurisdiction. The same implicit relation between domestic and international law lay behind the arguments for the embrace of prize law as a federal jurisdiction in the new republic of the United States.

the law of nations – a condition to which other polities, both within and without Europe, might aspire. Institutional changes in Spanish maritime law, and the response to the Spanish *guardacostas*, contributed to setting in place a logic that would influence legal politics in the late eighteenth-century Atlantic world and shape the formation of an ideology of European-centered international law.

Conclusion

By the middle decades of the eighteenth century, a global maritime culture had produced a diversification of ocean regulatory spheres and had laid the groundwork for a new (but not peaceful) legal regime of the sea. Oddly, regional differentiation developed out of the effects of mutual influence and circulating legal practices. In the Indian Ocean, political maneuvering shaped a more nearly Atlantic regime of maritime control characterized by jurisdictional claims over particular sea lanes. Non-European land-based polities advocated importing a system of maritime protection, the convoy, which had debuted in the Mediterranean and been tested in the Atlantic. The resulting regulatory order relied more on interimperial negotiation than on a connected network of legal forums and naval enforcers. The influence worked in the other direction, too, as Indian Ocean political pressures reverberated in the Atlantic world. Despite some attempts to impose a truly imperial maritime law, European empires extended prize courts vigorously only in the Atlantic, and the culminating campaign against piracy in the early decades of the eighteenth century was largely an Atlantic affair. A new kind of regionalism was being forged out of increasingly globalized maritime practices. Mariners in general, and pirates in particular, helped to shape this geographically variegated legal sea space, in part through their own strategies of hedging to sustain potential claims to legality and playing one power off against the other.

The English campaign against piracy in the 1720s should not be taken as representative of policies toward piracy in the long eighteenth century, and the increasingly desperate behavior of mariners labeled as pirates in this period should also not be understood as a sign of mariners' innate oppositional culture and attachment to custom over state law.[147] Both

[147] This is of course the central assertion of Linebaugh and Rediker, *Many-Headed Hydra*. Their chapter on Atlantic piracy argues that both extreme cases of "hydrarchy," the creation of a parallel social order under pirate rule, and the virulent suppression of piracy by the English crown were peculiar to the 1720s, but elsewhere the authors

trends followed decades of a more open-ended maritime politics at the turn of the eighteenth century, during which mariners challenged the legal order and promoted it by insisting on the legality of a range of actions. In doing so, they perpetuated aspects and changed the contours of a regulatory world made up of repeating imperial methods for adjudicating prize cases and ordering interimperial maritime actions. Both regulatory dimensions developed regional patterns; both depended on the shared understanding of ships at sea as law-bearing vessels tied to sovereign sponsors, tracing through their movements corridors of potential jurisdiction.

While emerging European understandings of international law and mariners' practices reinforced a pattern of regulatory regionalism of the seas in the first decades of the long eighteenth century, European empires were struggling to construct coherent maritime imperial policies – an elusive goal. The definition of the high seas as a special legal category responded to institutional tensions within separate imperial legal orders, and these institutional orders also replicated, with variations, systems for the proliferation or empowerment of colonial forums to handle maritime law. Meanwhile, jurisdictional jockeying among competing polities composed a broader maritime legal politics. By the middle of the eighteenth century, appealing to the law of nations by litigants and judges in prize cases had become routine. If this rhetoric was cheap talk, what conditions explain its embrace at a time when Britain's ascendance as a global naval power made the search for legal cover less imperative? And if the discourse reflected a new authority for international law, why did it occur in the context of waves of maritime violence featuring repeated flouting of its principles?

Explaining legal and rhetorical shifts of the eighteenth century depends on an understanding of trends in imperial legal administration. In eighteenth-century prize adjudication, to refer to the law of nations was after all to invoke the existence of not just other sovereigns but also other sovereigns' legal procedures, personnel, and courts. It mattered to both captors and captives where these courts were located, how many were functioning, and what their relation was to central government authority. In parallel reorganizations, European imperial powers officially extended into empire the authority to adjudicate prize cases over a period of several decades stretching from the 1670s through the first decades of the eighteenth century. Within British imperial law, this change featured the

suggest that pirates' loyalty to custom was relatively constant, and linked in unspecified ways to proto-revolutionary sentiments around the Atlantic.

establishment and jurisdictional enhancement of colonial vice admiralty courts, a move that was key to the British war on piracy in the 1720s. Parallel institutional changes in the French, Dutch, and Spanish empires fashioned prize law into a loose international regulatory framework – an early example of global administrative law – by the middle decades of the eighteenth century.[148] The framework did not guarantee or even encourage peaceful relations, but it did rely on an assumption of a certain degree of institutional continuity across empires, including similarities that went beyond the reliance on shared legal sources.

The account shows that we do not have to choose between writing the history of the impact of European imperial law on the wider world and constructing a narrative that emphasizes the autonomy and resilience of non-European legal orders. Nor do we need to separate narratives of European theories of the law of the sea and of European practice. Viewed in the context of maritime legal strategies, the contributions of Gentili and Grotius appear to be less starkly different from one another, and they can be understood as influential in a different way. In the wave of piracy and privateering at the end of the seventeenth century and into the first decades of the eighteenth century, both mariners and their sponsors embraced the full range of interpretive possibilities, stretching the terms of commissions (even forging them on a regular basis) and jockeying to announce the legitimacy of obscure issuing authorities as sovereign proxies.[149]

The jurisdictional tangles of maritime law flowed logically, in other words, from a world recognized by Gentili and Grotius in which the sea hosted multiple polities operating "in tension with one another."[150] Such

[148] Specifically, we might think about this institutional shift as an example of the formation of global regulatory functions out of domestic administrative law, as outlined by Benedict Kingsbury, Nico Krisch, and Richard B. Stewart, "The Emergence of Global Administrative Law," in *International Law and Justice Working Papers* (New York: Institute for International Law and Justice, New York University School of Law, 2005).

[149] Many of the legal issues addressed but not resolved by Gentili and Grotius continued beyond this period to roil interimperial maritime politics, including the rights of neutrals, the legality of prize proceedings conducted on the high seas, and the circumstances under which subordinate imperial polities might issue valid commissions. On neutrality, see Carl Jacob Kulsrud, *Maritime Neutrality to 1780: A History of the Main Principles Governing Neutrality and Belligerency to 1780* (Boston: Little, Brown, 1936). On debates about privateering more generally leading up to its abolition, see Francis R. Stark, *The Abolition of Privateering and the Declaration of Paris [1897]* (Honolulu: University Press of the Pacific, 2002).

[150] James Muldoon characterizes the extra-European legal order as "European condominium," or "Christendom without the pope." "Who Owns the Sea" (paper presented at "Sea Changes: Historicizing the Oceans," Universität Greifswald, July 2000).

a reading contributes to the larger project of reexamining "conventional wisdoms" in the history of international law and international relations.[151] It affirms the view that the international law of the period cannot be captured by describing a transition from a natural law basis of international jurisprudence to a positive international law; legal principles were invoked across the period in ways that were "jurisprudentially eclectic."[152] Gentili was not just embracing the positivism that seems to contrast with Grotius's reliance on natural law but also drawing from a wide legal repertoire and conceptualizing sea space as jurisdictionally complex. Like Gentili, Grotius sought to simplify definitions of the sea as a peculiar kind of legal arena but ended up also reaffirming widely circulating understandings of the uneven application of jurisdiction and sovereignty in ocean space. Interimperial politics and pervasive practices of privateering and piracy shaped these views. In both the real and the imagined legal order, ships and their captains moved as delegated legal authorities along intersecting paths, extending corridors of control, in turn weakly or strongly associated with jurisdiction, into an interimperial sea space that could not be owned but could be dominated.

If oceans were in some sense quintessentially global, it was not because they were assumed to be empty, vast, and lawless. Gentili's use of Roman sources to define pirates as the "enemies of all mankind" endured, though so did his flexibility in defining legal and illegal sponsorship. Grotius's emphasis on freedom of the seas was embraced, especially by later English promoters, but so was his recognition that parts of the sea could be militarized and controlled. Captains as agents of sovereigns carried law across the sea in imagined corridors of control that sometimes corresponded to areas of spectacular if sporadic sea raiding. Taking the measure of these trends, we can affirm that the long seventeenth century marked a turning point in the law of the sea, but one not captured by the usual narratives of the maritime origins of international law. In this period, Europeans articulated the basis of an international law of the sea as a complex tangle of jurisdictional strings that would operate as a framework for expanding violence into the next century.

[151] Keene, *Beyond the Anarchical Society*, 2.

[152] This is Armitage's phrase describing a similar blending of natural and positive law approaches in the Declaration of Independence. Armitage, *The Declaration of Independence*, 89.

4

Island Chains

Military Law and Convict Transportation

> Had I plantation of this isle, my lord, –
> . . . for no kind of traffic
> Would I admit; no name of magistrate:
> Letters should not be known: riches, poverty,
> And use of service – none: contract, succession,
> Bourn, bound of land, tilth, vineyard – none:
> No use of metal, corn, or wine, or oil:
> No occupation, all men idle, all:
> And women too, but innocent and pure:
> No sovereignty –
>
> – Shakespeare, *The Tempest*

> I was lord of the whole manor. . . . I might call myself king or emperor over the whole country which I had possession of; there were no rivals; I had no competitor, none to dispute sovereignty or command with me.
>
> – Daniel Defoe, *Robinson Crusoe*

Shakespeare's Gonzalo was entertaining a vision that belonged to a tradition of utopian imagery about island life that pervaded European colonial writings. Overseas posts strung along travel routes were an invitation to an "archipelagic imagination" already developed in medieval representations of islands as wild and holy places and as stopping points along spiritual itineraries.[1] Islands served as settings for reveries about primitive communalism and a revival of ancient custom. European imaginings of colonial landscapes as enchanted idylls – wondrous prospects – influenced

[1] Gillis, *Islands of the Mind.* The phrase and discussion of utopian visions are on p. 63; medieval representations of islands are discussed in Chapter 2 in this volume.

early colonial writings and took on new forms in the context of emerging representations of nature as both an object of scientific study and a setting for contemplation, leisure, and erotic pleasure.[2]

Yet, as in Gonzalo's musings, utopian images of islands as places of "no sovereignty" went hand in hand with visions of island rule as an exercise in despotism.[3] Gonzalo could not make sovereignty disappear without first imagining the island as his personal domain ("Had I plantation of this isle"). The imperative to control islands closely was related to their place in the political economy of militarily protected European commercial networks. Sheltering traders and fledgling settlements from attack by sea marauders and populations on shore, islands as sites of "garrison government" were familiar features of early European colonial enterprise, and variants of a more widespread pattern of military command over specialized colonial enclaves.[4] Meanwhile, islands' isolation and natural boundedness recommended their use as sites for imprisonment. Roman law had designated small Mediterranean islands as places of banishment, and European ships carried into wider oceanic circuits the long-standing practice of marooning intransigent mariners on small islands.[5] The earliest voyages beyond European territories carried convicts as forced settlers, sometimes to strategically located islands. These

[2] On the European discourse of wonder, see Greenblatt, *Marvelous Possessions.* On scientific approaches to nature and on ideologies of improvement in the context of nineteenth-century empire, see Richard Harry Drayton, *Nature's Government: Science, Imperial Britain, and the "Improvement" of the World* (New Haven, CT: Yale University Press, 2000). Alain Corbin, in *Lure of the Sea*, traces the origins of Europeans' appreciation of the seaside as a site of contemplation and leisure.

[3] Jonathan Lamb makes a similar point in noting that in prominent texts about South Sea islands, "the utopian possibilities of desert-island life are introduced at first as the bulwark against the forces of savagery, only to demonstrate in the end a cruelty whose impulse belongs not to the state of unimproved nature but to the degeneration of an ambitious civility." Jonathan Lamb, Vanessa Smith, and Nicholas Thomas, eds., *Exploration and Exchange: A South Seas Anthology, 1680–1900* (Chicago: University of Chicago Press, 2000), 31.

[4] The phrase is from Webb, *The Governors-General.*

[5] Alexander Selkirk, the seaman who lived in isolation on the larger of the Juan Fernández Islands, off the coast of Chile, for more than four years (and was probably Daniel Defoe's model for Robinson Crusoe) chose to take his chances alone on the island rather than continue to serve under a poorly qualified captain. Other mariners were put ashore – on that island, and on others – as punishment for infractions that ranged from insolence to sodomy to mutiny. The journal of Leendert Hasenbosch, a Dutch seaman "set ashore as a villain" on the small Atlantic island of Ascension, recounts the days up to his solitary death from thirst, after a Dutch captain ordered him left there, probably for the crime of sodomy. See Alex Ritsema, *A Dutch Castaway on Ascension Island in 1725* (Netherlands: A. Ritsema, 2006), 42.

overlapping uses of islands as sites of military garrisons, protected commercial nodes, agricultural stations, and places of natural confinement contributed to their growing association with captive labor and harsh disciplinary regimes.

The multiple real and imagined uses of islands influenced contrasting representations of island sovereignty. As naturally bounded spaces that could be thoroughly discovered and surveyed, islands seemed by their very nature to simplify the processes of taking possession and making dominion transparent.[6] What could be confusing about sovereignty over an island? Yet some of the same conditions that made islands seemingly easy objects of dominion rendered their rule a matter of legal complexity. Precisely because claims to islands referred to neatly bounded territories and implied a perfect match between authority and jurisdiction, individual or corporate authorities with control over islands often exercised an unusual degree of autonomy and presented novel challenges to imperial constitutions. Questions emerged about the authorization for tyrannical local rule, and about whether and in what measure imperial legal protections extended to island settlers, convicts, captives, and indigenous inhabitants. Like Robinson Crusoe's reign over his island, simple to describe when he was alone or with Friday but complicated as soon as his rescuers arrived, island sovereignty required negotiation and could involve unusual feats of legal imagination.

This chapter examines the problem of island rule in a particular and important context: the expansion of colonial convict transportation to island sites in the last decades of the eighteenth century and into the early nineteenth century. In this period, pretensions to comprehensive imperial schemes of penal servitude called attention to the contradictions between more ambitious goals of imperial legal ordering and the proliferation of enclaves of military rule and martial law. Sovereignty was problematic in island penal colonies not because there was much question about which imperial power ruled or whether it had the power to rule.

[6] Even in connection with the taking of islands as signs of possession, associations with prisons came up. Writing about his expedition's decision to settle on St. Croix, a small island in what is now the St. Croix River at the border between Maine and New Brunswick, Canada, Champlain wrote that he would thereafter "always be of the opinion that whosoever goes to a country to take possession of it should not make themselves prisoners upon islands." And Sir William Alexander wrote in "Encouragement to Colonies," in 1624, that the French had found "in the end . . . that a little Ile was but a kind of large prison." Both quotes appear in William Francis Ganong, *Champlain's Island: An Expanded Edition of Ste. Croix (Dochet) Island* (St. John: New Brunswick Museum, 2003), 96.

The problem lay in a linked set of contradictions: between supposedly integrated imperial systems of rule and the creation of new anomalous legal zones in empire, and between strengthening rhetoric about empires of liberty and the reliance on forced labor to expand and consolidate empires in a period of intense, global interimperial rivalry.[7]

Understanding this conjuncture requires placing it first within the longer history of banishment and convict transportation in European history, an exercise that allows us to glimpse the deeper structural features of the law conditioning the proliferation of imperial penal projects. The second task is to develop a wider comparative analysis for the period from the 1780s to the 1850s. Emphasis on the history of Botany Bay as the quintessential penal colony has tended to eclipse the study of convict transportation as a global phenomenon, while it has also encouraged a focus on the logic and expectation of a transition from penal colony to the territorial sovereignty of settler states.[8] This chapter considers a wider set of experiences, in particular the move within the Spanish empire to use military garrisons, or presidios, as penal colonies. The Spanish experience has received scant attention from historians, partly because the scale of convict transportation was small compared to earlier Portuguese and later English and French practices. Precisely because it sought to accommodate new imperial flows of convicts by adjusting existing colonial institutions, Spanish penal history helps to illuminate the logic of placing convicts under military rule, often on isolated island garrisons. The case also suggests new possibilities for tracing the connections between the militarization of empire and the constitutional challenges of the early nineteenth century. Contemporaries worried that enhancing military authority, even in contained spaces, might threaten constitutional projects in the metropole and in the nascent republics of Latin America.

Spanish convict transportation alters the lens through which we view English penal settlements by sharpening the focus on military and martial law. The connection is especially visible in British sites of secondary transportation, the small islands that composed a penal archipelago in

[7] Neuman, "Anomalous Zones," 1197. On this period as one of global forced migrations, see Emma Christopher, Cassandra Pybus, and Marcus Rediker, *Many Middle Passages: Forced Migration and the Making of the Modern World* (Berkeley: University of California Press, 2007).

[8] It is possible, of course, to view this transition not as a necessary outcome but as one impelled by legal and jurisdictional tangles. See Lisa Ford, *Settler Sovereignty: Jurisdiction and Indigenous People in America and Australia, 1788–1836* (Cambridge, MA: Harvard University Press, 2010).

the Pacific and Indian oceans.[9] Tracing the history of martial law in Norfolk Island in this chapter urges us to speculate on a broader discursive and structural link between the law of island penal colonies and the law of slave and postemancipation island colonies. The connection derived in part from the observation that delegating legal authority in empire invited men to behave as petty tyrants. Contemporaries did not always view this condition as undermining imperial constitutions, but the invocation of martial law and the strengthening of military authority prompted some observers to suggest that the layered systems of sovereignty inherent to empires might also threaten their future. Exceptions to imperial law, even in isolated pockets, might allow tyranny to migrate to other parts of empire or undermine the integrity of imperial legal systems. Such worries brought together questions about the constitutionality of penal servitude and anxieties about order in slave and postemancipation settings, reinforcing representations of islands as both models and anomalies of imperial legal ordering.

Convicts as Colonists

Across Europe, exile was a well-established criminal sentence, with clear and influential antecedents in Roman law. In its mildest form, banishment in Roman law required leaving a particular city or province in perpetuity or for a fixed term, with no effect on citizenship and no designated place of exile. More severe sentences of banishment involved the loss of civil rights and forfeiture of property or deportation to a fixed place. As in later European law, banishment served as a substitution for the penalty of death. It was overwhelmingly a sentence for crimes against the public order – political crimes – committed by persons of high status.

Four features of Roman legal practice are especially interesting as background to the developing uses of exile in European empires. First, the most common places of exile were islands, and *relegatio in insulam* (relegation to an island) became the preferred sentence for conspiracy, sedition, and similar acts. Early cases of banishment to islands mention the small island of Pandataria in the bay of Naples, Cercina off the coast

[9] On the Andaman Islands, see Clare Anderson, *Convicts in the Indian Ocean: Transportation from South Asia to Mauritius, 1815–53* (New York: St. Martin's Press, 2000); Satadru Sen, *Disciplining Punishment: Colonialism and Convict Society in the Andaman Islands* (Oxford: Oxford University Press, 2000); Aparna Vaidik, *Imperial Andamans: A Spatial History of Britain's Indian Ocean Colony, 1858–1921* (New York: Palgrave Macmillan, 2009).

of northern Africa, and Amorgos in the Aegean. In the early empire, the most common places for island deportation were other islands near the Italian coast, the Cyclades, Sardinia, Corsica, and the Balearic Islands. Second, there is some ambiguity in the historical record and perhaps also in Roman legal practice about whether exiles to islands were under the legal authority of Rome or of magistrates on the islands. Some exiles had guards to prevent them from leaving the islands, though most had freedom of movement within the designated place of exile. Punishments were developed for those who escaped places of banishment before the time fixed under their sentences. Third, banishment in Roman law could be a judicial or an executive punishment. Besides its use as a substitute for a sentence of death, exile (most often not to a fixed place) was sometimes ordered for people whose activities might disrupt public order: philosophers, foreigners, actors, astrologers, and Jews.[10] Finally, it is important to note that banishment in Roman law and practice was entirely separate from penal servitude, or the use of criminals for labor on public works, or in mines and quarries.

As with the influence of Roman law on the early modern European law of treason (discussed in Chapter 2), banishment in Roman law came into European legal systems not through a single source or as a fixed set of well-defined practices but as a resource with flexible interpretations and applications.[11] From the late medieval period, criminal exile found a place in the local and royal courts of all the European polities that would later sponsor transoceanic ventures. In Portugal, banishment could take the form of exile from a town or bishopric; to a specific place of exile for

[10] See Mary V. Braginton, "Exile under the Roman Emperors," *Classical Journal* 39, no. 7 (1944), 391–407; Robert G. Caldwell, "Exile as an Institution," *Political Science Quarterly* 58, no. 2 (1943), 239–62; Robinson, *Criminal Law*.

[11] Banishment was also used as punishment in other empires, so it is possible that it also entered through the circulation of other sources or news about other imperial practices, though I know of no studies of such cross-regional influences. In China, banishment became a key tool for colonizing the northwestern frontier regions brought into the Qing empire. Between 1758 and 1820, thousands of people were sent as exiles into the "new territories" of Xinjiang. Joanna Waley-Cohen, *Exile in Mid-Qing China: Banishment to Xinjiang, 1758–1820* (New Haven, CT: Yale University Press, 1991). In Islamic law, banishment also existed as a punishment. The Koran mentioned the punishment, and it was discussed in classical jurisprudence mainly as a punishment for banditry or illicit sex. Those sent into exile were almost exclusively males. The Ottoman criminal code describes banishment as a punishment for persons considered politically or socially dangerous, including Gypsies, lepers, irreligious people, and arsonists. Rudolph Peters, *Crime and Punishment in Islamic Law: Theory and Practice from the Sixteenth to the Twenty-First Century* (Cambridge: Cambridge University Press, 2005).

a term of years; to a designated place with or without a limited term, or for life; or from all of Portugal and any of its colonies for life.[12] In Spain, the term *destierro* was applied to a variety of punishments – including perpetual exile from a particular town or region and a sentence of military service or forced labor – for a range of of crimes, from theft to sedition. Spanish documents show scores of cases involving *destierro* between 1477 and 1505, many recorded because of requests for pardons for sentences of exile from a town or from the realm, or seizure of property.[13] The numerous applications for mercy suggest that local officials sometimes gave the sentence to rivals, unruly subordinates, or perceived social deviants. A *vecino* of the town of Villacomer in Ávila was sentenced to one hundred lashes and exile from the town for ten years for stealing livestock from the local lord. Inés de Mesa petitioned for a stay of her order of exile from Sanlucar de Alpechina for "lying with her father."[14] By the sixteenth century, Portugal, Spain, and France had adopted criminal sentences of forced labor in order to supply crews for the galley fleets assigned to protecting the coasts. The array of sentences of exile divided into two broad categories – banishment from the realm and galley service – depending on the high or low status of those receiving sentences.

The flexibility of the sentence made it a valuable tool in support of imperial ambitions. The Portuguese assigned convicts opportunistically and in risky schemes or encounters. When Pedro Álvares Cabral's ships touched the coast of Brazil in April of 1500, Cabral sent "a young convict," Alfonso Ribeiro, to go among the Tupi Indians and "learn their

[12] Timothy J. Coates, *Convicts and Orphans: Forced and State-Sponsored Colonizers in the Portuguese Empire, 1550–1755* (Stanford, CA: Stanford University Press, 2001), 22. Members of the clergy might also be banished to a monastery, with further restrictions on their writings and speech. In Spain and then in the Spanish empire, banishment of members of the clergy appears to have offered a way around limitations on royal jurisdiction over the clergy.

[13] Brief summaries of cases resulting in lifting of the sentence of exile ("alzamiento de destierro") in these years appear in the records of the Cancillería, Sellos de Corte, and the Consejo de Cámara de Castilla from the Archivo General de Simancas (hereafter AGS). They can be accessed on the Portal de Archivos Españoles (PARES, http://pares.mcu.es). Some, but not all, documents from various Spanish archives cited in this chapter may be accessed on this site.

[14] Sección Nobleza del Archivo Histórico Nacional (hereafter AHS), Castrillo, C.1, D.37; and AGS CCA-CED, 4, 131, 5. *Destierro* in these cases probably meant banishment from the local jurisdiction and exclusion from holding the rights of *vecinos*. On *vecindad*, see Herzog, *Defining Nations*. Herzog misleadingly translates *vecindad* as "citizenship" but defines it as a status of membership in a local political community and shows its importance in both early modern Spain and Spanish America.

manner of living and their customs."[15] Da Gama dispatched António Fernandes, a *degredado* (convict), to the interior region beyond Sofala to find out more about the gold trade.[16] Isabella and Ferdinand planned to send a contingent of condemned criminals to help colonize Hispaniola under Columbus in 1497.[17] The French instructed La Roque and Cartier to take criminals as colonists to New France in the early sixteenth century, and toward the end of the century De la Roche deposited sixty condemned men to settle Sable Island in the North Atlantic, where all but twelve soon died.[18] An English plan to send several convicts with Martin Frobisher's second voyage in 1577 was abandoned, but in 1615, James I established transportation as a reprieve for felons and designated several locations for exile, including imperial destinations in the East and West Indies and Newfoundland.[19] A member of the English East India Company, Thomas Aldworth, proposed in 1611 the annual shipment of one hundred convicts to the Cape of Good Hope; in 1615, ten convicts arrived and installed themselves briefly on Robben Island to evade hostile Khoikhoi on shore.[20] English officials began to urge sending convicts to Virginia very soon after the colony's founding, and the English employed criminal exiles to construct Tangier's sea barrier.[21]

[15] "Letter of Pedro Vaz de Caminha to King Manuel," in *The Voyage of Pedro Álvares Cabral to Brazil and India from Contemporary Documents and Narratives*, ed. William Brooks Greenlee (London: Printed for the Hakluyt Society, 1938), 3–32. On *degredados* in Brazil, see Geraldo Pieroni, *Vadios e ciganos, heréticos e bruxas: Os degredados no Brasil-Colônia* (Rio de Janeiro: Berstrand Brasil, 2000).

[16] On the basis of this voyage and a second trip in 1513, Fernandes reported that most of the gold was being traded at commercial fairs in the interior and that holding only the coastal factories of Sofala and Kilwa was unlikely to enhance the Portuguese share of the trade. Newitt, *History of Portuguese Overseas Expansion*, 87.

[17] Archivo General de Indias (hereafter AGI), Patronato, 295, N.35. In 1505, worried about disorder in the New World, the crown ordered a halt to banishing more criminals to the Indies. AHN, Diversos Colecciones, 41, N.22.

[18] On early French origins of convict transportation, see Jacques-Guy Petit, "La colonizzazione penale del sistema penitenziario francese," in *Le colonie penali nell'Europa dell'Ottocento: Atti del Convegno internazionale...: Porto Torres, 25 Maggio 2001*, Mario Da Passano, ed. (Rome: Carocci, 2004), 37–65.

[19] Gwenda Morgan and Peter Rushton, *Eighteenth-Century Criminal Transportation: The Formation of the Criminal Atlantic* (New York: Palgrave Macmillan, 2004), 9. Morgan and Rushton note that, as an imperial practice, transportation developed from "a convergence of policies towards both crime and poverty" (10).

[20] Harriet Deacon, ed., *The Island: A History of Robben Island, 1488–1990* (Cape Town: Mayibuye Books, 1996), 11–12.

[21] Attempts to regularize the process toward the end of the century included the 1679 Habeas Corpus Act prohibiting transportation without a trial. This act was the first in

These practices spawned movements of convicts within and across intraimperial regions. In the sixteenth century, Goan courts deported some convicted criminals to exile in Brazil, and to the Moluccas; judges in Angola sent men convicted of serious crimes to Brazil and exiles from Portugal who became repeat offenders to São Tomé and Príncipe; and Brazilian courts banished high-status criminals from the colony.[22] Spanish colonial courts also used *destierro* as a punishment. In the middle decades of the sixteenth century, the audiencia in Peru awarded sentences of exile from the viceroyalty for crimes ranging from murder to treason; some participants in Gonzalo Pizarro's rebellion were sentenced to *destierro* and the loss of their estates.[23] These cases involved only exclusion from towns or regions, but Spanish colonial courts also sometimes designated particular places of exile, sending criminals from Peru to New Spain, or from New Spain to the Philippines.[24] The Dutch East India Company utilized penal transportation and exile from an early date, creating a web of involuntary migration connecting nodes of company rule stretching from the Banda Islands to the Cape Colony.[25]

Certain underlying legal tensions were shared across these colonial projects. The first source of tension related to the juxtaposition of political and judicial sentences of banishment. Although legal distinctions could be sharply drawn, often ad hoc procedures associated with exile as

England formally establishing transportation as a sentence accompanying a pardon for another conviction.

[22] See Coates, *Convicts and Orphans*, 80.

[23] For example, see the 1572 petition sent to the Council of the Indies on behalf of Antonio de Heredia and Baltasar Pérez asking that the sentence of *destierro* pronounced for various violent acts committed in Lima be removed. AGI, Justicia, 445, N.2, R.4. And see the case against Pedro de Valdés, accused of lèse-majesté and treason in connection with Gonzalo Pizarro's rebellion. This case, begun in 1548 and still under review in 1559, shows that the slow pace typical of other parts of the system of justice applied to cases of exile (AGI, Justicia, 425, N.2).

[24] These flows, together with the assignment of convict laborers to more local public works projects, were probably not very substantial until the middle of the eighteenth century. On the assignment and sale of convict laborers sentenced in Mexico City, see Gabriel Haslip-Viera, *Crime and Punishment in Late Colonial Mexico City, 1692–1810* (Albuquerque: University of New Mexico Press, 1999), 104–8.

[25] For an excellent study of Dutch East India Company practices, see Ward, *Networks of Empire*. Ward notes that the Dutch did not engage in penal transportation from the metropole to the empire but extensively applied the punishments of penal transportation (mainly to "low-ranking Company servants, indigenes and Chinese people under Company jurisdiction, and slaves" [22–3]) and exile (usually reserved for indigenous elites but sometimes for lower-ranking locals defined as rebels) throughout the company's empire.

a punishment could also blur the differences. The second source of tension involved the open question of the legal authority over exiles once they reached their designated places of banishment. Even when metropolitan powers sought to fix this relation, an array of conditions intervened to change it, including the weakness of crown oversight of distant colonial courts, the economic and legal strategies of convicts, colonial authorities' anxieties about threats of military attack or insurrection, and the opportunism of local elites seeking to use the courts to enhance their control over resources, including labor. Such elements of uncertainty tended to inscribe extrajudicial actions into the heart of systems of exile and convict transportation.

These connections emerged clearly in the Portuguese empire, which blended systems of internal and external exile from an early date. In the fifteenth century, criminals who committed minor offenses were sentenced to internal exile, those judged guilty of more serious crimes were transported to garrisons in North Africa, and criminals convicted of the most serious offenses were either sentenced to labor in the galleys or shipped to the island of São Tomé.[26] On São Tomé, the unsettled status of *degredados* remained a key source of the political instability that plagued the island for the next century and a half. Escape attempts and rebellions by *degredados* were followed by the social and economic ascent of some criminal exiles, who then petitioned the crown for pardons and pursued opportunistic alliances with grantees, *fazendeiros* (landed estate owners), and merchants.[27] As sugar cultivation took off on the island, *degredados* began to play a key role in the slave trade and made up most of the island militia organized to keep the slaves in check.[28] Yet ruling elites and officials had little incentive to remove barriers to the advancement of *degredados*, especially because the island faced continual labor

[26] In the sixteenth century, Brazil and Portuguese Asia were also named as destinations for serious offenders. Coates, *Convicts and Orphans.*

[27] Only a year after the crown gave Álvaro da Caminha a grant over the island in 1493, a contingent of *degredados* attempted to escape to the mainland, hoping to join the ranks of *lançados* (Portuguese runaways) already probing river trade for profit. A second rebellion of *degredados* under Caminha's successor led to the imprisonment of some "rebels," later killed for attempting to escape. Caminha had brought not only convicts but also a shipment of perhaps as many as two thousand Jewish children who had been seized from their parents in Portugal. Robert Garfield, *A History of São Tomé Island, 1470–1655: The Key to Guinea* (San Francisco: Mellen Research University Press, 1992).

[28] The role of convicts in the militia became especially important in the seventeenth century in response to attacks by the English, French, and especially the Dutch. Garfield, *History of São Tomé Island*, 122.

shortages and welcomed the arrival of new shipments of convicts. The temptation was for powerful grantees to use the convict system to enhance their power and wealth. When the crown's anxieties about lax control over the island and especially lost revenue from unreported slave trading led to the appointment in 1516 of the first *ouvidor geral* (chief judge), the official found that the island's grantee (*donatario*), João de Mello, was routinely raiding the treasury and exceeding his legal authority. Under Mello, the local judge was convicting islanders of crimes with little evidence, probably with the goal of generating new *degredados* or extending the terms of exile for convicts in the service of local elites.[29] Mello finally went too far in this practice in 1521, when, on returning to São Tomé from Lisbon with more *degredados*, he ordered the ship's captain seized and declared him a convict for assignment on the island. In a process of secondary punishment that would become common in convict transportation systems, João de Mello himself was sentenced to be banished and confined to the island of Príncipe. São Tomé's record of ineffective royal control and ad hoc attempts to repress both *degredado* unruliness and slave revolts continued into the seventeenth century, leading one historian to characterize the island as occupying "a kind of limbo between the official and the unofficial empire."[30]

The legal peculiarities of São Tomé stemmed from the unresolved status of criminal exiles and the undefined authority over them by colonial officials. The same uncertainties took different forms in later colonies and in other empires. During the early decades of the eighteenth century, convict transportation began to be integrated into strategies of colonial settlement and interimperial rivalry, laying the groundwork for the global expansion of the systems toward the end of the century. In England, after a period at the beginning of the eighteenth century when shipments in convicts declined – mainly because vagrants and criminals were instead being pressed into service as soldiers and sailors – the 1718 Transportation Act established transportation as a sentence that the courts could impose directly as a punishment rather than indirectly as

[29] At about the same time, the island's first slave uprising took place, apparently with the leadership of some *forros* (free men). See Garfield, *History of São Tomé Island*.

[30] Newitt, *A History of Portuguese Overseas Expansion*, 126. The post of royal governor, created after Mello's banishment, rarely found willing candidates, and the bishopric also went unclaimed for decades. São Tomé came to share its status as a primary site of penal exile in the Portuguese empire with Angola, but the island setting meant that in effect the entire colony of São Tomé was a penal site; it had no jail. Coates, *Convicts and Orphans*, 122.

a form of conditional pardon for a sentence usually bearing another punishment.[31] The apparently subtle difference opened the way to a shift in the legal status of transported convicts because the Transportation Act effectively institutionalized servile bondage as an element of penal law.[32] Yet the legal status of convicts transported from Britain was not clearly stipulated and remained something to be worked out in practice.

In the next decades, Virginia and Maryland became the principal destinations for transported convicts until the American Revolution, receiving about 90 percent of convicts sent from Britain to the Americas; the total number transported to North America and the Caribbean between the 1660s and 1770s was about sixty thousand.[33] The surge in exiled convicts paralleled the well-documented rise in capital crimes in England. The most common offense associated with convict transportation was grand larceny, though stealing or receiving even very small amounts of property could also trigger criminal exile. An important element of transportation

[31] The full title of the act was "An Act for the further preventing Robbery, Burglary, and other Felonies; and for the more effectual Transportation of Felons and unlawful Exporters of Wool; and for declaring the Law upon some points relating to Pirates." See Alan Atkinson, "The Free-Born Englishman Transported: Convict Rights as a Measure of Eighteenth-Century Empire," *Past and Present* 44 (1994), 88–115.

[32] See Atkinson, "The Free-Born Englishman Transported," 97. English jurists had before characterized transportation as a form of banishment, in which bondage was prohibited. It is important to note that the innovation of awarding transportation as a direct sentence did not end the practice of ordering transportation in place of other punishments. Criminals convicted of offenses for which they could obtain benefit of clergy could receive sentences of transportation for seven years instead of burning or flogging, because clergyable offenses had become noncapital in practice; those convicted of non-clergyable offenses with capital sentences could receive mercy from the crown conditional on transportation for a fixed period. See Bruce Kercher, "Perish or Prosper: The Law and Convict Transportation in the British Empire, 1700–1850," *Law and History Review* 21, no. 3 (2003), 527–54, 530; for the place of transportation in the broader context of the criminal law in this period, see J. M. Beattie, *Crime and the Courts in England, 1660–1800* (Oxford: Clarendon, 1986), chap. 9. The term was often fixed at fourteen years for serious offenders transported to the Americas, though an interesting anomaly was that transported convicts were all considered on arrival to hold terms of seven years (see Atkinson, "The Free-Born Englishman Transported").

[33] The vast majority of convicts were shipped after 1700; before that date, an estimated 4,500 convicts were transported to the Americas, and the legal processes remained "somewhat vague and haphazard." Morgan and Rushton, *Eighteenth-Century Criminal Transportation*, 12. And see Peter Wilson Coldham, *Emigrants in Chains: A Social History of Forced Emigration to the Americas of Felons, Destitute Children, Political and Religious Non-Conformists, Vagabonds, Beggars and Other Undesirables, 1607–1776* (Baltimore: Genealogical Publishing, 1992). On seventeenth-century transportation patterns, see Abbot Emerson Smith, "The Transportation of Convicts to the American Colonies in the Seventeenth Century," *American Historical Review* 39, no. 2 (1934), 232–49.

to the Americas was that it was profitable. Shippers were willing to take convicts across the ocean because money could be made by selling the rights to their labor to private interests in American ports. Once assigned, the convicts functioned much like indentured servants, though they received no freedom dues when their longer sentences were completed. It was unclear whether they should be treated legally in the same way as indentured servants. Atkinson argues that until about the 1740s, convicts and indentured servants held roughly the same legal status; later, between 1740 and the Revolution, convicts were deprived of various legal prerogatives. In Virginia, they came to be exempt from the requirement of trial by juries composed of men from their local communities, disqualified from providing testimony in court, and barred from voting. Their legal status became both implicitly and explicitly more nearly associated with the status of slaves.[34] Still, the degree of "felony attaint" that applied in the colonies remained a matter of uncertainty and in practice appears to have been less extensive than it would have been in England.[35] The Transportation Act and patterns of transportation to the Americas established the practice as a colonial institution without resolving the fundamental tension between transportation as a form of exile and transportation as a category of bondage.

French legal practice presents yet another variation in this period, with results that also opened the door to novel legal moves later in the eighteenth century. Spieler has argued that French law in the ancien régime constructed the category of a legal nonperson within France and transposed the category to the empire with the exile of political prisoners and, then, common criminals. The "civil death" of some subjects moved to the colonies (first to French Guiana, later also to New Caledonia) marked these sites not as prisons but as forerunners of the concentration camp.[36] The mid-eighteenth-century end to the practice of condemning men to the galleys meanwhile began a long process of swelling the ranks of those eventually eligible for exile. Condemned criminals collected in

[34] Atkinson, "The Free-Born Englishman Transported," 144.

[35] See Kercher, "Perish or Prosper," 536–41.

[36] Miranda Spieler, "Empire and Underworld: Guiana in the French Legal Imagination c. 1789–1870," Ph.D. diss., Columbia University, 2005; and "The Legal Structure of Colonial Rule during the French Revolution," *William and Mary Quarterly* 66 (2009), 365–408. Spieler also notes the influence of the legal doctrine of the state of siege in the creation of French Guiana as an exceptional jurisdiction; this was a French variant on the European law of emergency. On the earliest disastrous shipment of convicts to French Guiana, see Emma Rothschild, "A Horrible Tragedy in the French Atlantic," *Past and Present*, no. 192 (2006), 67–108.

the *bagnes*, sites of imprisonment under naval administration at several ports, and this institutional arrangement provided the administrative framework for expanding transportation of convicts to imperial sites in the nineteenth century.

While the founding of Botany Bay and of French Guiana in some respects marked a turning point toward qualitatively different kinds of colonial penal servitude, a wider set of comparisons and a longer chronological perspective remind us that certain legal problems associated with these colonies were systemic, though magnified by conditions of the period. As we have seen, some form of convict transportation had emerged in every European empire through the adaptation of even older legal practices, and the legal status of convicts once transported remained uncertain. Toward the end of the eighteenth century, the phenomenon of colonial convict transportation shifted in scale, and at the same time, the stakes for defining the place of penal settlements within imperial administration became greater in the context of intensifying global inter-imperial rivalries. New efforts to plan and better control distant imperial projects coincided with campaigns to establish more extensive and comprehensive imperial controls. Shifting patterns of long-distance maritime trade created new incentives for establishing far-flung bases and defending sea approaches to distant spheres of influence. Britain's rising global hegemony facilitated the empire's first large-scale imperial resettlement plans.[37] Spanish and French anxieties in the wake of the Seven Years' War urged a shift toward more systematic forms of convict transportation in the context of global militarization, and new strategies of militarization. It was during this peculiar conjuncture that practices of penal exile were transformed into institutions of empire. Yet, significantly, the ambiguities of transportation as a legal mechanism remained, generating new variants. The period between 1780 and 1840 brought into sharp focus questions about the relation between local control of transported laborers and a broader system of imperial authority, particularly the place of military authority within imperial constitutions. A worried discourse about island

[37] Most notable was the movement of Acadians and their sponsorship as agrarian colonists. On the political tensions leading up to the resettlement of the Acadians, see Geoffrey Gilbert Plank, *An Unsettled Conquest: The British Campaign against the Peoples of Acadia* (Philadelphia: University of Pennsylvania Press, 2003). On the expulsion, see John Mack Faragher, *A Great and Noble Scheme: The Tragic Story of the Expulsion of the French Acadians from Their American Homeland* (New York: W. W. Norton, 2005); and Christopher Hodson, "Refugees, Acadians and the Social History of Empire, 1755–1785," Ph.D. diss. Northwestern University, 2004.

settlements as enclaves of martial law reached backward to the uncertainties of jurisdiction over criminal exiles in early modern practices of banishment and forward to the constitutional problems of imperial sovereignty in the late nineteenth century.

Presidios as Penal Colonies

In Spain as in France, the main penal institution before the late eighteenth century was neither imprisonment nor transportation, but the galleys. Low-status convicts were sentenced to the galleys for a set number of years, while high-status individuals were instead sent as exiles to the North African presidios. As in Portugal, Spanish forced laborers were gathered through a relay system that transported criminals from the places of their sentencing to collection points along the coast. In the sixteenth century, some Spanish convicts were also sentenced to labor at the mine of Almadén, a place of great importance in the empire because it provided mercury used in the production of silver. Legally, Almadén formed part of the galleys system; convicts were first sentenced to the galleys, then assigned to Almadén, considered a land equivalent of the galleys. By the seventeenth century, some convicts sentenced to galleys were being shipped instead to North African presidios, which earlier had been destinations for high-status exiles.[38] Forced labor in the galleys was eliminated in 1748. Almadén and the presidios remained as sites of punishment, and they acquired the status of places from which convicts were not expected to return.[39]

[38] At first glance, the shift toward the use of presidios for forced labor seems to parallel the broader trend in European punishment whereby low-status offenders increasingly received high-status punishments, a trend that ultimately produced a criminal sentencing regime in Europe much less harsh than its American equivalent (see Whitman, *Harsh Justice*). But the scenario is a bit more complicated because, as the presidios were converted into penal colonies over the seventeenth century, they came to be associated with the harsh labor discipline of the galleys. The records do not permit us to gauge whether and in what numbers high-status offenders were sentenced to hard labor in the overseas presidios. But as the discussion here shows, certainly not all presidiarios were low-status offenders. At least in the short run, the use of presidios as sites of exile seems to have produced a counterexample of the adaptation of a punishment for high-status offenders (overseas exile) to include punishment associated with lower-class offenders (hard labor in perpetuity). There continued to be some distinctions in punishment according to status, especially after 1771, when naval arsenals were designated as the destinations for those convicted of more serious crimes, while those guilty of minor offenses were exiled to the North African presidios.

[39] Around the same time, penal servitude was expanded for public works in Spain. The best overview of early Spanish penal servitude remains Ruth Pike, *Penal Servitude in Early Modern Spain* (Madison: University of Wisconsin Press, 1983), chap. 6.

The late eighteenth-century transformation of penal servitude into a broader imperial project rested on these foundations but responded directly to the vulnerability of Spanish colonies in the face of rising French and, especially, British power. Anxieties about commercial competition in the Pacific, concerns about the increasing volume of contraband in and around Spanish American colonies, eagerness to prevent the British and French from seizing strategically located points along important sea lanes, and worries that the British might repeat the capture of Havana and Manila – these preoccupations prompted Spanish investments in colonial fortifications and the creation of a series of new permanent garrisons. Spanish officials warned that it was essential for the empire to "populate and fortify the immense coasts and islands of our America from the River Plate, going round Cape Horn to Valdivia and Chiloé," and they worried that their efforts might be "too late."[40] Strategically located islands were special targets of imperial interest. After Commodore George Anson's visit to the Juan Fernandez Islands off Chile on his well-publicized circumnavigation of 1741, the Spanish began planning a settlement and presidio for the larger of the two islands (see Figure 4.1).

The plan for a greater military presence in empire from the start depended on forced labor. Constructed out of existing mechanisms of banishment and impressments, the project merged multiple forms of forced labor: the assignment of deserters; the exile of criminal convicts to work in colonial presidios, most notably those in Havana, San Juan, and the Philippines; and, in the California presidios, the coercion of Indian labor. The process turned presidios into peculiar legal zones, populated by both military and nonmilitary personnel serving under military command. Both groups had negligible room for legal maneuver, but civilian convicts in perpetual exile were especially sharply cut off from avenues for appeal and mercy.

After the end of the Seven Years' War, Spanish officials immediately adopted plans for major fortifications at Havana and San Juan, and these two sites became the principal destinations in the empire for deserters and convicts to labor in the construction of fortifications. Contingents were sent both directly from Spain and from other colonies. While most men sent from Spain were soldiers – deserters or soldiers convicted of

[40] This quote from a 1790 commentary on an agreement with Britain appears in Nuria Valverde and Antonio Furtado, "Space Production and Spanish Imperial Geopolitics," in ed., Daniela Bleichmar, Paula De Vos, Kristin Huffine, and Kevin Sheehan, *Science in the Spanish and Portuguese Empires: 1500–1800* (Stanford, CA: Stanford University Press, 2009) 198–215, 213. Valverde and Furtado call the shift in Spanish imperial policy a "reterritorialization of the empire of the seas" (214).

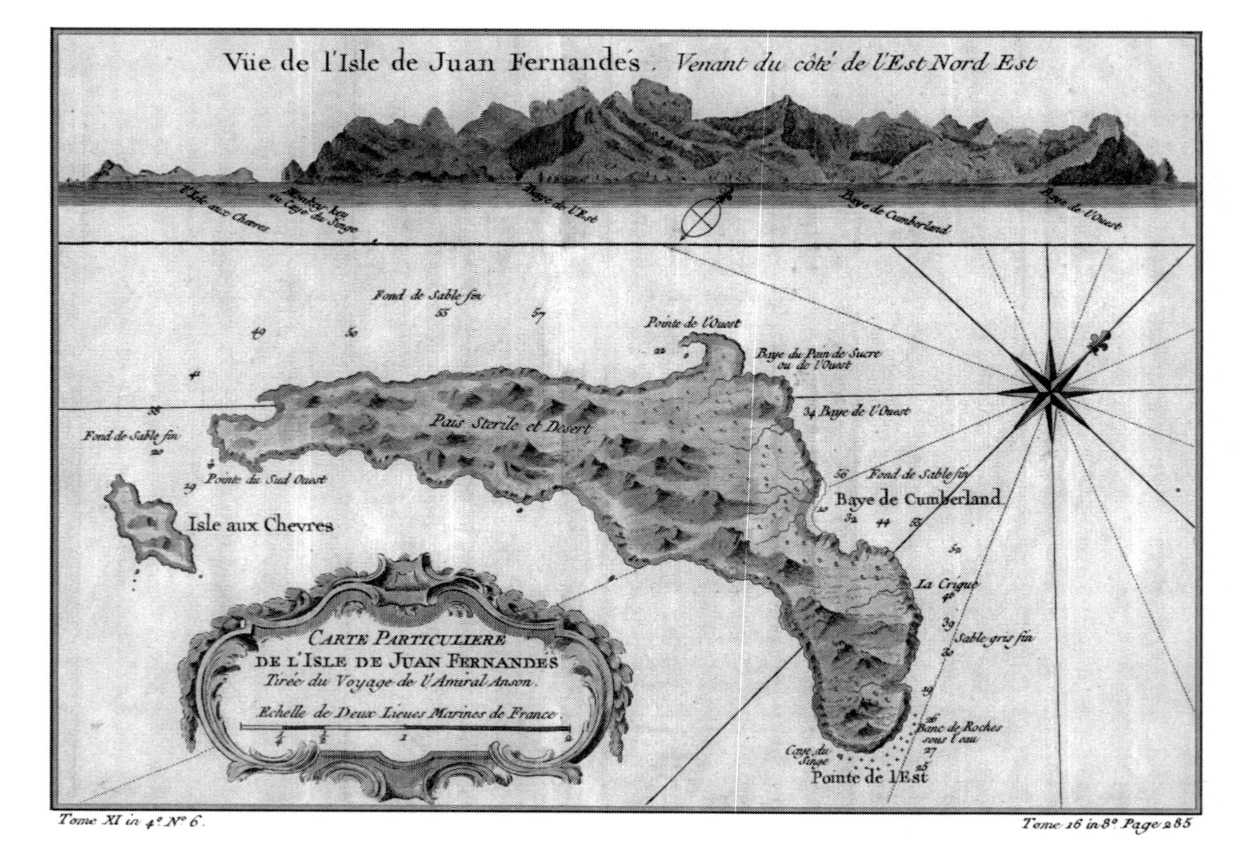

FIGURE 4.1. Map of Juan Fernández Island (c. 1750). Made by the French cartographer Jacques Bellin for Antoine François Prévost d'Exiles's *Histoire générale des voyages*, the map was based on surveys conducted when Commodore George Anson visited the island in 1741 on his voyage of circumnavigation. Anson's voyage called attention to the strategic importance of securing island stations along routes to the Pacific and prompted the Spaniards to found a settlement and presidio on the island in 1749.

crimes – most men transported to Havana and San Juan from other places in the Spanish empire originated in colonial criminal courts, with the largest contingent coming from New Spain, where most had been condemned for serious crimes. The criminal courts in New Spain also sentenced convicts to transportation to the Philippines, an expanding practice that had begun as early as the sixteenth century.[41] In the same way that men had been moved to the coast and held for assignment to the galleys, convicts and soldiers were amassed at Málaga or Cádiz for exile to the overseas presidios.

Besides these main channels for convict transportation – from various locations within Spain to Havana, Puerto Rico, the Philippines, and the African presidios, and with minor flows from New Spain to the Philippines and Havana – convicts moved in many smaller and more irregular circuits. In 1799, officials in Callao in Peru transported forty-nine convicts to help repair fortifications in San Diego de Acapulco, with the understanding that they should be returned as soon as the work was finished.[42] The governor of Louisiana received 240 prisoners to help build a canal in 1773, then asked to keep them for another year.[43] Various minor garrisons short on manpower requested some of the deserters and convicts massing for shipment to the main presidios. In March 1790, New Granada asked for "some of the Deserters and others convicted of minor crimes who were to be sent to Puerto Rico, Havana, and the Philippines." The officials complained that New Granada was especially short of Spanish-born soldiers, considered more reliable than creoles.[44] Movements of forced laborers around the empire included transfers of small groups of convicts and even individuals. In 1775, the governor of Puerto Rico acknowledged receipt in the presidio of three soldiers who had been condemned to death in Louisiana but whose sentences were converted to labor and confinement in the presidio of Puerto Rico for eight years.[45] Soldiers might be sentenced to terms of exile or presidio labor for nonviolent crimes or offenses other than desertion. José Freire, a soldier in Santo Domingo, was ordered to serve three years of exile in Havana for having secretly wed the daughter of a local merchant; he probably never

[41] Eva Maria St. Clair Segurado. "'Vagos, ociosos y malentretenidos': The Deportation of Mexicans to the Philippines in the Eighteenth Century" (paper presented at Conference of the American Historical Association, Atlanta, January 4–7, 2007).

[42] AGS, SGU,6979,55.

[43] AGS, SGU,7244,70.

[44] AGS, SGU,7057,6.

[45] AGI Santo Domingo, 2505.

served the sentence because the hearing was cut short when Toussaint L'Ouverture seized the city and the *escribano* fled to Cartagena.[46]

Spanish imperial transportation was decidedly a system, but it was one characterized by ad hoc adjustments at every level, particularly in the procurement of presidiarios in Spain and their distribution. The 1790 request from New Granada, for example, initiated several years of correspondence about the numbers of convicts available. Of the possible transportees being held in Cádiz, officials noted that they would have to exclude men convicted of murder, and others whose terms were almost completed. In 1792, Málaga jails held ninety-two men for possible shipment to New Granada, but a number of these were ultimately excluded, leaving only eighty-two. The commander in New Granada was still writing to urge Spanish officials to send more men in 1794, four years after the first request.[47] Even when sufficient numbers of deserters and criminals had been identified for transport, other problems surfaced in getting them to their destinations. In 1769, Spanish officials reported that they were holding hundreds of men, both deserters and "vagabonds," in Cádiz and hundreds more in El Ferrol. In response to complaints from Havana and Puerto Rico about the slow progress on fortifications and the need for more exiles as laborers, 250 convicts were ordered sent to Puerto Rico. But Cádiz officials balked at the cost and risks of transporting so many men, "especially these kinds of prisoners who by their nature require special guarding." The long trip across the Atlantic would expose the ships to the threat of mutinies, and, they argued, it was cheaper and safer to transport most of the men to the African garrisons and reserve only a few for the Americas.[48] The governor of Puerto Rico continued to press officials in Spain for more workers, writing in 1775 that the presidio had 442 forced laborers but needed 797 to complete the fortifications.[49]

[46] AGS, SGU,7165, 200. Rebellion also continued to be punished with exile. Of the participants in the 1780 uprising led by José Gabriel Túpac Amaru, sixteen were sentenced to death, six were absolved, and five were given sentences of *destierro* (AGI "Castas, correspondencia y expedienties sobre rebeliones" Microfilm C-516–517).

[47] AGS, SGU,7057,6.

[48] AGI Santo Domingo 2503.

[49] AGI Santo Domingo, 2505 no. 979. The fortifications in San Juan were nearly completed by 1784, leading officials to suspend regular shipments of presidiarios from abroad. Nevertheless, the presidio continued, with occasional arrivals of convicts from the outside, including some thirty-seven political prisoners from Spain as late as 1834. See Fernando Picó, *El día menos pensado: Historia de los presidiarios en Puerto Rico, 1793–1993* (Río Piedras, Puerto Rico: Ediciones Huracán, 1994), 26, 36.

Receiving presidiarios did not guarantee a solution to labor shortages in imperial garrisons. Desertion threatened at every step, from Spain to colonial presidios. Men whose acts of desertion had prompted their sentencing in the first place were willing to attempt it again. Some tried running away after they were sentenced and before they could be sent to presidios.[50] Havana officials complained continually about high levels of desertion, especially among presidiarios who were serving perpetual sentences.[51] Between 1778 and 1782, the total number of presidiarios in San Juan varied between 274 and 499; annual figures for desertion averaged 56, ranging between 10 and 20 percent of the total.[52] We get a hint of the frequency of desertion from the African presidios from a list of deserters drawn up by Spanish officials as they were preparing to abandon Oran in 1792. The document names 122 exiles who had disappeared in the previous few months from the garrison; most, presumably, had defected to nearby Muslim settlements.[53]

Illness and death also depleted the ranks of the presidio labor force. In 1774, the head of the fortification works in San Juan complained that the presidiarios sent from Spain included many now in "a deplorable state of health" and "useless" for more labor.[54] A presidiario at Puerto Rico complained that even when ordered confined to the hospital by the garrison doctor, men continued to work, some dying as a result.[55] The annual death rate for San Juan presidiarios between 1778 and 1782 reached as high as 13 percent.[56]

High rates of death and desertion reflected harsh conditions. At San Juan and Havana, the vast majority of presidiarios worked at the hard labor of constructing fortifications, while forced laborers elsewhere also assumed the heaviest tasks. As Hackel points out in his study of California presidios, soldiers not only found presidio work grueling but also objected that it placed them on the same level as common criminals, Indians, or

[50] One soldier sentenced to eight years in an African presidio deserted from the hospital in Málaga while awaiting transport. He was caught and received an additional two years on his sentence. AGS, SGU,7057,6.

[51] For example, AGI Santo Domingo, 2132.

[52] Pike provides yearly averages based on monthly reports for total numbers of presidiarios and deserters. Figures here are based on these averages. Pike, *Penal Servitude*, 147.

[53] AGS, SGU,7318,143.

[54] AGI Santo Domingo leg. 2505.

[55] "Bernardino de Valcárel," AGS, SGU,7136,9.

[56] Pike, *Penal Servitude*, 147. Percentage is calculated on figures derived by Pike as annual averages from monthly reports.

slaves. The California presidiario Miguel Periquez explained that the hard labor was the reason he had deserted from the Monterey garrison: "There was nothing we were not told to do: felling trees, building houses, carrying poles, mixing clay, making adobe, digging and carrying off the soil, cleaning up, making toilets – slaves could not have been treated worse."[57] A prisoner in San Juan complained that presidio sentences made men equal to "Thieves, Murderers, and other convicts."[58] The few writings of presidiarios describing the conditions emphasize the rampant corruption of the garrisons, with officials skimming off rations, using convicts as personal servants, and profiting in other ways from their control over forced laborers.[59]

The real novelty of presidio labor in this period lay not in the harsh or degrading conditions presidiarios faced but in their peculiar legal status. Presidiarios found themselves with practically no venues for appeal or even to plead for mercy. This legal limbo derived in part from the nature of exile as a sentence, and the frequency with which local officials ordered it without trial. It reflected, too, the trend of sentencing many soldiers and convicts to perpetual exile rather than fixed terms. Such sentences left the term open "until further providence" by the king.[60] Most important was that, for civilian prisoners, assignment to presidios effected a transfer into a system under military command, in which no routines existed for hearings to reconsider or reduce sentences. Civilians under military rule in distant imperial locations were under the jurisdiction of no court. The possibility of petitioning the king was of course never foreclosed, but it was not at all clear to presidiarios how or to whom they might present petitions. This legal condition resembled that of galley slaves but was otherwise highly unusual in the Spanish empire, where petitioning the king had long been a prerogative assumed to travel with Spanish subjects

[57] Steven W. Hackel, *Children of Coyote, Missionaries of Saint Francis: Indian-Spanish Relations in Colonial California, 1769–1850* (Chapel Hill: University of North Carolina Press, 2005), 288.

[58] "Bernardino de Valcárel," AGS, SGU,7136,9.

[59] Ibid. See also "Quejas de presidiarios," AGS SGU,7318,51.

[60] The language varied, but the indeterminate aspect of the sentence was the same. Ramón Terrazas was ordered moved from the presidio in Ceuta to the presidio in Puerto Rico "for the time willed by the crown" ("por el tiempo de Su Real voluntad.") "Ramón Terrazas. Destierro," AGS, SGU,7135,18. In the case of Justo de Córdoba, whom the governor of Cádiz sought to preserve from exile to a presidio on the grounds that his health was bad, the order confirming that he should be sent to "one of the American presidios" specified that he "would not be able to leave it without express Royal Order." "Justo de Córdoba, Destierro," AGS, SGU,7135,20.

and where all kinds of subjects routinely presented appeals to regional high courts (audiencias).[61]

The institutionalized departure from regular criminal procedure was apparently not lost on presidiarios. The vast majority left no records other than reports of their attempts to flee, but a few prisoners did commit their protests to paper. Bernardino de Valcárel was a lawyer who claimed he had been seized by troops who had transported him to Seville and then to Cádiz for embarkation to San Juan in 1791, all without any legal justification. To be treated in this manner, he wrote, was "to be punished without a hearing; to be made a criminal without any charges filed; [and] to close the case before it had been opened." Valcárel described the helplessness of the presidiarios once they had arrived in a place ruled "by many heads, all who give orders, and all who govern," and where convicts found themselves subjected to orders on all sides, and "their complaints have nowhere to go." In a year, Valcárel reported, he had not learned of any hearings or consideration of grievances. Arbitrary punishments were commonplace, and all the officials had presidiarios serving them rather than laboring on the fortifications. There was nothing for presidiarios to do except to dream about running away to the "Foreign Islands" nearby. Together with the plea that his identity be kept private for fear of reprisals, Valcárel proposed to officials in Spain that a separate jurisdiction be set up to operate independently of the hierarchy of the presidio and establish a regular legal channel for reviewing the complaints of the captive workers.[62]

Valcárel perhaps perished in the San Juan presidio; we do not know. The case of three presidiarios who complained about conditions in the Melilla garrison a year later suggests that appeals for intervention in the presidios fell on deaf ears. The petition to the king was signed by three presidiarios – Josef Arzia, Juan de la Isla, and Tomás Lerida – and it found its way to the official immediately in charge of the African presidios. The official refuted the presidiarios' charges that the governor was trading with the Moors, skimming excessive profits from presidio stores and taverns, and assigning as many as ten workers just to carry water to his house. He failed to mention one of the petition's central complaints, that the presidiarios were regularly brutally beaten and could not "ask for Justice" because to do so required appealing "to those who have to

[61] On the legal prerogative to petition the king, see Cañeque, *King's Living Image*. Both petitioning the king and taking cases directly to the audiencia were strategies open to all subjects, including Indians, who often used these tactics to get around local officials. See Serulnikov, *Subverting Colonial Authority*.

[62] "Bernardino de Valcárel, AGS, SGU,7136,9.

distribute it." The prisoners claimed that some presidiarios had been executed for appealing to the king. Officials seemed poised to retaliate against the petitioners, accusing them of forgery because their signatures did not match names on the presidio rolls and warning of the "bad consequences" for order that would follow if the men's complaints were credited.[63]

There were some voices for reform. Spanish officials had long recognized that concentrations of convict laborers generated peculiar problems, including the threat of disorder. Garrison commanders were careful to request only men who were convicted of minor offenses. Before the widespread labor shortages of the late eighteenth century, even deserters were sometimes turned away because of fears that they would spread criminality.[64] With the new practice of transporting criminals from Spain to the colonial presidios in the late eighteenth century, this same concern touched local Spanish officials. They began to worry about the ill effects of the return to Spanish cities of presidiarios who had completed their terms. Curiously, this worry seems to have been compounded by an attempt at reform by the crown. In response to reports from the presidios of rampant desertions, particularly by men sentenced to exile in perpetuity, the crown ordered in 1772 a fixed term of six years for desertion. The new policy prompted a complaint by the governor of Havana that a shortage of manpower would result, hindering work on the fortifications.[65] The measure appears also to have fueled anxieties about the disorderliness of returning presidiarios in Spain, and, in 1776, the crown directed that presidiarios freed in the colonies should not be returned to Spain unless they were married and had Spanish wives waiting for them. This was not the first time that officials had planned the release of convicts in situ. In 1774, the crown ordered that sick presidiarios judged by the head engineer in Puerto Rico as too weak for work should be distributed to "some places of that island," where they could be joined by other convicts as they completed their sentences.[66]

Had the numbers of presidiarios been greater, such measures might have signaled the beginning of a Botany Bay–style experiment in Puerto

[63] "Quejas de presidiarios," AGS, SGU,7318,51.

[64] As early as 1622, the governor of La Florida was writing to the Havana governor refusing entry to a shipment of vagabonds and men convicted of minor crimes (AGI Santo Domingo,868,L,F.189V–190V). A century later, Manila officials were complaining to the crown that New Spain was sending convicts who were disrupting the settlement and setting a bad example for *vecinos* of the city (AGI Filipinas, 342,L,10,F 52V–54V).

[65] AGI Santo Domingo leg. 2132.

[66] AGI Santo Domingo leg. 2505.

Rico, and perhaps elsewhere in the Spanish empire. Yet there was another factor, too, preventing the designation of entire islands as penal colonies in the way that Van Diemen's Land and Norfolk Island would be regarded by the British a few decades later. Spanish settlement and nonmilitary Spanish colonial hierarchies predated the surge in imperial convict transportation. While the transfer of convicts into military hands had the effect of strengthening military jurisdiction, confusion about the overlap between military and crown administration was also an inevitable result.[67] Many of the complications involved questions about the distribution of fiscal responsibilities for the presidiarios. In 1787, the crown clarified that soldiers convicted of desertion and other crimes were in fact entitled to receive payment while serving in presidios, an order that seems to have been directed toward abuses by presidio officials.[68] In 1790, the governor of Cádiz reported that he could not make a planned shipment of four hundred men from Oran to Havana because the funds now had to flow through the military rather than the Indies bureaucracy.[69] The question of fiscal responsibility arose again when the crown instructed in 1794 that presidiarios should pay for the costs of their own transport and maintenance. American presidio commanders debated whether the order applied to military as well as nonmilitary presidiarios; it had been addressed to "political magistrates" rather than "the military jurisdiction." In Havana, attention to the question was prompted by the arrival of two convicts sentenced in Guatemala who had to be maintained in the local hospital: who would pay, the authority responsible for their exile or the military garrison instructed to receive them?[70]

Even as the expansion of presidios strengthened the hand of military commanders in a general sense, officials had reason to advocate legal distinctions between deserting soldiers and nonmilitary criminals. Consider the move to convert longer sentences to a fixed six-year term. The measure was a response to high rates of desertion and included the possibility of reducing the six-year term to four years for good behavior. Officials in the Havana presidio noted that the provision would apply to 584 individuals and worried that the reform would slow progress on the works under way. The officials advocated exceptions for convicts whose

[67] There were other trends in play also enhancing the *fuero militar*, or military jurisdiction, especially the growing power and prestige of militias. See Lyle N. McAlister, *The "Fuero Militar" in New Spain, 1764–1800* (Gainesville: University Press of Florida, 1957).

[68] AGS, SGU,6863,74.

[69] AGS, SGU,7250,38.

[70] "Presidiarios Mantenimiento," AGS SGU,6919,19.

crimes were so "execrable...that they really excite no compassion." The governor of Havana reported that news of the measure was already inciting unrest and advocated authorizing officials in Havana with the power to exclude some men from having their terms reduced. The crown complied, declaring in 1778 that the provision would not apply to those "whose sentences contained a clause about being retained until the completion of their term or who had been condemned to Presidio in perpetuity for rebellious acts or disturbing the public peace." It was noted that the act had been intended as a onetime, "extraordinary" measure rather than an ongoing policy. These clarifications returned the power of summary judgment over presidiarios' terms of sentence to local commanders, who also took up the role of presenting and endorsing the petitions of those to whom the measure might still apply.[71]

The system of penal transportation from Spain to the colonies reached its peak in the late eighteenth century, but both the sentence and the penal establishments remained in place and served colonial officials into the next century. Many advocates of independence were banished to nearby island sites in the first decades of the nineteenth century, and the practice continued past the independence period with variants in the colonies of Puerto Rico, Cuba, and the Philippines, and in the new republics. Some new island sites were pressed into service, such as Isla de Pinos off the coast of Cuba, the destination for offenders in Havana in the 1860s and 1870s. Other island presidios that had served as penal settlements under the Spanish continued as sites of isolation for criminals and, especially, political offenders, such as Más a Tierra, the larger of the two Juan Fernández islands off the coast of Chile.[72] The presidios continued both to create singular opportunities for tyrannous rule by local commanders and to generate legal anomalies arising from the uncertain status of convicts

[71] The description of the exception by the governor of Havana uses the word *comuneros* for rebels. On the origins and other uses of the term in Latin America, see Chapter 2. The original describes the classes of men who were exceptions to the rule as follows: "aquellos cuyas sentencias tubieren la clausula de retención cumplido su tiempo o que hubiesen sido condenados a Presidio perpetuo por comuneros y pertubadores de la paz publica." AGI Santo Domingo leg. 2132.

[72] Chilean officials considered abandoning Más a Tierra, the larger of the Juan Fernández Islands. In 1812, the settlement there held seventy-three convicts, a small cadre of officials, eighty-eight soldiers, and a handful of free settlers. But a succession of governments found it a useful place to send political prisoners. The island's governance was altered numerous times in this period, and a series of controversies broke out over summary executions of rebellious convicts and soldiers. See Ralph Lee Woodward, *Robinson Crusoe's Island: A History of the Juan Fernández Islands* (Chapel Hill: University of North Carolina Press, 1969).

and the unstable relation between military and civilian jurisdictions. Both within the Spanish empire and in other European empires, the transfer of convicts to live under military rule in garrison penal colonies represented one facet of a wider process of an expanding role for military law in empire at the turn of the nineteenth century.

A "nursery of martial law"

When the American Revolution put a halt to the shipments of convicts to the North American colonies, British authorities began to imprison convicts on disabled ships, or hulks, in the Thames River. This measure was supposed to be temporary.[73] Prisoners, some still being sentenced to transportation by magistrates uncertain about alternatives, began to collect in overcrowded hulks and in local jails.[74] As early as 1778, officials were casting around for alternative sites for transportation and mentioned possible destinations in the East and West Indies, Nova Scotia, Florida, and the Falkland Islands.[75]

[73] It continued for eighty years. Even after the founding of Botany Bay, the hulks remained a staging place for convicts to be transported.

[74] Alan Frost argues that the buildup of prisoners in the hulks and the pressures by local jailers to accept more transfers into the hulks did not prompt the decision to pursue transportation, which had already been made. As he puts it, "transportation was the mode but not the motive of Britain's colonization of Australia." Alan Frost, *Botany Bay Mirages: Illusions of Australia's Convict Beginnings* (Carlton, Victoria: Melbourne University Press, 1994), 40. Others have argued against the notion that Botany Bay signified anything more than a response to the crisis of the cost and crowding of the hulks, showing that initial discussion of the site made scant mention of strategic interests, in particular the possibility of producing flax and hemp for the British navy. See, e.g., Mollie Gillen, "The Botany Bay Decision, 1786: Convicts, Not Empire," *English Historical Review* 97, no. 385 (1982), 740–66. Both sides appear to overstate the case. On the one hand, the argument against a broader strategic rationale for the founding of Botany Bay focuses narrowly on the question of official interest in finding sources for hemp, flax, and timber, without considering the broader political stakes and popular interest in imperial expansion in the Pacific, especially following Cook's voyages. On the other hand, we know that sustaining the hulks was controversial and, whether they were objectively crowded or not, that there were bottlenecks and problems in managing them experienced at all levels. The overseer of the hulks between 1776 and 1801, Duncan Campbell, wrote frequently to jails throughout England to instruct them to hold their prisoners until they could be accommodated on the hulks or transported. See *Convict Transportation and the Metropolis: The Letterbooks and Papers of Duncan Campbell (1726–1803) from the State Library of New South Wales* (Marlborough, Wiltshire, England: Adam Matthew Publications, microfilm).

[75] See A. G. L. Shaw, *Convicts and the Colonies: A Study of Penal Transportation from Great Britain and Ireland to Australia and Other Parts of the British Empire* (London: Faber and Faber, 1966), 43.

A House of Commons committee investigating the problem in 1785 learned from Joseph Banks that Botany Bay might be suitable, but its attention first focused on a proposed plan to transport convicts to the Island of Lemain, about fifty miles up the Gambia River.[76] Shaw tells us that the committee eventually "ruled out the Gambia site as too unhealthy," but we find that their investigation reveals as much concern with the colony's disciplinary order and legal viability as its disease environment.[77] The inquiry also shows the imagined promise and peculiar problems of an island site for a penal colony. The proposed plan envisioned sending an annual shipment of convicts to Lemain without any agent or commissioner. Convicts would be left to their own devices, presumably to raise crops and livestock, and they would receive only occasional visits from a captain of a guardship that would patrol the waters around the island to deter escapes or raids on nearby communities by the convicts. In addition to admitting that they knew of no European cultivators in the region and that mortality rates for Europeans were very high, a series of witnesses who had traveled in Africa as merchants or soldiers testified about anticipated problems of order. John Barnes, a merchant who had traded in the region and helped to develop the settlement plan, reported optimistically that Lemain appeared to be "a very fine Island" with a climate "generally

[76] "Minutes of Committee of House of Commons Respecting a Plan for Transporting Felons to the Island of Lee Maine in the River Gambia," The National Archives, Home Office (hereafter TNA HO) 7/1. See also Curtin's brief discussion of the debate about Lemain Island. Philip D. Curtin, *The Image of Africa: British Ideas and Action, 1780–1850* (Madison: University of Wisconsin Press, 1964), 92–5. Curtin notes that other African sites were considered, including São Tomé and southwestern Africa near the Orange River. Although, like Shaw (see *infra* note 77), Curtin places greater emphasis on British perceptions of the disease environment in Africa than on the preoccupation with questions of law and order, he does observe that the purchase of Lemain Island gave rise to confusion about sovereignty. As with other "anomalous" projects in African enclaves in the same period, he writes, Lemain Island was to be "recognized in some vague sense as British territory, but in fact the government had not the slightest intention of carrying out the normal obligations of a sovereign" (118).

[77] Shaw, *Convicts and the Colonies*, 46. This preoccupation with the problem of order runs through the records on the management of convicts in the hulks. Duncan Campbell, who held the government contract for the transportation of criminals from London after 1772, kept close records of disturbances on ships and in the hulks and advised ship captains on preparations for disciplining convicts in transit, as in a letter on February 27, 1786, advising, "You will find it best *to establish a proper* mode of *Order* as well among the convicts as your *Officers & Crew*." The same captain was told in November of 1786 that Campbell had no "wishes to stop the Avenues to mercy and therefore has no objections to the convict sending Petitions" if these were "drawn up with the proper Respect." *Convict Transportation and the Metropolis*, ff. 160 and 268.

esteemed much more healthy than lower down the river."[78] But he also predicted that convicts abandoned on the island would quickly be subsumed in a legal order of reciprocity dominated by surrounding African communities. Any disorderly acts of the convicts would endanger trade by leading locals to "revenge themselves among the Settlers."[79] The committee pressed the issue of order with another witness: "Could a colony of Convicts without order or Government be restrained in the Inland part of Africa from spreading themselves beyond a Spot advocated to them?" Impossible, came the answer, unless they were confined to irons.[80] The fate of a group of convicts sent earlier to Cape Coast Castle worried a military officer who testified. Those convicts had been "enlisted as Troops and were under Military Discipline with proper officers." They proved to be notoriously "riotous," and many deserted to Dutch forts or to unknown places "in the Country."[81] Committee members pressed witnesses on whether any convict settlement would be better managed under "Military Discipline Naval."[82] Not surprisingly, when their attention finally turned in May 1785 to the possibility of founding a penal settlement at Botany Bay, one of the first questions posed by the committee was about the need for military justice: "Should you or should you not think the use of Martial Law and prompt justice to be necessary in a colony so constituted?"[83]

As plans took shape for a convict fleet to Botany Bay, it became clear that the system for transporting convicts to the Americas, under charge of ship merchants who could profit by selling their labor assignments, would not be feasible elsewhere. With no existing British settlement or institutions in Australia, the government resolved to transport and settle the convicts under a system headed by a governor with unusually broad authority. New South Wales governors enjoyed powers to assign convicts to private masters, to award pardons, to command the colony's military officials and troops, and to act as sole arbiters in civil cases on appeal.

[78] TNA HO 7/1 ff. 16–16v.

[79] TNA HO 7/1, f. 23. Another man examined made the same point about the likelihood of retaliation by locals.

[80] TNA HO 7/1, ff. 33 and 33v.

[81] TNA HO 7/1, ff. 36v, 37.

[82] TNA HO 7/1, f. 60.

[83] TNA HO 7/1, f. 69. Suggestions for other sites for penal colonies included Gibraltar, the Cape Colony, Madagascar, Tristan da Cunha, Algiers, and stations serving the North Sea herring industry. Officials also continued to try shipping convicts to the Americas. After a ship sent to land at Georgia was turned away, it tried a succession of ports, including Honduras, Virginia, and Nova Scotia. On this attempt, and the larger debate leading up to Botany Bay, see Shaw, *Convicts and the Colonies*, chap. 2.

The colony's chief judge held the military title of judge advocate until 1809.[84] Acting as they saw it by necessity and in the absence of a legislature before 1824, governors pronounced new orders and regulations for the colony. The result was that, even as convicts were assigned to labor for private parties and began to contract their own labor under a parole system in which they received conditional permits known as tickets of leave, the colony had the characteristics of a vast penal system under a governor with civil and military authority.

As Bruce Kercher has noted, early New South Wales cannot be characterized as a society under martial law, except during a three-year period from 1792 to 1795, and again briefly after the rebellion against Governor William Bligh in 1808.[85] The first two judge advocates were instructed to apply "the rules and disciplines of war," but subsequent judge advocates, despite their military title, sought to administer English law while, in many cases, deviating from it to follow quickly developing local customs or to respond to the unusual conflicts of a penal settlement. In several key cases, the judges prevented military officers from asserting special prerogatives under the law.[86] But military officials also positioned themselves as the champions of justice in challenging the autocratic authority of the governors, an opposition that culminated in a coup against Governor Bligh in 1808, in the so-called Rum Rebellion. In declaring martial law on the heels of the rebellion, the officers constituting a new government announced their intention to reopen the courts and to "secure the impartial Administration of Justice, according the Laws of England."[87]

Though the colony did not operate under martial law during most of its early decades, the influence of military legal authority was complex and pervasive. The two brief periods of declared martial law were possible because of the power military officials held in the colony. Their

[84] See Kercher, "Perish or Prosper," esp. 542.

[85] Bruce Kercher, *Debt, Seduction, and Other Disasters: The Birth of Civil Law in Convict New South Wales* (Sydney: Federation Press, 1996); Bruce Kercher, "Resistance to Law under Autocracy," *Modern Law Review* 60, no. 6 (1997), 779–97.

[86] A case in 1796 involved the shooting of a pig belonging to a free settler, John Boston, by a soldier protecting land owned by an officer of the New South Wales corps. Boston's protests brought an order for soldiers to beat him, and Boston sued for damages. The mere fact that the court found in his favor, with the governor confirming the verdict on appeal, represented a victory for civilian over military rule, though the very small fine given to the soldiers reflected the persistent influence of the military. *Boston v. Laycock, McKellar, Faithfull and Eaddy* (1796) in "Decisions of the Superior Courts of New South Wales, 1788–1899," published by the Division of Law, Macquarie University, http://www.law.mq.edu.au/scnsw/index.htm.

[87] Kercher, *Debt, Seduction, and Other Disasters*, 39.

prominence placed officers in positions to influence a variety of legal outcomes. When Lachlan Macquarie was installed as governor two years after the rebellion against Bligh, he followed orders from London to recognize any rulings carried out by the court during the illegal interim. A more profound influence came from the mandated role of military officers on juries. In a penal colony dominated by convicts – who were barred from serving on juries – criminal trials operated with juries composed by law of seven commissioned officers appointed by the government. This arrangement continued even after the colony was placed on a new constitutional footing, with a legislature and Supreme Court, in 1824. In criminal trials of military personnel, the makeup of the jury influenced the result, as it did in the murder case brought against Captain Lowe for the murder of an Aborigine man in 1827.[88] The arrangement provoked little sustained opposition, though it did attract occasional critical comment. Supreme Court Justice Dowling noted in 1832 that the local jury had "very few if any of the incidents of a jury strictly and properly so called, and understood by the law of England."[89]

Early critics of the legal order of New South Wales did not focus on this institutional anomaly, though they regarded the autocratic rule of governors as an invitation to, and occasional equivalent of, martial rule. The most outspoken critic of governance in New South Wales, Jeremy Bentham, developed this critique in his *A Plea for the Constitution*, published in 1803.[90] Bentham's professional and personal stake in the panopticon scheme in England framed his criticism of New South Wales and focused his attention, especially in two earlier tracts, on the inability of a distant penal colony to serve as a deterrent for criminals in England, the greater costs of transportation compared to imprisonment in England, and the inevitable failure of convict discipline or reform in a distant penal

[88] *R. v. Lowe* (1827), *Australian*, 23 May 1827, in "Decisions of the Superior Courts." And for discussion of the case, see Ford, *Settler Sovereignty*.

[89] The case required a ruling on whether an undecided jury should be made to continue deliberating, and Dowling, in basing his decision in part on analogy to the English jury system, had to concede that juries in New South Wales provided few of the protections to Englishmen enshrined in the Magna Carta, in law, and in custom. *R. v. Sullivan* (1832), Dowling, *Proceedings of the Supreme Court*, Vol. 75, Archives Office of New South Wales, 2/3258, in "Decisions of the Superior Courts."

[90] Jeremy Bentham, *A Plea for the Constitution Shewing the Enormities Committed to the Oppression of British Subjects... In and by the Design, Foundation and Government of the Penal Colony of New South Wales: Including an Inquiry into the Right of the Crown to Legislate without Parliament in Trinidad and Other British Colonies* (London: Mawman, Poultry, 1803).

settlement.[91] As the possibilities of approval by the government of the panopticon faded, Bentham shifted his line of critique in *A Plea for the Constitution*, arguing that the penal settlement of New South Wales was unconstitutional.[92]

For Bentham, the essence of "the illegality of the government" of the colony lay in the absence in New South Wales of a legislative body combined with the de facto authority of governors to make laws in the colony.[93] This position was consistent with Bentham's developing view that legal order resided in positive law, specifically in the enactments of legislatures.[94] It also reflected his ongoing critique of colonialism; contrary to many of his disciples' representations of Bentham as a champion of the universal application of English-derived legislation, he was highly skeptical of the possibility of imposing appropriate legislation on distant parts of the empire.[95]

Bentham gave these broad positions a unique spin in his attack on the constitutionality of New South Wales, arguing that the legal framework for the founding of the colony converted it into a "nursery of martial law."[96] He signaled interlinking problems implied by the absence of a legislature: the creation of law by governors, the defense by magistrates of those in power, and the confinement of Britons, "free by law... in a state of bondage."[97] The inevitable autocratic actions of governors came under special attack as the equivalent of the rule of a "sea captain: for such has been the profession and rank, of every gentleman who has ever as yet been invested with this important office."[98] In obeying ordinances announced by the governor, the colony was laboring under a

[91] Jeremy Bentham, *Letters to Lord Pelham, Giving a Comparative View of the System of Penal Colonization in New South Wales* (London: Wilkes and Taylor, 1802).

[92] For an overview of Bentham's developing critique, see R. V. Jackson, "Jeremy Bentham and the New South Wales Convicts," *International Journal of Social Economics* 25, nos. 2–4 (1998), 370–80. See also the discussion of Bentham's views on New South Wales in John Gascoigne, *The Enlightenment and the Origins of European Australia* (Cambridge: Cambridge University Press, 2002), 41–4. Note that Gascoigne characterizes debates on the governance of early New South Wales as a widespread "consciousness that the colony was a constitutional anomaly" (44).

[93] Bentham, *A Plea for the Constitution*, v.

[94] For a clear and concise treatment of the significance of Bentham's position in international law of the period, see Armitage, *The Declaration of Independence*, 78–81.

[95] This view of Bentham as an anticolonial thinker is persuasively developed in Armitage, *The Declaration of Independence*, 78–81; and Jennifer Pitts, "Legislator of the World? A Rereading of Bentham on Colonies," *Political Theory* 31, no. 2 (2003), 200–34.

[96] Bentham, *A Plea for the Constitution*, 1.

[97] Bentham, *A Plea for the Constitution*, 2.

[98] Bentham, *A Plea for the Constitution*, 8.

mere "belief" in the lawful nature of these pronouncements.[99] Bentham approved the right of governors to give orders to military personnel in New South Wales and to convicts, but he questioned a governor's legal power over convicts whose terms had expired, their dependents, or "unblemished *settlers.*"[100] Bentham objected especially to the governor's exercise of power in preventing vessels from taking expiree convicts as passengers out of the colony. Constitutionally, such actions by the governor amounted to a usurpation of power, he argued. Bentham posed the critique as a challenge to the constitutionality of erecting a different structure of government in colonial settings – without explicit legislative authorization – from that of the metropole. He pointed to a history of legal cases establishing that the liberty of Englishmen traveled with them to distant territories: "Limited as the power of an English King is over Englishmen in England, in what book will he find that it is absolute over them every where else?"[101] New South Wales's legal flaw, according to Bentham, stemmed from its moment of foundation without a charter. There was no such thing as a colony without a charter, yet it would be impossible to write a charter for New South Wales because receiving one implied consent, and no constituency would accept a "charter to impower a free man to lead a life of slavery, and to be flogged as often as he endeavours to escape from it!"[102]

Bentham made it clear that he intended this critique of the legal foundations of New South Wales as a commentary on the question of the legitimacy of colonial government more generally. He recognized the claim by prominent jurists that the king's authority to legislate directly in a colony depended on whether the colony had been acquired by conquest or by consent; only in a conquered colony were legal directives by the crown legitimate actions.[103] Challenging this interpretation of the key cases of

[99] Bentham, *A Plea for the Constitution*, 8.

[100] Bentham, *A Plea for the Constitution*, 11. Emphasis in original.

[101] Bentham, *A Plea for the Constitution*, 18.

[102] Bentham, *A Plea for the Constitution*, 24.

[103] Bentham quoted at length from Mansfield's opinion in the so-called Grenada case, *Hall v. Campbell*, in which Mansfield reiterated (and accepted too readily, Bentham implies) the position, developed in Calvin's case in combination with a 1722 case challenging the legality of direct taxation by the crown in Jamaica, that the king could make laws for conquered territories but not for territories acquired in any other way. In *A Plea for the Constitution*, Bentham notes that Mansfield's ruling – which held that tax could only be imposed by an assembly of the island or by Parliament – should have addressed the narrower question of whether the king had the power to alter law in a colony acquired by means other than conquest. With feigned humility, as "an obscure ex-lawyer," Bentham suggests that whether legislation might be changed in a

colonial constitutional law, Bentham lamented the choice by men of law to go "fishing for drops of sense out of the extrajudicial ravings of Lord Coke" in Calvin's Case, rather than relying on the Magna Carta, the Bill of Rights, and Coke's own opinion in St. Alban's case. Here the court had disallowed an ordinance made in the town to enact a law infringing on rights protected under the Magna Carta. For Bentham, it was especially significant that Coke, in his opinion, argued that the ordinance would be illegitimate even if it "had been contained in the patent itself" incorporating the town. In other words, the case established that the crown did not have the power to make an exception of any piece of the realm by limiting within it the power of Parliament.[104] Bentham very explicitly related this argument to the American Revolution, surmising that it would never have occurred if English jurists had paid more attention to the view that English rule required Parliament's oversight, even over distant colonies.[105] By analogy, Bentham argued, New South Wales was a tyrannous regime in which the governor was de jure a limited monarch and de facto an absolute ruler.[106]

Having mounted this critique of the constitutional basis for the colony, Bentham returned to his particular concern with the legal foundations of

conquered colony is a question "still quite open." In his notes on the case, Bentham showed interest in the limits Mansfield placed on the king's legislative power; Bentham copied from the opinion a passage noting that even when the king had power to alter laws in a "conquered country" he was not authorized "to make any new change contrary to fundamental principles: he cannot exempt an inhabitant from that particular dominion; as, for instance, from the laws of trade, or from the power of parliament, or give him privileges exclusive of other subjects." Bentham papers at University College London (hereafter UCL), 166a, f. 133. Bentham was also interested to note that, even if Grenada had been at one point conquered, the king had given up his legislative prerogatives because he "had immediately and *unrecoverably* granted to all who were or should become inhabitants . . . that the subordinate legislation over the island should be exercised by an assembly with the consent of the governor and council, in like manner as the other islands belonging to the king" (Bentham Papers, UCL, 116a, f. 135).

104 On the St. Alban's case, see Bentham, *A Plea for the Constitution*, 18–19, quote at 16.

105 "If they had, nothing in the way of legislation would, from first to last, have been done in English-America, but *by* Parliament, or with *express* authority from Parliament. It would not then have been so much as dreamt of, that it was in the power of the King, by confederating with a part of his subjects, withdrawing themselves for this purpose to a vacant territory remote from the eye of Parliament – that it was in the power of his law-servants, by any such management, to oust Parliament of its rights: I mean its exclusive right of legislation, as established in the *St. Alban's* case. Dissension would then have been nipped in the bud: and the American war, with all its miseries, and all its waste of blood and treasure on all sides, would have been saved." Bentham, *A Plea for the Constitution*, 34.

106 Bentham, *A Plea for the Constitution*, 37.

convict discipline in the colony. He noted that the colony's criminal court was established under instructions to the governor and empowered to punish only crimes that would be considered "misdemeanours or felonies, treasons, or misprisions thereof" if committed "in this realm."[107] But the conditions of the penal colony quickly prompted the governor to criminalize a range of acts that would not fall into this category, such as distilling liquor or failing to surrender any boats to public authorities for use in fishing. Further, the criminal penalties for such crimes were to be improvised, exposing Britons to arbitrary punishment. Finally, Bentham argued that by extending the time of exile beyond the term of transportation and the period of bondage, transportation to New South Wales constituted a breach of the Habeas Corpus Act, with its clear proscription against sending subjects of England as prisoners "into ports, garrisons, islands, or places beyond the seas . . . within or without the dominions of his Majesty."[108] Every site "in which, without sufficient warrant, a man is kept against his will" became a prison. The whole island of Australia, he concluded, constituted a prison under the current legal order.[109]

A Plea for the Constitution did not address many of the legal issues that would become the focus of conflict in the colony in the coming decades: the nature of felony attaint, the legal status of Aborigines, or the composition of juries. Bentham did learn about the last two legal problems from his main source for all his writings on New South Wales, the journal of David Collins, the colony's first judge advocate.[110] Bentham noted

[107] Bentham, *A Plea for the Constitution*, 33. Bentham asks in a footnote, "What realm?" Added to the uncertainties arising from implying that the colony was a different realm, he adds the uncertainty of whether an act can be against the law in England, in Scotland, or in both together. Bentham, *A Plea for the Constitution*, 26n.

[108] Text of the act quoted in Bentham, *A Plea for the Constitution*, 53. And see Paul Halliday, *The Liberty of the Subject: Habeas Corpus from England to Empire* (Cambridge, MA: Harvard University Press, forthcoming).

[109] Bentham, *A Plea for the Constitution*, 55.

[110] David Collins and Philip Gidley King, *An Account of the English Colony in New South Wales: With Remarks on the Dispositions, Customs, Manners, &c. of the Native Inhabitants of That Country. To Which Are Added, Some Particulars of New Zealand; Compiled, by Permission, from the Mss. Of Lieutenant-Governor King* (London: Printed for T. Cadell Jun. and W. Davies, in the Strand, 1798). Bentham had numerous passages of Collins's journal copied out for his use, especially information about the dire conditions, including extreme drought and near famine, in the fledgling colony. Such data provided a wealth of support for Bentham's claims of the superiority of his panopticon scheme. Bentham seemed unsure what use to make of the pages of extracts copied under the heading "Native Hostility," in which Collins recounted such acts as a sentence of "severe corporal punishment" for a man convicted of killing an Aborigine. Bentham Papers, UCL, 116a, f. 66.

Collins's statement that the jury would never resemble the institution "ever dear and most congenial to Englishmen" until more settlers came to serve and reduce its "military appearance." This observation turned Bentham's thoughts to the anomaly of blended military and civilian law in the colony, and he scribbled in the margins of extracts from Collins's journal: "Martial law. Jury depends on free settlers." Below, he recorded a phrase that captured the crux of the difficulty he saw in combining a project for island self-sufficiency with distant sovereignty: "Such is the dilemma: the prosperity of the settlement depends upon a limited government – but the very existence of it depends upon an absolute one."[111]

Many of the conditions in the early New South Wales colony that Bentham learned about from Collins would disappear within several decades: famine abated as ranching and agriculture took hold and as contact with England became more frequent, free settlers arrived in greater numbers; emancipated convicts found political and legal avenues for promoting the expansion of their rights; and, in 1824, the colony gained both a legislature and a Supreme Court. The single issue raised by Bentham that seemed to persist as a target for his disciples was the continued existence of restrictions on the departure from the colony of emancipated convicts.[112] But Bentham had identified two broader themes that also continued at the center of discourse about convict transportation through midcentury. First, the presence of a legislature solved the Benthamite problem of the legitimacy of new law but did not remove questions about the relative influence in a wide range of cases of English law and local custom; the emerging legal order was very much a hybrid, contingent creation.[113] Second, the debate about the abolition of convict transportation connected closely to the problem of defining what constituted legitimate subordinate legal authority. Many convicts, like slaves, labored under the control of private persons whose disciplinary power derived from public authority. Bentham had no quarrel with expansive disciplinary power over convicts in prison systems; in fact, his panopticon scheme depended on it. But uncontrolled disciplinary power over all residents in one territory of the empire raised constitutional questions about the rights of imperial citizens and the sources of colonial authority.

The tendency identified by Bentham for the British empire to set space aside in which necessity motivated exceptions to the constitutional order

[111] Bentham Papers, UCL, 116a, f. 82.

[112] See Kercher, *Debt, Seduction, and Other Disasters.*

[113] Kercher, "Resistance to Law."

did not end as the economy improved and legal institutions were brought closer to constitutional norms in Australia. New South Wales gave rise to new and more restrictive penal settlements where transported convicts were awarded sentences of secondary transportation for additional, sometimes indeterminate, periods and under harsher conditions.[114] Historians have investigated these sites as places of purposeful experimentation in constructing penal regimes. Van Diemen's Land under Governor Arthur's autocratic rule between 1824 and 1836, and Norfolk Island under Alexander Maconochie, from 1840 to 1843, have taken their places as contrasting examples of prison discipline, the first as an instance of systematic harsh discipline, the second as an experiment in motivating prisoners through a system of "marks," or points, for good behavior.[115] Had Bentham looked beyond New South Wales in its early decades, he might have noted the unsettled governance structures of these colonies, their ad hoc legal practices, and the pattern they presented of a persistent blending of martial and civilian law.

"A beautiful island"

Norfolk Island received its English name from Captain James Cook, whose ship the *Resolution* sighted it in October of 1774, on Cook's second Pacific voyage. What the crew found on the small island situated about a thousand miles east of Australia turned out to be crucial in British plans for founding new settlements in the region.[116] The British navy was heavily dependent on finding wood for masts and flax for sail making, and the island was covered with flax bushes and tall pines, one of which Cook's carpenter used to fashion a new topmast. The wooded hills of the small island recalled landscapes familiar from home; George Foster

[114] Bentham was not entirely averse to setting space aside by combining the panopticon with transportation, and he even discussed with David Collins the possibility of erecting a panopticon-style establishment in Van Diemen's Land. See Gascoigne, *Enlightenment*, 131.

[115] Of course, Maconochie did much to establish the idea that the study of the penal colony offered insights into prison reform. Alexander Maconochie, *Australiana: Thoughts on Convict Management and Other Subjects Connected with the Australian Penal Colonies* (London: J. W. Parker, 1839). And see John Clay, *Maconochie's Experiment* (London: John Murray, 2001); Norval Morris, *Maconochie's Gentlemen: The Story of Norfolk Island and the Roots of Modern Prison Reform* (New York: Oxford University Press, 2002); John Hirst, "The Australian Experience: The Convict Colony," in Morris, *Maconochie's Gentlemen*, 235–65.

[116] See chapter 3 of Frost, *Botany Bay Mirages*, on the British interest in Pacific naval stores.

recorded in his journal from the voyage that "the melody of the birds was very pleasing in this little deserted spot, which if it had been of greater size, would have been unexceptionable for an European settlement."[117]

The British vision of Norfolk Island conformed to the pattern of global interimperial rivalries framing convict transportation as an imperial policy. The decision to found a penal settlement at Botany Bay not only emerged from a comparison of possible transportation sites but also belonged to a wider strategy of establishing British interests in the Pacific, with the specific goals of opposing French expansion in the region and imitating the success of American whalers, who had already appeared in the waters off New Zealand and were themselves in search of safe havens.[118] With its promise of naval supplies and provisions, and its potential as a stopping point along imagined sea lanes into the wider Pacific, Norfolk Island fit the pattern of the Juan Fernández Islands, the Falklands, and, in the wake of Cook's fatal encounter there, the Sandwich Islands as places considered vital to global imperial designs at the end of the eighteenth century.

On the arrival of the first fleet in Botany Bay in 1788, Governor Phillip quickly dispatched a mix of soldiers and convicts to form a small settlement at Norfolk Island under his lieutenant governor, Philip

[117] Quoted in Anne Salmond, *The Trial of the Cannibal Dog: The Remarkable Story of Captain Cook's Encounters in the South Seas* (New Haven, CT: Yale University Press, 2003), 282.

[118] The strategic value of penal colonies to larger goals of British commerce and influence in the region is discussed in Geoffrey Blainey, *The Tyranny of Distance: How Distance Shaped Australia's History* (Melbourne: Sun Books, 1966); K. M. Dallas, *Trading Posts or Penal Colonies: The Commercial Significance of Cook's New Holland Route to the Pacific* (Hobart: Fullers Bookshop, 1969); James F. H. Moore, *The Convicts of Van Diemen's Land, 1840–1853* (Hobart: Cat and Fiddle Press, 1976), 22. In *Botany Bay Mirages*, Frost emphasizes geopolitical considerations and the search for resources in the region to support the British navy. And for a related argument about the importance of strategic interests in prompting the founding of a penal colony in the Andamans, see Vaidik, *Imperial Andamans*. It is interesting to note that Spanish officials complained of the English settlements in Australia precisely because they viewed the projects as part of a strategy for dominion in the Pacific. The Spanish naval officer Alejandro Malaspina, who circumnavigated the world from 1786 to 1788, wrote that "the transportation of convicts" to Botany Bay "constituted the means and not the object of the enterprise." He warned that a Pacific crossing from the convict settlements "could bring to our defenceless Coasts two or three thousand castaway bandits to serve interpolated with an excellent body of regular Troops." Alejandro Malaspina, "Examen político de las colonias inglesas en el Mar Pacífico," quoted in Alessandro Malaspina, *The Malaspina Expedition, 1789–1794: Journal of the Voyage by Alejandro Malaspina* (London: Hakluyt Society, 2004), 3:77n4.

FIGURE 4.2. George Raper, Principal Settlement on Norfolk Island (1790). George Raper was a crew member of the HMS *Sirius*, one of the ships of the First Fleet. The *Sirius* was wrecked at Norfolk Island in March 1790. Raper made this image during the eleven months he spent on the island while Major Ross was serving as lieutenant governor. The blue and yellow flag in the foreground signaled landing conditions to approaching ships. George Raper, Principal Settlement on Norfolk Island [1790], nla.pic-an6054756, National Library of Australia.

Gidley King.[119] As a naval officer, King set his few charges, their numbers soon supplemented by more convicts shipped from Sydney, to a tightly scheduled round of agricultural tasks, and he punished transgressions by administering lashes after summary judgment. For its first two years, the settlement followed the familiar pattern of naval discipline moved on shore. The legal regime took a turn two years later, when King obtained permission to travel to England to recover from gout. The officer left in charge of the settlement, Major Ross, gathered the island's officers in March 1790, and declared martial law (the settlement in 1790 appears in Figure 4.2). As in New South Wales, where Ross had been serving as lieutenant governor, the immediate motive was the protection of dwindling

[119] Accompanying King were twenty-two men and women, including nine male convicts and six female convicts. An excellent account of the founding of the colony can be found in chapter 6 of Clay, *Maconochie's Experiment*.

stores.[120] A council of officers established procedures for composing a general court-martial and announced that "All Marauding or Plundering either of Public or Private Property" would henceforth be considered capital crimes.[121] Several months later, with the colony's conditions still dire, a series of proclamations authorized members of the council (a body made up of officers and a few others) to settle disputes and inflict punishments, and designated new capital crimes, including refusing to work, absconding "into the woods," hoarding tools, and not showing up for weekly rationing.[122] Most ominously, the council proclaimed that if a person engaging in any of these activities was killed, a court-martial would be assembled after the fact to acquit the killers. A few months later, three convicts, Benjamin Ingram, Charles Gray, and Thomas Jones, were charged for escaping to the woods; they were declared "freebooters" and ordered killed if apprehended.[123]

Back in London and unaware of these events, Philip King was already convinced that the island needed to be placed on a different legal footing. He composed a series of letters on his return voyage to Norfolk Island asking the Home Secretary for authorization to establish regular criminal and civil courts. Writing from Tenerife in April 1791, King begged for a set of law books and asked for "some arrangement being made respecting the Judicial proceedings at Norfolk Island."[124] In June, from the Cape Colony, he wrote again of the pressing need for courts and a "mode of inflicting punishments with some appearance of Legality," warning that in order to prevent disorder, he might be forced by necessity to inflict "the last & most dreadful of punishments."[125] On arrival in Norfolk Island, King reported that the settlement was now "an exact emblem of the Infernal Regions" and pleaded, "You will excuse me when I again remind you of the great necessity there is for some regular & authorized mode of distributing Justice."[126] The only way to reach a criminal court was to ship the accused to Port Jackson for trial. Witnesses had to be sent, too, and King lamented the interruptions to work in the small community.

[120] A long-awaited supply ship, the HMS *Sirius*, went aground off the island on March 19 – the day before the declaration of martial law. Its eighty-person crew survived but had to wait for rescue on the island, and their addition prompted new concerns about low rations.

[121] TNA, CO 201/9, f. 3v.

[122] The proclamation was issued on June 28, 1790. TNA, CO 201/9, ff. 5–7.

[123] Ibid., f. 7v.

[124] Ibid., f. 23.

[125] Ibid., ff. 47v.–48.

[126] Ibid., f. 50.

Acutely aware that he was presiding over a colony composed of small groups with potentially different standing in relation to his legal authority, King worried especially about the disruptive behavior of the "Marine Settlers," men from a wrecked ship sent from Sydney who had settled among the convicts and soldiers under his direct command. King saw these settlers as "unsubjected to any Laws" and doubted that he was "Warrantable in inflicting Corporal Punishments on them."[127] By the end of 1791, King had lost some of his scruples about such legal questions and contemplated placing the island under martial law again. But he still urged the formation of a court, one that he envisioned as a hybrid presided over by "civil and military justices," animated by a judge advocate, and "further aided by a jury chosen out of the Settlers."[128]

King and the others would have had little besides their personal experience, general knowledge, and the model of the courts of New South Wales to go on in designing such a court. A manual on martial law published in 1784 lamented that "so little hath been written on the Martial Law of England."[129] The most widely circulating law book in the empire of the late eighteenth century, Blackstone's *Commentaries*, citing Sir Matthew Hale for support, characterized martial law as "in truth and reality no law, but something indulged rather than allowed as law."[130] Blackstone was even critical of the functioning of military law as the basis of a disciplinary order for soldiers and military officials, noting that it retained "the characteristics of ancient servitude, concealed and precarious."[131] But the

[127] This appears in King's letter of September 29, 1791. Ibid., f. 52.

[128] Ibid, ff. 66–66v.

[129] Richard Joseph Sulivan, *Thoughts on Martial Law, with a Mode Recommended for Conducting the Proceedings of General Courts Martial*.... 2nd ed. (London: Printed for T. Becket, 1784), 1.

[130] The full quote shows that Blackstone recognized only the disciplinary functions of military law and favored tight restrictions on its use for other than members of the military: "Martial law, which is built upon no settled principles, but is entirely arbitrary in its decisions, is, as Sir Matthew Hale observes, in truth and reality no law, but something indulged rather than allowed as law. The necessity of order and discipline in an army, is the only thing which can give it countenance: and therefore it ought not to be permitted in time of peace, when the King's Courts are open for all persons to receive justice according to the laws of the land." Quoted in Alexander Fraser Tytler, *An Essay on Military Law, and the Practice of Courts Martial* (Edinburgh: Printed by Murray and Cochrane, 1800), 14. Tytler suggests that this passage by Blackstone must have been "penned in an unguarded moment" (13).

[131] Quoted in Robert B. Scott, *The Military Law of England (with All the Principal Authorities): Adapted to the General Use of the Army, in Its Various Duties and Relations, and the Practice of Courts Martial* (London: T. Goddard, 1810), xviii. This manual, and

real problem was the use of martial law as what one manual describes as an "extraordinary antidote" and "temporary restraint" in times of "disorder and turbulence."[132] This function, also criticized by Blackstone, was becoming better established in legislation and practice of the period. The 1788 statute in response to the rebellion in Ireland authorized martial law as a resource in any rebellious part of the kingdom. A treatise on martial law published in 1800 was vague in outlining the conditions and procedures under which the king or a delegated authority might declare martial law. Anyone declaring martial law must, it instructed, provide an explanation that certified "the necessity of this strong measure" without creating "unnecessary alarm."[133] Even if Ross, King, and subsequent commanders of Norfolk Island had been turning to law commentary for guidance on military or martial law – and there is no evidence that they ever did – they would have been supplied with little more than advice to justify their actions by pleading necessity and to make any procedures appear to conform to established practices. This much they could have surmised from a casual knowledge of military law and an interest in protecting their own careers.[134]

King more than his predecessor or successors appeared to be reluctant to declare martial law and was troubled by the deviations from what he took to be normal legal procedures that he felt forced to adopt in the colony. He reported his "perpetual anxiety . . . at the constant punishments, which are indispensable, & would be prevented if we had a regular Court of Justice."[135] By May 1792, King had improvised a system of rotating the duties of magistrate; King, an officer, the surgeon, and a member of the clergy took turns administering justice guided by two law books (Burn's *Justice* and Blackstone's *Commentaries*).[136] But he still

others of the period, acknowledged Blackstone's critique and suggested that it rested on an uncharacteristic misunderstanding.

[132] Tytler, *Essay on Military Law*, 378, 379, 51.

[133] Tytler, *Essay on Military Law*, 376.

[134] In fact, Major Ross's defense of his declaration of martial law follows this formula closely. In a letter to London written two days after the declaration of martial law, he wrote: "And when I consider the want of – perhaps – a sufficient authority for declaring Martial Law, which nothing but necessity would have induced me to do, being convinced that in our new state it is the only Law, by which the People can be kept in a subordinate state – we shall therefore trust to his Majesty & the British Parliament for such indemnification as the case may require. I hope & trust Your Excellency will authorise us to continue it, until we are supplied with Provisions, or at any rate that you will not forbid us." TNA, CO 201/9, f. 348.

[135] TNA, CO 201/9, f. 82.

[136] Ibid., ff. 100–100v.

complained almost a year later that in legal matters "we act without any authority whatever."[137]

The unusual mix of a soldier-citizenry with convicts and now a few emancipated convicts created the greatest challenge to legal administration on the island. A fight between soldiers and convicts at Christmas in 1793 prompted King to punish several of the soldiers, and this act produced more violence as the soldiers in barracks had reportedly "agreed... that no soldier should ever be punished on account of a Prisoner."[138] Still improvising, King identified twenty-nine soldiers as mutineers and took their weapons, arrested ten of the worst offenders, and formed the "Seamen Settlers" as a militia. He would not try the accused men by court-martial because he feared disruptions if he returned them to the barracks, so he sent them to New South Wales, where the court scolded King for the irregularity of throwing the men off the island without a trial. King must have appreciated the irony of the court's position; having been forced to create a set of ad hoc procedures combining magistracy and courts martial in controlling a convict population, King was now rebuked for not following military law procedures more closely to discipline the island's troops.

Uncertainties seemed to be at an end when a judge advocate was appointed for the island in August 1794. But the judge advocate did not sail until January 1796, and, when he did, he composed a letter at sea to London noting that by "a casual omission or oversight," the patent creating his post did not also establish a Court of Criminal Judicature for Norfolk Island. He was on his way to a serve as legal officer presiding over a nonexistent court.[139] A year after his arrival on the island, a state of legal confusion continued. A new island commander, John Townson, arrived in November 1797 to find the island suffering from "strange neglect" by Sydney at the same time that local production was faltering and a new crisis of provisions had emerged.[140] Townson complained of the effects on prisoners of continued uncertainty over the division of legal authority on the island; both he and King had pardoned convicts sentenced to

[137] From his letter of March 4, 1793. Ibid., f. 198.

[138] TNA, CO 201/10, f. 14.

[139] TNA, CO 201/18, f. 244.

[140] Ibid., f. 298. New South Wales saw its production levels rising, reducing its interest in provisions from Norfolk Island. And flax production on the island had never yielded much. In his first years as commander, King had brought two Maori men to teach them how to process the flax, but the men did not know how and King had finally returned them to New Zealand.

death before learning from the judge advocate that they had no power to do so. The judge advocate, for his part, soon discovered the need for improvisation; he began holding sessions of the Court of Criminal Judicature even though the court had never received authorization by Parliament and was functioning under royal charter – an arrangement that would have provided Bentham with more ammunition for accusations of unconstitutionality had he known about it. Records of the court's proceedings have not survived, but a single case recalls the actions of São Tomé courts in perpetuating a bound labor force and of the Spanish courts in condemning men to presidio labor in perpetuity. Convicted by the court of rape, Isaac Williams was condemned to death, then pardoned by the same court and sentenced to work for the government of Norfolk Island "until His Majesty's direction . . . is received."[141]

This period of quasi-legal, if sometimes well-intentioned, floundering turns out to have been Norfolk Island's finest hour as a penal settlement. The new commander appointed in 1800, Major Joseph Foveaux, instituted a disciplinary order featuring summary punishments, mainly severe flogging, for convicts and soldiers alike. Foveaux was also responsible for an explicit breach of legal procedure when he ordered the execution of two suspected mutineers, part of a larger group of Irishmen sent as political prisoners to Botany Bay and then on to Norfolk Island after being suspected of plotting insurrection at Parramatta. Foveaux pretended to turn to the judge advocate for advice, "perplexed" about how to proceed legally against the suspected ringleaders of the plot.[142] He then convened the island's officers, "both civil and military," and they "unanimously agreed" that the two men, and any others later shown to be involved, should be executed as "an immediate example."[143] Foveaux clearly realized that he would need to provide some justification for this act, so he wrote to King, now governor of New South Wales, and described a rationale based on two familiar principles: exception and necessity. The place was "widely different than any other part of the World," he wrote, and the prisoners there far worse than convicts in Port Jackson. With little guidance from the judge advocate, he argued, examples "if not exactly conformable to Law" were "indispensably necessary."[144] A series of other violent acts approved by Foveaux appeared nowhere in the public

[141] TNA CO 201/18, f. 258.
[142] TNA, CO 201/29, f. 21v.
[143] TNA, CO 201/29, f. 22 and 22v.
[144] TNA, CO 201/29, 22v.

record but have filtered into the historical record.[145] One such account followed Foveaux back to England, when John Mason, who had served on Norfolk Island as an assistant surgeon, undertook a campaign of letter writing to highly placed officials accusing Foveaux of having executed the two Irishmen "without trial or without proclaiming Martial Law" and of punishing soldiers by expelling them from the service and forcing them to labor with convicts "as Exiles in that distant colony." Foveaux, Mason wrote, had "usurped the Government of New South Wales assuming to himself the power of life and death . . . and under this illegal constitution" approved the executions of five more men.[146] Mason's language followed in a long tradition of attaching ancient rights to Britons no matter where in the empire they migrated; he was more original in arguing that such rights necessarily created the obligation of imperial legal oversight: "It is my wish . . . that the whole Empire may know that if two British subjects are hanged in any part of the British dominions however remote they may be, (even if two Roman Catholics) without trial or any form of Law whatever, or even their accusers being brought face to face, that their [*sic*] is a Tribunal some where, who will inquire whether these men were executed according to law, or murdered."[147] Mason appended charges of corruption: officers were forcing soldiers in their personal service, including convicts impressed for that purpose before being discharged and abandoned. Foveaux wrote from Cork to defend himself on the usual grounds, and he appears not to have suffered any penalty for his actions. As he rightly stated, the governor of New South Wales had not only excused but also praised him at the time for his quick response to the threat of mutiny.

Norfolk Island was abandoned in 1810, and departing troops burned the buildings and let dogs run wild in an effort to discourage the French from taking it over. But that was not the end of the island's life as a penal settlement. As New South Wales officials continued to press for the creation of sites of secondary punishment for transported convicts found guilty of additional crimes, attention turned again to Norfolk Island in the 1820s. This time there was no pretense of producing flax for the navy or foodstuffs for New South Wales. Governor Thomas Brisbane explained that convicts sent to Norfolk Island would be "forever excluded from all hope of return" and would "have forfeited all claim to the

[145] See Clay, *Maconochie's Experiment*.

[146] TNA, CO 201/71, ff. 3–3v.

[147] TNA, CO 201/71, f. 5.

protection of the law." He added that "if it were not too repugnant to the laws of England, I should consider it very fitting to have Norfolk Island completely under Martial Law."[148]

Between 1827 and 1840, Norfolk Island was operated as a particularly brutal prison camp. A series of military commandants approved severe flogging for convicts breaking even the smallest rules of a regime that kept them under lock and guard in a prison complex and on mandatory work crews. The degraded conditions and hopeless plight of the convicts gave rise to a desperate practice: a group of convicts would draw straws to designate a murderer and his victim, and the other participants would stand as witnesses. Then the whole party, including the accused, would have to be transported to Sydney for the trial. The pact prevented convicts, many of whom were Catholics, from having to take their own lives, and promised to provide a brief respite – one that almost always resulted in hanging for the accused murderer and any accomplices – from the hellish conditions on the island.[149] Norfolk Island in these years stands as the epitome of nearly perfect autocratic rule of an island penal colony.

The attempted reform of this harsh regime under Captain Alexander Maconochie between 1840 and 1843 has attracted attention from prison reformers and historians of prisons as one of the first attempts to apply a system of rewards in place of corporal punishment. We cannot recount that history here, but it is worth noting that Maconochie's failure on Norfolk Island rested, paradoxically, on the few controls that did exist on the authority of island commanders. Maconochie ignored instructions to apply his point scheme, the "mark system," only to new prisoners, and officials in New South Wales and London refused to approve his plan to reward prisoners who had accumulated a certain number of marks by moving them off the island. Writing from Sydney, Governor Gipps expressed his concern that such changes would alter the function of

[148] Quoted in Clay, *Maconochie's Experiment*, 114.

[149] For example, John McDonald and Francis Mullins were tried and hanged for striking Thomas Smith with a hammer, with intent to kill him. The *Sydney Herald* reported that at trial, one defendant stated that "striking Smith was for the purpose of getting up to Sydney, that they might have some chance of escaping from the gaol or hulk, but not with intent to murder him." *R. v. McDonnel and Miller* (1832), *Sydney Herald*, February 27, 1832, in "Decisions of the Superior Courts." Other, less elaborately planned acts of violence on the island seem to have been carried out with the aim of getting to Sydney. A man convicted of assault was reported to have said that "prisoners on the island did not care what they said or of what they accused one another, in order to get to Sydney." *R. v. Welsh*, *Australian* (1831), *Sydney Gazette*, January 11, 1831, in "Decisions of the Superior Courts."

Norfolk Island as a place of "great and salutary dread" for the convict population of New South Wales.[150] Under Gipps's influence, the Colonial Office in London authorized Maconochie's removal. The official rationale for refusing to reward men for accumulating marks by freeing them rested on an argument about the need for strict observance of the law; because terms of transportation were defined by statute and awarded in court, there was no legal basis for an island commander to alter them. Too late to preserve Maconochie in his post, Gipps eventually came to recognize some of the benefits of his system of marks, and he noted that one of the principal "torments" of the prisoners was the isolation of the place. He even came to question "the superiority of insular penitentiaries."[151]

The application of the term *penitentiary* to Norfolk Island is perhaps misleading. In this second phase of the island's history as a penal settlement comprising the period from 1827 to 1855, when the island's designation as a place of transportation ended, its governance continued earlier patterns of scant regulation of the disciplinary power of military commanders and the dearth of civilian legal institutions. In 1845, the island's ex-chaplain, T. B. Naylor, complained in a letter to Lord Stanley of the unique legal position of the island. With no criminal court, serious crimes were tried by a visiting barrister from Van Diemen's Land presiding over a court of five officers. Quite apart from "the deviation from constitutional practice which marks this proceeding" and the bias of "officers in the military charge of prisoners" trying them, Naylor was incensed at the delay that followed when any capital case had to be decided by referral to Van Diemen's Land, a judgment from which there was no appeal.[152] He cited the example of a case tried in May 1845, in which two men were found guilty of murder. The case was referred to Van Diemen's Land, and confirmation of the sentence arrived in August, but officials noticed irregularities in the paperwork. After some discussion of the warrant's "glaring inaccuracies," the commandant and sheriff told the men they would not be hanged – then changed their minds and had them executed. Naylor wrote, "In no other spot in the British dominions could such an outrage have been perpetrated but here."[153] The convicts, he complained, existed in a state of controlled isolation, in which all letters, visits, complaints, and attempts to secure release had to flow through the hands of

[150] Clay, *Maconochie's Experiment*, 160.
[151] Quoted in Clay, *Maconochie's Experiment*, 235.
[152] TNA, CO 885/2/27, p. 21.
[153] Ibid, p. 22.

officials. Civil cases could be appealed but not criminal cases, and criminal trials were governed by anomalous rules: "No copy of the indictment is allowed; no traverse is permitted in felonies, although, strangely enough, in misdemeanors. The accused may not have known what witnesses were to be brought against him until they appeared in the box.... He may suddenly be called upon to plead to a perfectly new charge, wholly differing from the one on which he was committed."[154]

Although to a different degree, this period continued the earlier legal confusion and the claims by local officials of the necessity of extralegal proceedings and actions.[155] If the legal tangles were less intricate in the 1840s, it was partly because the multiple categories for inhabitants – convicts, convict-settlers, soldiers, soldier-settlers, and convict-soldiers – were now collapsed into only two: prisoners and officials. Under both early and late regimes, martial law constituted a procedural model as well as a permanent threat. In both periods, the island was distinguished from other parts of the penal archipelago as a place of no return, where indeterminate sentences and lack of recourse placed convicts in a state of legal suspension. No reform ever altered this condition. The legal limbo of convicts transported to Norfolk Island would have been familiar to a presidiario in San Juan half a century before, and half a world away.

Militarism and Imperial Constitutions

Convict transportation in all its varieties between 1780 and 1850 fit into a pattern of proliferating forms of coerced labor and formed part of a wider imperial project of moving forced laborers around the globe. The various categories of forced labor shared a structural relation to state law. Captive workers fell under the immediate legal authority of delegated private or public powers. Slave owners, masters of assigned convicts or servants, governors of penal colonies, and ship captains had authority to administer severe summary punishments, and in this sense slave colonies, penal colonies, and military encampments formed different but related parts of a single problem of imperial legal ordering. The issues raised

[154] Ibid., p. 30.

[155] Though Van Diemen's Land had a different court system, its officials still complained of irregularities in the administration of law related to its continued role as a place of primary transportation after convict transportation to New South Wales was ended in 1840. The solicitor general of Van Diemen's Land found "great confusion in the law department of the Government of this colony, arising from the anomalous nature" of the duties required of poorly trained officials. TNA CO 881/1/21a, p. 3.

were not merely administrative but also constitutional, if we define this term in its broadest sense.[156] Sources for the authorization of delegated legal authority remained murky. The scope and nature of control over delegated authority also lacked precise definitions. We often think of these constitutional concerns in tracing the tensions between colonial interests and metropolitan authority; they were also very much a part of forced labor arrangements horizontally replicated across imperial arenas.[157]

This angle shows us new connections between forced labor in penal colonies and the forced labor of slaves. Martial law and transportation were familiar tools of legal authority in Caribbean slave societies, where they responded to a similar search by officials and elites for a legal framework for repression – and raised similar questions about the limits of the law in sustaining regimes of force. Banishment took its place among punishments for slaves suspected of rebellion in the Caribbean. Courts in eighteenth-century St. Domingue, for example, sent slaves suspected of fomenting rebellion to the "wild coast" of Honduras.[158] Spanish officials responded to this practice by monitoring French ships suspected of reconnoitering to deposit rebellious slaves "on our coasts and islands."[159] In the early nineteenth century, officials declared martial law in Barbados in 1805 and 1816, and in Demerara in 1823, in response to slave rebellions. The Demerara case provoked commentary in England from critics, especially abolitionists, who questioned the constitutionality of extending martial law beyond the moment of crisis when whites were in actual danger of attack. The House of Commons debate focused attention on the imperial constitutional issue of whether an unlimited prerogative

156 Here I would follow Daniel Hulsebosch's suggestion "to think of constitutions not as documents but rather as relationships among jurisdictions and people mediated through highly charged legal terms." *Constituting Empire: New York and the Transformation of Constitutionalism in the Atlantic World, 1664–1830* (Chapel Hill: University of North Carolina Press, 2005), 77.

157 Christopher Brown observes that the main challenge facing emancipationists was constitutional: "Reducing the power masters held over slaves required, in some way, reducing the power slaveholders possessed in the governance of colonial societies.... Even if emancipationists could generate momentum for slavery reform, did the crown or Parliament have the standing and resources to make such measures enforceable by law?" Christopher Leslie Brown, *Moral Capital: Foundations of British Abolitionism* (Chapel Hill: University of North Carolina Press, 2006), 240–1.

158 Laurent Dubois, *A Colony of Citizens: Revolution and Slave Emancipation in the French Caribbean, 1787–1804* (Chapel Hill: University of North Carolina Press, 2004), 296–7.

159 Officials in Cartagena worried that the French ship *La Filipina* entering the harbor in 1792 was part of a convoy carrying rebel slaves to deposit along the coast. AGS, SGU, 7237,52.

of declaring and sustaining martial law in the hands of colonists violated the sovereignty of Parliament. As one critic of the colonists argued, upholding "the rule of justice" in the empire required recognizing that "the claims of the slave owners are admitted but the dominion of Parliament indisputable – that we are sovereign alike over the White and the Black."[160]

The Demerara debate foreshadowed later controversies about the constitutionality of martial law in empire in pitting metropolitan critics against colonial officials. But it is worth noting that colonial officials were already finding both transportation and martial law to be awkward aids in their efforts to structure a legal framework for repression. Consider the response to the 1816 slave rebellion in Barbados, which prompted both the declaration of martial law and the plan to transport some rebels off the island. Writing to the secretary of state for war and colonies in the aftermath of the insurrection and its repression, Captain General James Leith recorded the legal uncertainties of how to deal with slaves suspected of being involved in the rebellion. Under martial law, in the two weeks after the outbreak of the revolt, 144 executions were carried out, many "on the Spur of the Moment, and many of them in the Fields," and Leith hoped that orders to conduct "more formal trials" would have better effect in calming the island.[161] But the question remained of how to deal with prisoners after the removal of martial law. About seventy had been tried and sentenced to death, and another one hundred had not been tried. Officials appointed a board of field officers to pass judgment on these slaves under a 1688 statute, "an old and extremely defective Law of the Island... which is unfortunately the only act... which takes cognizance of the Crime."[162] The board, Leith noted, would follow that act in trying to "conform to the modern Usages of War."[163] In effect, martial law declared by royal appointees had been substituted by a regime like martial law authorized by the Barbados council. To complete the legal uncertainties of the repression, Leith proposed to find a place to transport the slaves under sentences of death. "No British or Foreign colony would receive the Prisoners," he realized, and he wished for a tiny island with a British garrison, where the rebellious slaves could become charges of

[160] Emília Viotti da Costa, *Crowns of Glory, Tears of Blood: The Demerara Slave Rebellion of 1823* (New York: Oxford University Press, 1994), 289; and see Kostal, *Jurisprudence of Power*, 201–2.

[161] CO 28/85, f. 38.

[162] Ibid., f. 36v.

[163] Ibid., f. 37.

the British military.[164] The episode highlights similarities to legal posturing in Norfolk Island and elsewhere; officials improvised, inventing new procedures and citing familiar rationales that would allow them to place punishment in a recognizable imperial legal framework.

At the same time that martial law was coming to be regarded as "dormant as domestic jurisprudence," it was, in this ad hoc way, gaining traction as a tool in empire.[165] Martial law was declared in Ceylon, in 1817 and 1848; Jamaica, in 1831–1832 and 1865; the Cape Colony, in 1835, 1846, and 1850–1851; Canada, in 1837–1838; Cephalonia, in 1849; India, in 1857–1858; and St. Vincent, in 1862.[166] By the mid-nineteenth century in the British empire, the application of martial law in a post-emancipation setting had the potential to move to the center of debates about the imperial constitution. The best-studied episode is the controversy in England about the legality of acts under martial law after the Morant Bay uprising in Jamaica, in 1865. The governor of Jamaica, Edward Eyre, declared martial law over a part of the island after a crowd attacked the Morant Bay courthouse and killed eighteen people, including the chief magistrate.[167] It was the execution of a prominent opposition politician, George Gordon, under martial law after the immediate threat of the uprising had been quelled that attracted critical comment in England and became the object of public and private prosecutions. Gordon had been arrested in Kingston, an area explicitly exempted from martial law, and then ordered by Eyre to be transferred to a jurisdiction under martial law to be tried by court martial. His alleged crime was political agitation encouraging the revolt. Gordon was described as "coloured" in Jamaica and regarded as a member of a rising Jamaican political elite that was culturally close to the white, British Jamaican ruling group. Liberals in England led by John Stuart Mill saw this series of events as an

[164] Leith mentions that "a place like the Island of Bregue or Crab Island" would be perfect if British troops were stationed there. Crab Island referred to Vieques, near Puerto Rico. Ibid., f. 37v.

[165] Kostal, *Jurisprudence of Power*, 194. And see also Hussain, *Jurisprudence of Emergency*.

[166] Kostal, *Jurisprudence of Power*, 201.

[167] If the response to the attack had been limited to the violent repression targeting black Jamaicans in the district around Morant Bay in the weeks after the rebellion, the events probably would not have developed into a major political and legal controversy. As Governor Eyre would later explain in his defense, he was relying on Jamaican legislation approving martial law in times of emergency that dated from the era of slavery. The rebellion is discussed in Hussain, *Jurisprudence of Emergency*, but the most thorough analysis is Kostal, *Jurisprudence of Power*.

opportunity to challenge the constitutionality of martial law. As Rande Kostal has shown in tracing all facets of the debate, the controversy also raised broader questions about the imperial constitution: From what imperial source did the authority arise for either colonial legislatures or colonial governors to declare martial law? Was there such a thing as "imperial citizenship" that guaranteed British subjects the same rights everywhere in empire, or could location alter legal status? The debate urged new attempts to clarify the law of martial law, with particular attention to the question of whether martial law constituted a suspension of common law or its continuation in another form. Liberal critics of Eyre were driven by the worry that exceptions to the rule of law anywhere in empire might erode liberty in the metropolitan center.[168]

The legal politics about transportation and the rule of penal colonies surveyed in this chapter remind us that these late nineteenth-century questions about the imperial constitution belonged to long traditions of metropolitan and imperial discourse and practice. They were also not exclusive to Atlantic colonial governance or to debates about the legal prerogatives and political power of slaveholders. Small and geographically dispersed attempts to construct a legally coherent disciplinary order for penal colonies remind us of the pervasive and structural nature of conflicts over the relation between local, delegated legal authority and imperial governance. This history also helps us to keep in mind the spatial referents that were never far from the political imagination of colonial officials: island solutions to problems of imperial sovereignty.

Consider how challenges of ruling an empire of islands and anxieties about the corrupting influence of anomalous enclaves continued to be intertwined in Spain and its empire. The proliferation of presidios in the late eighteenth century, as we have seen, reflected the militarization of empire in this period, a trend with uneven geographic effects, and one that took on new significance and trajectories in the struggles over sovereignty in new Latin American polities of the early nineteenth century. Historians have described Latin American constitutionalism as a movement responding to peculiar regional conditions by privileging order over rights.[169] We know, too, that the late eighteenth-century militarization

[168] Kostal observes that the deeper explanation of the intensity of the controversy is that the mid-Victorian "moral imagination . . . fundamentally was a legal imagination." Kostal, *Jurisprudence of Power*, 20.

[169] Jeremy Adelman, *Sovereignty and Revolution in the Iberian Atlantic* (Princeton, NJ: Princeton University Press, 2006); and see also Ivan Jaksic, *Andrés Bello: Scholarship and Nation-Building in Nineteenth-Century Latin America* (Cambridge: Cambridge University Press, 2001).

of empire forms part of the story of refashioned "legacies" of colonialism in the region.[170] But the institutions, practices, and conflicts that carried military law as a constitutional problem into the nineteenth century have not been clearly traced.

We cannot do them justice here, but a few connections deserve mention. Local militias in the late colonial period took on new legal and political roles and resulted in many places in an expanded scope for military jurisdiction, or the *fuero militar*. Having long operated as one of an array of subordinate legal jurisdictions, the *fuero militar* gained importance as subjects who were not strictly speaking in the military (such as members of militias, or suppliers of services to the military) found it advantageous to claim the right to have the *fuero militar* applied to them.[171] Militarization of elites and persisting concerns about military defense meanwhile helped to move military commanders closer to the reins of power in colonial polities. The movement was evident in many parts of the Spanish empire at the turn of the nineteenth century, but the trajectory was uneven across the empire. It fit, too, within a wider political discourse about the imperial constitution.

[170] The way that colonial militarism influenced postcolonial law and politics has, however, not been deeply explored. One simplistic strand of argument has been that colonial militarism prepared the way for caudillismo and clientelism by promoting a cult of rule by individual military commanders, beginning with conquistadores. See John J. Johnson, *The Military and Society in Latin America* (Stanford, CA: Stanford University Press, 1964). A volume intended to provide a more sophisticated analysis of "colonial legacies" mentions this approach but does not provide analysis of the military in the nineteenth century. Jeremy Adelman, "Introduction," *Colonial Legacies: The Problem of Persistence in Latin American History*, ed. Jeremy Adelman (New York: Routledge, 1999), 1–13, 9. Other case studies offer to examine the "close relationship . . . between authoritarianism and militarism during the immediate post-Independence period" but focus on the military and politics rather than law. Linda Alexander Rodríguez, "Authoritarianism and Militarism," in *Rank and Privilege: The Military and Society in Latin America*, ed. Linda Alexander Rodríguez (Wilmington, DE: Rowman and Littlefield, 1994), 37–54, 38. In general, caudillismo and militarism in the early nineteenth century are viewed as sources of disorder, though I have suggested elsewhere that caudillos acted as legal authorities within their spheres of influence and that their contests with emerging state authority may be partly understood as variants of jurisdictional politics (Benton, *Law and Colonial Cultures*, chap. 6). On political disorder, see Brian Loveman and Thomas M. Davies Jr., "Instability, Violence, and the Age of Caudillos," *The Politics of Antipolitics: The Military in Latin America*, ed. Brian Loveman and Thomas M. Davies (Wilmington, DE: Rowman and Littlefield, 1997), 15–28; and on the legal control of the countryside as an element of national legal politics in the nineteenth century, see Benton, *Law and Colonial Cultures*, chap. 6.

[171] McAlister, "*The Fuero Militar*." On the militia's role in social mobility and social hierarchy in the eighteenth century, see Jorge I. Dominguez, "International War and Government Modernization: The Military – A Case Study," in Rodríguez, *Rank and Privilege*, 1–36.

In Spain, the liberal authors of successive constitutions simultaneously advocated the incorporation of the colonies in a single political community and enumerated the distinctive social and political qualities that marked the colonies as legally exceptional. As Josep Fradera has noted, Spanish liberals' goal of separating military and political power was viewed as unworkable in colonies whose loyalty was in question.[172] In the colonies, the relation of military to political power developed along several trajectories. In Cuba and Puerto Rico, colonial governance was reconfigured under captains general who held both political and military power. Together with the Philippines, these were the "island imperial enclaves" of a reconstituted empire.[173] Elsewhere, the series of conflicts across the empire in the decades following the Napoleonic invasion of Spain cast militarism in a new light. Forms of "militarized politics" corresponded to new patterns of spatial fragmentation, as rural armed forces challenged and in some cases eclipsed the power of urban centers controlled by merchant elites.[174]

The continual warfare prompted legal elites to place a premium on order, however it was produced. As fledgling governments actively sought international recognition, their negotiations in Europe tended to revolve around the promise to pay debts and the demonstration of strong government institutions. Chilean leaders in the 1820s, for example, struggled to establish a constitutional order while their representatives in London lamented their inability to provide "proof to the British government that Chile is . . . on its way to consolidating government institutions."[175] The project of establishing international legitimacy and the problem of constitution writing converged, illustrated by the efforts of Andrés Bello, the region's leading codifier. Bello approached the delicate problem of providing institutional continuity with the colonial state by insisting that Spanish imperial rule had never represented "a *ferocious* tyranny."[176] A student

[172] For an excellent analysis of the conflicting goals of Spanish liberals and the definition of the colonies as legally exceptional, see Josep Maria Fradera, *Gobernar colonias* (Barcelona: Ediciones Península, 1999), 71–125.

[173] The colonies shared the conditions of major fortification projects, influential militias, rapidly growing agricultural export economies, and fiscal drains on other parts of the empire. Josep Maria Fradera, *Colonias para después de un imperio* (Barcelona: Edicions Bellaterra, 2005), 31–2.

[174] Adelman, *Sovereignty and Revolution*, 261.

[175] Jaksic, *Andrés Bello*, 97.

[176] Jaksic, *Andrés Bello*, 135, emphasis in original; and see chapter 10 in Matthew C. Mirow, *Latin American Law: A History of Private Law and Institutions in Spanish America* (Austin: University of Texas Press, 2004).

of Bentham's writings, Bello endorsed a subtle shift of emphasis from lawmaking to the enforcement of order as the fundamental condition of sovereignty.[177] All the elements of militarization of the late-colonial and revolutionary decades found reinforcement in the 1833 constitution and its political aftermath: a merging of elite and military leadership in a repressive and politically influential national guard; "extraordinary faculties" of the president, including suspending the constitution and civil liberties; and the declaration of a state of siege in specific provinces. Some sort of state of emergency prevailed in Chile for half the years between 1833 and 1861.

In this context, Bello both espoused Bentham's vision of codification as key to political order and cited Bentham's vision of the panopticon as inspiration for the construction of a system of prisons that would reinforce that order. The penal colony at Juan Fernández on the island of Más a Tierra held a symbolically central place in debates about the political and legal order. Between 1814 and 1854, the colony housed a mix of political prisoners and common criminals. It was closed at several intervals, the longest between 1837 and 1851, in response to what Bello called "repeated escapes, rebellions, and bloody scenes."[178] In promoting penitentiaries as an alternative, Bello also provided a twist to Bentham's critique of penal colonies. The problem with Juan Fernández, Bello suggested, was that it was structurally flawed. Confining men in a "deserted and distant island" would always create motives for escape, opportunities for overcoming guards, and a tendency toward corruption among officials in charge. Such a place would require "constant and close

[177] Bello asserted, "The ability to participate in public affairs is infinitely less important than the ability to secure life and property." Jaksic, *Andrés Bello*, 178.

[178] Andrés Bello, "El presidio ambulante," in *Sistema carcelario en Chile: Visiones, realidades y proyectos (1816–1916)*, ed. Marco Antonio León León (Santiago, Chile: Dirección de Bibliotecas, Archivos y Museos, Centro de Investigaciones Diego Barros Arana, 1996), 69–71, 70; my translation. The detailed history of these events cannot be presented here, but it is worth noting that the Chilean state experimented with different regimes, including an attempt to run the island under a private contract, in an effort to continue to utilize it as a penal colony. The first political prisoners were antiroyalists, but subsequent republican regimes also banished political rivals to the island. A mutiny uniting soldiers and inmates in 1834 garnered special public attention when the newly appointed English governor of the presidio, Thomas Sutcliffe, was tried and acquitted in Santiago on charges of prompting the mutiny through cruel and arbitrary acts. See chapter 4 of Marco Antonio León León, *Encierro y corrección: La configuración de un sistema de prisiones en Chile: 1800–1911*, vol. 2 (Santiago: Universidad Central de Chile, Facultad de Ciencias Jurídicas y Sociales, 2003) and Woodward, *Robinson Crusoe's Island.*

inspection by disinterested observers," as if the presidio itself were a cell within a panopticon.[179] It is interesting that the lesson drawn by Bello and by others associated with the Portales regime was that the death penalty was an irreplaceable tool of the state. For Bello, the continual disturbances in Juan Fernández showed that "the death penalty is today the only effective punishment."[180]

A similar adaptation of penal settlements in the politics of postindependence Latin American occurred elsewhere in the region. In the 1790s, in the worried response to the outbreak of violence on St. Domingue, officials in Havana considered sending leaders of black auxiliary forces to the presidio on Isla de Pinos.[181] Ordered not to fuel the disturbance by selling "French slaves" to Puerto Rico, officials also sent captured slaves to Isla de Pinos.[182] Nearly a century later, in the 1870s, the small island was being used as a place of internal exile for "insurrectionists."[183] Some new penal stations were created in the immediate postindependence period, such as Puerto Luis on the Falkland Islands in 1828, and still others were founded in the second half of the nineteenth century in both Spanish colonies and new republics.[184] In a tract published in 1871, *El presidio político en Cuba*, José Martí described the horrific treatment of presidiarios, which he regarded as proof of the emptiness of rhetoric about the glories of the empire: "National unity dishonors, flogs, and murders there. And stirs, exalts, and inspires here."[185]

[179] Andrés Bello, "Establecimientos de confinación para los delincuentes," in León León, *Sistema carcelario en Chile*, 47–8.

[180] Andrés Bello, "Establecimientos de confinación para los delincuentes," in León León, *Sistema carcelario en Chile*, 47. Portales emphasized this point in the prosecution of a political opponent, Ramón Freire, sentenced by the courts to exile rather than death, as Portales insisted was just. He followed this case with legislation to force judges to justify their sentences, a move designed specifically to tighten controls over the judiciary. See León León, *Encierro y corrección*, 55.

[181] ES 41091.AGI/1.16417.1.6/ESATDO, 5B, N. 176.

[182] ES.47161.AGS/1.1.19.12/SGU, Leg 1, SGU, Leg, 7163, 7.

[183] There are about one hundred files documenting such cases in the Archivo Histórico Nacional (hereafter AHN), Ultramar. For example, AHN ULTRAMAR,4386,EXP.6 reports on twenty-one people sentenced to deportation to Isla de Pinos for disloyalty.

[184] Puerto Princesa was founded on the island of Palawan in the Philippines in 1852; a penal colony was founded at Fernando Po in 1879 to house prisoners from Cuba; Argentina created a penal colony on Isla de los Estados (the Malvinas or Falkland Islands) that operated between 1899 and 1902, when it was moved to Tierra del Fuego; Mexico opened a penal settlement on the Islas Marías in 1905; Panama founded a penal colony on Coibo in 1919; and Ecuador used Isabella Island for prisoners between 1946 and 1959.

[185] José Martí and Celina Manzoni, *El presidio político en Cuba, último diario y otros textos* (Buenos Aires: Editorial Biblos, 1995), 59. ("La integridad nacional deshonra, azota, asesina allá. Y conmueve, engrandezca, entusiasme aquí.")

The imperial transportation system of the late eighteenth century had put many of these sites in place, while the longer practice of confinement in presidios and exile to islands provided precedents. But the legal and political significance of the presidios shifted in the context of constitutional and republican politics, and in nineteenth-century imperial politics. In Chile, the presidio itself came to signify the dangers of a sphere outside the close control of the nascent state. Elites, including central figures in the construction of the new constitutional and legal order, viewed the presidio as simultaneously too far outside the ambit of state control and insufficiently harsh. Such associations fit within a broader pattern of association that Ricardo Salvatore, writing about the embrace of capital punishment in mid-nineteenth-century Argentina, calls the union of "death and liberalism."[186] At the same time, presidios as places of exclusion could serve as symbols of the unevenly distributed benefits of continued Spanish sovereignty – "blood stains," as Martí wrote.[187] Both discourses played a role in shaping constitutional orders that paired the maintenance of central political authority with the temporal exception of the state of siege and the spatial and legal anomaly of the military prison for civilians.

Conclusion

Historians have been somewhat reluctant to view the shifting schemes for the legal ordering of penal colonies as forming part of an imperial constitutional politics. One reason is easy to locate: the proliferation of penal colonies coincided with the rise of penitentiary systems in Europe and the United States, and transportation often entered public discussion as an alternative to incarceration for criminals at home. This comparison neutralized considerations of imperial sovereignty; there was no question, even for Bentham, that European governments had the power to restrain and punish criminals, at home or abroad. If penal colonies were prisons, their governors could be styled as wardens. Even if some wardens might treat prisoners harshly, their prerogative to punish, and the sovereign power of the state behind them, was not in dispute.

In practice, as we have seen, the delegated legal authority of penal colonies was anything but simple to define. Most, if not all, penal colonies

[186] Ricardo Donato Salvatore, "Death and Liberalism: Capital Punishment after the Fall of Rosas," in *Crime and Punishment in Latin America: Law and Society since Late Colonial Times*, ed. Ricardo Donato Salvatore, Carlos Aguirre, and G. M. Joseph (Durham, NC: Duke University Press, 2001), 308–41.

[187] Martí and Manzoni, *El Presidio Político*, 40.

had inhabitants other than convicts, and the presence of soldiers and settlers automatically posed the anomalous situation of nonconvicts living under a disciplinary order not intended for them. Further, penal colonies, like other forced labor regimes, posed perpetual risks to order. The threat of mutiny prompted not just occasional exceptional violence but also its institutionalization. The suspension of law came to be built into the legal fabric, even though the authority for declaring a state of exception and the type of law to be installed remained undefined.[188] Martial law provided the connection between these constitutional questions. Very little about military law and martial law was settled in this period.[189] We have seen that military legal authority was associated with the routine management of the disciplinary order of the armed forces and also with the application of the laws of war in moments of "necessity," supposedly to protect public order. As Bentham recognized, the application of martial law in any colonial setting raised constitutional issues about the authority for its declaration, the scope of its application, and its duration.

Penal colonies were shaped by several streams of law – the law of exile and the law of emergency – and there was ambiguity in both areas of law. The legal tradition of banishment left undefined the nature of jurisdiction over criminals in places of exile. In European convict transportation, a range of practices grew up to fill this void, and they were only partly directed from imperial centers. The shifting and uncertain legal status of British convicts in Maryland and Virginia in the middle decades of the eighteenth century is an example of this process; the diversity of economic roles for convicts in the Portuguese empire is another. The continuities between galley labor under French and Spanish law and convict transportation to overseas penal stations established military officials as legal authorities in sites of exile. But this seemingly simple transition contained hidden discontinuities, as transportation either depended on or created a status of "legal nonperson" for convicts arriving in (and rarely leaving) the penal archipelago.[190] Military law meanwhile entered penal settlements

[188] Nasser Hussain has argued persuasively that the rationale for declaring martial law in empire eventually came to rest on Europeans' perception that the racial and cultural differences of colonial subjects created a constant threat of insurrection. Colonial law came to be infused with what Hussain calls a "jurisprudence of emergency." Hussain, *Jurisprudence of Emergency*.

[189] Or, indeed, later. For an excellent discussion of the lineage of jurists' writings on martial law in Britain, see Kostal, *Jurisprudence of Power*.

[190] Spieler, "Empire and Underworld."

through two doors. Through one, the regime of military discipline encompassed civilians in distant places; through another, officials invoked martial law to respond to situations of vaguely defined emergency.

Both streams of law – the law of criminal exile and military or martial law – had built-in spatial associations that the project of imperial penal colonization tended to reinforce. The Roman law of banishment had provided for the isolation of criminals on islands. Imperial policy retained and revived this purposeful isolation – and not merely an undifferentiated sending away – in convict transportation systems, especially in the designation of distant island destinations such as São Tomé, Príncipe, Ceylon, Sable Island, the Juan Fernández Islands, Van Diemen's Land, and Norfolk Island, or in the proximate island prisons of Deer Island in Boston Harbor, Robben Island off the Cape Colony, Isla de Pinos off Cuba, and the Islas Marías near Mexico. This colonial history in turn deepened the association of islands and convict exiles. It is not surprising to find Captain George Marby writing to the British secretary of state for the Home Department in 1837 to extol "the advantages presented by the Eastern side of Greenland" as a site "peculiarly fitted to be used as a Transportation Settlement" because its isolation made "escape impossible."[191] Still later, in 1875, the Real Academia de Ciencias Morales y Políticas in Madrid sponsored an essay contest on the subject of whether Spain should found penal colonies in the Marianas Islands or the islands of the Gulf of Guinea like "the English [had done] at Botany Bay."[192] Also citing the example of Botany Bay, the French settled a new shipment of convicts on the Îles du Salut off French Guiana in 1852 and declared New Caledonia a site for transportation in 1863.[193] In the early twentieth century, Devil's Island, one of the Îles du Salut and only one of multiple staging areas for

[191] TNA, HO 44/30 ff. 59–60, f. 59.

[192] The winning submission imagined a penal system staged across multiple sets of islands, with convicts completing a period of agricultural labor in Corisco and Annobon before being sent to a third island in the Gulf of Guinea or on Saypan and Tinian before being transported to the Marianas. Francisco Lastres y Juiz and Eduardo Martínez, *La colonización penitenciaria de las Marianas y Fernando Póo* (Madrid: Imprenta y Librería de Eduardo Martínez, 1878), 66.

[193] The French considered other sites, including western Australia, Madagascar, Sierra Leone, and St. Domingue. On the influence of Botany Bay, see chapter 7 in Leslie R. Marchant, *France Australe: The French Search for the Southland and Subsequent Explorations and Plans to Found a Penal Colony and Strategic Base in South Western Australia 1503–1826* (Perth: Scott Four Colour Print, 1998). And see Colin Forster, *France and Botany Bay: The Lure of a Penal Colony* (Carlton South: Melbourne University Press, 1996).

convicts in French Guiana, entered transnational popular culture as a symbol for the horrors of penal exile.[194]

In the imagined legal geography of convict transportation, nature would corral criminals, military rule would ensure order, and systemic violence would respond to vaguely defined necessity. Anxieties about security influenced the selection of sites by officials at home, as we saw in the discussion of Lemain Island as a potential place of convict settlement. On penal islands themselves, as at Norfolk Island, martial law was imposed by local commanders who worried that mutineers would run amok and slaughter officials, soldiers, and their families. The same isolation that gave prisoners no escape would prevent settlers and officials from fleeing in the case of insurrection. Because island garrisons were often founded under the same naval officials who transported convicts to build them, the term *mutiny* was not a casual reference but a purposeful transposition of understandings of islands as similar to ships at sea: vulnerabilities to insurrection justified extraordinary measures by commanders to preserve order. Other associations of the dangers of island insurrection would have filtered through circulating stories about slave rebellions in the Atlantic world. In defending his actions on Norfolk Island, Foveaux could count on his audience's familiarity with descriptions of fear of extermination of a small controlling island cadre at the hands of a group of desperate and disenfranchised men.

Penal colonies' aura of extralegality did have real effect. Presidiarios disappeared from the historical record almost without protest because they were so nearly completely deprived of legal recourse. Captain Foveaux commanded his reign of terror without serious challenge, except from a disgruntled assistant surgeon with a penchant for letter writing. But the legal isolation of prisoners, the weak institutional protections, and the harsh repression of commanders should not lead us to characterize penal colonies as lawless places. Military law did not boast a well-established or intricate jurisprudence, and martial law tended to excuse ad hoc excesses and exemplary punishment like the execution of mutineers at Norfolk Island or Más a Tierra. Yet regimes of martial law did operate under a kind of law, and they did have a definable place in the imperial order. It was precisely these qualities that connected the penal colonies to a broader constitutional politics.

[194] Devil's Island did not acquire this reputation until after 1894, when it was reserved for political offenders who were not made to work but were entirely isolated. On the broader cultural discourse about French Guiana in the twentieth century, see Peter Redfield, *Space in the Tropics: From Convicts to Rockets in French Guiana* (Berkeley: University of California Press, 2000).

Questions raised by the legal administration of penal colonies applied to colonial rule more generally, and by an easy analogy to the constitutional politics of slavery. In particular, island penal colony rule depended on an understanding of sovereignty that authorized spatial exceptions to institutionalized restraints on the exercise of delegated legal authority. The worry expressed by Bentham and others that such exceptions might erode the rule of law were rhetorical positions without great force in the early nineteenth century, but they would emerge later in the context of controversies about the rights of imperial citizens. Spatially uneven imperial legal regimes raised the prospect of a permanent differentiated rights regime. Even more so than the temporal exception of the declaration of martial law, penal colonies as "nurseries" of martial law cradled constitutional contradictions. Designed to expand and defend empire as a unified system, convict transportation multiplied pockets of legal anomaly that challenged emerging visions of imperial order.

5

Landlocked

Colonial Enclaves and the Problem of Quasi-Sovereignty

> The feudal constitution naturally diffused itself into long ramifications of subordinate authority. To this general temper of the government was added the peculiar form of the country, broken by mountains into many subdivisions scarcely accessible but to the natives, and guarded by passes, or perplexed with intricacies, through which national justice could not find its way.
>
> – Samuel Johnson, *A Journey to the Western Islands of Scotland*

"Mountains Come First"

To gaze at the mountains from the plains in the sixteenth-century Mediterranean world was to look back in time, according to Braudel.[1] Mountains were both geologically old and socially primeval: they bore evidence of prehistoric folding and ancient, inland seas, as well as the marks of settlement from eras before the coastal plains were made safe from disease and enemies. Rome's impact was muted, and religious conversion – both Christianization and Islamization – developed more slowly than on the plains. These Mediterranean "hilltop worlds" were worlds apart, "semi-deserted" and "half-wild" zones of refuge for religious sects and "aberrant cults."[2] Yet, despite their reputation for slow change and inhabitants' "primitive credulity," mountainous regions could also experience rapid and violent shifts as the result of conquest and reconquest by plains

[1] "Mountains Come First" is Braudel's heading for the section on mountain geography referred to in this paragraph. Fernand Braudel, *The Mediterranean and the Mediterranean World in the Age of Philip II* (New York: Harper and Row, 1976), 1:25.

[2] Braudel, *Mediterranean*, 34, 29, 37.

polities, most of which established only tenuous control over the highlands.[3]

Like Johnson's mid-eighteenth-century musings about the craggy landscape of the Scottish islands blocking "national justice," Braudel's portrait of mountain and hill regions as reserves for ancient practices promoted their association with legal primitivism. Vendettas in Corsica and other hilly enclaves thrived because feudal justice had not penetrated there. The legal system of the hills and mountains was as undeveloped as the aristocracy, so that such regions became zones "of liberty, democracy, and peasant 'republics.'"[4] The story was the same across the Mediterranean: in the hill villages of Greece, Albania, and Lebanon, "Turkish despotism" fared poorly.[5] Even as trade, transhumance, and the seasonal labor migrations of mountain dwellers connected highland and lowland regions, perceptions of deep cultural and institutional differences persisted.

The contrast between the civilized plains and the primitive mountains belonged to an intellectual tradition with classical roots, an early modern lineage, an Enlightenment reprise, and – no doubt subtly influencing Braudel – a nineteenth-century evolutionary twist. The mountains were "magic" because their geography suspended time. The imperfect penetration of civilization from below produced not just cultural difference but backwardness. Change occurred only as a result of disruptions from the outside, usually in the form of attempts at conquest from below. Unlike sixteenth-century lowlanders, Braudel did not engage in cruel caricature of highlanders, but it is easy to imagine how his portrayal of mountain regions as shelters for earlier forms of legal culture might promote confusion between historical description and analysis of a politically charged discourse.[6]

Since Braudel, some historians have tried to disentangle lowlanders' perceptions from the lived conditions and legal politics of mountain regions. There is considerable evidence that the boundaries between lowlands and highlands were porous in most times and places, crossed by intermediary groups and by migrants, especially plains peoples moving into hill regions to escape the reach of lowlands rulers, religious orthodoxy,

[3] Braudel, *Mediterranean*, 37. Note that Braudel distinguishes between mountain and hill regions but not consistently.

[4] Braudel, *Mediterranean*, 40.

[5] Braudel, *Mediterranean*, 40.

[6] Braudel, *Mediterranean*, 46.

and taxes.[7] Regional histories overturn the mythical narrative of "original peoples" living in isolated mountain regions and sheltered from the influences of more dynamic lowland civilizations. Mountain peoples participated in the construction of state institutions and borders. And mountain regions entered a broader political and cultural discourse as symbols of qualities other than backwardness. Colonial elites often portrayed the mountains as a healthful refuge from the degenerating environment of the hot plains, which in colonial settings posed a danger to European constitutions.[8]

Despite these currents, associations of hill country with archaic practices were powerful and persistent. For James Scott, the "magic" of the mountains lies precisely in the resilience of a discourse about backwardness in the face of contradictory findings.[9] This stereotype carried across centuries, found application in a wide variety of European and colonial settings, and had deep roots in other empires and world regions, including China and the lowland polities of Southeast Asia. One wonders whether the tension between highlands and lowlands might constitute a fundamental element in human history, much like the relation between nomadic and settled populations. Scott distills the historical sociology of mountain regions and their relation to political power into two statements: "civilizations 'don't know how to climb,'" and "people, sometimes collectively, sometimes individually, 'climb' to escape them."[10]

This chapter explores the ways that this relation, real or imagined, shaped law. In particular, it argues that categorizing mountain and

[7] On porousness, see James C. Scott, "La montagne et la liberté, ou pourquoi les civilisations ne savent pas grimper," *Critique Internationale* 11 (2001), 85–104, 86. My translation.

[8] For a study of the differences and convergences of the views of highlanders and lowlanders about the political status of mountain regions, see Peter Sahlins, *Boundaries: The Making of France and Spain in the Pyrenees* (Berkeley: University of California Press, 1991). For an analysis of representations of a mountain region in a national discourse on enlightenment, see Kären Wigen, "Discovering the Japanese Alps: Meiji Mountaineering and the Quest for Geographical Enlightenment," *Journal of Japanese Studies* 31, no. 1 (2005), 1–26. And on the British colonial discourse about mountains as healthful zones that contrasted to the dangerous climate of the tropical plains, see David Arnold, *Colonizing the Body: State Medicine and Epidemic Disease in Nineteenth-Century India* (Berkeley: University of California Press, 1993); Mark Harrison, *Climates and Constitutions: Health, Race, Environment and British Imperialism in India, 1600–1850* (New York: Oxford University Press, 1999); and especially Dane Keith Kennedy, *The Magic Mountains: Hill Stations and the British Raj* (Berkeley: University of California Press, 1996).

[9] Scott, "Montagne et la liberté," 89.

[10] Scott, "Montagne et la liberté," 96, my translation.

hill regions as distinctive political and cultural spaces helped to inform applications of international law in empire. Viewed as primitive areas with the potential to become increasingly, but never fully, modern, hill regions were seen as zones in perpetual transition. They might attain, and would be rewarded with, only the kind and amount of law that matched their level of development. Imperial governance seemed to require colonizers to hold legal prerogatives in reserve. The notion that sovereign functions could be parceled out and assigned to territories as they developed was related, in turn, to a new version of an old idea of sovereignty as divisible, made up of a bundle of separable traits. The thin air of mountain regions could support only a thin collection of sovereign attributes, while lowland colonial territories, or even highland polities that attempted to consolidate naturally occurring petty states, sustained a mix of sovereign rights producing petty despotism. This supposed tendency toward despotism paradoxically affirmed the greater purity of forms of sovereignty in the hills and at times suggested that they were deserving of more autonomy. Rule over hill territories required more than a simple extension of imperial legal administration; it demanded solutions for the problem of incorporating different categories of subjects and multiple separate polities within empire.

The link to international law also emerged from portrayals of highlanders as belligerents, capable of gathering effective fighting forces but not of staffing bureaucratic legal institutions. European officials represented hill regions as tending toward violence, and they developed this angle into a rationale for intervention. The "primitive" nature of sovereignty in hill regions suggested that they should be left alone, allowed to turn their militarism inward rather than outward toward the imperial state and to struggle much like small states in conflict within an international order without an overarching political authority.[11] At the same time, any measure of sovereignty by subordinate entities figured as a potential challenge to imperial sovereignty, so the legal politics of hill regions entered directly into broader debates about the imperial constitution.

Talk about the rule of hill regions figured in several extended crises of legitimacy for European empires. Casting around for solutions to

[11] Or, alternatively, to fight for the imperial state. On perceptions of military prowess among highlanders, see Heather Streets, *Martial Races: The Military, Race and Masculinity in British Imperial Culture, 1857–1914* (Manchester, U.K.: Manchester University Press, 2004).

the problem of incorporating remote peoples and polities in empire, European jurists and colonial officials tried various strategies for reconciling imperial rule with territorial unevenness and jurisdictional complexity. One such extended moment involved sixteenth-century debates over the Spanish crown's moral and political right to rule the peoples of the overseas Spanish empire. This chapter begins with a brief look at how broader Spanish debates about the legal status of Indians included representations of mountain regions, dispersed settlements, and small polities as less-than-fully-integrated parts of empire. The exercise allows us to identify some strands of legal discourse that would reappear in much later debates about the incorporation of semisovereign polities in European empire. The chapter then turns to the late nineteenth century, when a shift toward more expansive territorial claims of empire-states again focused sharp attention on the problem of polities and peoples who occupied positions simultaneously within and without the imperial legal order. In this period, and in the very different context of expansive territorial empires, colonial highland regions did not define a moving frontier but instead formed enclave territories, discrete zones embedded within areas of more direct colonial rule. Represented as metaphorical high ground stranded above "the rising tide of... civilization," enclave territories became the focus of elaborate efforts to define quasi-sovereignty and fix its place within international law.[12]

The problems of refining the definition of quasi-sovereignty and fitting it within broader frameworks of law was taken up in the late nineteenth century by both international lawyers and colonial officials – overlapping groups, as we shall see.[13] Both sets of writers ultimately argued for the limits of applying international law to systems of quasi-sovereignty and at times imagined imperial power as trending irreversibly toward a unified system of sovereignty. In this view, the law of empire represented

[12] Wilkinson uses this phrase to describe U.S. officials' perceptions of Indian enclaves within Western states. Charles F. Wilkinson, *American Indians, Time, and the Law: Native Societies in a Modern Constitutional Democracy* (New Haven, CT: Yale University Press, 1987), 17. Lee-Warner used the same metaphor in writing of the Indian princely states as comprising "vast tracts of territory left above the tide of British conquest as it rose and submerged" the rest of India. William Lee-Warner, *The Protected Princes of India* (London: Macmillan, 1894).

[13] *Quasi-sovereignty* is chosen here to encompass a number of terms used to describe arrangements of shared or limited sovereignty, including *semisovereignty*, *paramountcy*, *protectorates*, and *indirect rule*. International lawyers have developed some distinctions among these terms, so it seems preferable to choose a term not commonly used by them to refer to the class of arrangements of divided rule.

a disaggregated variant of the law of nation-states. Yet, even as they contributed to this emerging perspective, colonial officials faced a legal politics that simultaneously urged them to articulate a third position: the view that imperial law had distinctive qualities. I explore this process in analyzing a legal crisis in the Indian princely state of Baroda and the connection of this case to evolving notions of the imperial legal order. In this case and in general, attention to the problem of quasi-sovereignty was instrumental in converting the business of imperial legal administration into a jurisprudence of imperial constitutional law.[14]

Understanding quasi-sovereignty as a problem of imperial constitutional law allows us to connect debates in India to legal politics in other late nineteenth-century colonial (and national) settings. The last section of this chapter traces the very different results of legal politics regarding quasi-sovereignty in Basutoland in southern Africa and Indian law in the United States. The comparative context illuminates several dimensions of quasi-sovereignty as a constitutional problem. First, it calls attention to the global circulation of ideas about quasi-sovereignty. Phrases denoting a category in between "foreign" and "domestic" migrated across empires and regions. Second, the comparisons remind us of the open-endedness of the legal politics of quasi-sovereignty, with outcomes ranging from the establishment of rationales for broad legal intervention in U.S. Indian reservations to the creation in Basutoland of a formally independent nation-state. Third, juxtaposing the legal history of Indian princely states with the history of other dependent polities helps to highlight the spatial dimension of quasi-sovereignty. The enclave pattern of semisovereign territories surrounded by areas of more direct colonial rule generated similar jurisdictional tensions that in turn prompted both periodic suspensions of law and the creation of new categories of legal distinction. Quasi-sovereign states came to be imagined everywhere as anomalous legal spaces, where the application of imperial law defied easy categorization and seemed even to require the occasional suspension of law.

Hill Polities

Perhaps not surprisingly given its imaginative power, elements of the European discourse about the hills as places of legal primitivism found

[14] I am adapting here Hulsebosch's argument, in *Constituting Empire*, about the influence of imperial legal politics on the emergence of a new kind of constitutional law in eighteenth-century New York. For a discussion of global parallels to the scenario described in Hulsebosch, see Benton, "Constitutions and Empires."

their way into European colonial settings from the sixteenth century on. They also became intertwined with problems of sovereignty already present in Europe but exacerbated in the construction of colonial rule. Discourse about hill peoples fit within a broader set of questions about the definition of civility, debates about whether "barbarians" held natural rights, and controversies over the moral and legal foundations for conquest. Writings about such issues generated speculation about the qualities of small polities and their preservation as semiautonomous units within empire.

Precedents for associating the hills with political isolation and conflict were easy to find. Spanish conquistadors and officials could draw on relatively fresh anxieties about the Alpujarras, the mountains south of Granada, as a preserve of unconverted and politically dangerous Moors. The rebellions at the turn of the sixteenth century reinforced the fear that the mountains harbored a permanent "fifth column" of unbelievers, a worry that continued right up until the expulsion of the Moriscos that began in 1609. England on the eve of imperial expansion had its own "magic" hill regions, a Celtic fringe regarded by London elites as a sphere of cultural and legal primitiveness. Giraldus Cambrensis's influential *Topography of Ireland* (1188) characterized Ireland as a place of anarchy where "every one may do just as he pleases."[15] Subsequent chroniclers lumped together inhabitants of Ireland, the Anglo-Scottish border region, and the Scottish Highlands and islands as barbarous peoples, naturally resistant to agriculture and government. Writing in the late fourteenth century, John of Fordun echoed widely circulated views in portraying Scots highlanders and islanders as belonging to "a savage and untamed nation, rude and independent... hostile to the English people and language... and exceedingly cruel."[16]

Associating the plains and high plateaus with civility, royal control, and church authority, while painting the highlands as places good for sheltering heretics and forming horizontal solidarities, matched a broader

[15] Andrew Hadfield and John McVeagh, *Strangers to That Land: British Perceptions of Ireland from the Reformation to the Famine* (Gerrards Cross, U.K.: Colin Smythe, 1994), 29, and see 7, 25.

[16] Jane H. Ohlmeyer, "'Civilizinge of those Rude Partes': Colonization within Britain and Ireland, 1580s–1640s," *The Oxford History of the British Empire, Volume I: The Origins of Empire* (Oxford: 1998), 124–147, ed. Nicholas P. Canny (Oxford: Oxford University Press, 1998), 131. Ohlmeyer gives an excellent overview of this discourse in the seventeenth century. Schama traces its continuation in the eighteenth century, linking an "eighteenth-century obsession with primitive virtue" to representations of Alpine herdsmen as "primitive democrats." Schama, *Landscape and Memory* (New York: Vintage, 1995), 479–80.

understanding of the town as a marker of civility.[17] This idea had classical and medieval roots and was reinforced especially in the Iberian reconquest, when Christian rule advanced through a pattern of founding towns and endowing them with ruling councils and law codes (*fueros*). In England, the marches were associated with wildness and lawlessness, and in England and France, garrisons or bastides dotted volatile territories and sharply distinguished the order within from surrounding expanses beyond their control. Such arrangements were legally different in important ways; in Roman administration, towns with municipal councils exercised jurisdiction within their walls and in surrounding areas that might include hamlets and villages, whereas garrisons operated within a military hierarchy and had less expansive legal prerogatives. But the strategies were spatially similar in their effects: the creation of uneven borderlands where a series of enclaves shaped concentric zones, rather than a moving line, marking the advance of royal, military, or state control.[18]

This contrast between the town or garrison and the surrounding countryside found visible expression in Renaissance town views contrasting the angular streets and buildings of the foreground with the distant backdrop of undulating hills. The mere presence of the town implied the domestication of the hills, which in most of these images appeared as unthreatening, even bucolic. The imagination of a tamed nature in the service of the town also worked its way into chorography, and into descriptions of ideal town sites that positioned forests and hills as resources for settlements. This convention was easily transposed to representations of colonial towns, though with a noticeable shift toward depicting mountains more frequently as wild regions beyond the domesticated spaces of towns and harbors (see Figure 5.1). In Spanish America, the gridiron of newly founded towns came to be even more sharply distinguished from the surrounding countryside, often represented in early colonial maps in the pictographic style of indigenous mapping as a cluster of discrete hills.[19] Despite a different legal status for towns in New England and

[17] The correlate image in classical thought was one of the heights as a zone associated with the sacred origins of life and a place of communication with the divine world. On "mountain sacredness," see Schama, *Landscape and Memory*, 408. And see María Eugenia Petit-Breuilh Sepúlveda, *Naturaleza y desastres en Hispanoamérica: La visión de los indígenas* (Madrid: Sílex, 2006), 77.

[18] Kagan and Marías, *Urban Images*, 26–7. Topographical differences matched this pattern unevenly because advance garrisons and captured towns were themselves often situated on hills in command of coveted valleys.

[19] On hybrid styles of mapping this distinction, see Kagan and Marías, *Urban Images*, 14. On hybrid styles more generally, and pictographic representations of hills, see Mundy, *Mapping of New Spain*.

FIGURE 5.1. Port Called Nombre de Dios (c. 1590). This image from the so-called Drake Manuscript (*Histoire naturelle des Indes*) contrasts the domesticated space of the harbor and port with the wild mountains behind. Pierpont Morgan Library, New York. MA 3900, fol. 97. The caption (part of which is visible here) emphasizes this distinction, noting that the port "is located in a mountainous region where the air is heavy and unhealthy and the Spaniard cannot live there for a long time." (Text in translation from Pierpont Morgan Library, *Histoire naturelle des Indes: The Drake Manuscript in the Pierpont Morgan Library.* [New York: W.W. Norton, 1996], 266.)

Virginia, and a greater emphasis on dispersed settlement as the pattern best suited to the extension of agriculture, towns in British North America were also depicted as bastions of civility in the midst of politically volatile and dangerous backcountry.[20] Views of trading posts and garrisons marked town space off from surrounding countryside even more sharply by fortifications encircling enclaves of European rule.

Such imagery was connected with Europeans' assertions of Roman analogies in describing overseas colonization. In New World chronicles in particular, Roman comparisons were invoked partly to highlight the military prowess of European forces – a rhetorical strategy of "besting the ancients" – and partly as shorthand references to the contrast between the civility of Europeans with the barbarity of Indians. Yet Roman analogies were applied flexibly.[21] A common trope was the representation of Indians as having some of the qualities and virtues of early Iberians or ancient Britons before the conquest by Rome.[22] This analogy permitted critics of the treatment of Indians in the Spanish empire to merge historical revisionism – disdain for Rome as a symbol of tyranny – with an argument against classifying Indians as barbarians.[23]

The Spanish debate about dominion in the Indies has received much attention by historians, and I need not outline the various positions taken here.[24] Significant for our purposes is the connection between Roman analogies and the representation of some places and peoples in the New World as practicing forms of political association that fell between wildness and *policía*, a term referring to a congeries of qualities associated with civility. Comparing Indians to early Iberians (and ancient Britons)

[20] See the introduction and chap. 1 of Evan Haefeli and Kevin Sweeney, *Captors and Captives: The 1704 French and Indian Raid on Deerfield* (Amherst: University of Massachusetts Press, 2003).

[21] On "besting the ancients," see David A. Lupher, *Romans in a New World: Classical Models in Sixteenth-Century Spanish America* (Ann Arbor: University of Michigan Press, 2003), chap. 1.

[22] Lupher, *Romans in a New World*, chap. 1; Ohlmeyer, "Civilizinge of those Rude Partes"; Sabine MacCormack, *On the Wings of Time: Rome, the Incas, Spain, and Peru* (Princeton, NJ: Princeton University Press, 2007), Pagden, *Lords of All the World*, chap. 1.

[23] Lupher, *Romans in a New World*, 219.

[24] For useful overviews, see Colin M. MacLachlan, *Spain's Empire in the New World: The Role of Ideas in Institutional and Social Change* (Berkeley: University of California Press, 1988); James Muldoon, *The Americas in the Spanish World Order: The Justification for Conquest in the Seventeenth Century* (Philadelphia: University of Pennsylvania Press, 1994); and Anthony Pagden, *Spanish Imperialism and the Political Imagination: Studies in European and Spanish-American Social and Political Theory, 1513–1830* (New Haven, CT: Yale University Press, 1990).

involved extolling a specific set of traits, many of them positive: bravery, martial skills, and governance through flexible forms of political mobilization.[25] Even for writers less insistent than Las Casas that Indians were not "barbarians," such positive qualities, together with evidence of orderly governance, raised the challenge of characterizing the legal status of Indians. They appeared not so enlightened as sixteenth-century Christian Spaniards but at least as civilized as their forbears.[26] In describing Indians' level of civility, Spanish chroniclers found especially useful the late medieval notion of *behetría*, a term from the thirteenth century that referred to a corporate community holding the prerogative to select its own lord, one who then occupied a nonheritable position. The label seemed apt to describe the practice in some New World Indian communities of creating temporary political and military leaders, mainly in time of war. Juan de Acosta, for example, wrote in his *Historia natural y moral de las Indias* (1589): "In this way is governed most of the New World, where there are no kingdoms founded or republics established, no known dynasties of princes or kings, though there are some lords and leaders who are like knights advantaged more than commoners."[27]

Matching topographical distinctions with degrees of civility in New World societies was a tricky exercise.[28] Spaniards encountered the most

[25] Although the parallel was also framed in negative terms, as when Las Casas argued that the barbarism of early Iberians was "much worse" than that of the indigenous inhabitants of New Spain. See Lupher, *Romans in a New World*, 219.

[26] Spanish observers understood that the conquest itself had pushed some Indians into remote and dispersed settlements. López de Velasco in his 1574 *Geografía y descripción universal de las Indias*, for example, theorized that the conquest had destroyed towns and caused Indians to become "scattered in the wild and in the most rugged places," where they lived "without government." Juan López de Velasco, *Geografía y descripción universal de las Indias*, ed. Marco Jiménez de la Espada (Madrid: Atlas, 1971), 73. Traveling into northern New Spain toward the end of his sojourn across North America, Cabeza de Vaca reported seeing Indians who "went hidden through the mountains, fleeing to avoid being killed or made slaves by the Christians." Quoted in Adorno, *The Polemics of Possession*, 263. The policy of *reducciones*, or forced settlement of Indians in towns, was designed to bring Indians under Spanish authority and missionary influence.

[27] José de Acosta, *Historia natural y moral de las Indias* (Madrid: Historia 16, 1987), 405. My translation. On *behetría*, see Harald Braun, *Juan de Mariana and Early Modern Spanish Political Thought* (Burlington, VT: Ashgate, 2007), 36. For another Spanish chronicler's use of the term, see MacCormack, *On the Wings of Time*, 90, 184, 207.

[28] Spaniards were clearly aware of Indians' own sets of associations with highland regions. Chroniclers describe local rituals showing a regard for mountains, especially volcanoes, as sacred places inhabited by divine figures and characterized by cosmic struggles between opposite forces (fire and ice, air and earth, hot and cold). Petit-Breuilh Sepúlveda notes a striking homology between this "cult of the heights" ("el culto de las alturas") in the

powerful New World polities in the Mexican highlands and the Andes. Still, entrenched ideas about rough highlanders could be put to work. Acosta described the Chichimecas as the "oldest and first inhabitants" of New Spain and suggested that they had always preferred the remote mountains and continued to live "in the most rugged and the thickest parts of the sierra." Indians living *en behetría* inhabited settled communities and were at least amenable to civilizing forces.[29] Both groups had "left the best and most fertile land unpopulated," so when agricultural Indians from the north moved in, they were able to settle in and cultivate the high plains.[30] This narrative neatly merged the bits of information Spaniards possessed about the history of the central valley of Mexico with classical and medieval notions of the link between settlement and civility. Encounters in the Andes inspired slightly different Roman analogies. The Incas themselves were compared to Romans, and their rule over surrounding communities, small polities in what later became Colombia and Ecuador, here also described as more primitive (but not wholly barbarous) *behetrías*, was seen as analogous to Roman imperium.[31] Placing the Incas at the top of a hierarchy of Indians with lesser or greater degrees of *policía* did not turn the topographic hierarchy on its head. The more Hispanized coastal areas of Peru continued to be contrasted to the mountainous regions, seen as less susceptible to Spanish cultural influences and more protective of indigenous forms of law and justice.[32]

Spanish commentators regarded war as perhaps the natural tendency of small, splintered polities. Writing about the Araucanians, who launched a successful revolt against Spanish rule in Chile in the mid-sixteenth century, Gerónimo de Vivar commented that they "had from ancient times engaged in wars against each other, for they were all divided into factions, one group of lords fighting another."[33] In the view of Spanish writers, the continual warfare had produced some positive effects, in particular leading to the consolidation of Incan rule.[34] The Araucanians were

Americas and European mythic associations with mountains. On all these points, see Petit-Breuilh Sepúlveda, *Naturaleza y desastres*, 77–80.

[29] Acosta, *Historia natural*, 438–9. My translation.

[30] Acosta, *Historia natural*, 441. My translation.

[31] See MacCormack, *On the Wings of Time*, 90, 184, 207.

[32] This pattern matched linguistic differences between Pacific coastal areas where the conquest brought the greatest change and Andean regions where Quechua and Aymara continued to dominate. MacCormack, *On the Wings of Time*, 19.

[33] Gerónimo de Vivar, *Crónica y relación copiosa y verdadera de los Reinos de Chile* (1558), quoted in Lupher, *Romans in a New World*, 309.

[34] Lupher, *Romans in a New World*, 91.

lauded for their "great tenacity and determination" as they "defended their lands against such fierce enemies as are the Spaniards."[35] It was hard to let go of the notion that some Indians possessed a deeply politically conditioned tendency to embrace violence. In the late eighteenth century, even as Indians across the Andes engaged in multiforum legal appeals to oppose excessive tribute exactions, colonial officials portrayed them as rebels seeking to unseat Spanish authority and "live without any subjection whatsoever, as is their natural propensity."[36]

This narrative of small, warlike Indian polities and peoples in perpetual conflict played on Roman themes while also offering support for one argument for the legitimacy of Spanish rule. Just as the Romans had, according to Francisco de Vitoria, "come into possession of the world" by "right of war," Spaniards had been justified in the conquest because they had come to the aid of one or another of the continually warring factions.[37] Las Casas developed a similar view in defending the Spaniards' legitimate intervention in Mexico as allies of the Tlaxcalans. He also went further in arguing that the Indians could withhold consent to Spanish rule. He distinguished, in other words, between the "universal imperial jurisdiction" awarded by the pope to the Spanish kings and "the power of exercising supreme jurisdiction" that would follow from Indian consent.[38] Some historians emphasize the novelty of this formulation as an expression of the idea of individually held natural rights.[39] It certainly reflected widely circulating ideas about the nature of small polities nominally within but effectively outside the orbit of Spanish rule.

Spanish commentators were uncomfortable about the implied recognition of the limits to Spanish sovereignty in the New World. As James Muldoon has shown, when the seventeenth century brought the more urgent threat of competing claims by other European empires, leading jurists reverted to the argument that the legitimacy of the Spanish

[35] This is from Ercilla's epic poem *La araucana*, from a passage translated and quoted in Lupher, *Romans in a New World*, 359n17.

[36] Quoted in Serulnikov, *Subverting Colonial Authority*, 134. Serulnikov's book chronicles Indian legal strategies before and during the Bourbon reforms.

[37] Vitoria is quoted by Lupher, *Romans in a New World*, 73. Vitoria even argued that because the Indians possessed natural rights, including the right to self-defense, and no one could renounce such rights, the Spanish could intervene to protect victims of human sacrifices or cannibalism even without being asked. Brian Tierney, *The Idea of Natural Rights: Studies on Natural Rights, Natural Law, and Church Law, 1150–1625* (Grand Rapids, MI: William B. Eerdmans, 2001), 281.

[38] Tierney, *Idea of Natural Rights*, 283–4.

[39] For a compelling argument of this interpretation, see Tierney, *Idea of Natural Rights*, 283–7.

conquest rested on the papal donation.[40] This renewed effort to simplify the basis for Spanish rule battled both empirical evidence of the uneven reach of Spanish authority and the long tradition of multiple and conflicting definitions of imperium: as a composite political community and as a single realm.[41] The discourse about the archaic nature of New World societies defined such polities as lying within the empire but spatially and also metaphorically placed them on its precarious margins. Though sustained by Roman analogies, this formulation depended on an understanding of early modern empire as a different sort of construct than the Roman empire, with its pretense to world dominion. Now the application of *ius gentium* implied the existence of multiple polities inside the empire that retained in different degrees some measure of formally recognized authority in relation to sovereign power.

I do not want to assert that the history of layered or uneven sovereignty in empire depended on the discourse about the backwardness of remote hill regions. Nor do I want to suggest that this trope transferred without change across continents and centuries. But it is useful to see that references to primitive sovereignty in remote hill regions packed a certain symbolic punch within broader debates about the structure and legitimacy of imperial rule. European observers of empire and colonial officials cited Roman precedents and drew from similar late medieval imagery contrasting markers of civility with symbols of wildness. They both admired and feared quick mobilizations under leaders who seemed to rise from nowhere. And they preserved prejudices about hill regions as places of imperfect rule, semicivility, and peculiar virtues. We see these influences in anxieties about hill regions as places of refuge from New World slavery, when, in Jamaica, Brazil, New Spain, and elsewhere, maroons used topography to their advantage in protecting communities of runaway slaves. We see them later, too, in French pronouncements about the differences between lowland Arabs and highland Kabyles in Algeria, and in Portuguese and Brazilian worries about the political volatility of the nineteenth-century *sertão*.[42] The associations surfaced once again in the

[40] Muldoon, in *The Americas in the Spanish World Order*, outlines in detail the arguments of Juan de Solórzano. Solórzano understood that the approach of Las Casas, as well as that of his rival Sepúlveda, who argued that the barbarous nature of the Indians created the right of a civilized people to rule them, could easily be adopted by other European empires in support of their own competing claims.

[41] Pagden, *Lords of All the World*, 17.

[42] French officials noted the Kabyles' aggressiveness but saw it as fundamentally different from that of Arabs because the Kabyles were violent in self-defense. They also speculated on the similarities and possible shared origins of Kabyle law with Roman law. See Patricia M. E. Lorcin, *Imperial Identities: Stereotyping, Prejudice and Race in Colonial Algeria*

construction of a British imperial army featuring "martial races" originating mainly in highland regions and mobilized especially in the defense of the contested mountains of Central Asia.[43] Ideas about the legal, martial, and political characteristics of mountain peoples were also reproduced in the nascent field of human geography in efforts to create a typology of societies formed in response to geographic conditions.[44] Then again in the late nineteenth century, ideas about the legal primitivism of hill country would enter into the center of debates about international law and its applications in empire. One problem was very old: how to incorporate in empire polities sitting both within and without the imperial legal order. The political conditions of empire and the emerging model of global governance would suggest different solutions from those of the sixteenth century. Familiar tropes about ancient practices in high places would inform new strategies for reconciling part sovereignties and expansive imperial authority.

Inventing Quasi-Sovereignty

International lawyers in the second half of the nineteenth century embraced an emerging model of an international legal community composed of states recognized as "civilized" by the societies already considered members of the international community.[45] Efforts to fix a

(London: I. B. Tauris, 1999), especially chaps. 1 and 7. And another example: the Brazilian *sertão* was not just the dry backcountry; it was a region of low hills. Coastal elites labeled the region as one of barbarism, where inhabitants "neither recognized nor obeyed" the laws. Robert M. Levine, *Vale of Tears: Revisiting the Canudos Massacre in Northeastern Brazil, 1893–1897* (Berkeley: University of California Press, 1995), 79–80, 152.

43 This project brought together metropolitan and colonial discourses by joining representations of Scottish highlanders, Sikhs, and Gurkhas. It drew on older ideas about highlanders and modified them, for example in portraying these groups as especially loyal to the imperial state. Streets traces the direct relation between this developing discourse and interimperial competition for the control of Afghanistan. Streets, *Martial Races*, 146–7.

44 Writing in 1911 in a work aimed at advancing a system of "anthropo-geography" developed by Friedrich Ratzel, Ellen Churchill Semple touches on all the themes discussed in this section in relation to mountain communities, including the fierceness of "highland warfare," their tendency toward "political dismemberment" into "minute mountain states," their role in relation to the plains as "asylums of refuge for displaced peoples," and their status as "museums of social antiquities." Ellen Churchill Semple, *Influences of Geographic Environment, on the Basis of Ratzel's System of Anthropo-Geography* (New York: H. Holt, 1911), 590, 593, 595, 599.

45 See Gerrit W. Gong, *The Standard of "Civilization" in International Society* (New York: Oxford University Press, 1984). See also Martti Koskenniemi, *The Gentle Civilizer of*

classification system encountered the problem of how to characterize a dependent imperial subpolity that was "outside the scope of law and yet within it, lacking international capacity and yet necessarily possessing it."[46] Two solutions emerged. One was descriptive; states could be placed along a continuum stretching from, at one end, American federalism as a case in which states had retained significant jurisdictional prerogatives but could not engage in foreign policy to, at the other end, polities with some measure of control over external sovereignty such as the German states under the Holy Roman Empire; Tunis in relation to France; Zanzibar under the protection of England; and the tributary polities of the Mughal and Chinese empires. Indian princely states fell somewhere in the middle of this continuum.[47] The other solution was to apply international law by analogy to systems of imperial subpolities.[48] These states could be understood as relating to one another and at times to the imperial power in the same way as nation-states in the international order, with the difference that the imperial government possessed legal hegemony as the dominant political entity. In this sense, imperial administration represented a perfected international order, one without the Austinian problem of the absence of an overarching legal authority.[49] The international

Nations: The Rise and Fall of International Law, 1870–1960 (Cambridge: Cambridge University Press, 2005).

[46] Anghie, *Making of International Law*, 81.

[47] These examples are all provided by Westlake, in L. Oppenheim, ed., *The Collected Papers of John Westlake on Public International Law* (Cambridge: Cambridge University Press, 1914), 88–9, 182, 198.

[48] See Westlake's statement on international law by analogy, for example. Oppenheim, *Collected Papers*, 232.

[49] To a certain extent, this position also emerged out of the writings of imperial administrators. We see it foreshadowed in early nineteenth-century writings on the subsidiary alliance system in India. Wellesley, for example, noted in 1804 that British military power sustained by subsidiary forces in Indian states and supplemented by British political pressures enabled "the British power to control the causes of... internal warfare" and to guarantee to each state "the unmolested exercise of its separate authority within the limits of its established dominion, under the general protection of the British power." "Letter to the Secret Committee of the Court of Directors," extracted in S. V. Desika Char, *Readings in the Constitutional History of India, 1757–1947* (Delhi: Oxford University Press, 1983), 191–2. This view generalized the terms of treaties between the East India Company and the larger Indian states. The treaties took the form of agreements between independent states and emphasized the commitment of both sides to "mutual defence and protection against all enemies" while also committing the Indian ruler, "in the event of any differences arising," to accept "whatever adjustment" was decided on by the "Company's Government" after it weighed "matters in the scale of truth and justice." "Treaty of General Defensive Alliance Concluded by the Company with the Nizam of Hyderabad, 12 October 1800," in Desika Char, *Readings*,

community gave some recognition to such "protected" states as having international personality – or control over external sovereignty – even though they clearly had only limited capacity to form international relations.[50] Neither of these solutions, of course, truly disposed of the legal challenges posed by quasi-sovereignty. As Antony Anghie has observed, it was unclear how polities that possessed and yet did not possess sovereignty fit within a schema pairing degrees of civilization with graduated membership in international society.[51] And rendering empire as a kind of international system begged the question of when and where, and in the interests of whom and what, it was permissible to subvert treaties, suspend law, or otherwise ignore agreements between states in the imperial system.

The Indian princely states appeared to occupy a special place in these debates. These states comprised areas that had never come under the direct control of the British government, and they numbered in the hundreds – various estimates over a fifty-year period placed the number of states at 693, 620, and 562, covering an area larger than one-third of the region and encompassing about a quarter of its population.[52] The states

189–92. For similar treaties from this period, see C. U. Aitchison, ed., *A Collection of Treaties, Engagements, and Sunnuds, Relating to India and Neighboring Countries [1862–1865]* (Calcutta: Printed by G. A. Savielle and P. M. Cranenburgh, Bengal Print, 1865).

[50] Another point of comparison was extraterritoriality, specifically claims to jurisdiction over Europeans resident in foreign nations. Extraterritorial claims by Europeans in the Ottoman Empire, China, and elsewhere in the long nineteenth century influenced thinking about quasi-sovereignty, but the parallel was not perfect. In most such cases, territorial enclaves were defined as having European or mixed jurisdiction; they were not native territories of quasi-sovereign status within areas of direct colonial rule. On extraterritoriality, see Benton, *Law and Colonial Cultures*, chap. 6. And see especially the interesting study by Mary Lewis of jurisdictional politics involving imperial subjects in Tunisia at the turn of the twentieth century. Lewis moves beyond traditional approaches to extraterritoriality in analyzing a complex legal politics linking imperial rivalry, strategic claims to nationality by subjects crossing imperial borders, and shifting definitions of Tunisian sovereignty. "Geographies of Power: The Tunisian Civic Order, Jurisdictional Politics, and Imperial Rivalry in the Mediterranean, 1881–1935," *The Journal of Modern History* 80 (December, 2008): 791–830.

[51] Anghie, in *Making of International Law*, notes that the problem "was never satisfactorily denied or resolved" (81).

[52] An estimate produced by a retired deputy surveyor general in 1833 calculated that the area of native states with treaties of alliance with the British covered a little more than 41 percent of the territory of the raj. Barbara N. Ramusack, *The Indian Princes and Their States* (Cambridge: Cambridge University Press, 2004), 52–3. A report for the government of India in 1875 estimated that the states covered more than 590,000 square miles with nearly 56 million inhabitants (Political and Secret Department, "Indian Native States Approximate Area, Population, Revenue, and Military Force," May, 1875; IOR

seemed to international lawyers to represent an intermediate case in the continuum from subordinate society to semiautonomous and potentially independent state. They retained significant control over internal affairs while being stripped of rights to engage in foreign relations. Their regulation seemed to belong to the realm of imperial administration rather than international law. Yet, even for John Westlake, who asserted that by the 1890s the basis of rule over Indian states had completed the shift "from an international to an imperial basis," international law continued to have the power of analogy.[53] Arguing that the imperial power only appeared to share sovereignty with the princely states but also trying to account for the continued deference to aspects of Indian state sovereignty, Westlake remarked that equating the states with "the dominions of the Queen" and regarding their subjects as holding a status analogous to that of the queen's subjects represented "niceties of speech handed down from other days and now devoid of international significance." It might be politically expedient to make comparisons "for purposes internal to the empire," but such comparisons should be regarded as legal fictions.[54]

Westlake drew support for his position from British colonial officials' accounts of legal relations with the Indian states, but he drew very selectively on this record. He suggested, for example, that it was a matter of settled law from 1857 on that the subjects of Indian princely states were British subjects.[55] Westlake argued, too, that although the power of the executive and the application of imperial legislation were constrained inside native states, they were in theory unlimited. Whenever necessary, the imperial power could enact legislation – as it had in the case of control of the slave trade – that would apply across the empire. Westlake acknowledged that the intricacies of sovereignty in native states had "at

L/PS/18/D). In 1909, the *Imperial Gazetteer of India* counted 693 states (Ramusack, p. 2). By 1929, in part as a result the consolidation of smaller states, a process approved by the larger states in order to secure their political influence and restrict membership in the Chamber of Princes, the estimated number was 562. L. F. Rushbrook Williams, *The British Crown and the Indian States: An Outline Sketch Drawn up on Behalf of the Standing Committee of the Chamber of Princes by the Directorate of the Chamber's Special Organisation* (London: P. S. King and Son, 1929).

[53] Oppenheim, *Collected Papers*, 232.

[54] Oppenheim, *Collected Papers*, 220.

[55] More precisely, Westlake thought that this principle had been proved by the Baroda case discussed in this paper because the British had asserted their right to "try" an Indian prince. The British execution of the brother of the ruler of Manipur in 1891 for leading the revolt that placed his brother in power was regarded by Westlake as confirmation that not just rulers but also the inhabitants of Indian princely states were British subjects. See Oppenheim, *Collected Papers*, "The Indian Empire," 222–3.

times perplexed the men who with high education and great practical ability have moulded that empire," but he also thought that the attempts to delineate the legal puzzles of Indian states had probably been "needlessly intricate."[56] There was nothing especially complex about a growing and, he thought, irreversible, imperial power.

The progression of British power in India seemed to Westlake to parallel territorial consolidation. Imperial authority had spread to the interior of India from coastal enclaves at Bombay, Madras, and Calcutta, gradually to overtake the plains and then, finally, the mountain regions.[57] This progression was emblematic of a general process of naturally expansive imperial influence that could be measured by the spread of imperial jurisdiction: "It is true that in inland places there may be a greater difficulty of maintaining effective jurisdiction than on the coast," Westlake wrote, but as communications and settlement progressed, "the means of government will advance with parallel steps."[58] The shifting of law in India "from an international to an imperial basis" depended on the gradual formation of a single legal framework for territory.

Westlake's account shows a set of wider assumptions at work about the linked processes of expanding imperial legal authority and the formation of Indian national space. As Goswami has shown, at the same time that the political imagination of a national territory was forming out of a complex array of transnational processes, uneven capitalist change continued to create territorial unevenness.[59] Other territorial anomalies were meanwhile being produced by imperial legal politics. The Indian national imaginary did not immediately occlude what Cooper has called "the imperatives of thinking like an empire."[60] The impulse to claim

[56] Oppenheim, *Collected Papers*, 223, 232.

[57] Oppenheim, *Collected Papers*, 215.

[58] John Westlake, "Territorial Sovereignty, Especially with Relation to Uncivilized Regions," in Oppenheim, *Collected Papers*, 186. In relying heavily on Lee-Warner's account of the history of British relations with Indian princely states, Westlake would have also been influenced by Lee-Warner's representation as the princely states as islands of territory left over from an imperial push from the coasts. The "ring-fence" policy of the early raj had promoted the autonomy of Indian states as buffer zones responsible for their own protection on the edges of British-controlled districts. As British influence advanced from the coasts, Indian state territories were encircled. See Lee-Warner, *Protected Princes of India.*

[59] Goswami, however, emphasizes territorial consolidation. Manu Goswami, *Producing India: From Colonial Economy to National Space* (Chicago: University of Chicago Press, 2004).

[60] Frederick Cooper, *Colonialism in Question: Theory, Knowledge, History* (Berkeley: University of California Press, 2005), 189.

territorial sovereignty over bounded space occurred alongside the imperial project of devising a system of territorial differentiation recognizing degrees of sovereignty for colonial enclaves. Quasi-sovereignty came to be defined as a coherent system at precisely the same time that imperial legal politics revealed it to be unworkable. Driving this contradiction were repeating legal conflicts blurring the boundaries between internal and external sovereignty in colonial enclaves: border disputes, jurisdictional tangles, and controversies about the application of imperial legislation. In critical moments when the messy legal politics defied administrative ordering and confused categories of sovereignty, political interventions trumped legal rules. The result was more than a gap between theory and practice. The core characteristics of systems of divided sovereignty came to be the occasional outright suspension of law.

British musings about the distinctive qualities of hill regions contributed to this process. Hill regions had no cultural uniformity and spread from the foothills of the Himalayas to the interior of southern India. British observers insisted on cataloging similarities arising from the contrast of these regions with the plains. Writings about the hills were infused with "nostalgic intent" and evoked images of an English past of simpler village life. The hills were also seen as an antidote to the politically and physically degraded environment of the plains.[61] These associations were partly the basis for James Tod's identification of the Rajput polities as examples of European feudalism in an influential report for the East India Company published as *Annals and Antiquities of Rathast'han* in 1823. The "feudal" label would prove somewhat controversial among British officials, but the idea matched a more general discourse about the hills as places relatively protected from the influences of sequential invaders, both Mughal and Maratha. Elphinstone's 1821 *Report on the Territories Conquered from the Paishwa*, for example, describes the "grand geographical feature" of western India as the "chain of ghauts" transecting the region from north to south. Offering the Bhils as an example, Elphinstone contrasted the unruly inhabitants of the hills with the "sober, frugal, industrious" peasants of the plain who were more vulnerable to the oppression by "coarse, ignorant, rapacious and oppressive" Maratha rulers. Yet Elphinstone did not condemn Maratha rule, mainly because the government's corruption left subjects "the means of procuring [justice] for themselves." Hill regions especially benefited from being left alone. A British policy of imitating "the Native system" and acting

[61] Kennedy, *Magic Mountains*, 3.

only to remove obvious sources of corruption would, he argued, allow legal change to continue to occur slowly, permitting the development of society "to keep pace with that of the laws."[62] This account, and others like it, combined an image of remote regions as pristine and primitive with the view that the British should emulate Indian political models and encourage – through contained conflict – a natural progression toward a more advanced legal order. The hills were seen as naturally chaotic because of their division into petty states. Yet they were also imagined as peculiarly suited to imperial government because conflict, combined with primitive forms of sovereignty, supposedly made the states amenable to rule by a paramount power.

This pairing of legal evolution and legal geography received careful elaboration by a handful of officials in the Foreign Office within the British government of India, a colonial project energetically pursued between 1870 and the end of the century.[63] The Foreign Office was responsible for the relations between the British government of India with Afghanistan, the Persian Gulf states, and Burma, as well as with the numerous "Native States" of India.[64] With very little coastal land, the territories of native states interrupted or partially surrounded districts claimed under direct British administration. Some of the princely states – Hyderabad and Mysore, to name just two – were large and politically formidable, a condition that makes the discourse about native states as small and scattered hill polities all the more notable. The problem of defining the sovereign status of the states fell to Foreign Office officials, who sought to deduce from the mass of records of treaties, legal conflicts, and political crises a comprehensive doctrine of what was labeled "political law" and the foundations of a branch of Indian constitutionalism. This effort has been treated somewhat peripherally by historians, in part

[62] Mountstuart Elphinstone, *Territories Conquered from the Paishwa; a Report* (Delhi: Oriental Publishers, 1973), 1, 8, 7, 87, 94; James Tod, *Annals and Antiquities of Rajast'han, or the Central and Western Rajpoot States of India* (London: Smith, 1829).

[63] Throughout this chapter, when I use the phrase "government of India," I will be referring to the British government of India, the highest administrative authority of the British in India.

[64] Sir Charles Aitchison led attempts to centralize foreign affairs in the hands of the government of India in Calcutta as foreign secretary between 1870 and 1877. He succeeded in placing Zanzibar and the Persian Gulf under the Foreign Office, while the government of Bombay retained oversight of Sind, Upper Sind, Baluchistan, and Khelat. See I. F. S. Copland, "The Baroda Crisis of 1873–77: A Study in Government Rivalry," *Modern Asian Studies* 2, no. 2 (1968), 97–123.

because the princely states were quickly and clearly made subordinate to the British.[65] Many of the princes were key allies of the British during the 1857 rebellion – as Lord Canning famously put it, they were the "breakwaters" of the wave of rebellion that swept the region – and post-1857 policy toward the states was influenced by the evident desire by most princes and British officials to preserve a close political alliance. But the record of relations between the British and the native princes is hardly one of simple accommodation and collaboration. Nor was the project of systematizing the legal administration of empire an easy exercise. Most of the tensions surrounding the legal and political status of the princely states were never in fact resolved, and they emerged directly from conflicts and cases that often opposed princely and imperial authority. Further, the conflicts, and the debates they engendered, directly influenced broader definitions of British Indian rule. In particular, the anomalous legal situation of princely territories informed distinctions among other British Indian territories. Beyond British-Indian relations, the conflicts connected to debates about the relation between imperial and international law, and the nature of indirect rule.

An interesting window into the development of British legal policy toward princely states is provided by the writings of Sir Charles Lewis Tupper, an official in the British Punjab government from 1890 to 1899 and later a member of the Viceroy's Council. Tupper wrote both a general treatise on Indian "protectorates" and a four-volume report intended to

[65] The best comprehensive history of the Indian princely states is by Ramusack (*The Indian Princes and Their States*), who correctly notes the "muddled tedium" of most histories of the princely states (2). Ramusack provides a brief overview of efforts of colonial officials to produce what she calls "bureaucratic codifications" of relations with princely states (92–8). Another valuable study of indirect rule and the residency system is Michael Herbert Fisher, *Indirect Rule in India: Residents and the Residency System, 1764–1858* (New York: Oxford University Press, 1998). Fisher's study ends before the period covered here but shows that British thinking about paramountcy was well developed before the mid-nineteenth century and featured earlier the idea of preserving domestic sovereignty while removing sovereignty beyond the borders of dependent polities. Yet before 1858, Fisher observes, wide divisions of opinion about indirect rule were evident, and there was "inconsistent development of official British policy with respect to sovereignty" (13). On the careers of officials of the Foreign Office, see William Murray Hogben, "The Foreign and Political Department of the Government of India, 1876–1919: A Study in Imperial Careers and Attitudes" (Ph.D. diss., University of Toronto, 1973). For an interesting legal case involving an Indian prince that reveals a certain reverence in popular culture in Bengal for petty princes in the early twentieth century, see Partha Chatterjee, *A Princely Impostor? The Strange and Universal History of the Kumar of Bhawal* (Princeton, NJ: Princeton University Press, 2002).

serve as a manual on British law and policy toward the native states.[66] The report, published in 1895, built on the work of two officials of the Foreign Office: H. Mortimer Durand, the author of a volume of "leading cases" involving the governance of princely states, and Sir Charles Aitchison, who served as foreign secretary between 1870 and 1877. The report compiled multiple volumes of treaties, engagements, and sanads guiding relations of the government of India and the native states. Disagreements among these men and others within the Foreign Office were surprisingly minor. All endorsed the view that the relation between princely states and the British government should be regulated not according to international law or municipal law but through something that Tupper called "political law," the foundations of which were the doctrine of "divisible sovereignty" and "usage."[67]

For Tupper, drawing on Elphinstone's report, Sir Alfred Lyall's writings on Rajputana, and works by other British officials, including Henry Sumner Maine, renderings of both sovereignty and usage depended on understanding the history of hill regions. "Indian political law" as positive law had its roots in a pre-British Indian past, and in "the hills and comparatively inaccessible tracts left aside by successive streams of invasion."[68] Tupper identified these regions as comprising "the Punjab frontier, the Punjab hills, parts of Central and Southern India, and... nearly the whole of the country shown in the maps as belonging to native states."[69] The regions had preserved "a phase of sovereignty" that was "earlier than territorial sovereignty" and based on "tribal ownership of the soil."[70] Left to themselves, Tupper explained, the Indian rajas had historically shown a tendency "to range themselves, whether by compulsion or otherwise, under the hegemony of some paramount

[66] Charles Lewis Tupper, *Our Indian Protectorate. An Introduction to the Study of the Relations between the British Government and Its Indian Feudatories* (London: Longmans, 1893); Charles Lewis Tupper, ed., *Indian Political Practice: A Collection of the Decisions of the Government of India in Political Cases. Compiled by C. L. Tupper. [1895]* 4 vols. (Delhi: B. R. Publishing, 1974).

[67] The term *political* was to distinguish the action of officials with regard to native states from diplomacy, the term for dealings between sovereign states. Tupper, *Our Indian Protectorate*, 6. Tupper also rejects the term *international law*. The phrase "political law" is thus designed specifically to reflect the British control over the assignment of the attributes of sovereignty.

[68] On the "Indian past," see Tupper, *Our Indian Protectorate*, 9, 132.

[69] Tupper, *Our Indian Protectorate*, 131.

[70] Tupper, *Our Indian Protectorate*, 131, 167.

power."[71] In danger of imminent destruction by conquerors, the petty states were being rescued and preserved under British paramountcy.[72]

While emphasizing their basic similarities, Tupper also distinguished among different forms of primitive sovereignty in various hill regions. The states of Rajputana, for example, displayed a form of sovereignty defined as "midway between tribal chiefship and territorial chiefship," with those states closer to the plains and therefore more exposed to the Mughal and Maratha influences tending toward feudalism. In contrast, the highest regions of the Punjab hills represented "an earlier formation" of tribal suzerainties.[73] Yet none of the regions, even the cases approaching territorial sovereignty, could claim national territorial sovereignty, defined as a purely European construct distinguishing British from Indian conceptions of political community.

This understanding of sovereignty in hill regions fortified the argument that British rule was based on a political arrangement – paramountcy – which was in turn founded on prior, indigenous political forms. As Tupper put it, "Our present conception of an empire comprising districts under direct administration and dependent states held by subordinate or tributary chieftains is really indigenous."[74] This "native" construction of paramountcy was seen to be congruent with European understandings of limited sovereignty. Rather than signifying a quality that a state either possessed or failed to retain, sovereignty could be held by degrees, with full sovereignty reserved for the imperial power.[75]

[71] Tupper, *Our Indian Protectorate*, 143.

[72] Tupper, *Our Indian Protectorate*, 151.

[73] Tupper, *Our Indian Protectorate*, 147–8. Tupper is basing these observations on the work of Sir Alfred Lyall. Alfred Comyn Lyall, *Asiatic Studies, Religious and Social* (London: J. Murray, 1882). He quotes Lyall's characterization of the eastern portion of Rajputana as "rapidly sliding into the normal type of ordinary Oriental government, irresponsible personal despotism." Tupper, *Our Indian Protectorate*, 148.

[74] Tupper, *Our Indian Protectorate*, 153.

[75] In 1930, the rulers of native states turned this argument on its head, arguing that because sovereignty was divisible the princely states retained any trait of sovereignty that had not been formally ceded to the British. Similarly, members of the Chamber of Princes resolved that just because a particular right of a state was confirmed in a sanad issued by the government of India, this did not mean that the paramount power had created that right, only that it had recognized an existing right. K. M. Panikkar, *The Indian Princes in Council: A Record of the Chancellorship of His Highness, the Maharaja of Patiala, 1926–1931 and 1933–1936* (London: Oxford University Press, 1936). On Indian states' argument that they retained any right of sovereignty that had not been transferred, see Kadayam Ramachandra Ramabhadra Sastry, *Indian States and Responsible Government* (Allahabad: Allahabad Law Journal, 1939).

The notion of divisible sovereignty was articulated most clearly by Henry Sumner Maine, who proposed the idea in opposition to John Austin's definition of sovereignty as an attribute only of nation-states. It is helpful to understand this concept in the context of Maine's quasi-evolutionary understanding of legal development presented in *Ancient Law*, "the only legal best seller" of the century.[76] The best-known element of this work is Maine's thesis that law in society progressed "from status to contract," but the mechanisms for historical changes in law described by Maine were both more complex and vaguer than this phrase implies.[77] In Maine's view, legal evolution occurred in response to, and in harmony with, changing social conditions, but the speed and direction of change were not inevitable. Jurists had a special responsibility to adjust law in ways that would encourage gradual change, a task possible only through appreciation of the historical basis for existing law. Maine's thought came to have more than a theoretical connection to imperial policy when he went to India in 1862 – a year after the publication of *Ancient Law* – to serve as law member of the Governor General's Council. He wrote a series of minutes in India that profoundly influenced officials in the Foreign Office formulating Indian political law. Aspects of Tupper's approach to Indian sovereignty precisely imitated Maine's historical jurisprudence. Maine came to argue that the British had a responsibility to guide the speed of legal and political development in India so that it was neither too slow nor too fast. Like Braudel's "magic mountains," Maine's India operated in a wholly different time so that the British were obligated "to make their watches keep time in two longitudes at once."[78] Only exceptional leadership by jurists and lawyers would protect against "the capacity for law to become separated from the society it was supposed to reflect."[79]

It was this context that gave meaning to Maine's formulation of the notion of divisible sovereignty and provided the key to its application by

[76] The phrase is from A. W. B. Simpson, quoted in Raymond Cocks, *Sir Henry Maine: A Study in Victorian Jurisprudence* (Cambridge: Cambridge University Press, 1988), 1.

[77] Maine identified three main processes within law that could produce change in order that the law would conform more closely to social conditions. These "instrumentalities" were legal fictions, equity, and legislation. Maine never succeeded in developing a coherent theory about how such mechanisms worked. He did become increasingly convinced that careful jurists could help to guide effective change, a belief that informed his strong support for codification later in his career.

[78] Quoted in Cocks, *Sir Henry Maine*, 86.

[79] This is Cocks's useful summation of Maine's central concern in *Ancient Law*. Cocks, *Sir Henry Maine*, 108.

British officials of the Foreign Office. The way to preserve earlier political and legal formations and to provide for their gradual change was to affirm the existence of quasi-sovereignty in these polities. Maine explained the argument clearly in his minute of 1864 written in response to a question raised about the nature of sovereignty in Kathiawar. The region had been under the suzerainty of the Marathas, with tribute paid yearly to the gaekwar, the ruler of Baroda. The British had the yearly exactions by the gaekwar converted into fixed tribute, and, in 1820, administration of the region was ceded to the British, who guaranteed collection and payment of the tribute.[80] British officials regarded Kathiawar as a quintessential example of an anarchical region whose remote hills harbored multiple petty chieftainships in perpetual conflict. The British established a court of criminal justice in 1831 and another forum for adjudicating land cases, the Rajasthanik Court, in the same year. In the early 1860s, proposals to reassign some villages within the region, to enact measures against robberies across jurisdictions, and to regulate the district's mints raised questions among British officials about whether the region should be considered foreign or British territory and, if foreign, whether intervention in internal governance was permissible. The governor of Bombay argued that the territory was part of British India because there was no evidence that the Kathiawar "chiefs" exercised sovereignty.[81] Members of the Bombay Council agreed, citing Elphinstone's report to argue that the polities of Kathiawar had long recognized sovereignty as residing in the suzerain power. On this basis, the Bombay government approved a plan by the political agent to consolidate and reorder the region's multiple petty jurisdictions.

In approving the plan for legal reorganization, the viceroy reached a different conclusion about Kathiawar's status. Its residents, he argued,

[80] Gujarat and Kathiawar had been divided between the *peshwa* and the gaekwar. Part of the region under the control of the *peshwa* became British territory under the 1807–1808 settlement agreement. In 1862, a proposal to cede this territory back to the *thákur* of Bhaunagar was one of the issues that prompted the question of whether Kathiawar should be considered foreign or British territory. For more on Kathiawar, see John McLeod, *Sovereignty, Power, Control: Politics in the State of Western India, 1916–1947* (Leiden: Brill, 1999), 15–25.

[81] The governor of Bombay, Sir Bartle Frere, made the specific distinction between jurisdiction, which he recognized the petty states to hold, and the "power of making war and peace, and of compelling allegiance under penalty of treason," which he saw as the sole prerogatives of the imperial government. Quoted in Ian Copland, *The British Raj and the Indian Princes: Paramountcy in Western India, 1857–1930* (Bombay: Orient Longman, 1982), 106.

owed allegiance to the crown but were not subject to British laws or administration. Although the British government retained the right to intervene "from time to time" when necessary to correct "evils and abuses," Kathiawar could not be considered British territory. Support for this "half-formed theory," as Tupper described the policy and its rationale, was drawn from Wheaton's writings on limited sovereignty.[82] But it was Maine who provided in his 1864 minute the explicit theory of sovereignty that could compass a dependent state with quasi-sovereignty under British rule: "Sovereignty is a term which, in international law, indicates a well-ascertained assemblage of separate powers or privileges. . . . A sovereign who possesses the whole of this aggregate of rights is called an *independent* sovereign; but there is not, nor has there ever been, anything in international law to prevent some of those rights being lodged with one possessor, and some with another. Sovereignty has always been regarded as divisible." The Kathiawar states had "been permitted," Maine observed, to exercise some sovereign rights, but "by far the largest part of the sovereignty . . . resided in practice with the British Government, and among the rights which it has exercised appears to me to be an almost unlimited right of interference for the better order of the States." Maine added that the obligation to intervene was enhanced by "the fact . . . that our government of India has in a sense been the cause of this anarchy in Kathiawar" by preventing the states from engaging in the "natural process" of armed conflict among themselves. Maine concluded that Kathiawar must "be properly styled foreign territory."[83]

Tupper viewed the Kathiawar decision, and Maine's minute in particular, as the foundation for Indian political law. For Tupper, the recommendation that Kathiawar "be properly styled foreign territory" was not just legally but also historically correct; it translated an indigenous arrangement of petty states under a suzerain power into "Western phraseology" and signaled a distinction between the "primitive violence" of pre-British India and the "civilized rule" of the raj.[84] There were other revealing, but still vague, parts of Maine's minute that would take on more definite form as relations with princely states developed. Kathiawar, in Maine's

[82] Tupper's assessment and the phrases quoted from the February 1864 minute by the Viceroy, Sir John Lawrence, are in Tupper, *Indian Political Practice*, 1:218. For a detailed analysis of the Kathiawar debate, see Copland, *British Raj and the Indian Princes*, 98–122; McLeod, *Sovereignty, Power, Control*, 15–25; Tupper, *Our Indian Protectorate.*

[83] "Kattywar States; Sovereignty," minutes by the Hon. Sir H. S. Maine, 22 March 1864, IOR V/27/100/3, 35–8.

[84] Tupper, *Indian Political Practice*, 1:220.

words, had been "permitted" the exercise of sovereign rights. This wording implied, as subsequent policy debates would affirm, the view that sovereignty was held as an exclusive property of the imperial power and some of its attributes merely awarded, conditionally, to native states. Only "immunity from foreign laws" approached the nature of an inherent sovereign right, but this prerogative, too, might occasionally be swept away in the course of an act of "interference" by the British.[85] The only theoretical limit on intervention was that it be undertaken in the interest of restoring or promoting order and good governance.

Perhaps most striking about Maine's minute of 1864 is not that it contained the outlines of British policy toward native territories for the next half century but that it left so many aspects of the relation undefined. It was impossible to deduce from the definition of a part-foreign and part-sovereign territory the arrangements that might pertain to jurisdiction. Not surprisingly, jurisdictional disputes – in turn intricately related to revenue questions – continued to dominate daily relations between the British government of India and the Indian states. Further, the vagueness of the criteria for acts of intervention that violated states' sovereignty, while clearly serving the interests of the British government, was destined also to create uncertainty and controversy about the distinction between political and legal actions with regard to the states. Underlying this problem was the equivocation in Maine's minute about the applicability of international law to the relation between the British government and the Indian states. Maine rested the rationale for intervention on principles of international law; the situation of Kathiawar, he wrote, exactly paralleled the hypothetical case of "a group of little independent States in the middle of Europe... hastening to utter anarchy." Their "theoretical independence" would never deter "the greater powers" from interfering to restore order. Yet, at the same time, Maine tried to distance the Indian situation from international law. The mere consideration of these questions seemed to enhance imperial authority. By defining native states' sovereignty, the British government had diminished it; by articulating a right to contain warfare, the British had removed interstate relations from the realm of international relations.[86]

[85] "Kattywar States; Sovereignty," IOR V/27/100/3, 35–8.

[86] "Kattywar States; Sovereignty," IOR V/27/100/3, 35–38. This understanding was consistent with a parallel move by the colonial state to claim a prerogative to make the rules for the plural legal order and, in the process, set itself up as the dominant legal authority. See Benton, *Law and Colonial Cultures*, chap. 4.

Perhaps anticipating the conflicts that would highlight these ambiguities, Maine's 1864 minute held up "usage" as the only steady source for guidelines on British policy toward the Indian states: "The mode or degree in which sovereignty is distributed between the British Government and any given Native State is always a question of fact, which has to be separately decided in each case, and to which no general rules apply." In other words, British policy itself formed guiding precedents, while the precise mix of sovereign rights in princely states would be deduced "from the *de facto* relations of these States with the British Government." Tupper generalized this principle as one establishing "usage" as the preeminent source of "political law."[87]

It is tempting to construe these principles as providing rationales for the exercise of unconstrained power. But this view would ignore several political and legal realities. First, British preoccupation with preserving the princes as allies after the events of 1857 created persistent pressure from within to accommodate their authority. Second, though they were sometimes labeled as collaborators, the rulers and subjects of native states repeatedly and routinely challenged British jurisdiction and extralegal interventions. Third, British policy was riddled with contradictions. The tension between efforts to systematize relations with Indian states and insistence on the purely political nature of British intervention continued. Often it was minor colonial agents who demanded greater precision in law and higher British officials who saw legal guidelines as a potential constraint on power. Yet officials at both levels remained committed to the project of articulating the legal basis of differentiated rule. One result was an implied claim that the law itself generated the conditions for extralegal action. Another was the creation of increasingly elaborate schemata for classifying different types of legal territories within both British India and the native states. These moves responded to a series of disputes and political crises clustered in just the first decade following the Kathiawar decision.

"Bare sovereignty"

If British officials looked to debates about Kathiawar for definitions of sovereignty in princely states, they considered the Baroda case a reference point for subsequent interventions in native state administration. As it has come to be summarized, the case seems simple enough: Toward

[87] "Kattywar States; Sovereignty," IOR V/27/100/3, 35–8.

the end of 1874, the British resident in Baroda, Colonel Robert Phayre, reported an attempt on his life. Someone had poisoned his morning sherbet, and suspicion fell almost immediately on household servants thought to be working for Baroda's ruler, the gaekwar, Malhar Rao. The viceroy appointed a commission composed of three British officials and three prominent Indians from other princely states to render an opinion on the charges, and the panel was divided, with the British officials convinced of the gaekwar's guilt and the Indian appointees declaring that there was insufficient evidence of his involvement. The British government then ordered the gaekwar deposed, not on the basis of the attempt to poison the resident but on the broader charge of "misrule," which was supported in part by reference to an earlier commission report detailing revenue irregularities and acts of oppression. Malhar Rao was sent into exile and an heir chosen by the British government from among several minors proposed as candidates for succession. According to Tupper and other later observers, the actions simultaneously affirmed British control over succession in princely states and established the right to intervene to counter "misrule."[88] By refraining from annexing Baroda, the government of India sought to reassure other native rulers that the pre-1857 policy of annexation would not be resumed while also reinforcing the authority of residents, who were officially empowered only to offer native rulers guidance and advice on internal affairs.

The crisis was more complex than this narrative suggests. Rather than resolving questions of British authority, the case pointed to the central and persistent legal puzzles of quasi-sovereignty. While the immediate catalyst was the apparent attempt to poison Colonel Phayre, the background to the accusation was a struggle between the gaekwar and the resident centering on legal administration, especially jurisdictional arrangements. Baroda's geography helped to shape this legal politics (see Figure 5.2). The gaekwar's territories were noncontiguous and mostly landlocked, surrounded by areas that were formally part of British India

[88] The Baroda case was routinely cited as a precedent-setting case for intervention on the basis of charges of misgovernment. Tupper framed the case in this way, characterizing it as "pre-eminently a leading case" that established "the principle that incorrigible misrule is a disqualification for sovereign power." Tupper, *Indian Political Practice*, 1:49. Westlake defined the precedent somewhat differently, emphasizing that the investigation of the gaekwar for the alleged poisoning was founded on an understanding that rulers of Indian states owed allegiance to the queen and the relation of the British monarch to the ruler was one "of sovereign to subject." John Westlake, "The Empire of India," in Oppenheim, *Collected Papers*, 221. For more on this argument in relation to the "trial" of the gaekwar, see *supra* note 55.

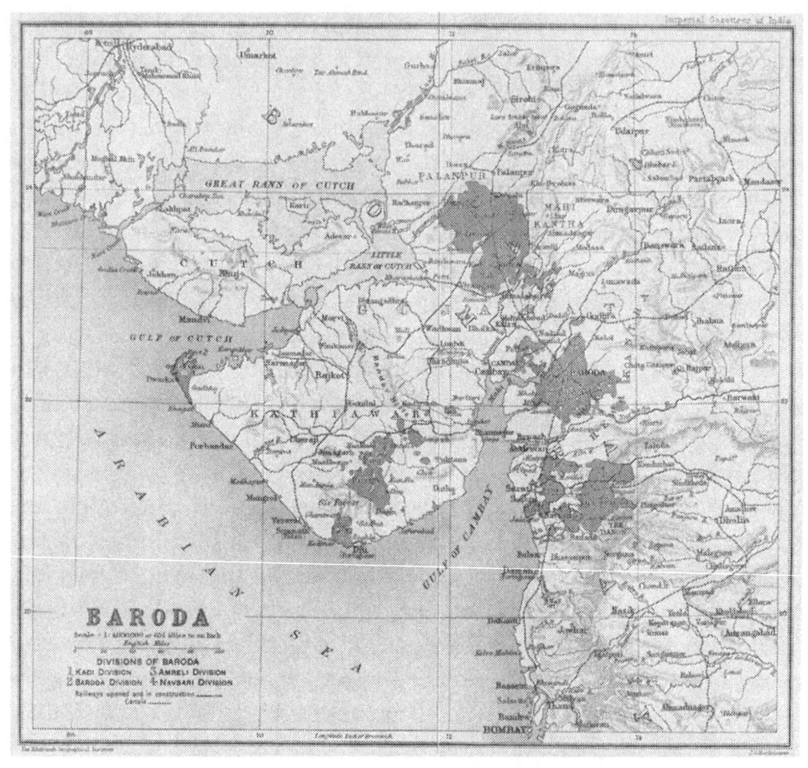

FIGURE 5.2. Map of Baroda (1907–1909). This map highlights the four divisions of Baroda and shows the state's disaggregated territories. *Imperial Gazetteer of India*, new ed., published under the authority of His Majesty's Secretary of State for India in Council. Oxford: Clarendon Press, 1907–1909, vol. 7, opposite page 64.

or other native states. Baroda contained both low plains, where cotton had recently become the main crop, and a diverse array of hill regions ranged along the state's noncontiguous borders. The legal administration of the hills was a subject of special conflict between the gaekwar and the Bombay government and the object of particular attention from Colonel Phayre. The British government's unwillingness to clarify jurisdictional rules or impose unpopular arrangements formed part of a more general, inchoate position on the limits of law in native states. The intractability of everyday legal politics helped to prepare the way for the British government's extralegal actions late in the crisis.

The crisis also resulted in part from tensions between Phayre, who appealed to the government to sweep away the legal ambiguities of quasi-sovereignty, and higher officials who tried to perpetuate uncertainty as a matter of policy. Phayre had not been in Baroda for long. The Bombay government appointed him in 1873, over the objections of officials of the government of India in Calcutta.[89] In long and detailed letters to his superiors, Phayre cuts an officious figure.[90] He was strident in demanding more precise and aggressive rulings from Bombay to strengthen the authority of the resident in Baroda, and he displayed little tact in his dealings with either British officials or the gaekwar. Reading his correspondence, one begins to suspect that there were others besides the Baroda ruler who took pleasure in imagining him dead. Certainly toward the end of the crisis, Bombay and Calcutta officials would agree on wanting him moved out of the way.

One of Phayre's first communications as resident to the Bombay government echoed his predecessor's praise for the gaekwar as someone who was "very intelligent and ready to hear about what I have to urge upon questions of importance."[91] Only a month later, Phayre's tone had changed, and he was warning that if the government did not address festering problems in Baroda, the situation would "culminate in a general outbreak of some sort or other."[92] In summarizing Phayre's objections, historians have emphasized tensions between the gaekwar and local elites, particularly complaints about excessive taxation and, later, Phayre's open hostility toward the gaekwar's chosen dewan.[93] But a larger volume of Phayre's correspondence was taken up with legal matters. The gaekwar's hill territories bordering British Indian districts were a particular source of trouble. Baroda subjects were moving into British territory, some

[89] Copland sees the case mainly as the byproduct of the political rivalry of the Bombay government and the Viceroy's Council in Calcutta. Copland, "The Baroda Crisis of 1873–77."

[90] Phayre's behavior recalls Greg Dening's portrait of Captain Bligh as an official who was simply very bad at inspiring loyalty in interlocutors or subordinates. Greg Dening, *Mr Bligh's Bad Language: Passion, Power, and Theatre on the Bounty* (Cambridge: Cambridge University Press, 1992).

[91] IOR R/2/481/55 f. 29. After the attempted poisoning, Phayre claimed that the gaekwar had made overtures to bribe him soon after he arrived in Baroda. When that effort failed, the gaekwar began a campaign of "sorcery" involving a servant "going about Baroda with a middle sized magic bottle" with Phayre's name inscribed in English and Persian. This display was followed by "persecution and insult" and, after the British government, at Phayre's urging, issued a statement calling for administrative reform, "an active system of retaliation." IOR R/2/474/2, ff. 25–6.

[92] IOR R/2/474/2, f. 37.

[93] This is Ian Copland's view, in "Baroda Crisis of 1873–74," in the most careful and comprehensive accounting of the crisis.

conducting raids and robberies along the border and taking refuge in the gaekwar's dominions. The British had no clear legal basis for arresting or prosecuting suspects in such cases.[94] Nor could the resident act against British subjects or the subjects of other native states who were entering Baroda territory to commit crimes; the gaekwar had sole criminal jurisdiction in his territory, except with regard to European British subjects. Phayre complained that the gaekwar's courts could not be trusted. British subjects' rights were "systematically disregarded," criminal proceedings were especially lax, and Phayre claimed that rumors were rampant about the use of torture and the forgery of evidence.[95] By July 1873 – just four months into his tenure as resident – Phayre was urging the Bombay government to award him sole authority to determine whether individual cases should be tried in British or Baroda courts. If the gaekwar resisted the resident's authority, Phayre proposed, the government should seize from him all criminal jurisdiction with regard to British subjects.[96]

British officials sent back mixed messages. They took Phayre's complaints seriously enough to appoint a commission to assess the state of governance in Baroda. But action in response to Phayre's repeated requests for the expansion of his legal authority, and even for clarification of the resident's role, was slow in coming. Phayre was instead instructed not to encourage the gaekwar's subjects to lodge complaints with Phayre because he had "no legal authority to grant them redress." The resident was also warned to avoid "any language calculated to cause irritation" to the Baroda ruler.[97]

Undeterred, Phayre was in full campaign against the gaekwar by early 1874.[98] He pressed the government to create a British criminal court at Baroda for trying British subjects and hectored Bombay officials to enhance his jurisdiction to try the suspects in a number of dacoity cases,

[94] The chief constable from an adjacent British territory wrote: "Supposing a robbery has taken place and the perpetrators escape into the Guikwar territory, and if any one was suspected of having committed it, yet neither our police nor the complainant can according to law touch him." IOR R/2/481/55, f. 69.

[95] IOR R/2/481/55, f. 212.

[96] IOR P/481, p. 122.

[97] IOR R/2/481/55, f. 82.

[98] He penned a detailed account of Malhar Rao's "course of treason, murder, and every conceivable act of lawlessness, for the last 16 years." IOR R/2/481/55, f. 69. Phayre accused the gaekwar of having participated in the rebellion of 1857 by participating in a conspiracy against the British spreading across Baroda's borders to neighboring British districts. He also cited evidence that Malhar Rao had taken a leading role, never proved, in the conspiracy to kill his brother, then the gaekwar, and replace him on the throne in 1863. IOR R/2/481/55, f. 88.

eliciting the support of antidacoity officials.[99] The peculiar jurisdictional tangles in Baroda were illustrated by "a case of dacoity upon the property of a British subject residing at [the British district of] Ahmedabad, which had meanwhile been committed in gaekwar territory by a gang of robbers from Rajpootana."[100] Phayre was adamant in stating that mere negotiation with the gaekwar to sort out legal responsibilities in such cases would fail; the Baroda ruler jealously guarded his legal authority and was resisting the resident's advice about the disposition of cases involving British subjects or border raids.[101] The response from Bombay continued to be anything but encouraging. In May 1874, the government resolved that it was "not expedient to press the gaekwar to give the Resident jurisdiction."[102] A few months later, Bombay officials were more explicit and instructed Phayre to give up his campaign; British subjects apprehended in British territory for crimes committed in Baroda were to be surrendered to Baroda authorities.[103]

One of the issues pressed by Phayre was the nature of criminal jurisdiction in the cantonment and residency bazaar. The question had come up nearly twenty years before, when officials worried about the lack of clear provisions about whether the British or the gaekwar held jurisdiction on a site that was "situated in the territories of a foreign state."[104] In 1867, the Bombay government declared that the British held only military jurisdiction inside the cantonment but could exercise a wider jurisdiction if the gaekwar consented. Officials assumed that he would cooperate, but he turned out to be "very tenacious" in asserting his judicial authority in

[99] The general superintendent for the suppression of thuggee and dacoity wrote in June 1873: "It would seem that the Resident has no judicial authority to dispose of any other criminal cases but those which may be committed within the Cantonment of Baroda, and that the Assistant Resident has no criminal jurisdiction whatever," and he described this position of the British political authorities in Baroda as "exceptional." IOR P/752 Government of India Foreign Department Proceedings, April 1874, Judicial, No. 2, p. 2.

[100] IOR P/752, Government of India Foreign Department Proceedings, April 1874, Judicial, No. 69, p. 73.

[101] Phayre wrote, "It appears to me to be vain to expect that, put the case how we may, the Durbar will voluntarily consent to surrender what they wrongly conceive it is for their dignity and honor to retain." The gaekwar bristled at the existing requirement that he produce witnesses before the resident to establish a prima facie case against any British subject before proceeding to trial in one of his courts. IOR P/752, Government of India Foreign Department Proceedings, April 1874, Judicial, No. 81, p. 98.

[102] IOR P/752, Government of India Foreign Department Proceedings, April 1874, Judicial, No. 82, pp. 98–9.

[103] IOR P/481, p. 122.

[104] IOR R/2/487/71 f. 3.

both criminal and civil cases.[105] Though Malhar Rao eventually agreed that a British magistrate might operate under his jurisdiction, Phayre was complaining in 1874 about irregularities in procedure and continued uncertainties about the exercise of criminal jurisdiction. He wrote to Hyderabad seeking information on jurisdictional arrangements in the cantonment there, and he appealed to Bombay for guidance in a case of camp followers arrested for murder outside the cantonment; he thought they should be returned to the British for trial.[106]

Phayre was calling attention to questions that were being raised, usually in less strident tones, by British officials in other native states. The problem of cantonment jurisdiction, for example, had recently gained the attention of the government because of an appeal brought in 1872 from the cantonment of Secunderabad, in Hyderabad. A woman whose cantonment house had been attached in a civil suit sought to delay action in the case by appealing to the Privy Council. The Hyderabad resident inquired whether the appeal was proper, as his jurisdiction in the case was merely delegated by the nizam and the majority of residents inside the cantonment were the nizam's subjects. The government of India ruled that jurisdiction flowed from the occupation of the cantonment by British troops and was "*a matter of fact.*" The petitioner had no right to appeal to the Privy Council, but the council of the government of India might decide to hear an appeal and might issue "any injunctions they think fit."[107] In a subsequent case in Deesa, the government affirmed British jurisdiction in the cantonment, which was described as native territory that for legal purposes was to be treated as British territory. Such cases seemed to establish the principle that native states had no jurisdiction in cantonments, while the states retained a property labeled by one official as "bare sovereignty."[108] Even this erasure of effective sovereignty did not clear away conflict over the actual exercise of jurisdiction, as relations in Baroda clearly showed. It in fact distinguished a form of sovereignty from jurisdiction.[109]

[105] Ibid. f. 17(a).

[106] In 1875, Phayre complained that an arrangement dating from 1853, whereby the British agreed to hand over to the gaekwar any of his subjects arrested for crimes committed in the cantonment and the gaekwar was to transfer camp followers suspected in crimes committed outside the camp, was breaking down.

[107] The case is covered in Tupper, *Indian Political Practice*, 3:17–19.

[108] Quoted in Tupper, *Indian Political Practice*, 3:20.

[109] Further attention should be paid to the use of the term *bare sovereignty* in the decades from 1870 to 1920. It appears at times to have been used to mean (in analogy with the theological use of the term to represent an unmediated power by God) an unlimited or

The issue of jurisdiction over British subjects was also prevalent in other native states, and guiding principles also left considerable room for interpretation and maneuver. The British government distinguished between European British subjects and Indian British subjects in a ruling in 1871 directing that no native state would be permitted "to try a European British subject according to its own forms of Procedure and punish him according to its own laws."[110] In 1873, the native states of Travancore and Cochin announced an extradition agreement, prompting a debate among British officials about whether to insist on inserting a clause excepting European subjects from transfer for prosecution in either state. Travancore had earlier tried a European British subject, Liddell, for misappropriating state funds, and the government of India had decided not to intervene. Now the governor general instructed the Foreign Office not to alter the Travancore-Cochin agreement; despite imperial legislation prohibiting native states' jurisdiction over European subjects, imperial officials insisted that the question should be treated "as one of many undefined matters" subject to ad hoc regulation.[111] It was possible, the viceroy asserted, to imagine other cases in which a European offender should be left to be tried in native courts, and the best policy was not to form a firm rule – and certainly to avoid recognizing that treaties with or between native states were authoritative sources for such a rule.

If the seemingly fixed legal status of European British subjects was open-ended, that of Indian British subjects was even more uncertain. At the same time that Phayre was worrying about the vagaries of jurisdiction

unadorned power. See Elisha Mulford, *The Republic of God: An Institute of Theology* (Boston: Houghton, Mifflin, 1881), 6; Elisha Mulford, *The Nation: The Foundations of Civil Order and Political Life in the United States* (New York: Hurd and Houghton, 1871), 51. At other times, it appears to have been used in ways similar to its meaning here, that is, to signify a residual, minimalist, or nominal form of sovereignty distinguished from jurisdiction. For example, the Italian foreign affairs minister complained that the effect of the Berlin Conference was to establish a "*de facto* possession of territories by some Powers that leaves to others a bare sovereignty which consists of nothing." Tommaso Tittoni, Bernardo Quaranta di San Severino, and Maggiorino Ferraris, *Italy's Foreign and Colonial Policy: A Selection from the Speeches Delivered in the Italian Parliament by the Italian Foreign Affairs Minister, Senator Tommaso Tittoni, During His Six Years of Office (1903–1909)* (Smith, Elder, 1914), 124.

110 IOR P/752, Government of India Foreign Department Proceedings, September 1873, Judicial, No. 6, p. 7. Quoted in "Remarks by the Advocate General," H. S. Cunningham, written on June 13, 1872.

111 IOR P/752, Government of India Foreign Department Proceedings, September, 1873, Judicial, No. 8, p. 10.

over British subjects in Baroda, the issue was being raised by the political agent of Hill Tipperah, a native state bordering British India territory in Bengal. As in Baroda, the question of order in the hills, and on the border, was prompting the political agent to call for British jurisdiction. British subjects were said to be committing crimes and escaping into Hill Tipperah, where there were "great facilities for evading justice."[112] Here, as in Baroda, the government instructed that assuming jurisdiction would be "inexpedient" and that nothing should be done.[113]

Indeterminacy was being articulated as policy – even as a core principle of an imperial law based on divisible sovereignty. Commenting on the Liddell case, the government of India insisted on the importance of not specifying legal arrangements in treaties or other agreements with native states. "To do so would, in our opinion, reduce the right which we claim to exercise as the Paramount Power in India to a matter of negotiation between us and those over whom we assert the right." The position left open the possibility of action "when our interference is imperatively called for by the administration of justice in such States."[114] Even if the government wished for further precision, some legal advisers argued, the "infinite variety" of arrangements in native states, with different portions of sovereignty permitted to various native rules, made this goal impossible. Defining "in precise terms where in each case the ruling Prince merges into a British subject seems *beyond the power of language* in the present state of our relations and of our information."[115]

It is no wonder that his superiors found Phayre's insistence on precision in matters of jurisdiction so disruptive. In November 1874, when he was probably on the verge of being removed from office by Calcutta officials, Phayre raised the alarm about the attempt to poison him and insisted there was "no reasonable hope" for a fair investigation with the gaekwar

[112] IOR P/752, Government of India, Foreign Department Proceedings, July 1874, Judicial, No. 60, p. 58. IOR P/752 No. 60.

[113] IOR P/752, Government of India, Foreign Department Proceedings, July 1874, No. 63, p. 64. At issue was whether political agents in Hill Tipperah would be required to try native British subjects accused of crimes. There was a mild objection to any diminution in the raja's prerogative on this account, and a more forceful advocacy by the political agent that without some change in this direction, Hill Tipperah would remain "an exception to the general rule." IOR P/752 Government of India, Foreign Department Proceedings, July 1874, No. 61, p. 60.

[114] IOR P/752, Government of India Foreign Department Proceedings, September 1873, Judicial, No. 9, p. 14.

[115] IOR L/PS/20/MEMO31/24, "Note for the Bhaonagan Case" by E. Perry, December 11, 1875. Emphasis added.

in power. The viceroy sent Sir Lewis Pelly to Baroda in December to head up a special commission; Phayre was sacked.[116] Although Pelly's appointment marked a turning point in the power struggle between Bombay and Calcutta, it was not at all certain that the result would be direct intervention in Baroda governance. Pelly's early reports stated that the main problems in the state flowed from the recent collapse of cotton prices – a condition with global causes – and the resulting attempt by the state to shore up its financing through increased taxation.[117] Financial reforms, together with some greater clarity and stability in the government's policies toward Baroda, were perhaps all that was needed. But it was no longer possible to ignore the poisoning charge when Pelly's investigation produced the confession of a servant who said he had tried to poison Phayre at the behest of the gaekwar. This confession was followed by admissions of guilt by three others. Now Calcutta officials had to act.

The government had, however, no formal criminal jurisdiction over the gaekwar or his subjects. Any proceeding would have to be extrajudicial. Summarizing British actions later, the viceroy allowed that the commission convened to consider the charges of poisoning and spying "was not constituted as, or intended to be, a judicial tribunal."[118] The decision to suspend the gaekwar while the inquiry was under way was also "not based on considerations of law. It was an act of State, carried out by the Paramount Power."[119] In another extrajudicial move, it was decided not to press charges against the men who had confessed to involvement; they were sent for indefinite terms of imprisonment to points ranging from Aden to Burma. When the commission returned its opinion, perfectly

[116] Pelly's appointment by the government of India was an affront to the Bombay government. See Copland, "Baroda Crisis of 1873–77."

[117] "The main origin of the present revenue difficulties is, in my opinion, to be found among the consequences of the rebellion in the United States," Pelly reported (BL Mss Eur F/126/83, f. 3). As the price of cotton had gone up, more land was reserved for its cultivation and less for food production. Though cotton prices had recently fallen, Pelly found, rents were still high and cultivators were unable to pay. Pelly wondered, too, whether some agriculturalists might have been encouraged by the British in their opposition to the gaekwar.

[118] IOR Mss Eur F/126/88, f. 5. In its charge to the commission, the government of India stated that if the charges were proved, it would be tantamount to treason. This statement, Westlake later argued, established that the government's rationale for what Westlake incorrectly called a "trial" was that the gaekwar was a subject of the queen and owed allegiance to the crown. See Westlake, "The Empire of India," in Oppenheim, *Collected Papers*, 222, and *supra* note 88.

[119] IOR Mss Eur F/126/88, f. 4. The native members of the commission were also accused of a form of jury nullification, of basing their opinions more on "political feeling than on consideration of the evidence." Ibid., f. 9.

divided along British and Indian lines, the government could not rest the decision to depose the Baroda leader on the poisoning charges. But the charge of "misrule" also appeared flawed, since neither the first commission's findings in 1874 nor the government of Bombay, nor even Pelly, had recommended that the gaekwar be permanently deposed for the irregularities of rule observed before the poisoning charge surfaced. It was left for the viceroy to argue that the action was taken "on general grounds" that included some very recent missteps by the gaekwar and factored in lingering suspicions, though not proven charges, in the poisoning case.[120]

The enclave location of the state also provided an argument for intervention. Conditions in Baroda under the gaekwar "contained the elements of serious disturbance, which, owing to the manner in which the territories of the British Government and the Gaekwar are intermingled, might have been greatly prejudicial to the interest of British subjects and to the peace and order of Her Majesty's dominions."[121] The ultimate rationale for extrajudicial action was the appeal to order. Phayre and other officials had certainly understood this logic when they had portrayed Baroda as a refuge for plunderers and a threat to the peace of adjoining districts.

The Baroda case did not make law so much as it pointed to the limits of law in regulating relations between the British government and the native states. These limits existed not just in the case for deposition because of misrule but in the more routine management of legal matters arising from minor cases and unsolved jurisdictional questions. The same Foreign Office officials who prided themselves on systematizing legal relations with the native states also developed and refined the notion that paramountcy resided mainly in the prerogative of the imperial power to decide where law ended and politics began. More precisely, the colonial state claimed the power not to decide – to remain silent on questions that were "beyond the power of language."

Territorial Anomalies

The political fallout from Malhar Rao's deposition was less than some officials had feared, and less than others had hoped. Calcutta officials who saw the Baroda case as an opening for asserting stronger authority over the Bombay presidency were mainly disappointed. A number of ambitious schemes for political reorganization were scuttled, and the

[120] Ibid., f. 9.
[121] The Viceroy's Minute of April 29, 1875, IOR F/126/88.

principal gain for Calcutta was control over the Baroda residency. One of the schemes for reorganization was interesting for the way it called on a familiar, romanticized notion of simpler governance in the hills. Pelly and Meade, the heads of the two Baroda commissions, came to champion the idea of consolidating Baroda and the Kathiawar states into a consortium of Gujarat-Maratha states. The idea was prefigured in a postscript to one of Pelly's letters to the viceroy in the midst of the crisis. Pelly had been stationed in Rajputana before coming to Baroda, and he suggested that if Baroda had been structured as "a congeries of States," the crisis would never have occurred; order would have been attained through "force of routine and system" guided by the Foreign Office.[122] The comment was in part intended to reinforce the claims of the government to intervene in Baroda, but it also called on the widely circulating notion that a multiplicity of Indian states in tension with one another formed a purer political system, one that was more amenable to imperial rule. The same phenomenon, of course, could perpetuate disorder and delay progress. By design, the idea that the outcome was contingent on the methods of careful rule – dependent, in other words, precisely on the qualities that Phayre had lacked but men like Pelly and Aitcheson claimed to possess – implied that imperial governance was both science and art, and that the men of the Foreign Office were its most gifted players.

For a brief time, at least, their efforts were in fact central to shaping imperial space. Debates about how to deal with the legal ambiguities of native states influenced broader efforts to designate categories of colonial territory according to their different relationships to law. A reflection on jurisdictional problems in native states made the connection explicitly, noting that "the root of the difficulty" appeared to be that the government of India's administrative powers had a larger scope than its legislative powers. The administrative power of the government in native states was vast and allowed for "growth and extension"; the government's legislative capacity – its authority to extend laws passed by the Legislative Council to the territories of native states – was "very definitely marked off." Although British laws might be in force in a given native state, they derived their standing as law not from legislative but from executive authority through the actions of the governor general in council "executing powers delegating to him by a foreign ruler." The result was to form territories that were "at once foreign to us and not foreign.... Such a state of things is very peculiar and anomalous, and must issue sooner or

[122] BL Mss F 126/83, f. 10.

later in practical difficulty."[123] By way of illustration of the anomalies, the letter called attention to two cases of legal confusion. In one, a subject of Jaipur was convicted in Rajputana and sent to an Agra jail, under British control. When a British official wanted to move the prisoner, he was asked for a warrant, but because the man was not a British subject, he did not have authority to obtain one. Effectively, the man had been made into a legal nonperson by transfer into custody in a British district.[124]

This problem was related to the broader uncertainty about the application of imperial government regulations and laws in "outlying districts" deemed to be unsuited for them. In 1870, Parliament established a process for local authorities to apply to the council for "dereglationising Acts" intended "to remove those districts from beyond the pale of the law." Despite this and other attempts to fix a procedure and guidelines for determining when and where the general enactments were legally in force, there was considerable confusion about the standing of various districts. Beginning in 1870, judicial officials undertook a massive review of the record of relevant legislation. Because the standing of a number of native territories was in question – some areas were still technically quasi-sovereign but operated legally as if integral to British India – any territory whose status was uncertain was excepted from the resulting schedule. The Scheduled Districts Act, passed in 1874, listed those districts that would be "excluded from the acts we pass for the rest of the country." These territories comprised "remote or backward tracts or provinces of British India" in which legislation and ordinary jurisdiction had never been in operation, or had been removed. Some territories, including some scheduled districts, remained subject to 1870 decisions on their status.

[123] IOR P/752, Government of India Foreign Department Proceedings, July 1875, Judicial, No. 14, pp. 9–10.

[124] In a memorandum about these issues, James Fitzjames Stephen disagreed that the legal problems were intractable. Any "persons brought into the country by force" were subject to British law as soon as they entered British territory. Stephen asserted that the only constraint on making laws investing British courts with the power to try subjects of native states (even if they committed crimes there) was political. And there could be no objection to carrying out a sentence passed in a native court: "A man commits an offence on the Holkar State Railway. He is brought before a Nimar Magistrate sitting in British territory under the executive authority of the Viceroy, and sentenced to imprisonment. It is surely incorrect to say that such a man is punished by British law for an offence committed in Native territory. He is punished by Native law for an offence committed in Native territory by a Native Court which, by the permission of the British Government, sits in British territory, and the sentence of which is executed by British officials." Memorandum by Mr. Stephen upon the issues disposed of by Despatch (Judicial) No. 55, dated December 23, 1875, IOR L/PS/18/D118.

As Tupper summarized later, the legislation, together with existing practice and policy regarding native states, created five kinds of legal territory: three kinds of territory in British India and two kinds of territory in native states, depending on the statutes and agreements determining exemptions from British enactments and jurisdiction. Within British India, the exceptional territories making up the two minor categories represented "wild, remote, or peculiar districts or provinces."[125] Within native states, "exceptional portions" operated under laws established through executive order of the governor general in council.[126] The legislation of 1875 had been partly prompted by the legal anomalies of native states, but in practice it did little to address them while creating new categories of legal exception within British India.

One need not have a very active imagination to guess that this schema did not put an end to questions about legal administration in the various territories, nor, even, resolve controversies about the designation of some districts as British or native. But the legal typology created and linked two kinds of legal backwardness, one of regions considered remote that were inside British India and another of native state territories that had not received British law. Exclusion from British jurisdiction and legislation was clearly tied to representations of remoteness, wildness, and disorder.[127] Hill regions, within both British India and native states, continued to form the quintessential examples of such legal primitiveness.

A last example will help to illustrate this point. The Dangs, an area that lay along the border of Baroda and the British district of Khandesh, was characterized by the British as a composite of chiefdoms, whose main inhabitants, the Bhils, repeatedly leased the lands for forestry to the British.[128] In 1889, the Bombay government sought to declare the Dangs a part of British India. The arguments both in favor and against this proposal relied on representations of the Bhils as culturally and legally

[125] Tupper, *Indian Political Practice*, 1:241.

[126] As Maine had noted in 1864, the British government had no authority to extend British laws into native territory; they could only be applied.

[127] On the British discourse on "wildness," see Ajay Skaria, *Hybrid Histories: Forests, Frontiers and Wildness in Western India* (Oxford: Oxford University Press, 1999). See also Vaidik, *Imperial Andamans*, chap. 1. It is worth noting that this discourse was not limited to European empires. See especially Emma Teng, *Taiwan's Imagined Geography: Chinese Colonial Travel Writing and Pictures, 1683–1895* (Cambridge, MA: Harvard University Asia Center, 2004).

[128] Skaria (*Hybrid Histories*) provides a detailed history of British relations with the Bhils. The forest leases were in 1832 and 1862. The Baroda gaekwar had unsuccessfully presented claims to sovereignty over part of the region beginning in the 1860s.

backward. If the Bhils were incapable of exercising civil or criminal jurisdiction, then by default legal administration should fall to the British.[129] But the Bhils' legal primitivism also suggested that they were not ready for direct rule: "In this wild country the introduction of laws and regulations seems likely to lead to embarrassment and difficulty. The Government of India are disposed to think that, for a backward community like the Dáng Bhíls, the strongest and most effective form of control is the personal rule of a British officer untrammeled by anything but executive orders from his own Government."[130] As in Baroda, part of the issue was intergovernmental rivalry and a desire on the part of the central government to block Bombay's control; but, as with Pelly's comments comparing Baroda to Rajputana, the government's response also rested on understandings of the natural fit between legally primitive petty states and the less complicated oversight of an imperial executive with unspecified power. Here, as elsewhere, the uncertainty of the Bhils' status urged a political solution with a spatial referent – undefined executive authority over a legally anomalous zone.

Comparative Puzzles

International lawyers in the second half of the nineteenth century came to define membership in international society as restricted to those polities recognized as civilized by the societies already considered members of the international community. As Anghie has shown, efforts to fix a classification system pairing degrees of civilization with graduated membership in international society produced inconsistency and confusion: "The ambivalent status of the non-European entity, outside the scope of law and yet within it, lacking international capacity and yet necessarily possessing it . . . was never satisfactorily denied or resolved."[131] Anghie views the efforts to grapple with quasi-sovereignty as a result of the contradiction posed by expansive imperial claims and the continued recognition of the capacity of non-European polities to enter into treaties.

This observation is useful as far as it goes. In India, British officials did assert the right to disregard treaties and other agreements with princely states, and this move, seen as voiding any claims of the states'

[129] British power had "not been questioned though never defined." Letter from W. Lee-Warner, Esq. Secretary to Government, to Secretary to the Government of India, February 22, 1889, Bombay Castle, Political Department. IOR R/3505 No. 350.

[130] Tupper, *Indian Political Practice*, 1:245.

[131] Anghie, *Making of International Law*, 81.

international personality, drove the effort to find another way of defining their status in international law. But Anghie's important goal of analyzing "the constitutive effect of colonialism on sovereignty" cannot be achieved only by observing trends within European international law.[132] Quasi-sovereignty was a construct also shaped by repeating problems of legal administration in empire-states. Intellectual and political-legal currents cannot be separated. To begin with, much of the intellectual work of defining quasi-sovereignty was not being done in Europe and the United States but in empire. The material for Westlake, and for other international lawyers writing about Indian princely states, was supplied by colonial officials, whose elaborate legal typologies were being constructed not to resolve intellectual puzzles so much as to respond to ongoing legal conflicts and provide a guide for colonial administrators in an imperial future they saw as extending indefinitely.[133] Maine, and at a lower profile, Tupper and Lee-Warner, straddled the worlds of imperial officials and metropolitan intellectuals. They were acutely aware of the forces ranged against the easy incorporation of enclave colonial territories into the legal order of empire. Local rulers insisted on retaining jurisdiction, and they advanced arguments about territorial sovereignty that invoked both international law arguments and a discourse about the virtues of customary law.[134] Colonial officials' efforts to systematize rule meanwhile

[132] Anghie, *Making of International Law*, 37.

[133] On the importance of colonial officials in the crafting of British ideologies of governance in India, see Martha McLaren, *British India and British Scotland, 1780–1830: Career Building, Empire Building, and a Scottish School of Thought on Indian Governance* (Akron, Ohio: University of Akron Press, 2001).

[134] For example, in the debate about the treaty of extradition negotiated by Travancore and Cochin in 1873, British officials ultimately approved the treaty but explicitly denied the arguments of the dewan of Travancore based on international law in defending the states' rights to form the agreement. It is important to note that the dewan, Madava Row, was not taking a particularly radical stance, suggesting at one point that the agreement could incorporate a statement requiring approval of the resident for any extradition of a European British subject (IOR P/752, Government of India, Foreign Department Proceedings, September 1873, Judicial, No. 5). The responses of British officials to this case prompted one of the clearest statements of the perceived tight connection between paramountcy and indeterminacy in the imperial government's posture toward the native states: "The Dewan of Travancore appeals to the maxims of international law, which regulate the relations of independent and co-equal European States. I do not concur in the line of argument, though I do not blame the Minister for advocating the rights of his sovereign with dignity and spirit. There *is* a paramount power in the British Crown, of which the extent is wisely left undefined. There *is* a subordination in the Native States which is understood, but not explained. I may affirm, however, with safety, that the Paramount Power intervenes only on grounds of general policy where the interests of the Indian people, or the safety of the British power, are

resulted in further territorial classifications as they distinguished different kinds of anomalous legal zones and applied confusing and contradictory legal policies. Conflicts like those in Baroda about control at borders, ambiguities of subjecthood, and the vagaries of applying imperial legislation were repeated in other Indian princely states and elsewhere, with variations.

While nineteenth-century jurists embraced comparisons across a broad range of "protectorates," they turned away from comparisons between Indian native states and "uncivilized" colonial enclaves.[135] Westlake, for example, insisted on distinguishing between Indian princely states and protectorates in "uncivilized" regions. Yet his analysis of their qualities was not so very different; he viewed sovereignty in both kinds of places as effectively "in suspense" – in uncivilized regions, because they were stateless and would inevitably be subsumed by imperial governance; and in civilized regions, because recognition of autonomy was merely a political convenience and could be removed at any time.[136]

Despite Westlake's reluctance to make such connections, a discourse about hill country and legal primitivism promoted comparisons across disparate colonial enclave territories. Consider just one example, that of Basutoland, the region of hills, mountains, and high plateaus between Natal, the Orange Free State, and Griqualand East in southern Africa. The region fit the image of a refuge from successive upheavals emanating from conflicts nearer to the coast.[137] European visitors to its rugged mountains commented on the landscape as a natural complement to a politics of primitive solidarities and charismatic leadership. Thomas Arbousset, a missionary with the Paris Evangelical Missionary Society, developed these themes in his account of travels with the Sotho (or Basuto) leader Moshoeshoe in 1840 through the Drakensburg Mountains. Moshoeshoe was interested in visiting the place of his childhood and seemed also to view the trip as an opportunity to identify other highland areas the

at stake. Irrespective of those features of sovereign right which Native States have, for the most part, ceded or circumscribed by Treaty, there are certainly some of which they have been silently, but effectually, deprived" (IOR P/752, Government of India, Foreign Department Proceedings, September 1873, Judicial, No. 9, pp. 12–13). And see previous discussion of the Lidell case.

135 See Gong, *Standard of "Civilization"*; and see also Koskenniemi, *The Gentle Civilizer of Nations*.

136 Westlake, "Territorial Sovereignty," in Oppenheim, *Collected Papers*, 183.

137 The *mfecane* had propelled a diverse set of polities into the high tablelands, and Boer and Griqua incursions also threatened to displace agricultural and pastoral settlements along the region's shifting borders, pushing various groups to higher ground.

Sotho might inhabit if incursions from the plains intensified.[138] Arbousset's impressions of the hill country alternated between "pleasant" and "frightful." He was struck by the "natural delight" of the hills but found the first large mountain cavern he entered to be a perfect image of hell.[139] Arbousset remarked on the contrast between his own impressions of nature and those of the region's inhabitants. Like the caves in which they took shelter, the hill peoples were inward looking, he reported, and "little disposed towards imaginative insight." Unlike Moshoeshoe, whom Arbousset praised for his "deep yearning for complete knowledge," the people were incapable of appreciating the powerful landscapes around them. The mountains were for them an unremarkable backdrop – at most, a refuge: "Born in the wilderness, they are used to it. What delights us most are things such as its vastness, its fears, its gloomy stillness, its burning sands, and its refreshing oases.... But such things are of little account to them." After scaling one of the highest peaks in Maloti, a region of low mountains on the edge of Natal, Arbousset was amazed that Moshoeshoe commented wondrously on the beauty of the place. This sort of admiration of nature was, for an African, "quite exceptional."[140]

This account fits within a long European tradition of remarking on Moshoeshoe's exceptional qualities. Moshoeshoe pursued a balanced program of diplomacy and warfare, seeking protection against Boer settlers by negotiating a shifting alliance with British and Cape authorities and fighting to retain power over the region's many smaller polities. His maneuvering contributed to the British government's decision in 1854 to abandon the Orange River Sovereignty, a territory comprising the Boer settlements and Basutoland that had been annexed in 1848. Instability in the region, especially warfare between the Basuto and Boers, led to further intervention by the British – invited by Moshoeshoe, who had come to view British authority as essential protection from Boer incursions. But after the British government insisted on annexation by the Cape Colony, a period of direct administration by the Cape government from 1871 to

[138] The terms *Basuto* and *Basutoland* were British creations; speakers of the Sotho language (*Sesotho* to native speakers) refer to themselves as *Basotho*, and the territory they inhabit *Lesotho*. I use *Basuto* and *Basutoland* here because they appeared commonly in documents at the time. Historians have also tended to adopt the term. See Sandra Burman, ed., *The Justice of the Queen's Government: The Cape's Administration of Basutoland, 1871–1884* (Leiden: Afrika-Studiecentrum, 1976), 1–2.

[139] Thomas Arbousset, *Missionary Excursion into the Blue Mountains, Being an Account of King Moshoeshoe's Expedition from Thaba-Bosiu to the Sources of the Malibamatso River in the Year 1840* (Morija, Lesotho: Morija Archives, n.d.), 58–61.

[140] Arbousset, *Missionary Excursion*, 92, 146.

1884 ended in revolt, and a return to indirect rule under British imperial authority. The region eventually became the seat of Lesotho, an independent country subject to the economic and political constraints of its enclave geography within the territory of South Africa. This narrative is often told as a story of political acumen on one side and shortsightedness mixed with errors in judgment on the other, as successive British and Cape officials underestimated Sotho power. While there is no doubt that the outcomes owed a great deal to the skill of Sotho leaders, especially Moshoeshoe, it is worth noting that a personality-centered explanation for Basuto success was embraced and promoted by contemporary British colonial officials. We can guess at some of the reasons for the appeal of this story.

The corollary of the view that Moshoeshoe was an exceptional leader was that the rest of the Basuto were politically primitive. The failure of successive colonial officials to establish order could be seen as arising partly from the natural volatility of the place and the difficulties of understanding its mercurial political order.[141] Emphasizing a Basuto legal primitivism featuring fractional, personal rule and an aversion to institutions seemed to help explain why colonial interventions in the region were necessary – and why they failed. These views received careful elaboration in the writings of George Theal, an official in the Native Affairs Department at the Cape, on the origins of Basuto political life in the introductions to three volumes of documents involving relations with the Basuto published in 1893.[142]

Like his contemporary Tupper, Theal was looking back on the internal colonial correspondence involving various phases of quasi-sovereignty between 1848 and 1881. He wrote that the Basuto were "physically inferior" to lowland Africans and, at the time that French missionaries

[141] At the same time, portraying some colonial officials as insufficiently flexible also worked to shift attention from contradictions inherent in the system of colonial rule. The mysteries of local political culture and the limitations of individual magistrates were themes intertwined in British assessments of the career of Hamilton Hope. He had been a magistrate in Basutoland, where he was known for his brutality and "imperious style." When serving as magistrate of the neighboring Qumbu district, he was killed in the Gun War of 1880–1881; he was attending a ritual that he expected to affirm the supremacy of the British magistrate before a group of supposedly allied warriors. Sean Redding, *Sorcery and Sovereignty: Taxation, Power, and Rebellion in South Africa, 1880–1963* (Athens: Ohio University Press, 2006), 31. On Hope's death, see Clifton Crais, *The Politics of Evil: Magic, State Power, and the Political Imagination in South Africa* (Cambridge: Cambridge University Press, 2002), chap. 1.

[142] George MacCall Theal, ed., *Basutoland Records: Copies of Official Documents of Various Kinds, Accounts of Travellers... [Etc.]*, 3 vols. (Cape Town, W.A. Richards & Sons: 1883).

were invited to settle among them in 1833, that they were "in such a condition that progress towards a higher kind of life, unless directed from some agency external to themselves, was nearly impossible."[143] Going beyond mere assertions of the Basuto's need for a civilizing mission, Theal included elements of utopian primitivism in his portrait of Basuto law and politics. The chief, he explained, could not own land but could only alienate it in parts, and only temporarily. The consent of the tribe in council was always required for new laws and treaties. At a number of key points in British-Basuto relations, Theal explained, Moshoeshoe was willing but unable to sign agreements with the British because "his people" would not accept them.[144] Just as sovereignty resided in the people, law derived not from the chief but from ancient custom: "The people composing the Basuto tribe were inheritors of a system of common law admirably adapted to the circumstances in which they lived. It had come down to them from a period so remote that its origin was lost in the mists of antiquity."[145] Yet despite its emphasis on "perfect freedom of speech" for every individual and for "always deciding cases according to precedent," Basuto common law was not to be confused with the common law of England; it was "adapted to people in a rude state of society" and generated a legal order that tolerated cruelty, protected chiefs' privileges, and treated many serious crimes as mere civil offenses. The system was also, if left in isolation, frozen in time: "The traditional laws meeting all the circumstances of barbarian life, it was only when something abnormal occurred through contact with civilization that new ones were needed."[146]

[143] Theal, *Basutoland Records*, 2:iv, xii.

[144] For example, when the British proposed in 1852 an agreement to abandon the controversial boundary between Boer and Basutho territory along the Caledon River to recognize Moshoeshoe's supremacy over petty chiefs in the region, and to withdraw from any interference in internal affairs, the Basutho people withheld their consent. There appears to be little evidence for this conclusion. Moshoeshoe was in a strong position at the time, having defeated a British force in 1851, and even without a formal agreement to withdraw, the British entered a period in which their authority, as Theal concedes, was "merely nominal." "Introduction" in Theal, *Basutoland Records*, 2:lv.

[145] "Introduction" in Theal, *Basutoland Records*, 3:xv. Theal's comments echoed a British discourse on the "ancient constitution" of India and, like the outlines of the plan for quasi-sovereignty in Basutoland, seemed to draw on imperial officials' experiences in and knowledge of India. See Robert Travers, *Ideology and Empire in Eighteenth-Century India: The British in Bengal, 1757–93* (New York: Cambridge University Press, 2007); and Thomas R. Metcalf, *Imperial Connections: India in the Indian Ocean Arena, 1860–1920* (Berkeley: University of California Press, 2007).

[146] Theal, *Basutoland Records*, 3:xv–xvi.

In many respects this picture of legal primitivism was more sympathetic than British views of law among the nearby Boer settlements. Here, Theal reported, "Individuals could commit almost any crime without being brought to punishment. There was neither a police nor a regularly constituted tribunal of justice."[147] In the 1830s, as the numbers of Boer settlers grew, Cape officials briefly regarded recognizing the jurisdiction of Moshoeshoe as preferable to, and perhaps made necessary by, the state of lawlessness in territories that were effectively beyond the reach of colonial laws. British perspectives on Basuto legal primitivism were also relevant to colonial officials' profound ambivalence about intervention in Moshoeshoe's battles with other chiefs in the region. After 1848, the British promoted the independence of smaller polities over which Moshoeshoe had claimed suzerainty; in part motivated by the desire to counterbalance and contain Moshoeshoe's power, the policy drew strength from an implicit assumption that a system of multiple, small chieftainships exercising primitive sovereignty was natural to the region, a better fit given its stage of development than a political order built on the suzerainty of one leader.

The centrality of legal politics in the creation and re-creation of Basuto as a territorial enclave is striking.[148] While major struggles focused on such issues as the collection of the hut tax, the enforcement of marriage regulations, and Basuto disarmament in the rebellion that led to the end of Cape administration, conflicts over the structure of shared legal authority were both routine and occasionally explosive. During the twelve years that Basutoland came under direct administration of the Cape, colonial officials sought to undermine chiefs' legal authority while carefully preserving elements of their legitimacy. Basuto leaders, for their part, often sought accommodations on matters of principle but violently opposed specific acts by Cape-appointed magistrates that threatened to undermine local legal prerogatives in settling disputes, imposing fines, and fixing punishments.[149]

[147] Theal, *Basutoland Records*, 3:xx.

[148] See Sandra Burman, *Chiefdom Politics and Alien Laws: Basutoland under Cape Rule 1871–1884* (London: Macmillan, 1981). The following account is based largely on Burman's narrative; see also Burman, ed., *The Justice of the Queen's Government*; and, for the broader set of state practices involved in colonial consolidation, Crais, *The Politics of Evil*, chap. 2.

[149] For example, in the explosion of raiding between Boers and Basuto after 1854, leaders of the Orange Free State routinely demanded restitution for Basuto cattle raids and the surrender of Basuto men accused of violent crimes for their trial by Orange Free State courts. The Basuto occasionally made some restitution for raids, but Moshoeshoe never

The Basuto revolt against Cape authority in the 1880s prompted an attempt to introduce an arrangement modeled directly on British relations with Indian princely states. In the midst of the rebellion, the military commander at the Cape, Major-General Charles Gordon, proposed a system explicitly based on British Indian models in which Basuto internal affairs would be left alone and the British would assume control of the region's external sovereignty. Drawing from Indian examples, Gordon wanted to remove magistrates from Basutoland and replace them with a resident and two subresidents, charging these men mainly with overseeing Basuto relations with adjoining territories. Significantly, the proposal was rejected by Cape officials, who argued that the Basuto had no polity but were "simply a collection of jarring clans held together for the time by animosity against us."[150] As with the Bhils in India, such ideas could be placed in the service of opposite solutions. The pressures toward creating an enclave status for Basutoland emanated not so much from these debates as from the continued raiding and legal indeterminacy along a border where Boers and Basutos intermingled, and from Basuto leaders' repeated insistence that Cape officials held only the equivalent of bare sovereignty. Participants in the conflicts of the 1870s and 1880s would not have predicted Basutoland's return to British indirect rule and eventual transformation into Lesotho. Only slight differences in the political context might have produced an outcome more like the quasi-sovereignty of Indian princely states or the status of Indian reservations in the United States.[151]

The comparison of Indians to Indians was one embraced, curiously, by nineteenth-century international lawyers and colonial officials.

gave in to the request for jurisdiction over border crimes. The Basuto leader eventually agreed to recognize a long-disputed boundary between the polities but refused the Boer demand that he accept a magistrate in Basuto territory to curb border infractions. Even in the Gun War that ended Cape sovereignty, the controversy over disarmament became a crisis only when the chiefs rejected the right of Cape-appointed magistrates to interfere in chiefs' actions to punish subjects who had refused orders not to give up their guns. Burman, *Chiefdom Politics and Alien Laws.*

[150] Burman, *Chiefdom Politics and Alien Laws*, 165.

[151] The term *outcome* requires qualification. Conflicts over jurisdiction and shared sovereignty continued into the twentieth century, though the term *quasi-sovereignty* fell out of use and tensions over sovereignty took on new forms in the context of Indian nationalism. In the 1920s, the Chamber of Princes, composed of representatives of the larger princely states, asserted that the sovereign rights of the states were inherent rights rather than dependent on the paramount power (or any subsequent government) for their creation. See Ian Copland, *The Princes of India in the Endgame of Empire, 1917–1947* (Cambridge: Cambridge University Press, 2002); Panikkar, *Indian Princes in Council.*

Apparently drawing on John Marshall's phrase defining American Indian nations within the United States as "domestic dependent nations," Twiss described Indian native states in his 1861 book *The Law of Nations* as "protected dependent states," and this formulation was later picked up and repeated by other writers.[152] The timing of this attention to Marshall's words is curious. By the time they were being invoked as part of a model for treating Indian princely states, Marshall's opinion had come to be largely overshadowed by a different approach to U.S. Indian law that proposed a theoretically nearly unlimited federal power to interfere with Indian jurisdiction and property. An important shift began with Congress's legislation in 1871 to ban further treaties with American Indian nations. The end of the treaty regime was followed by the decline of tribal governance and the effective transfer of power by the 1880s to officials of the Bureau of Indian Affairs. The reservation system, established through a series of forced agreements whereby Indians gave up large tracts of land in return for assurances of internal sovereignty, was then nearly dismantled as a result of the 1887 General Allotment Act, or Dawes Act, which created the mechanisms for the eventual transfer of some 86 million acres of land out of Indian hands. The result was a patchwork pattern of land ownership in which lands under Indian, non-Indian, and corporate control were interspersed, and "Indian country" came to be traversed by private railroads and state and federal highways. These trends exacerbated some jurisdictional tensions at the same time that they strengthened the hand of state and federal officials seeking rationales for further authority over disputes involving Indians and local resources.[153]

The precedent set by the Supreme Court in favor of a system of "measured separatism" did, in its broadest outlines, resemble the theoretical outlines of British paramountcy in India, and this line of legal thinking and policy was not a complete dead-letter.[154] In *Ex parte Crow Dog*, in 1883, the Court upheld the right of the Brulé Sioux Indians to judge and punish an Indian for the murder of another Indian and held that Congress

[152] Travers Twiss, *The Law of Nations Considered as Independent Political Communities: On the Rights and Duties of Nations in Time of Peace [1884]* (Littleton, CO: Fred B. Rothman, 1985), 27. Twiss is cited approvingly by Tupper, *Our Indian Protectorate*, 4. Marshall's phrase is from *Cherokee Nation v. Georgia*, 30 U.S. 1, 33 (1831).

[153] This account summarizes a complex history of Indian law and policy. For an overview, see Francis Paul Prucha, *The Great Father: The United States Government and the American Indians* (Lincoln: University of Nebraska Press, 1984); Wilkinson, *American Indians.*

[154] The phrase is from Wilkinson, *American Indians*, 16, 22.

had never established federal jurisdiction over Indian subjects committing crimes on Indian land. In *Talton v. Mayes*, decided in 1886, the Court went on to exempt Indian tribes from the requirement of conducting a grand jury proceeding under the Fifth Amendment because tribal law predated the writing of the Constitution. These decisions kept alive a line of legal reasoning and a tradition in policy based on the assumption of effective Indian internal sovereignty.[155] But they also elicited a backlash. In part prompted by the *Crow Dog* decision, Congress passed the Major Crimes Act in 1885 to establish federal jurisdiction over Indians anywhere who were charged with crimes of murder, manslaughter, rape, assault with intent to kill, arson, burglary, and larceny. The law was upheld in *United States v. Kagama* the next year, in a ruling that seemed to establish definitively the power of the federal government to determine unilaterally the kind and amount of autonomy that would be awarded to Indians, including those with organized governments in clearly bounded territories.

Uniting both strands of Indian jurisprudence was an effort to distinguish federal from state prerogatives to intercede in Indian affairs. Any possibility for upholding Indian sovereignty depended on claims to effective governance, which in turn was restricted to nations with formally bounded reservations, enclave territories now largely engulfed by state lands. Deborah Rosen notes that this pattern emerged out of the efforts of states to assert jurisdictional claims over Indians, in part by advancing arguments about the varying status, condition, or location of Indian groups so that, for example, state encroachments were especially legally effective against Indians living interspersed with whites or in scattered territories.[156] Advocates of expanding federal jurisdiction cited the need to protect Indians from aggressive acts and property seizures by the states, or by white settlers ranged around the borders of Indian lands. Many of the legal problems that carried forward into the next century were related to this enclave geography, and to "the dilemma of porous reservation boundaries": cases involving continued questions

[155] On the federal rulings from *Ex parte Crow Dog*, 109 U.S. 556 (1883) to *Talton v. Mayes*, 163 U.S. 376 (1886), and to the Major Crimes Act of 1885, see Sidney L. Harring, *Crow Dog's Case: American Indian Sovereignty, Tribal Law, and United States Law in the Nineteenth Century* (Cambridge: Cambridge University Press, 1994).

[156] These arguments had to be posed constitutionally as assertions of states' rights to except Indians from federal oversight. See Deborah A. Rosen, *American Indians and State Law: Sovereignty, Race, and Citizenship, 1790–1880* (Lincoln: University of Nebraska Press, 2007), chap. 2.

about jurisdiction, challenges to definitions of citizenship and tribal membership, and questions about the application of legislation in Indian territory.[157]

In contrast to nineteenth-century India, there was less debate about whether American Indian law developed within a constitutional framework rather than within a regime of international law. Yet we still observe a systemic tendency toward territorial anomalies, and the legal administration of American Indian lands formed only one part of a wider pattern. The administration of newly acquired territories by the United States created a variegated legal landscape. Most newly acquired territories had been or would be converted into states. But even when statehood was the eventual outcome, administration of the territories posed resilient legal puzzles, including "constitutionally bizarre" arrangements such as the peacetime military administration of the territory of California in the two years before statehood, and the definition of U.S. "sovereignty without sovereignty" in Panama and the Pacific guano islands.[158] Continuing political and legal jockeying over the definition of state sovereignty reinforced understandings of sovereignty as implying partial or limited prerogatives. Loose analogies to federalism applied widely. State sovereignty, as Deborah Rosen notes, became "a paradigm for imagining the status of Indian tribes" at the same time that states' expanding jurisdictional claims eroded Indian sovereignty.[159] Such comparisons often remained implicit given the potential political explosiveness of grouping Indian territories with other part-sovereign entities. But in the context of the U.S. brush with formal empire at the turn of the century, the parallel became a matter of law. Echoing Marshall in the Cherokee cases, Justice White wrote in his concurrence in *Downes v. Bidwell* (1901) that Puerto Rico should be considered "foreign to the United States in a domestic sense."[160]

[157] The phrase is from Brad Asher, *Beyond the Reservation: Indians, Settlers, and the Law in Washington Territory, 1853–1889* (Norman: University of Oklahoma Press, 1999), 195. Asher argues that Indian law beneath the federal level was "inherently unstable." On local jurisdictional complexities, see also Ford, *Settler Sovereignty.* And for a rich study and explicit argument about the importance of state and territorial law in defining Indian citizenship, see Rosen, *American Indians and State Law.*

[158] See Benton, "Constitutions and Empires"; Christina Duffy Burnett, "The Edges of Empire and the Limits of Sovereignty: American Guano Islands," *American Quarterly* 57, no. 3 (2005), 779–803; Gary Lawson and Guy Seidman, *The Constitution of Empire: Territorial Expansion and American Legal History* (New Haven, CT: Yale University Press, 2004), pt. 2.

[159] Rosen, *American Indians and State Law*, 22.

[160] *Downes v. Bidwell*, 182 U.S. 244 (1901). Christina Burnett argues that the "epochal significance" of the *Insular Cases* was not that they created a category of attenuated

A formula for the constitutional recognition of legally anomalous enclaves surrounded by U.S. national space was relied on to describe the legal status of a colonial territory outside the country's borders.

I do not want to follow nineteenth-century writings in insisting on strained comparisons of Indians to Indians. These histories, and the geographies they produced, are very different.[161] In both settings, though, legally anomalous enclave territories played a symbolically important role in wider processes of incorporating territory into empire-states. And during the same decades of the nineteenth century, legal schemata promoting a vision of semiautonomous subpolities – a form of quasi-sovereignty – gave way slowly, through political acts framed by discourse about the limits of law, to a regime of intervention. Both national and imperial constitutionalism promoted uncertainty and, at the same time, the transposition of arrangements for enclave rule to other legally anomalous territories.

These examples help to remind us of the variety of settings in which enclave territories developed because and in spite of imperial legal policies. In the United States, a constitutional formula for the protection of quasi-sovereignty produced a legal regime of intervention in the nineteenth century combined with continued recognition of territorial anomalies. In Basutoland, an apparent trend toward legal integration led

sovereignty for territorial acquisitions outside the United States but that they provided for the possibility of *de*annexation. Christina Duffy Burnett, "*Untied* States: American Expansion and Territorial Deannexation," *University of Chicago Law Review* 72 (2005), 797–880.

[161] The geographic discourse associated with these histories also appears to be very different, though we do not yet know enough about the links between legal and geographic imaginations in the western United States. There is a good deal of scholarship on representations of the West as a great desert and on the imagined "Great Basin" of the intermountain West, and there are obvious links to strategies for pushing Indians onto arid lands. Limerick, *Desert Passages*; Richard V. Francaviglia, *Mapping and Imagination in the Great Basin: A Cartographic History* (Reno: University of Nevada Press, 2005). But we also get a hint of a more complex set of associations between topography and legal status of Indians in histories tracing representations of "wild Indians" outside Spanish settlements of the Southwest or in the unsuccessful attempts by Utes to hold onto a vast territory on the western slope of the Rockies. James Brooks, *Captives and Cousins: Slavery, Kinship, and Community in the Southwest Borderlands* (Chapel Hill: University of North Carolina Press, 2002); and Ned Blackhawk, *Violence over the Land: Indians and Empires in the Early American West* (Cambridge, MA: Harvard University Press, 2006). On eastern Indians and geographic imagination, see Timothy Silver, *A New Face on the Countryside: Indians, Colonists, and Slaves in South Atlantic Forests, 1500–1800* (New York: Cambridge University Press, 1990). The links between geographic discourse and law deserve closer scrutiny in both periods.

unexpectedly to the creation of a permanent enclave state. Events in Baroda illustrate the close connections, apparent in all these cases, between routine legal tensions and the rationale for political intervention. Visions of the hardiness of primitive law blended with projections of its inevitable demise, while designs on territorial absorption also recognized repeated territorial variation. Everywhere, seemingly small legal disputes rose quickly to the level of constitutional challenges or political crises. In enclave territories surrounded or partially engulfed by territories of direct rule, jurisdictional conflicts at the borders and controversies about subjecthood or citizenship blurred distinctions between internal and external sovereignty. Fumbling to define situations that had no clear place within municipal or international law, officials sought ways to make the repeated suspension of law an integral rather than exceptional part of the legal order.

Conclusion

Quasi-sovereignty was more than a theoretical device with a brief history within international law. The legal politics of divisible sovereignty in empire generated sharp conflicts and stimulated new ways of thinking about imperial law. Intended to reconcile colonialism and international law, the legal project of devising a typology of states within empire instead established new sets of constitutional issues at the center of what was being defined as a distinctive imperial legal order. Seeking to mark clearly the scope of autonomy for subpolities produced an elaborate set of legal territories in empire. And as Indian princes and other indigenous elites held tenaciously to jurisdiction over internal affairs and even maneuvered for some elements of external sovereignty, colonial officials were driven to describe with greater precision the terms of intervention as a political act situated at the edges of law. No amount of wishful thinking on the part of international lawyers could make an imperial law dominated by these preoccupations disappear. In fact, borrowings from international law served mainly to highlight the peculiarities of law in empire: a tendency toward more, not less, territorial irregularity and the probability that the terms of relations between imperial powers and colonial quasi-states would sometimes be defined as standing outside the law.

Tracing this development of imperial law suggests that we need to push still further in revising historical narratives of the international order. The history of quasi-sovereignty in the late nineteenth century reminds us that empires retained their international significance in an imagined world of territorially homogeneous and bounded states.[162] Comparisons show that within empires and also some nation-states, conflicts over sovereignty produced similar jurisdictional tensions, uneven patterns of legal geography, and discourse about dependent polities. The usual statement that international law struggled to accommodate empire and eventually rendered it obsolete might be turned around. That is, the colonial project that Westlake had described as "needlessly intricate" in its parsing of sovereignty generated a robust constitutionalism that increasingly referenced international law for style, not substance. In the process, imperial jurisprudence pointed to the limitations of both international and municipal law as comprehensive frameworks for the global order.

As we saw in the previous chapter, imperial legal politics encouraged calls for the suspension of law, together with routines for setting space aside and designating it as legally anomalous. In quasi-sovereign colonial enclaves, repeated conflicts over border control, jurisdictional tensions, and attempts to define the application of imperial legislation created an environment in which routine legal disputes could quickly generate political crises – creating the institutionalization of intervention "by necessity." The limits of law in these cases both originated in and helped to create spatial irregularities in empire. Acts of intervention that would have been politically unremarkable if applied to territories of direct rule took on the quality of exceptional acts when applied to colonial enclaves, engendering an association between holes in the imperial map and silences in the law.

The late nineteenth-century legal politics of colonial enclaves had an immediate and direct effect on ideological and theoretical formulations within European international law. Colonial officials did not merely provide the raw material for metropolitan jurists. They used categories and approaches with a long history and molded them to new contexts. We cannot draw a straight line from Acosta to Tupper, or from Braudel's sixteenth-century lowlanders worrying about Moors in the Alpujarras to the residents of Cape Town considering the problem of Basutoland. At the same time, the continuities of discourse about the spatial (and topographical) separation of legally archaic societies help to explain some of the late nineteenth-century formulations, for example, the notion that one rationale for imperial rule lay in the moral imperative to check the tendency of small hill polities to engage in mutual aggression. The same

[162] On this point, see also Jane Burbank and Frederick Cooper, *Empires in World History* (Princeton, NJ: Princeton University Press, forthcoming).

tendency toward aggression, founded in egalitarian forms of political association, appeared to explain why such polities were not ready for full incorporation into the imperial legal order.

The discourse about archaic law in the hills – quintessential settings for zones of quasi-sovereignty – both contributed to the impulse to create separate legal spaces and helped to make this spatial and legal exceptionalism appear natural. The legal primitivism associated with the hills was transposed onto other landscapes, and it offered a useful explanation for the legal anomalies of other places, even while it affirmed the expectation of their eventual absorption. Like the trope of the tropics, the image of timeless colonial hills was related to a broader Orientalism, to be sure, but it also reflected a legal politics creating differentiated colonial territories rather than consolidated zones of homogeneous and subordinated otherness. The very notion of divided sovereignty seemed linked to the natural political and cultural fissures of enclave regions. Their singularity signaled the spatial and temporal limits of law.

6

Bare Sovereignty and Empire

We know sovereignty when we see it – at least we think we do. Post-nineteenth-century definitions of sovereignty highlight the ambition to control what and who crosses borders as well as the power to make laws to regulate what happens within them. *State sovereignty* and *national sovereignty* are terms that have lodged themselves in our political vocabulary to such a degree that they appear to have no logical substitutes. Yet we also know that sovereignty is often more myth than reality, more a story that polities tell about their own power than a definite quality they possess. Most boundaries are porous and many are contested, and states cannot consistently enforce laws to regulate activities across and within borders. And as we have seen, territory plays tricks. Mere patches of regulated land may appear to signify claims to vast holdings, while integral "sovereign" space may fracture into many odd-shaped pieces. The problem is not just that tumultuous times and distant realms produce unmanageable complexity. Political space everywhere generates irregularities: polities and subpolities secure exemptions from legislation, jurisdictions guard their autonomy, and subjects and citizens seek to expand or protect extraterritorial legal rights. Peculiar forms of attenuated and partial sovereignty are as common to political life as acts of corruption, and they are politically more far reaching in their effects.

How do we reconcile these two kinds of knowledge about sovereignty, our certainty about its definition and our recognition of its elusiveness? One way would be to refine the theoretical understanding of sovereignty; another, to retell its history. This book has sought to contribute to each of these projects. By definition and in practice, sovereignty in empire formed as multiple agents positioned themselves to act as subjects of and proxies for imperial powers, and as polities and populations negotiated scope for their own autonomy, sometimes urging radical reconfigurations of rule. Theories of divided sovereignty came into play early and developed in connection with the problems of imagining and ordering colonial rule. The strength and persistence of arrangements of layered and divided sovereignty made a difference in the structure of the global legal regime. By the end of the nineteenth century, such patterns posed a sharp challenge to claims about the basis of international law in the agreements formed by separate and equal sovereign states. Multiple anomalous legal spaces in European empires developed not merely in opposition to imperial centers but also in response to shifting interimperial relations and cross-imperial comparisons, forming in the process part of a broader, geographically uneven regulatory web, or another source of international law.

This way of viewing imperial sovereignty contrasts with older accounts of the history of sovereignty in Western Europe. Those histories emphasized the emergence of territorial nation-states in response to military competition and capital formation. Differences of interpretation within this narrative addressed the question of the timing of the transition to territorial sovereignty, sometimes placed in the seventeenth century, more often associated with the eighteenth century, and often fixed confidently in the nineteenth century.[1] We now know that the impulse to territorial rule and the legal politics that transcended or splintered territory were parallel and not mutually exclusive processes. European polities retained and created their own anomalous enclaves and loosely configured corridors of imperial control that defied easy categorization, even alongside tendencies to define and protect borders. Recent studies have emphasized the close kinship between European state formation and the political structuring of empires, both understood as open-ended processes in which pronouncements about sovereignty conflicted with the realities of composite polities, jurisdictional tensions, and intrastate violence.[2]

[1] See Hendrik Spruyt, *The Sovereign State and Its Competitors: An Analysis of Systems Change* (Princeton, NJ: Princeton University Press, 1996); Charles Tilly, *Coercion, Capital, and European States, AD 990–1992*, rev. ed. (Cambridge, MA: Wiley-Blackwell, 2007); Thomas Ertman, *Birth of the Leviathan: Building States and Regimes in Medieval and Early Modern Europe* (Cambridge: Cambridge University Press, 1997).

[2] James Muldoon, in *Empire and Order*, has advocated understanding state and empire formation as parallel processes. In *Colonialism in Question*, Frederick Cooper recommends the term *empire-states*. Studies of the interrelation between state formation and early empire have explored a wider and more nuanced set of connections. See especially M. J. Braddick, *State Formation in Early Modern England, c. 1550–1700* (Cambridge: Cambridge University Press, 2000). For the late colonial period, Sen, in *Distant Sovereignty*,

Still, the idea of sovereignty as a quality defined first and foremost by territorial control continues to exert influence. Though attentive to the halting and incomplete progression to nation-state sovereignty, Stephen Krasner describes three kinds of modern sovereignty – Westphalian, domestic, and international – and presents territorial control as a critical element of each. Westphalian sovereignty claims involve the exclusion of external political actors from the political structures of a given territory; domestic sovereignty refers to the actual ability of political authorities to control processes inside the borders of their polities; and international sovereignty is a function of states' capacities to control flows across those borders.[3] Leaving aside the question of whether these definitions are useful for analysis of the interstate order of the twentieth and twenty-first centuries, we see the dangers, and also the temptation, of applying Krasner's notions of sovereignty to the early modern world, and to Europe's overseas empires. Although European powers aggressively pursued territorial acquisitions throughout the period under study here, they also often placed other goals ahead of territorial control and consolidation, including the protection of commercial networks and routes, and strategic responses to moves by imperial rivals. Interimperial conflicts encouraged an emphasis on symbolic demonstrations of power and authority rather than the control of borders and the creation of institutions evenly distributed across space.[4] Practical adaptations of theoretically vibrant notions of divided sovereignty permitted experiments in partial or mixed sovereignty, arrangements that appeared consistent with the structure of plural legal orders and varieties of geographic formations.

This book has explored the production of variegated legal spaces of empire, zones that emerged as legal practices responded to interimperial rivalries, intraimperial politics, and local conflicts, and that combined with selective elements of geographic discourse. These processes raised problems for contemporaries struggling to define the nature of the global legal community, and they pose challenges to historians seeking to

probes a number of promising avenues for analyzing links between colonial state formation in India and the development of the nineteenth-century British state, noting that phenomena in empire that "may appear to be novel or deviant aspects of colonial administration thrust upon it by the force of circumstance turn out on closer inspection to be strikingly consistent with the overall paradigm of policial culture in contemporary England" (4). At the same time, Sen suggests that there were some distinctive features of the "distant and disputed sovereignty" of empire (xvii).

[3] Stephen D. Krasner, *Sovereignty: Organized Hypocrisy* (Princeton, NJ: Princeton University Press, 1999), chap. 1.

[4] This point is made by Maier, *Among Empires*, 101.

construct a narrative of the origins and development of sovereignty, and of the interstate order. It was, and is, difficult to fit empires, with their stubbornly composite forms of rule and layered systems of sovereignty, either into frameworks of global integration modeled loosely on Roman ideas about world dominion or within models of a global community of nation-states.[5] The challenge is further complicated by evidence of the continual production in empires of new legal and geographic variations. Where we might expect to find a progression toward a simplified project of territorial control as empires embraced more fully the "territorial imperative" in later centuries, we instead see processes generating new sources of spatial and legal differentiation.[6]

In seeking to draw larger lessons from these histories, one is tempted to look to the writings of Carl Schmitt, and the related theories of Giorgio Agamben, for clues about how best to understand a systemic tendency to produce moments and spaces of exception in empire. The controversial jurist Schmitt viewed the "bracketing" of a zone of war outside Europe as an essential element of the self-fashioning of Europe as a zone of peace and the seat of international norms. He saw this development as in turn linked inextricably to the emergence of a global system of nation-states "because international law regulating relations between empires could not be converted easily into a firm bracketing of war," that is, into a coherent global spatial order.[7] In this world order, imperial sovereignty became irrelevant, or, more precisely, relevant only for its preservation of types of polities (colonies and protectorates) not yet subsumed under the category of states.

This formulation seems to describe a legal distinction between European and extra-European arenas that corresponds to a well-documented discourse, with many historical variants, delineating the differences between metropolitan and colonial law. But it is important to separate

[5] On the awkward fit of Roman imperial models, see especially Pagden, *Lords of All the World*, chap. 1. On the problem of empires within an international legal order of nation-states, see Keene, *Beyond the Anarchical Society*; and Anghie, *Making of International Law*.

[6] Thus, historians of U.S. empire and other scholars using imperial history as a lens through which to view nineteenth- and twentieth-century imperialism have also moved toward this conclusion. Ann Laura Stoler asks, "What if we begin not with a model of empire based on fixed, imperial cartographies but with one dependent on shifting categories and moving parts whose designated borders at any one time were not necessarily the force fields in which they operated or the limits of them?" She concludes that the result is an image of empire as a composite of zones of different "degrees of sovereignty." "On Degrees of Imperial Sovereignty," *Public Culture* 18, no. 1 (2006), 125-46, 138. And see Amy Kaplan, "Where Is Guantánamo?" *American Quarterly* 57, no. 3 (2005), 831–58.

[7] Schmitt, *Nomos of the Earth*, 55.

Schmitt's formula from historical accounts of European discourse.[8] Viewing colonial territories as spheres of legal exception was, after all, overdetermined. European international lawyers working for European states would not have chosen to imagine a global legal order centering around a region outside Europe, nor would they have elevated a different kind of political formation to primacy in the international system in place of the nation-state. A European preference for describing the global order as an interstate system centered in Europe does not make this formulation either useful as theory or accurate as historical narrative. As the case studies of this book have shown, a broad array of legal routines extended law transregionally, and European sojourners and settlers enthusiastically embraced law as a framework for accumulating knowledge about the extra-European world, defining membership in distant political communities, positioning themselves for patronage and authority, and interacting with indigenous peoples and polities. A binary distinction between European and extra-European legal zones gives us little to work with in describing or analyzing the patterns of varation within and across European empires resulting from this legal politics.

Schmitt's other main insight into sovereignty seems to offer a more promising point of departure for the study of imperial sovereignty. Schmitt defines the sovereign as "he who decides on the exception."[9] For Schmitt, the sovereign decision is an act simultaneously inside and outside the juridical order; the sovereign steps outside the law to decide, but the authority to decide derives from law. As Agamben summarizes Schmitt's view, "what is at issue in the sovereign exception is . . . the very condition of possibility of juridical rule, and, along with it, the very meaning of State authority."[10] Going further, Agamben argues that the exception constitutes the rule by representing the suspension of the rule. Eliding "the rule" and "the rule of law" – a problematic confusion that I will discuss in a moment – both Schmitt and Agamben represent the declaration of martial law and the state of siege as quintessential acts of the suspension

[8] For example, we should not read Eliga Gould's study of representations of Europe as a zone of law and the outer Atlantic as a zone of lawlessness ("Zones of Law") as an exercise in applying Schmitt's ideas. Nor should we understand European discourse, either Schmittian variants or much older approaches, as accurate historical accounts of legal geography.

[9] In this construction, the exception creates the general rule, which in turn constructs its meaning in relation to "a regular, everyday frame of life to which it can be factually applied." Carl Schmitt, *Political Theology: Four Chapters on the Concept of Sovereignty* (Chicago: University of Chicago Press, 2005), 5.

[10] Giorgio Agamben, *Homo Sacer: Sovereign Power and Bare Life* (Stanford, CA: Stanford University Press, 1998), 17.

of law. The possibilities for violence created in the "state of exception" flow from exclusionary acts that simultaneously include violence in the juridical order.[11]

Neither Schmitt nor Agamben, it must be said, reveals a particular interest in, or knowledge of, the world outside Europe. Nasser Hussain takes up the task of relating their ideas to an understanding of law in empire in analyzing the suspension of law in the nineteenth-century British empire.[12] Hussain argues that emergency played a crucial role in the constitution of imperial sovereignty, and he follows Schmitt in understanding emergency measures (the suspension of habeas corpus and the declaration of martial law) as exceptions to the rule of law that were simultaneously deeply rooted in the juridical order. He views colonial settings as distinctive not because the suspension of law was unique to them but because the relation of emergency to sovereignty became more clearly visible in them. Because part of Hussain's argument rests on his observation that emergency came to be invoked with greater frequency in the colonies than in the metropole, the effect of this approach is to suggest an association between empire and the state of exception.[13] But this construction grows out of an interest in using the history of empire to illuminate the workings of modern state sovereignty rather than elaborating the dynamics of imperial sovereignty. Hussain approvingly quotes Chatterjee, who notes "the inherent impossibility of completing the project of the modern state without superseding the conditions of colonial rule." Like Anghie, who focuses on the challenge posed to international legal theory by the complexities of imperial sovereignty, Hussain reads colonial history as a lesson about the blockages to a system of state sovereignty. He wants to reveal "the colonial as an iteration of the modern."[14]

This construction reminds us that embedded within Schmitt's and Agamben's approaches lies a narrative of historical progression in which

[11] I simplify a good deal of difference on this point. Schmitt, in opposition to Walter Benjamin, who defines "pure violence" as residing outside the law, wants to "reinscribe violence within a juridical context," in Agamben's words. Giorgio Agamben, *State of Exception* (Chicago: University of Chicago Press, 2005), 59. Agamben, for his part, criticizes Schmitt's basis for this view in a flawed distinction between constituent power and constituted power, and he offers a variant in which the "state of exception" becomes a "juridical void" that is nevertheless maintained in relation to the juridical order because it holds "a decisive strategic relevance" (51).

[12] Hussain, *Jurisprudence of Emergency*.

[13] Achille Mbembe urges the same association, characterizing colonies as "the location par excellence where the controls and guarantees of judicial order can be suspended." "Necropolitics," *Public Culture* 15, no. 1 (2003): 24.

[14] Hussain, *Jurisprudence of Emergency*, 7.

the exception becomes ever more closely identified with the rule. Agamben states this point clearly: "The state of exception comes more and more to the fore as a fundamental political structure and begins to become the rule."[15] If we identify empire as a site of the frequent suspension of law and link it to the state of exception, we then import a narrative about empire as occupying an earlier historical stage before the emergence of modern state sovereignty. Replacing the familiar Whiggish logic of this sequence is the idea of a gradual movement toward naturalizing the exception as a property of sovereignty.

There is a great deal that is intriguing about this analytic move. As we saw in tracing the constitutional afterlife of penal colonies, there is no doubt that the contained experiments with martial law influenced the wider political culture, and we need some conceptual framework for describing and tracing this influence. The bleeding of exceptionalism into dominant political structures offers one approach to this shift. Yet there are also troubling elements of the approach. Like Schmitt's construction of the extra-European world as a zone of lawlessness, the identity between empire and exception can lead us to replace investigations of the legal politics and spatial history of empire with interpretations of metropolitan discourses about empire. For example, accounts of anxieties about the effects of the denigration of rights in empire on the body politic in the metropole might be substituted for an analysis of variants of rights regimes in empire.[16] Also, the paradoxical effect of privileging something called modern state sovereignty as the outcome of a long historical sequence is to preserve certain assumptions about state sovereignty that tie it to imagined Westphalian competencies, especially, as Hussain remarks without critique, "the state's obligations to maintain its territories and institutional integrity."[17] Neither of these points is

[15] Agamben, *Homo Sacer*, 20. For Agamben, this blurring of exception and norm involves a gradual merging of "bare life" – life stripped of its political significance – with sovereignty.

[16] On the difference between institutional and ideological comparisons of the rule of law, see Lauren Benton, "Not Just a Concept: Institutions and the 'Rule of Law'" *Journal of Asian Studies* 68 (2009): 63–8. For an example of an analysis of legal strategies on the construction of a distinctive imperial rights regime, see Jane Burbank, *Russian Peasants Go to Court: Legal Culture in the Countryside, 1905–1917* (Bloomington: Indiana University Press, 2004).

[17] Hussain, *Jurisprudence of Emergency*, 22. Similarly, Herzog, in *Defining Nations*, makes an important point in insisting on the contribution of processes constituting local communities and the formation of the states in which these communities were embedded. But she gives more attention to the goal of illuminating "state and nation formation in Europe" than the objective of understanding imperial sovereignty (6).

trivial.[18] But rather than pursuing them further here, I want to focus on a third problem illuminated by the case studies of this book: representing empires as zones of exception oversimplifies imperial sovereignty. I should note that I am not referring to distinctions we might draw between ideological representations of the rule of law in Europe and "rule by law" in empire.[19] Rather, I want to consider in the rest of this chapter the implications of taking into consideration the two aspects of imperial sovereignty explored in this book – the portability of subjecthood and the delegation of legal authority – and the uneven imperial geographies they helped to create.

It is helpful to begin by pointing out some problems arising from Agamben's purposeful confusion of "the rule" with "the rule of law." He blends the two concepts by defining "the rule" as always referencing a wider context of repeated behaviors that constitute a normative order: "The law has a regulative character and is a 'rule' not because it commands and proscribes, but because it must first of all create the sphere of its own reference in real life and *make that reference regular.*"[20] The rule announces more than sanction, then. Its very expression depends on the recognition of the exceptional case, which, as we have seen, is included in the juridical order at the same time that it is formally excluded. In Agamben's view, a subtler understanding of the rule as a normative statement nested within a habitus, a context of norms, provides the basis for a meaningful analogy with the rule of law. The analogy is clearly an imperfect one. There are many ways in which the rule of law is distinguished from the rule even in its subtlest rendering, and these distinctions turn out to be especially important to an understanding of imperial sovereignty.

Consider first the evidence from this book showing that legal politics and geographic discourse combined to carry legally sanctioned coercive

[18] Nor is the implied Eurocentrism of a focus on European sovereignty as the quintessential example of modern state sovereignty. This problem cannot be removed just by railing against Eurocentrism or by acts of recentering global history. As A. Dirlik points out, it makes no sense to seek to correct the Eurocentrism of the study of European empires because a particular and important kind of global power cohered in the metropolitan powers. "Confounding Metaphors, Inventions of the World: What Is World History For?" in *Writing World History, 1800–2000*, ed. Benedikt Stuchtey and Eckhardt Fuchs, (New York: Oxford University Press, 2003), 91–133.

[19] This approach leaves comparison at the level of ideology. For an example of this approach, see Jonathan Ocko and David Gilmartin, "State, Sovereignty, and the People: A Comparison of the 'Rule of Law' in China and India," *Journal of Asian Studies* 68, no. 1 (2008), 1–46; and my critique: Benton, "Not Just a Concept."

[20] Agamben, *Homo Sacer*, 26 (emphasis in original).

violence in directed streams to places far from imperial centers of power. In the politics of treason in the early modern Atlantic, European sojourners understood that the legality of their actions depended directly on crown support, and this connection required cultivation and might be withdrawn at any time. Rather than reducing violence in the name of law in remote regions, the reserved right to judge capital crimes and execute traitors in the metropole produced incentives to charge rivals with treason in distant regions and to link the threat of legal jeopardy to exemplary punishments. We found, too, that the strategic efforts by mariners to maintain connections to sovereigns often involved favoring legal arguments about legitimate sponsorship and sometimes led mariners to reinforce the power of captains. The rehearsal of legal stories justifying violence on the seas brought that violence under a complex regulatory structure that recognized the thrust of parallel jurisdictional claims into sea space.

Such examples teach us that law traveled with effects that were considerably more complex than the production of lawlessness and exceptional violence. Whereas Agamben's approach applied to empires might suggest the analogy of a universe of mappable concentrations of matter, imperial history conjures up comparisons to a universe in which contortions like wormholes and black holes challenge our spatial imagination and cannot be conventionally mapped. There is no doubt that sovereignty sometimes seemed simply to diminish in force with distance and that at times it prompted experiments in despotism or countersovereignty. More often it developed in twists and turns, with authority and its contours of control distributed unevenly across space and time. Pockets of legal anomaly created in empire appear more often as patterned variations of legal ordering than as instances of exception, though the two may be related. Precisely because they defied easy categorization, such variations were imaginatively rendered in discourses about geography and referenced in elaborate practices of legal posturing.

It may be helpful in trying to understand one effect, the somewhat counterintuitive strengthening of power both at the core and at irregularly placed distant points, to digress here in order to recall Jean Bodin's writings on sovereignty. Bodin's sixteenth-century tract on sovereignty is notable for its utter lack of attention, and even mention, of territory.[21] Bodin's definition of sovereignty was fundamentally juridical.

[21] Jean Bodin, *On Sovereignty: Four Chapters from the Six Books of the Commonwealth*, trans. Julian H. Franklin (Cambridge: Cambridge University Press, 1992). The treatise

He outlined a series of "marks of sovereignty," the most important of which was the "power to give law to all . . . subjects in general and to each in particular" without the consent or approval of anyone else.[22] Several other marks of sovereignty also depended on the law: the authority to review appeals from inferior magistrates, the power of pardon, the power to confer capital sentences, and the authority to require "subjects and liege vassals to swear that they will be loyal without exception to the person to whom their oath is owed." These marks of sovereignty were contained within more general legal powers of the sovereign: to make law, to act as judge, and to appoint judges.[23] Bodin did not omit territory as a category through some oversight. His view was consistent with an early modern construction of sovereignty as spatially elastic. Because subjects could be located anywhere, and the tie between sovereign and subject was defined as a legal relationship, legal authority was not bound territorially.

Rather than imagining a sovereign territory like one that would fit within Krasner's schema, European sojourners and settlers who inhabited the world of the long sixteenth, seventeenth, and eighteenth centuries mainly thought of empires in terms closer to those of Bodin: as the products of the uneven extension of sovereign rule, embodied in the law. Territorial control was a contingent element of imperial rule, not a property firmly associated with sovereign jurisdiction, and subjecthood was defined by a set of political and legal relationships shaped by strategic maneuvering and interpretation, and subject to challenge. As a result, a volatile legal politics involved political actors in establishing and protecting their ties to sovereigns and to local political communities, and in defining and redefining the geographical extent of crown, semiprivate, and corporate authority. To claim sovereignty implied certain responsibilities for the administration of justice, with obligations flowing in both directions. Empire changed the conditions, and some of the stakes, of membership in political communities, but continuities in political and legal strategies were more noticeable than ruptures. Disputes invoking claims and accusations about loyalty, maladministration of justice, and the delegation or usurpation of legal authority in imperial settings can be read as discourses about sovereignty, but of course for imperial actors the

circulated widely in Latin and was especially embraced by English theorists. Most scholarly attention to Bodin's ideas has revolved around the question of to what degree his views of sovereignty exalted or limited the power of the sovereign and prepared a shift to a notion of power as an abstract quality of the state.

22 Bodin, *On Sovereignty*, 59.

23 Bodin, *On Sovereignty*, 59. And see Orr, *Treason and the State*, 35.

stakes were also both lower and higher: lower, because conflicts focused on particular interests and goals of discrete groups; higher, because outcomes could mean catastrophic loss – of life, patronage, property, commercial rights, and political influence – and irreparable damage to the viability of empire itself. At the same time, as many commentators on Bodin have correctly observed, his juridical understanding of sovereignty endorsed a historically novel form of absolutist power. A juridical construction of sovereignty awarded it properties that could simultaneously cohere and travel.

It is particularly important to note that the significance of allegiance in the construction of complex imperial sovereignties continued into the nineteenth century. In nineteenth-century British India, as we have seen, devising formulas for sovereignty over an array of territories with different legal relations to the imperial center involved isolating allegiance to the crown as one of a set of sovereign properties that transcended the empire, undergirding British authority in realms where most other capacities of sovereignty were recognized as residing in the hands of local authorities. In 1891, less than two decades after the Baroda case analyzed in Chapter 5, for example, allegiance to the queen was cited as the fundamental quality of an overarching sovereignty in justifying intervention in the princely state of Manipur to put down a rebellion and execute one of its leaders.[24] Of course, imperial governments' demands of allegiance did not prevent colonial governments from advancing their own claims to loyalty from subjects. As we saw in tracing the second career of treason in the Atlantic world, a legal politics focused on loyalty to distant sovereigns in early periods of reconnaissance and settlement provided a reference point for much-later conflicts in which colonial institutions, rather than distant sovereigns, exacted oaths of allegiance. In the nineteenth century, liberal thinkers would point to the portability of subjecthood and allegiance in arguing that the rights of imperial citizens, as well as their obligations to sovereign powers, extended throughout empire. As elements of political culture and focal points of legal conflict, loyalty and disloyalty assumed a variety of meanings and remained important to the dynamics of imperial authority. The rule might generate (and incorporate) exceptions as simultaneously external to and implied by the rule, but the rule of law contemplated no externalities because it implied the circulation of law in different forms into all spaces of sovereignty.

[24] See Chapter 5, note 55, in this volume.

This point brings us to another aspect of the rule of law that distinguishes it from the rule. In legal orders, the normative context providing meaning to the rule consists in part of more law.[25] In other words, the patterns of social interaction shaping the regularities of social life constitute law and not just norms influencing law. Like the old joke about the mythic structural support for the world being turtles all the way down, the cultural context of norms is law all the way down. This pervasive legal-cultural context converts exceptional moments of apparent legal rupture into experiments in other kinds of law. Agamben explicitly resists this point: "The state of exception is not a special kind of law (like the law of war); rather, insofar as it is a suspension of the juridical order itself, it defines law's threshold or limit concept."[26] But histories of imperial law tell another story. The layering of overlapping, semi-sovereign authorities within empires generated a lumpy juridical order, in which legal actors, even rogues (pirates, as we have seen, or isolated and autocratic garrison commanders), engaged in creative legal posturing. They sought not merely to give their actions the color of law but also to render them secure parts of a recognized administrative order. Subjects did not consider themselves to be operating within a "special kind of law" but rather, at most, to be producing logical variations in the law of the empire.

We can glimpse the implications briefly by returning to the problem, raised by Hussain, Kostal, Spieler, and others, and investigated in the legal history of island penal colonies in Chapter 4, of the apparent suspension of law in empire. A different way of describing the suspension of law is as the substitution of one kind of authorization of delegated legal authority for another. Martial law, for example, represents both the suspension of law considered normal and its replacement with military authority operating within a different legal idiom. In colonial settings, this condition, broadly defined, did not require extraordinary measures because its possibility was embedded in a structure of imperial sovereignty in which delegated legal authority in one form or another was always present. One

[25] Schmitt, of course, argues that the sovereign's decision remains within the juridical order, so a Schmittian approach might not dispute this point. But the subtle difference is meaningful; attention to distant sovereignty shifts attention, in effect, from the constitutional moment of the sovereign decision to the routine constitution of sovereignty through the delegation of part-sovereign capacities. And Agamben explicitly associates the "state of exception" with a "juridical void." Agamben, *State of Exception*, 51; and see *supra* note 11.

[26] Agamben, *State of Exception*, 4.

important effect of this structural logic is that acts for the suspension of law in empire did not reference only, or primarily, metropolitan law as the normative order being held in suspension but occurred as variations of (sometimes imagined) similar structures and acts elsewhere in empire. Declaring martial law on Norfolk Island in this sense drew from the routine employment of military commanders in colonial governance. The same logic promoted a symbolic and "horizontal" link between the treatment of convicts and the legal status of slaves in the late eighteenth century.[27] A second implication is that structures and practices of imperial sovereignty depended on conflicts organized around alternative positions about the relation of multiple authorities and of overlapping regulatory frameworks. The law of martial law was contingent, in other words, on interpretations of the imperial constitution. Rather than operating as imitators or implementers of the arbitrary power of sovereigns, local authorities were constitutionally authorized to innovate, providing a degree of legitimacy to anomalous practices that might not be politically sustained in centers of power.[28]

Perhaps I am proposing only subtle differences between a story about the origins of modern state sovereignty and a more open-ended narrative about the persistence of empires and states composed of varied and sometimes-overlapping fields of partial sovereignty. Yet I think there is evidence for the greater explanatory power of the second view. Agamben's approach helpfully corrects Foucault's linking of governmentality to modernity, which, in emphasizing the ways power drafted the social categories through which rule is constructed, ironically helped to shift attention toward diffuse and subtle state power and away from a range of other forms of violence. Agamben's correction reinserts violence as an uncontrolled force in the state of exception that came to be gradually normalized as a condition of sovereignty. This approach does not precisely capture, though, the many forms of imperial violence that simultaneously depended on the state's coercive authority and announced the legitimacy of violence by delegated proxies. Slaveowners meting out "justice" in

[27] This connection is also noted by Kerry Ward, in *Networks of Empire*, who views Dutch East India Company policies of penal transportation and slavery as linked aspects of a broader project of forced migration. This is one of an array of examples of discourses moving across imperial arenas with effects at least as important as those of the more-studied "vertical" movements between metropole and colony.

[28] This view can be contrasted with Agamben's position in *State of Exception* that "the state of exception is not a dictatorship (whether constitutional or unconstitutional, commissarial or sovereign) but a space devoid of law" (50).

punishing their slaves are only the clearest of many examples. One must certainly read the harsh punishments of slaves as deeply intertwined with their racial exclusion, just as violence against convicted criminals can be viewed as a phenomenon linked to their conversion, through sentencing, to the status of legal outsiders. But these and other forms of outsourcing of violence were also integral to layered systems of sovereignty in which the sovereign's claim to a monopoly on coercive power was consistent with the authorization of weakly regulated violence in the sovereign's name. This view reminds us that the rule of law is not necessarily associated with republican or liberal political formations.[29] Nor does exceptional violence indicate an absence or mitigation of the force of law. Rather, sovereignty implies the extension of law beyond the center, not as a gradually dissipating force but as a set of relationships that, through spatial and temporal prisms, may endow distant actors with greater specific powers.

This point leads us to the third observation that, unlike an abstract rule, the rule of law depends on peculiar kinds of rules. They are rules about rule, or statements about ordering that encompass the relation between rule and exception, and the structural relation of multiple arenas of law and political authority.[30] The normative and/or legal context

[29] On this disconnect between the rule of law and liberalism, see Brian Z. Tamanaha, *On the Rule of Law: History, Politics, Theory* (Cambridge: Cambridge University Press, 2004).

[30] See the discussion in Benton, *Law and Colonial Cultures*, chap. 6. In thinking about rules about rule, we might build on H. L. A. Hart's notion that legal systems have a "rule of recognition" that determines which other rules are valid (*The Concept of Law*, eds., Penelope Bulloch and Joseph Raz, New York: Clarendon Press, 1994, 2nd ed.). But Hart's formulation poses particular problems in thinking about law and empire (and they are not the usual critiques of Hart's understanding of the relation of law and morality). The approach assumes without explanation that rules become internalized across the legal order and that the relation between what Hart called primary and secondary rules would be consistent throughout that order – though starkly different in primitive, "pre-law" societies. As critics have observed, these and other qualities make Hart's ideas about rules rather limited for understanding spatially and culturally complex or diverse legal systems. See Malcolm Wood, "Rule, Rules, and Law," in *The Jurisprudence of Orthodoxy: Queen's University Essays and* H. L. A. *Hart*, eds., Philip Leith and Peter Ingram (New York: Routledge, 1988), 27–60; and Peter Fitzpatrick, *Modernism and the Grounds of Law* (Cambridge: Cambridge University Press, 2001), 96–7. However, Scott Shapiro suggests that the utility of the rule of recognition can be retained if we understand it as "a shared plan which sets out the constitutional order of a legal system." Shapiro's proposal seems to me promising and his analysis of a "shared plan" is close to my discussion of rules about rule as an aspect of imperial constitutions. "What is the Rule of Recognition (and Does it Exist)?" Yale Law School, Public Law Working Paper No. 184. Available at SSRN: http://ssrn.com/abstract=1304645.

of the rule of law is a constitutional order, and the rules about rule compose constitutions, including and especially imperial constitutions. These arrangements do not have to be written and often exist in the familiar form of overlapping discourses rather than doctrines.[31] The rule of law is also, in this approach, a more elaborate social and political construction than the rule because routine or mundane legal conflicts can escalate quickly into constitutional conflicts. Think of the way that the actions of the British government in India to investigate the attempted murder of a resident raised constitutional questions about the limits of imperial law, or how the trial and punishment of a politician in Jamaica prompted an extended debate about the existence and definition of imperial citizenship. In a broad – indeed, global – pattern of imperial legal change, the impulse of simplifying a jumbled, multi-jurisdictional legal order in colonial settings merged with the pressures created by legal conflicts to produce hierarchically ordered legal systems with an undefined and shifting relation to imperial states.[32] Not surprisingly, jurists and legal officials looked to international law for models for imagining the structure and function of imperial law. This move did nothing to contain the recurring crises calling for revised definitions of rules about distant and delegated rule, but it did give rise both to new forms of imperial sovereignty and to newly robust claims about state sovereignty.[33]

This framing helps us to make sense of the history of quasi-sovereignty in the late nineteenth century. In one sustained exercise to try to construct a formal model that accommodated both expansive power and irregular, negotiated sovereignty, imperial officials and international lawyers devised a coherent typology of polities with different degrees of sovereignty. Attempting to enumerate the subset of qualities of sovereignty held by, and granted to, quasi-sovereign entities within European empire, jurists imagined an imperial order that reserved full sovereignty for European imperial governments while defining precisely the nature of partial sovereignty in subordinate but semi-independent

[31] Hulsebosch, *Constituting Empire*, 77.

[32] For elaboration of this point, see Benton, *Law and Colonial Cultures*; and Benton, "Constitutions and Empires."

[33] As Armitage has argued, new declarations of sovereignty from the late eighteenth century onward presented the historically novel claim that polities within empire might become – would become – sovereign states. Armitage, *The Declaration of Independence*. See also Daniel Hulsebosch and David Golove, "On an Equal Footing: Constitution-Making and the Law of Nations in the Early American Republic" (paper presented at the Legal History Colloquium, New York University School of Law, January 21, 2009).

colonial polities. The task for imperial administrators became one of tinkering continually with these typologies of rule in order to be able to label the different patterns of articulated legal authority represented by hundreds of small states and zones of anomaly within the empire. In the new context of an international order explicitly described as resting on sovereign nation-states, the old challenges of defining political membership and limiting local authority persisted and posed novel challenges.

It is once again tempting to adopt the conceptual aid of exception to talk about this project. Certainly the finding that the problems of Indian princely states could not be ordered within international or municipal law but required the exercise of political prerogatives by the ruling power implies a suspension of law and even appears to create a zone of legal exception. But the solution to the limits of law went further in announcing a new jurisprudence – imperial law – as a hybrid of municipal law and international law that could encompass divided sovereignty. The politics surrounding this move combined talk about the limits of law with claims about the transcendent nature of a particular subset of markers of sovereignty: allegiance to the imperial power, a monopoly of the imperial government over foreign relations, and an open-ended and vaguely defined responsibility to good government that would justify ad hoc impositions on local autonomy. In embracing the idea of the limits of law, imperial officials simultaneously were inverting the idea of the exception. That is, they represented political intervention as an unexceptional prerogative of imperial power. They also defined local autonomy as bare sovereignty, a political and legal condition that remained unchanged when imperial intervention occurred because it implied only a very limited scope for local authority. In practice, quasi-sovereign entities might exercise something very close to the full range of sovereign prerogatives without posing a challenge to imperial rule precisely because their relation to sovereign power was defined as subordinate and because the requirement of allegiance did not need to reside in visible structures. Imperial power could also then be seen as exercising a version of bare sovereignty, without changing the calculus of rule.

We have in view a critique of Agamben that is rather different from some critical commentary. Some scholars have emphasized the drawback that Agamben has failed to appreciate resistance to sovereignty and its violence, noting, for example, that resistance sometimes takes the form of "usurping sovereign power over bare life."[34] What happens,

[34] Ewa Plonowska Ziarek, "Bare Life on Strike: Notes on the Biopolitics of Race and Gender," in *The Agamben Effect*, ed. Alison Ross (Durham, NC: Duke University Press,

though, if we view usurpation of elements of sovereign power as a recurring tendency, structurally even more prominent than the rejection of authority or the movement toward a substitute totalizing power? As the examples explored in this book have shown, sites of bare sovereignty, a partial and often-minimalist construction of sovereign authority, pervaded empires.[35] Not surprisingly, politics took many forms, not all of them oppositional to claims of sovereignty. The legal politics of layered sovereignty in empire created opportunities and incentives for counter sovereignties, to be sure – the imagined breakaway kingdom of Aguirre, discussed in Chapter 2, is an example. Far more commonly, conflicts involved appeals to semiautonomous but still formally subordinate authorities. Legal actors making such appeals continued to reference and recognize imperial sovereignty. They even framed many of their efforts as empire building – attempts to extend the reach of the law, realign parts of empire, or enable entities within empire to respond flexibly and forcefully to local and other imperial challenges.[36]

In addition to responding to a fluid legal politics, reconfigurations of imperial sovereignty drew on conventions and proposed new labels for zones of legal variation. Geographic tropes such as rivers and sea lanes

2007), 100; cf. Pal Ahluvalia, "Death and Politics: Empire and the 'New' Politics of Resistance," in *The Postcolonial and the Global*, ed. Revathi Krishnaswamy and John C. Hawley (Minneapolis: University of Minnesota Press, 2008).

[35] I pick up the term *bare sovereignty* from the commentary of a British official on the political power retained by Indian princely states in their cantonments (see Chapter 5 in this volume, especially note 109). In generalizing it, I retain an emphasis on a minimalist authority distinguished from jurisdiction. The term has been used in slightly different ways in other commentary on Agamben; see, e.g., Costas Douzinas, "Speaking Law: On Bare Theological and Cosmopolitan Sovereignty," in *International Law and Its Others*, ed. Anne Orford (Cambridge: Cambridge University Press, 2006), 35–57. Douzinas defines "bare sovereignty" as "the coming together of jurisdiction, law and politics in community," and he represents jurisdiction as "the expression of the emergence of a communal space and common identity" (40) It is more useful, I think, to place in view a common but not necessary (and in fact unstable) link to jurisdiction and, more importantly, to unlink the existence of decentered sovereignty from community, and certainly from a common identity. Neither must be present, even in imagined form, for a decentered legal authority to claim, or be defined as holding, partial sovereignty. Otherwise, we would have to recognize the slave master's authority as one connected to the community of the plantation. My use of *bare sovereignty* is closer to that of Peter Fitzpatrick, who unfortunately follows Agamben in his "effort to place sovereignty socially in the modern period." "Bare Sovereignty: Homo Sacer and the Insistence of Law," *Theory & Event* 5, no. 2 (2001).

[36] This point is made somewhat differently by Peter Fitzpatrick, who characterizes sovereignty as a response to the tensions between the impulse to describe society as "a positively set totality" and its representation as "a collection of distinct particularities." *Modernism and the Grounds of Law*, 52. And see Fitzpatrick, "Bare Sovereignty."

signified, at times more prominently than at others, corridors of imperial control that, in turn, sat uneasily within spheres of influence. Islands and hill regions figured as imperial enclaves whose characteristics posed problems of legal order. These and other geographic categories, such as forests, the tropics, and even regions named only by ordinal directions, like the "south" or "southern latitudes," were often referred to in ways that evoked remoteness, or wildness.[37] This quality of being off the map often corresponded to representations of barbarism, with all that the label implied as a contrast to imperial centers as seats of civility. Yet there was more to this contrast than the juxtaposition of center and periphery, civilization and barbarism, law and lawlessness.[38] A diverse array of geographic categories became salient descriptors of varieties of spheres of imperial sovereignty. The geographic tropes came to evoke particular patterns of the extension of law, from the emphasis on loyal subjecthood and its opposite in early Atlantic riverine regions to the associations of pure but volatile forms of political solidarity in the interior hill regions of increasingly powerful nineteenth-century colonies. Law was never absent in such constructions – even when conflicts prompted talk about the limits of law. Nor were legal controls understood as simply dissipating in remote regions, creating zones of attenuated sovereignty. The extension of law associated with geographic elements instead modeled precise patterns: corridors as conduits for law and enclaves corresponding to differently configured elements of sovereignty. Expectations about such patterns attached to geographic descriptions in extended historical moments, so that the references became an integral part of discourses about empire and interimperial relations. For example, islands had long signaled pristine wildness, but their heightened significance as markers of maritime control in the context of intensifying global rivalries at the end of the eighteenth century nurtured the view that the natural qualities of islands made them both places of perfect imperial control and sites of semiauthorized petty despotism.

[37] Nicolás Wey Gómez, *The Tropics of Empire: Why Columbus Sailed South to the Indies* (Cambridge, MA: MIT Press, 2008). On wildness, see Vaidik, *Imperial Andamans*, chap. 1.

[38] It is helpful to turn here to Lefebvre's *Production of Space*. He writes of the pervasive influence of what he calls "constitutive dualities" on the representation of social space. These repeating dualities "underpin more complex... pluralities and multiplicities" (411). Understanding constitutive dualities helps us to make sense of the "problematic of space," but analyzing the production of social space is incomplete without the study of empirically observable patterns of "spatial practice" (413).

Attention to this fluid discourse merging geography and law helps to move us beyond the expectation that varieties of imperial territories awaited incorporation into sovereign states. Contemporary scholars saw fragmented geographies as integral to and even constitutive of imperial sovereignty from an early date.[39] Atlantic imaginings of riverine regions as entries into new continents where subjecthood became strained played directly into European interpretations and applications of a legal politics of possession informed by Roman private law. Gentili and Grotius were responding directly to pressures to defend imperial interests in preparing arguments about the thrust of law into ocean space through the actions of private persons and sovereign agents. Bentham regarded New South Wales as an unconstitutional experiment because it nurtured the selective suppression of Englishmen's rights and encouraged petty autocrats. Such conditions called into question the viability of imperial constitutions. And Maine, along with other figures who straddled colonial administration and the world of scholarship on international law, wrote about divided sovereignty to reconcile the legal variations of imperial territories and the newly prominent view of territorial sovereignty as a property of member states of the international legal community. These moves responded to, and found application in, the strategies of legal actors in empire: leaders of Atlantic expeditions adopting flexible approaches to claiming territory under law, mariners affirming the legitimacy of sovereign rights to conduct sea raiding, convicts and penal station commanders struggling to define the operation of martial law, and Indian princes and their advisers maneuvering to expand and protect legal prerogatives under imperial law.

In these examples, divided sovereignty appears less as a temporary concession to particular challenges of administering empire and more as a central premise of rule with an enduring influence on both imperial geographies and global regulation. Subjecthood and citizenship featured as fluid categories permitting the spatially irregular extension of legal authority.[40] The legal politics of indigenous peoples produced another

[39] Here I follow Keene (*Beyond the Anarchical Society*), Anghie (*Making of International Law*), and others who have recognized that empire formed a special problem for theorists of international law. But I also want to push beyond their focus on fragments of empire as an intellectual challenge to international lawyers to reveal the connections between efforts to characterize divided sovereignty and legal-political processes in empire.

[40] On this point and its relevance to understanding citizenship in the nineteenth-century world, see especially Adam McKeown, *Melancholy Order: Asian Migration and the Globalization of Borders* (New York: Columbia University Press, 2008).

source of geographic unevenness, which in turn influenced Europeans' territorial strategies.[41] And structures of delegated power – the key operational element of divided sovereignty – favored the exercise of legal authority over pieces of empire. Creating a coherent account of such variety called for nimble thinking. In particular, it urged blurring distinctions between natural and positive law, in part by recognizing that inter-imperial disputants in the early modern world might invoke natural law principles, cite treaty regimes, or follow norms implied by the actions and interactions of imperial agents. The last phenomenon as a source of international law developed out of the parallel and mutually intelligible thrust of the jurisdiction of empires into imperfectly controlled territories and ocean spaces. That legal actors and observers conflated international and imperial law under these conditions should come as no surprise. Empires appeared at times as more controllable models of a global order of splintered polities. The layered sovereignty of empire seemed to ensure an uneven distribution of political protections and rights, while the continued existence of empires appeared at times to color interstate agreements as elaborate legal fictions.

Returning from these observations to consider Agamben's embedded historical narrative about the gradual folding into modern sovereignty of the state of exception, we would give a different interpretation to the historical significance of the zones of legal variation, or the anomalous legal spaces, constituting European empires. The anomalies of empire I have studied appear to be widely replicated configurations of rule, so much so that we might say that they capture something fundamental about the political imagination of European empire between 1400 and 1900. In early centuries, attention to anomalies corresponded to a wider discourse about the singularities of experience and the wonders of the world beyond Europe. Later observers struggled to reconcile consistent categories of partial sovereignties with newly appearing spatial and legal variations, sometimes describing particular cases as odd or anomalous. Epistemologies of cosmography, geography, and law awarded a place of privilege to anomalies in the accumulation of knowledge and the development of understandings of global order. Anomalies required explanation. They not only introduced new intricacies into existing frameworks but

[41] Writing about European and Indian encounters in the Arkansas Valley, Kathleen DuVal makes this point in noting that "Europeans gained their sovereignty vis-à-vis one another in part by piggy-backing on Indians' sovereignty." *The Native Ground: Indians and Colonists in the Heart of the Continent* (Philadelphia: University of Pennsylvania Press, 2006), 8.

also made diversity of legal administration rather than legal integration a permanent expectation. Because observers compared irregular formations not just to the metropole but also to other constituent parts of empire, anomalies signified variations rather than exceptions. This "modular condition of empire" rendered imperial sovereignty elusive while challenging understandings of global order.[42]

If such patterns tell us something important about empires and their interactions between 1400 and 1900, they may also illuminate more recent examples of legal anomaly. The rationale for creating military commissions at Guantánamo Bay, and the choice of an island garrison, reveal some continuities with the processes examined in this book. The transfer of elements of sovereignty, including negotiations over a status akin to bare sovereignty in such places as Iraq and Afghanistan, points in the same direction. For some problems in law, such as the delineation of jurisdiction on U.S. Indian reservations or the contested prerogatives of embedded, subordinate, and part-sovereign enclaves, such as Gaza, the continuities are very explicit. I leave aside for now the interesting problem of tracing these histories. It is enough to show the ways in which a search for sovereignty in European overseas empires before the end of the nineteenth century merged geographic discourse and law, shaping a world of repeating fragments – an interimperial legal regime in pieces.

[42] This is Ward's useful phrase. *Networks of Empire*, 56.

Bibliography

List of Archives and Abbreviations

Archivo General de Indias, Seville (AGI)
Archivo General de Simancas, Valladolid (AGS)
Archivo Histórico Nacional, Madrid (AHN)
The National Archives, Kew, Richmond, Surrey (TNA)
  Home Office, 1700–2002 (HO)
  Colonial Office, 1570–1990 (CO)
British Library, London (BL)
  India Office Records (IOR)
University College of London (UCL)
  Bentham Papers

Works Cited

Acosta, José de. *Historia natural y moral de las Indias*. Madrid: Historia 16, 1987.

Acuña, Cristóbal de. Acarete du Biscay, Jean Grillet, and François Béchamel. *Voyages and Discoveries in South-America, the First up the River of Amazons to Quito in Peru, and Back Again to Brazil, Perform'd at the Command of the King of Spain by Christopher D'acugna: The Second up the River of Plata, and Thence by Land to the Mines of Potosi by Mons. Acarete: The Third from Cayenne into Guiana, in Search of the Lake of Parima, Reputed the Richest Place in the World by M. Grillet and Bechamel: Done into English from the Originals, Being the Only Accounts of Those Parts Hitherto Extant: The Whole Illustrated with Notes and Maps*. London: Printed for S. Buckley, 1698.

______. "A New Discovery of the Great River of the Amazons." In *Expeditions into the Valley of the Amazons, 1539, 1540, 1639*, ed. and translated by Clements Markham. London: Printed for the Hakluyt Society, 1859.

Adelman, Jeremy. *Republic of Capital: Buenos Aires and the Legal Transformation of the Atlantic World*. Stanford, CA: Stanford University Press, 1999.

———. *Sovereignty and Revolution in the Iberian Atlantic*. Princeton, NJ: Princeton University Press, 2006.

———. "An Age of Imperial Revolutions." *American Historical Review* 113, no. 2 (2008): 319–40.

Adelman, Jeremy, ed. *Colonial Legacies: The Problem of Persistence in Latin American History*. New York: Routledge, 1999.

Adelman, Jeremy, and Stephen Aron. "From Borderlands to Borders: Empires, Nation-States, and the Peoples in Between in North American History." *American Historical Review* 104, no. 3 (1999): 814–40.

Adorno, Rolena. *The Polemics of Possession in Spanish American Narrative*. New Haven, CT: Yale University Press, 2007.

Adorno, Rolena, and Patrick Charles Pautz. *Álvar Núñez Cabeza de Vaca: His Account, His Life, and the Expedition of Pánfilo de Narváez*. 3 vols. Lincoln: University of Nebraska Press, 1999.

Agamben, Giorgio. *Homo Sacer: Sovereign Power and Bare Life*. Stanford, CA: Stanford University Press, 1998.

———. *State of Exception*. Chicago: University of Chicago Press, 2005.

Ahluvalia, Pal. "Death and Politics: Empire and the 'New' Politics of Resistance." In *The Postcolonial and the Global*, ed. Revathi Krishnaswamy and John C. Hawley, 166–77. Minneapolis: University of Minnesota Press, 2008.

Aitchison, C. U., ed. *A Collection of Treaties, Engagements, and Sunnuds, Relating to India and Neighboring Countries [1862–1865]*. Calcutta: Printed by G. A. Savielle and P. M. Cranenburgh, Bengal Print, 1865.

Alexandrowicz, Charles Henry. *An Introduction to the History of the Law of Nations in the East Indies: (16th, 17th and 18th Centuries)*. Oxford: Clarendon, 1967.

Alfonso X. *Leyes De Los Adelantados Mayores: Regulations, Attributed to Alfonso X of Castile, Concerning the King's Vicar in the Judiciary and in Territorial Administration*. Ed., Robert A. MacDonald. New York: Hispanic Seminary of Medieval Studies, 2000.

Álvarez, Adela Repetto. "Traición y justicia en los tiempos de Felipe II, 1565–1570." *Fundación para la Historia de España* 3 (2000): 37–56.

Anand, Ram. *Origins and Development of the Law of the Sea*. The Hague: Martinus Nijhoff, 1983.

Anderson, Clare. *Convicts in the Indian Ocean: Transportation from South Asia to Mauritius, 1815–53*. New York: St. Martin's Press, 2000.

Anghie, Antony. *Imperialism, Sovereignty, and the Making of International Law*. Cambridge: Cambridge University Press, 2007.

Antigallican. *A Series of Letters Relating to the Antigallican Private Ship of War, and Her Lawful Prize the Penthievre . . . The Whole Containing an Unparalleled Scene of Cruelty, Perjury, and Injustice. With Proper Observations. By an Antigallican*. London: Sold by W. Owen, 1758.

Appelbaum, Robert, and John Wood Sweet, eds. *Envisioning an English Empire: Jamestown and the Making of the North Atlantic World*. Philadelphia: University of Pennsylvania Press, 2005.

Arbousset, Thomas. *Missionary Excursion into the Blue Mountains, Being an Account of King Moshoeshoe's Expedition from Thaba-Bosiu to the Sources of the Malibamatso River in the Year 1840*. Morija, Lesotho: Morija Archives, n.d.

Armitage, David. *The Ideological Origins of the British Empire*. Cambridge: Cambridge University Press, 2000.

______. *The Declaration of Independence: A Global History*. Cambridge, MA: Harvard University Press, 2007.

______. David Armitage and Michael Braddick, eds. *The British Atlantic World, 1500–1800*, second edition. New York: Palgrave Macmillan, 2009.

Arnold, David. *Colonizing the Body: State Medicine and Epidemic Disease in Nineteenth-Century India*. Berkeley: University of California Press, 1993.

Asher, Brad. *Beyond the Reservation: Indians, Settlers, and the Law in Washington Territory, 1853–1889*. Norman: University of Oklahoma Press, 1999.

Atkinson, Alan. "The Free-Born Englishman Transported: Convict Rights as a Measure of Eighteenth-Century Empire." *Past and Present* 44 (1994): 88–115.

Baker, Alan R. H. *Geography and History: Bridging the Divide*. Cambridge: Cambridge University Press, 2003.

Banks, Kenneth J. *Chasing Empire Across the Sea: Communications and the State in the French Atlantic, 1713–1763*. Montreal: McGill-Queen's University Press, 2002.

Barrell, John. *Imagining the King's Death: Figurative Treason, Fantasies of Regicide, 1793–1796*. Oxford: Oxford University Press, 2000.

Barrera-Osorio, Antonio. "Nature and Experience in the New World: Spain and England in the Making of the New Science." In Navarro Brótons, *Más allá de la leyenda negra*, 121–35.

______. "Empiricism in the Spanish Atlantic World." In Delbourgo, *Science and Empire in the Atlantic World*, 177–202.

Battenberg, Friedrich, and Filippo Ranieri, eds. *Geschichte Der Zentraljustiz in Mitteleuropa: Festschrift für Bernhard Diestelkamp zum 65. Geburtstag*. Weimar: Böhlau, 1994.

Baud, Michiel, and Willem van Schendel. "Toward a Comparative History of Borderlands." *Journal of World History* 8, no. 2 (1997): 211–42.

Bauer, Ralph. *The Cultural Geography of Colonial American Literatures: Empire, Travel, Modernity*. Cambridge: Cambridge University Press, 2003.

______. "A New World of Secrets: Occult Philosophy and Local Knowledge in the Sixteenth-Century Atlantic." In Delbourgo, *Science and Empire in the Atlantic World*, 99–126.

Bayly, C. A. *The Birth of the Modern World, 1780–1914: Global Connections and Comparisons*. Malden, MA: Blackwell, 2004.

Beattie, J. M. *Crime and the Courts in England, 1660–1800*. Oxford: Clarendon, 1986.

Beaulac, Stéphane. *The Power of Language in the Making of International Law: The Word Sovereignty in Bodin and Vattel and the Myth of Westphalia*. Leiden: Martinus Nijhoff, 2004.

Bellamy, John G. *The Law of Treason in England in the Later Middle Ages*. Cambridge: Cambridge University Press, 1970.

Bentham, Jeremy. *Letters to Lord Pelham, Giving a Comparative View of the System of Penal Colonization in New South Wales*. London: Wilkes and Taylor, 1802.

______. *A Plea for the Constitution Shewing the Enormities Committed to the Oppression of British Subjects... In and by the Design, Foundation and Government of the Penal Colony of New South Wales: Including an Inquiry into the Right of the Crown to Legislate without Parliament in Trinidad and Other British Colonies*. London: Mawman, Poultry, 1803.

Benton, Lauren. "Not Just a Concept: Institutions and the 'Rule of Law.'" *Journal of Asian Studies* 68, no. 1 (2008): 63–8.

______. "The Legal Regime of the South Atlantic World: Jurisdictional Complexity as Institutional Order." *Journal of World History* 11, no. 1 (2000): 27–56.

______. *Law and Colonial Cultures: Legal Regimes in World History, 1400–1900*. Cambridge: Cambridge University Press, 2002.

______. "Legal Spaces of Empire: Piracy and the Origins of Ocean Regionalism." *Comparative Studies in Society and History* 47, no. 4 (2005): 700–24.

______. "Constitutions and Empires." *Law & Social Inquiry* 31 (2006): 177–98.

______. "Empires of Exception: History, Law, and the Problem of IMperial Sovereignty." *Quaderni di Relazioni Internaxionali* (2007, December): 54–67.

______. "From International Law to Imperial Constitutions: The Probelm of Quasi-Sovereignty, 1870–1900." *Law and History Review* 26 (2008): 595–620.

______. "The British Atlantic in Global Context." In Armitage, *The British Atlantic World*, 271–89.

Benton, Lauren, and Benjamin Straumann. "Acquiring Empire by Law: From Roman Doctrine to Early Modern European Practice." *Law and History Review* (forthcoming).

Biggar, Henry Percival, ed. *The Works of Samuel de Champlain*. Toronto: Champlain Society, 1922.

Bilder, Mary Sarah. *The Transatlantic Constitution: Colonial Legal Culture and the Empire*. Cambridge, MA: Harvard University Press, 2004.

Black, Jeremy. *Maps and History: Constructing Images of the Past*. New Haven, CT: Yale University Press, 1997.

Blackhawk, Ned. *Violence over the Land: Indians and Empires in the Early American West*. Cambridge: Harvard University Press, 2006.

Blainey, Geoffrey. *The Tyranny of Distance: How Distance Shaped Australia's History*. Melbourne: Sun Books, 1966.

Blansett, Lisa. "John Smith Maps Virginia." In Appelbaum and Sweet, *Envisioning an English Empire*, 68–91.

Blázquez Martín, Diego. *Herejía y traición: Las doctrinas de la persecución religiosa en el siglo XVI*. Madrid: Dykinson, 2001.

Bleichmar, Daniela, Paula De Vos, Kristin Huffine, and Kevin Sheehan, eds. *Science in the Spanish and Portuguese Empires: 1500–1800*. Stanford, CA: Stanford University Press, 2009.

Blom, Hans W., ed. *Property, Piracy and Punishment: Hugo Grotius on War and booty in De Iure Praedae – Concepts and Contexts*. Leiden: Brill, 2009.

Bodin, Jean. *On Sovereignty: Four Chapters from the Six Books of the Commonwealth*. Translated by Julian H. Franklin. Cambridge: Cambridge University Press, 1992.

Borschberg, Peter. *Hugo Grotius, the Portuguese, and Free Trade in the East Indies*. Honolulu: University of Hawaii Press, 2009.

———. "Grotius, Maritime Intra-Asian Trade and the Portuguese Estado da Índia: Problems, Perspectives and Insights from *De iure praedae*," in Blom, *Property, Piracy and Punishment*, 31–60.

———. *Hugo Grotius' Commentarius in Theses XI: An Early Treatise on Sovereignty, the Just War, and the Legitimacy of the Dutch Revolt*. Berne: Peter Lang, 1994.

Bose, Sugata. *A Hundred Horizons: The Indian Ocean in the Age of Global Empire*. Cambridge, MA: Harvard University Press, 2006.

Bourne, William, and E. G. R. Taylor. *A Regiment for the Sea, and Other Writings on Navigation*. Cambridge: Published for the Hakluyt Society at the University Press, 1963.

Boxer, C. R. *The Tragic History of the Sea, 1589–1622*. Cambridge: Cambridge University Press, 1959.

Braddick, M. J. *State Formation in Early Modern England, c. 1550–1700*. Cambridge: Cambridge University Press, 2000.

Bradley, Peter T. *The Lure of Peru: A Study of Maritime Intrusion into the South Sea, 1598–1701*. New York: St. Martin's Press, 1989.

Braginton, Mary V. "Exile under the Roman Emperors." *Classical Journal* 39, no. 7 (1944): 391–407.

Brantlinger, Patrick. *Rule of Darkness: British Literature and Imperialism, 1830–1914*. Ithaca, NY: Cornell University Press, 1988.

Braudel, Fernand. *The Mediterranean and the Mediterranean World in the Age of Philip II*. Vol. 1. New York: Harper & Row, 1976.

Braun, Harald E. *Juan de Mariana and Early Modern Spanish Political Thought*. Burlington, VT: Ashgate, 2007.

Brooks, George E. *Eurafricans in Western Africa*. Athens: Ohio University Press, 2003.

Brooks, James. *Captives and Cousins: Slavery, Kinship, and Community in the Southwest Borderlands*. Chapel Hill: University of North Carolina Press, 2002.

Brotton, Jerry. *Trading Territories: Mapping the Early Modern World*. London: Reaktion Books, 1997.

———. "Terrestrial Globalism: Mapping the Globe in Early Modern Europe." In *Mappings*, ed. Denis E. Cosgrove, 71–89. London: Reaction Books, 1999.

Brown, Christopher Leslie. *Moral Capital: Foundations of British Abolitionism*. Chapel Hill: University of North Carolina Press, 2006.

Burbank, Jane. *Russian Peasants Go to Court: Legal Culture in the Countryside, 1905–1917*. Bloomington: Indiana University Press, 2004.

———. "Thinking Like an Empire: Estate, Law, and Rights in the Early Twentieth Century." In Burbank, *Russian Empire*, 196–217.

Burbank, Jane, and Frederick Cooper. *Empires in World History*. Princeton, NJ: Princeton University Press, forthcoming.

Burbank, Jane, Mark von Hagen, and A. V. Remnev, eds. *Russian Empire: Space, People, Power, 1700–1930*. Bloomington: Indiana University Press, 2007.

Burman, Sandra. *Chiefdom Politics and Alien Laws: Basutoland under Cape Rule 1871–1884*. London: Macmillan, 1981.

Burman, Sandra, ed. *The Justice of the Queen's Government: The Cape's Administration of Basutoland, 1871–1884*. Leiden: Afrika-Studiecentrum, 1976.

Burnett, Christina Duffy. "The Edges of Empire and the Limits of Sovereignty: American Guano Islands." *American Quarterly* 57, no. 3 (2005): 779–803.

———. "*Untied* States: American Expansion and Territorial Deannexation." *University of Chicago Law Review* 72 (2005): 797–880.

Burnett, D. Graham. *Masters of All They Surveyed: Exploration, Geography, and a British El Dorado*. Chicago: University of Chicago Press, 2000.

Bushnell, Amy Turner. Situado *and* Sabana: *Spain's Support System for the Presidio and Mission Provinces of Florida*. New York: American Museum of Natural History, 1994.

Ca' da Mosto, Alvise, Antonio Malfante, Diogo Gomes, and João de Barros. *The Voyages of Cadamosto and Other Documents on Western Africa in the Second Half of the Fifteenth Century*. Translated by G. R. Crone. London: Hakluyt Society, 1937.

Caldwell, Robert G. "Exile as an Institution." *Political Science Quarterly* 58, no. 2 (1943): 239–62.

Cabeza de Vaca, Álvar Nuñez. *Naufragios y comentarios*. Mexico City: Porrúa, 1988.

Cabeza de Vaca, Álvar Nuñez. *Chronicle of the Narváez Expedition*. Translated by Fanny Bandelier. New York: Penguin Books, 2002.

Camões, Luís Vaz de. *The Lusíads*. Translated by Landeg White. Oxford: Oxford University Press, 1997.

Campbell, Duncan. *Convict Transportation and the Metropolis: The Letterbooks and Papers of Duncan Campbell (1726–1803) from the State Library of New South Wales*. Marlborough, Wiltshire, England: Adam Matthew Publications, microfilm.

Cañeque, Alejandro. *The King's Living Image: The Culture and Politics of Viceregal Power in Colonial Mexico*. New York: Routledge, 2004.

Cañizares-Esguerra, Jorge. *Nature, Empire, and Nation: Explorations of the History of Science in the Iberian World*. Stanford, CA: Stanford University Press, 2006.

Canny, Nicholas, ed. *The Origins of Empire*. Oxford: Oxford University Press, 1998

Carter, Paul. *The Road to Botany Bay: An Essay in Spatial History*. London: Faber and Faber, 1987.

Casale, Giancarlo. "The Ottoman 'Discovery' of the Indian Ocean in the 16th Century." In *Seascapes: Maritime Histories, Global Cultures, and Transoceanic Exchanges*, ed. Jerry Bentley, Renate Bridenthal, and Kären Widen, 87–104. Honolulu: University of Hawaii Press, 2007.

Castro, José de Antequera y. *Colección general de documentos, que contiene los sucesos tocantes a la segunda época de las conmociones de los regulares de la Compañía en el Paraguay, y señaladamente la persecucion, que hicieron a Don Josef de Antequera y Castro*. Vol. 3. Madrid: Imprenta Real de la Gaceta, 1769.

Cayton, Andrew R. "'When Shall We Cease to Have Judases?' The Blount Conspiracy and the Limits of the 'Extended Republic,'" in *Launching the "Extended Republic": The Federalist Era*, ed. Ronald Hoffman and Peter J. Albert (Charlottesville: University Press of Virginia, 1996), 156–89.

Certeau, Michel de. *The Practice of Everyday Life*. Translated by Steven Rendall. Berkeley: University of California Press, 2002.

Chapin, Bradley. *The American Law of Treason: Revolutionary and Early National Origins*. Seattle: University of Washington Press, 1964.

Chaplin, Joyce E. *The First Scientific American: Benjamin Franklin and the Pursuit of Genius*. New York: Basic Books, 2006.

———. "Knowing the Ocean: Benjamin Franklin and the Circulation of Atlantic Knowledge," in Delbourgo, *Science and Empire in the Atlantic World*, 73–96.

Chatterjee, Partha. *A Princely Impostor? The Strange and Universal History of the Kumar of Bhawal*. Princeton, NJ: Princeton University Press, 2002.

Christopher, Emma, Cassandra Pybus, and Marcus Rediker, eds. *Many Middle Passages: Forced Migration and the Making of the Modern World*. Berkeley: University of California Press, 2007.

Clay, John. *Maconochie's Experiment*. London: John Murray, 2001.

Coates, Timothy J. *Convicts and Orphans: Forced and State-Sponsored Colonizers in the Portuguese Empire, 1550–1755*. Stanford, CA: Stanford University Press, 2001.

Cocks, Raymond. *Sir Henry Maine: A Study in Victorian Jurisprudence*. Cambridge: Cambridge University Press, 1988.

Coldham, Peter Wilson. *Emigrants in Chains: A Social History of Forced Emigration to the Americas of Felons, Destitute Children, Political and Religious Non-Conformists, Vagabonds, Beggars and Other Undesirables, 1607–1776*. Baltimore: Genealogical Publishing, 1992.

Collins, David, and Philip Gidley King. *An Account of the English Colony in New South Wales: With Remarks on the Dispositions, Customs, Manners, &c. of the Native Inhabitants of That Country. To Which Are Added, Some Particulars of New Zealand; Compiled, by Permission, from the Mss. Of Lieutenant-Governor King*. London: Printed for T. Cadell Jun. and W. Davies, in the Strand, 1798.

Columbus, Christopher. *The Four Voyages of Columbus: A History in Eight Documents Including Five by Christopher Columbus, in the Original Spanish, with English Translations*. Ed. Lionel Cecil Jane. New York: Dover Publications, 1988.

Conrad, Robert Edgar, ed. *Children of God's Fire: A Documentary History of Black Slavery in Brazil*. Princeton, NJ: Princeton University Press, 1983.

Cooper, Frederick. "Empire Multiplied." *Comparative Studies in Society and History* 46 (2004): 247–72.

———. "Globalization." In *Colonialism in Question: Theory, Knowledge, History*, 91–112. Berkeley: University of California Press, 2005.

———. "Alternatives to Empire: France and Africa after World War II." In *The State of Sovereignty: Territories, Laws, Populations*, ed. Doughlas Howland and Louise WHite, 94–123. Bloomington, IN: Indiana University Press, 2009.

Copland, I. F. S. "The Baroda Crisis of 1873–77: A Study in Government Rivalry." *Modern Asian Studies* 2, no. 2 (1968): 97–123.

Copland, Ian. *The British Raj and the Indian Princes: Paramountcy in Western India, 1857–1930*. Bombay: Orient Longman, 1982.

———. *The Princes of India in the Endgame of Empire, 1917–1947*. Cambridge: Cambridge University Press, 2002.

Corbin, Alain. *The Lure of the Sea: The Discovery of the Seaside in the Western World, 1750–1840*. Berkeley: University of California Press, 1994.

Corcoran, Paul. "John Locke on the Possession of Land: Native Title vs. the 'Principle' of *Vacuum Domicilium*." In Australasian Political Studies Association Annual Conference. Melbourne: Monash University, 2007. Refereed papers, political theory: http://arts.monash.edu.au/psi/news-and-events/apsa/refereed-papers/index.php.

Cormack, Lesley B. *Charting an Empire: Geography at the English Universities, 1580–1620*. Chicago: University of Chicago Press, 1997.

Cortesão, Armando, and Avelino Teixeira da Mota, eds. *Portugaliae Monumenta Cartographica*. Vol. 1. Lisbon: Imprensa Nacional-Casa da Moeda, 1960.

Cosgrove, Denis E., ed. *Mappings*. London: Reaktion Books, 1999.

———. *Apollo's Eye: A Cartographic Genealogy of the Earth in the Western Imagination*. Baltimore: Johns Hopkins University Press, 2001.

Costa, Emília Viotti da. *Crowns of Glory, Tears of Blood: The Demerara Slave Rebellion of 1823*. New York: Oxford University Press, 1994.

Crais, Clifton. *The Politics of Evil: Magic, State Power, and the Political Imagination in South Africa*. Cambridge: Cambridge University Press, 2002.

Crump, Helen Josephine. *Colonial Admiralty Jurisdiction in the Seventeenth Century*. London: Published for the Royal Empire Society by Longmans, Green, 1931.

Cruz Barney, Oscar. *El régimen jurídico del corso marítimo: El mundo indiano y el México del siglo XIX*. Mexico City: Universidad Nacional Autónoma de México, 1997.

Cunliffe, Barry. *Facing the Ocean: The Atlantic and Its Peoples, 8000 BC–AD 1500* Oxford: Oxford University Press, 2001.

Curtin, Philip D. *The Image of Africa: British Ideas and Action, 1780–1850*. Madison: University of Wisconsin Press, 1964.

Cuttler, S. H. *The Law of Treason and Treason Trials in Later Medieval France*. Cambridge: Cambridge University Press, 1981.

Da Passano, Mario, ed. *Le colonie penali nell'Europa dell'Ottocento: Atti del Convegno internazionale...: Porto Torres, 25 Maggio 2001*. Rome: Carocci, 2004.

Dallas, K. M. *Trading Posts or Penal Colonies: The Commercial Significance of Cook's New Holland Route to the Pacific*. Hobart, Australia: Fullers Bookshop, 1969.

Daston, Lorraine, and Katharine Park. *Wonders and the Order of Nature, 1150–1750*. New York: Zone Books, 2001.

Davenport, Frances and C. O. Paullin, eds. *European Treaties Bearing on the History of the United States and Its Dependencies*. Washington, D.C.: Carnegie Institution of Washington, 1917.

Davis, Natalie Zemon. *Fiction in the Archives: Pardon Tales and Their Tellers in Sixteenth-Century France*. Stanford, CA: Stanford University Press, 1987.

Deacon, Harriet, ed. *The Island: A History of Robben Island, 1488–1990*. Cape Town: Mayibuye Books, 1996.

Deacon, Margaret. *Scientists and the Sea, 1650–1900: A Study of Marine Science.* London: Academic Press, 1971.
De Vos, Paula. "The Rare, the Singular, and the Extraordinary: Natural History and the Collection of Curiosities in the Spanish Empire." In Bleichmar, *Science in the Spanish and Portuguese Empires*, 271–289. Stanford, CA: Stanford University Press, 2009.
Delbourgo, James and Nicholas Dew, eds., *Science and Empire in the Atlantic World.* New York: Routledge, 2008.
Dirlik, Arif. "Confounding Metaphors, Inventions of the World: What Is World History Good For?" In *Writing World History, 1800–2000*, ed. Benedikt Stuchtey and Eckhardt Fuchs. New York: Oxford University Press.
Division of Law, Macquarie University, "Decisions of the Superior Courts of New South Wales, 1788–1899," http://www.law.mq.edu.au/scnsw/.
Dening, Greg. *Mr. Bligh's Bad Language: Passion, Power, and Theatre on the Bounty.* Cambridge: Cambridge University Press, 1992.
Desika Char, S. V. *Readings in the Constitutional History of India, 1757–1947.* Delhi: Oxford University Press, 1983.
Dominguez, Jorte I. "International War and Government Modernization: The Military – A Case Study." In Rodríguez, *Rank and Privilege*, 1–36.
Douzinas, Costas. "Speaking Law: On Bare Theological and Cosmopolitan Sovereignty." In *International Law and Its Others*, ed. Anne Orford, 35–57. Cambridge: Cambridge University Press, 2006.
Drake, James David. *King Philip's War: Civil War in New England, 1675–1676.* Amherst: University of Massachusetts Press, 1999.
Drayton, Richard Harry. *Nature's Government: Science, Imperial Britain, and the "Improvement" of the World.* New Haven, CT: Yale University Press, 2000.
Driver, Felix. *Geography Militant: Cultures of Exploration and Empire.* Oxford, U.K.: Blackwell Publishers, 2001.
Dubois, Laurent. *A Colony of Citizens: Revolution and Slave Emancipation in the French Caribbean, 1787–1804.* Chapel Hill: University of North Carolina Press, 2004.
Dunn, O. C., and James E. Kelley, eds. *The* Diario *of Christopher Columbus's First Voyage to America, 1492–1493.* Norman: University of Oklahoma Press, 1989.
DuVal, Kathleen. *The Native Ground: Indians and Colonists in the Heart of the Continent.* Philadelphia: University of Pennsylvania Press, 2006.
Earle, Peter. *The Sack of Panamá: Sir Henry Morgan's Adventures on the Spanish Main.* New York: Viking Press, 1981.
______. *The Pirate Wars.* London: Methuen, 2003.
Edney, Matthew H. *Mapping an Empire: The Geographical Construction of British India, 1765–1843.* Chicago: University of Chicago Press, 1997.
Elliott, J. H. *Empires of the Atlantic World: Britain and Spain in America, 1492–1830.* New Haven, CT: Yale University Press, 2006.
Elphinstone, Mountstuart. *Territories Conquered from the Paishwa; A Report.* Delhi: Oriental Publishers, 1973.
Ertman, Thomas. *Birth of the Leviathan: Building States and Regimes in Medieval and Early Modern Europe.* Cambridge: Cambridge University Press, 1997.

Fairén Guillén, Víctor. *Los procesos penales de Antonio Pérez*. Zaragoza, Spain: El Justicia de Aragón, 2003.

Faragher, John Mack. *A Great and Noble Scheme: The Tragic Story of the Expulsion of the French Acadians from Their American Homeland*. New York: W.W. Norton, 2005.

Feldman, Lawrence H., ed. *Lost Shores, Forgotten Peoples: Spanish Explorations of the South East Maya Lowlands: Chronicles of the New World Order*. Durham, NC: Duke University Press, 2000.

Findlen, Paula. "A Jesuit's Books in the New World: Athanasius Kircher and his American Readers." In *Athanasius Kircher: The Last Man Who Knew Everything*, ed. Paula Findlen, 316–50. New York: Routledge, 2004.

Fisher, Michael Herbert. *Indirect Rule in India: Residents and the Residency System, 1764–1858*. New York: Oxford University Press, 1998.

Fitzmaurice, Andrew. *Humanism and America: An Intellectual History of English Colonisation, 1500–1625*. Cambridge: Cambridge University Press, 2003.

Fitzpatrick, Peter. "Bare Sovereignty: Homo Sacer and the Insistence of Law." *Theory and Event* 5, no. 2 (2001).

______. *Modernism and the Grounds of Law*. Cambridge: Cambridge University Press, 2001.

Flynn, Dennis O., and Arturo Giráldez. "Cycles of Silver: Global Economic Unity through the Mid-Eighteenth Century." *Journal of World History* 13 (2002), 391–427.

Force, Peter, ed. *Tracts and Other Papers, Relating Principally to the Origin, Settlement, and Progress of the Colonies in North America, from the Discovery of the Country to the Year 1776*. Washington, D.C.: Printed by P. Force, 1836.

Ford, Lisa. *Settler Sovereignty: Jurisdiction and Indigenous People in America and Australia, 1788–1836*. Cambridge: Harvard University Press, 2010.

Forster, Colin. *France and Botany Bay: The Lure of a Penal Colony*. Carlton South, Victoria: Melbourne University Press, 1996.

Fradera, Josep Maria. *Gobernar colonias*. Barcelona: Ediciones Península, 1999.

______. *Colonias para después de un imperio*. Barcelona: Edicions Bellaterra, 2005.

Francaviglia, Richard V. *Mapping and Imagination in the Great Basin: A Cartographic History*. Reno: University of Nevada Press, 2005.

Frost, Alan. *Botany Bay Mirages: Illusions of Australia's Convict Beginnings*. Carlton, Victoria: Melbourne University Press, 1994.

Furtado, Júnia Ferreira. "The Indies of Knowledge, or the Imaginary Geography of the Discoveries of Gold in Brazil." In Bleichmar, *Science in the Spanish and Portuguese Empires*, 178–215.

Gallup-Diaz, Ignacio. *The Door of the Seas and Key to the Universe: Indian Politics and Imperial Rivalry in the Darién, 1640–1750*. New York: Columbia University Press, 2004.

Games, Alison. *The Web of Empire: English Cosmopolitans in an Age of Expansion, 1560–1660*. New York: Oxford University Press, 2008.

Ganong, William Francis. *Champlain's Island: An Expanded Edition of Ste. Croix (Dochet) Island*. Saint John: New Brunswick Museum, 2003.

Ganson, Barbara Anne. *The Guaraní under Spanish Rule in the Río de la Plata*. Stanford, CA: Stanford University Press, 2003.

Garfield, Robert. *A History of Sâo Tomé Island, 1470–1655: The Key to Guinea.* San Francisco: Mellen Research University Press, 1992.

Gascoigne, John. *The Enlightenment and the Origins of European Australia.* Cambridge: Cambridge University Press, 2002.

Gentili, Alberico. *Hispanicae advocationis, libri dvo [1613].* Translated by Frank Frost Abbott. Vol. 2. New York: Oxford University Press, 1921.

______. *De iure belli librie tres.* Translated by John Carew Rolfe. Oxford, U.K.: Clarendon Press, 1933.

Ghachem, Malick W. "Introduction: Slavery and Citizenship in the Age of the Atlantic Revolutions." *Historical Reflections* 29, no. 1 (2003): 7–17.

Gill, Anton. *The Devil's Mariner: A Life of William Dampier, Pirate and Explorer, 1651–1715.* London: Michael Joseph, 1997.

Gillen, Mollie. "The Botany Bay Decision, 1786: Convicts, Not Empire." *English Historical Review* 97, no. 385 (1982): 740–66.

Gillis, John. *Islands of the Mind: How the Human Imagination Created the Atlantic World.* New York: Palgrave Macmillan, 2004.

Glete, Jan. *Warfare at Sea, 1500–1650: Maritime Conflicts and the Transformation of Europe.* New York: Routledge, 2000. *The Grand Pyrate, or, the Life and Death of Capt. George Cusack, the Great Sea-Robber with an Accompt of All His Notorious Robberies Both at Sea and Land: Together with His Tryal, Condemnation, and Execution/Taken by an Impartial Hand.* London: Printed for Jonathan Edwin, 1676.

Goldsmith, Jack L., and Eric A. Posner. *The Limits of International Law.* Oxford: Oxford University Press, 2005.

Gong, Gerrit W. *The Standard of "Civilization" in International Society.* New York: Oxford University Press, 1984.

González, Juan García. "Traición y alevosía en la alta Edad Media." *Annuario de Historia del Derecho Español* (1962): 323–46.

Goswami, Manu. *Producing India: From Colonial Economy to National Space.* Chicago: University of Chicago Press, 2004.

Gould, Eliga. "Zones of Law, Zones of Violence: The Legal Geography of the British Atlantic, circa 1772." *William and Mary Quarterly* 60, no. 3 (2003): 471–510.

______. "Entangled Atlantic Histories: A Response from the Anglo-American Periphery." *American Historical Review* 112 (2007): 764–86.

Green, Samuel A. *The Boundary Line between Massachusetts and New Hampshire: From the Merrimack River to the Connecticut: A Paper Read before the Old Residents' Historical Association of Lowell, on December 21, 1893, the Twenty-Fifth Anniversary of the Formation of the Society.* Lowell, MA: Lowell Courier, 1894.

Greenblatt, Stephen Jay. *Marvelous Possessions: The Wonder of the New World.* Chicago: University of Chicago Press, 1991.

Greene, Jack P. *Peripheries and Center: Constitutional Development in the Extended Polities of the British Empire and the United States, 1607–1788.* Athens: University of Georgia Press, 1986.

Greenlee, William Brooks, ed. *The Voyage of Pedro Álvares Cabral to Brazil and India from Contemporary Documents and Narratives.* London: Printed for the Hakluyt Society, 1938.

Gregory, Derek. *The Colonial Present: Afghanistan, Palestine, Iraq.* Malden, MA: Blackwell Publishing, 2004.

Grossberg, Michael and Christopher Tomlins, eds. *The Cambridge History of Law in America, Vol. I, Early America (1580–1815).* Cambridge: Cambridge University Press, 2008.

Grotius, Hugo. *The Free Sea.* Translated by Richard Hakluyt, ed. David Armitage. Indianapolis: Liberty Fund, 2004.

______. *The Rights of War and Peace*, 3 vols, ed. Richard Tuck. Indianapolis: Liberty Fund, 2005.

______. *Commentary on the Law of Prize and Booty.* Translated by Gwladys L. Williams, ed. Martine Julia van Ittersum. Indianapolis: Liberty Fund, 2006.

Hackel, Steven W. *Children of Coyote, Missionaries of Saint Francis: Indian-Spanish Relations in Colonial California, 1769–1850.* Chapel Hill: University of North Carolina Press, 2005.

Hadfield, Andrew. *Literature, Travel, and Colonial Writing in the English Renaissance, 1545–1625.* Oxford: Oxford University Press, 2007.

Hadfield, Andrew, and John McVeagh. *Strangers to That Land: British Perceptions of Ireland from the Reformation to the Famine.* Gerrards Cross, U.K.: Colin Smythe, 1994.

Haefeli, Evan, and Kevin Sweeney. *Captors and Captives: The 1704 French and Indian Raid on Deerfield.* Amherst: University of Massachusetts Press, 2003.

Haliczer, Stephen. *The* Comuneros *of Castile: The Forging of a Revolution, 1475–1521.* Madison: University of Wisconsin Press, 1981.

Halliday, Paul. *The Liberty of the Subject: Habeas Corpus from England to Empire.* Cambridge, MA: Harvard University Press, forthcoming.

Hancock, David. *Oceans of Wine: Madeira and the Emergence of American Trade and Taste.* New Haven, CT: Yale University Press, 2009.

Harley, J. B. "New England Cartography and the Native Americans." In J. B. Harley, *The New Nature of Maps*, ed. Paul Laxton, 169–97. Baltimore: Johns Hopkins University Press, 2001.

______. "Rereading the Maps of the Columbian Encounter." *Annals of the Association of American Geographers* 82, no. 3 (1992): 522–36.

Harley, J. B., and David Woodward, eds. *: Cartography in the Traditional Islamic and South Asian Societies.* Vol. 2, bk. 1, *The History of Cartography.* Chicago: University of Chicago Press, 1992.

______. *Cartography in the Traditional East and Southeast Asian Societies.* Vol. 2, bk. 2, *The History of Cartography.* Chicago: University of Chicago Press, 1995.

Harring, Sidney L. *Crow Dog's Case: American Indian Sovereignty, Tribal Law, and United States Law in the Nineteenth Century.* Cambridge: Cambridge University Press, 1994.

Harrison, Mark. *Climates and Constitutions: Health, Race, Environment and British Imperialism in India, 1600–1850.* New York: Oxford University Press, 1999.

Hart, H. L. A. *The Concept of Law.* eds., Penelope Bulloch and Joseph Raz 2nd ed. New York: Clarendon Press, 1994.

Haskell, Alexander B. "'The Affections of the People': Ideology and the Politics of State Building in Colonial Virginia, 1607–1754." Ph.D. diss., Johns Hopkins University, 2004.

Haslip-Viera, Gabriel. *Crime and Punishment in Late Colonial Mexico City, 1692–1810*. Albuquerque: University of New Mexico Press, 1999.

Herzog, Tamar. *Defining Nations: Immigrants and Citizens in Early Modern Spain and Spanish America*. New Haven, CT: Yale University Press, 2003.

High Court of Admiralty, England and Wales. *The Tryals of Joseph Dawson, Edward Forseith, William May, [Brace] William Bishop, James Lewis, and John Sparkes for Several Piracies and Robberies by Them Committed in the Company of Every the Grand Pirate, near the Coasts of the East-Indies, and Several Other Places on the Seas: Giving an Account of Their Villainous Robberies and Barbarities: At the Admiralty Sessions, Begun at the Old-Baily on the 29th of October, 1696, and Ended on the 6th of November*. London: Printed by John Everingham, 1696.

Hinderaker, Eric, and Peter C. Mancall. *At the Edge of Empire: The Backcountry in British North America*. Baltimore: Johns Hopkins University Press, 2003.

Hirst, John. "The Australian Experience: The Convict Colony." In Morris, *Maconochie's Gentlemen*, 235–65.

Hodson, Christopher. "Refugees, Acadians and the Social History of Empire, 1755–1785," Ph.D. diss. Northwestern University, 2004.

Hoffer, Peter Charles. *The Treason Trials of Aaron Burr*. Lawrence: University Press of Kansas, 2008.

Hoffman, Ronald, and Peter J. Albert. *Launching the "Extended Republic": The Federalist Era*. Charlottesville: University Press of Virginia, 1996.

Hogben, William Murray. "The Foreign and Political Department of the Government of India, 1876–1919: A Study in Imperial Careers and Attitudes." Ph.D. diss., University of Toronto, 1973.

Horn, James. *Adapting to a New World: English Society in the Seventeenth-Century Chesapeake*. Chapel Hill: University of North Carolina Press, 1994.

______. "The Conquest of Eden: Possession and Dominion in Early Virginia." In Appelbaum and Sweet, *Envisioning an English Empire*, 25–48.

Howard, David A. *Conquistador in Chains: Cabeza de Vaca and the Indians of the Americas*. Tuscaloosa: University of Alabama Press, 1997.

Howe, Adrian. "The Bayard Treason Trial: Dramatizing Anglo-Dutch Politics in Early Eighteenth-Century New York City." *William and Mary Quarterly* 47, no. 1 (1990): 57–89.

Hulsebosch, Daniel, and David Golove. "On an Equal Footing: Constitution-Making and the Law of Nations in the Early American Republic." Paper presented at The Legal History Colloquium, New York University School of Law, January 21, 2009.

Hulsebosch, Daniel. *Constituting Empire: New York and the Transformation of Constitutionalism in the Atlantic World, 1664–1830*. Chapel Hill: University of North Carolina Press, 2005.

Hurst, James Willard. *The Law of Treason in the United States: Collected Essays*. Westport, CT: Greenwood, 1971.

Hussain, Nasser. *The Jurisprudence of Emergency: Colonialism and the Rule of Law*. Ann Arbor: University of Michigan Press, 2003.

Jackson, Bernard S. "Analogy in Legal Science: Some Comparative Observations." In *Legal Knowledge and Analogy: Fragments of Legal Epistemology, Hermeneutics, and Linguistics*, ed. Patrick Nerhot, 145–64. Dordrecht, The Netherlands: Kluwar, 1991.

Jackson, R. V. "Jeremy Bentham and the New South Wales Convicts." *International Journal of Social Economics* 25, no. 2–4 (1998): 370–80.

Jaksic, Ivan. *Andrés Bello: Scholarship and Nation-Building in Nineteenth-Century Latin America*. Cambridge: Cambridge University Press, 2001.

Jameson, J. Franklin, ed. *Privateering and Piracy in the Colonial Period: Illustrated Documents*. New York: Augustus M. Kelley, 1970.

Jobson, Richard. *The Discovery of River Gambra (1623) by Richard Jobson*. London: Hakluyt Society, 1999.

Johnson, Captain Charles. *A General History of the Robberies and Murders of the Most Notorious Pyrates, and Also Their Policies, Discipline and Government, from Their First Rise and Settlement in the Island of Providence,... With the Remarkable Actions and Adventures of the Two Female Pyrates, Mary Read and Anne Bonny. To Which Is Prefix'd an Account of the Famous Captain Avery... By Captain Charles Johnson*. London: Printed for Ch. Rivington, J. Lacy, and J. Stone, 1724.

Johnson, John J. *The Military and Society in Latin America*. Stanford, CA: Stanford University Press, 1964.

Kagan, Richard L. *Lawsuits and Litigants in Castile, 1500–1700*. Chapel Hill: University of North Carolina Press, 1981.

Kagan, Richard L., and Fernando Marías. *Urban Images of the Hispanic World, 1493–1793*. New Haven, CT: Yale University Press, 2000.

Kantorowicz, Ernst Hartwig. *The King's Two Bodies: A Study in Medieval Political Theology*. Princeton, NJ: Princeton University Press, 1957.

Kaplan, Amy. "Where Is Guantánamo?" *American Quarterly* 57, no. 3 (2005): 831–58.

Karras, Alan. *Sojourners in the Sun: Scottish Migrants in Jamaica and the Chesapeake, 1740–1800*. Ithaca, NY: Cornell University Press, 1992.

Keene, Edward. *Beyond the Anarchical Society: Grotius, Colonialism and Order in World Politics*. Cambridge: Cambridge University Press, 2002.

Keller, Arthur Schopenhauer, Oliver James Lissitzyn, and Frederick Justin Mann. *Creation of Rights of Sovereignty through Symbolic Acts, 1400–1800*. New York: Columbia University Press, 1938.

Kelley, Donald R. *The Human Measure: Social Thought in the Western Legal Tradition*. Cambridge, MA: Harvard University Press, 1990.

Kempe, Michael. "Beyond the Law: The Image of Piracy in the Legal Writings of Hugo Grotius." In Blom, *Property, Piracy and Punishment*, 379–96.

Kennedy, Dane Keith. *The Magic Mountains: Hill Stations and the British Raj*. Berkeley: University of California Press, 1996.

Kercher, Bruce. *Debt, Seduction, and Other Disasters: The Birth of Civil Law in Convict New South Wales*. Sydney: Federation Press, 1996.

———. "Resistance to Law under Autocracy." *Modern Law Review* 60, no. 6 (1997): 779–97.

———. "Perish or Prosper: The Law and Convict Transportation in the British Empire, 1700–1850." *Law and History Review* 21, no. 3 (2003): 527–54.

Kesselring, K. J. *Mercy and Authority in the Tudor State.* Cambridge: Cambridge University Press, 2003.

Kingsbury, Benedict, Nico Krisch, and Richard B. Stewart. "The Emergence of Global Administrative Law." In *International Law and Justice Working Papers.* New York: Institute for International Law and Justice, New York University School of Law, 2005.

Koskenniemi, Martti. *The Gentle Civilizer of Nations: The Rise and Fall of International Law 1870–1960.* Cambridge: Cambridge University Press, 2005.

Kostal, R. W. *A Jurisprudence of Power: Victorian Empire and the Rule of Law.* Oxford: Oxford University Press, 2005.

Krasner, Stephen D. *Sovereignty: Organized Hypocrisy.* Princeton, NJ: Princeton University Press, 1999.

Kulsrud, Carl Jacob. *Maritime Neutrality to 1780: A History of the Main Principles Governing Neutrality and Belligerency to 1780.* Boston: Little, Brown, 1936.

Kupperman, Karen Ordahl. "The Puzzle of the American Climate in the Early Colonial Period." *American Historical Review* 87 (1982): 1262–80.

———. "English Perceptions of Treachery, 1583–1640: The Case of the American 'Savages.'" *Historical Journal* 20, no. 2 (1977): 263–87.

———. *The Jamestown Project.* Cambridge, MA: Belknap Press, 2007.

Lake, Peter, and Michael Questier. "Agency, Appropriation and Rhetoric under the Gallows: Puritans, Romanists and the State in Early Modern England." *Past and Present,* 153 (1996): 64–107.

Lamb, Jonathan, Vanessa Smith, and Nicholas Thomas, eds. *Exploration and Exchange: A South Seas Anthology, 1680–1900.* Chicago: University of Chicago Press, 2000.

Lane, Frederic Chapin. *Venice, a Maritime Republic.* Baltimore: Johns Hopkins University Press, 1973.

Lastres y Juiz, Francisco, and Eduardo Martínez. *La colonización penitenciaria de las Marianas y Fernando Póo.* Madrid: Imprenta y Librería de Eduardo Martínez, 1878.

Laudonnière, René. *Three Voyages.* Tuscaloosa: University of Alabama Press, 2001.

Lawson, Gary, and Guy Seidman. *The Constitution of Empire: Territorial Expansion and American Legal History.* New Haven, CT: Yale University Press, 2004.

Lee, Robert E. *Blackbeard the Pirate: A Reappraisal of His Life and Times.* Winston-Salem, NC: John F. Blair, 2002 [1974].

Lee-Warner, William. *The Protected Princes of India.* London: Macmillan, 1894.

Leed, Eric J., *The Mind of the Traveler: From Gilgamesh to Global Tourism.* New York: Basic Books, 1991.

Lefebvre, Henri. *The Production of Space.* Translated by Donald Nicholson-Smith. Malden, MA: Blackwell, 2004.

Lemon, Rebecca. *Treason by Words: Literature, Law, and Rebellion in Shakespeare's England.* Ithaca, NY: Cornell University Press, 2006.

León León, Marco Antonio, ed. *Sistema carcelario en Chile: Visiones, realidades y proyectos (1816–1916)*. Santiago, Chile: Dirección de Bibliotecas, Archivos y Museos, Centro de Investigaciones Diego Barros Arrana, 1996.

León León, Marco Antonio. *Encierro y corrección: La configuración de un sistema de prisiones en Chile: 1800–1911*. Vol. 2. Santiago: Universidad Central de Chile, Facultad de Ciencias Jurídicas y Sociales, 2003.

Lepore, Jill. *The Name of War: King Philip's War and the Origins of American Identity*. New York: Vintage Books, 1999.

Levack, Brian P. *The Civil Lawyers in England, 1603–1641: A Political Study*. Oxford: Clarendon Press, 1973.

Levine, Robert M. *Vale of Tears: Revisiting the Canudos Massacre in Northeastern Brazil, 1893–1897*. Berkeley: University of California Press, 1995.

Lewis, Martin W. "Dividing the Ocean Sea." *Geographical Review* 89, no. 2 (1999): 188–214.

Lewis, Mary Dewhurst. "Geographies of Power: The Tunisian Civic Order, Jurisdictional Politics, and Imperial Rivalry in the Mediterranean, 1881–1935." *The Journal of Modern History* 80 (December, 2008): 791–830.

Limerick, Patricia Nelson. *Desert Passages: Encounters with the American Deserts*. Albuquerque: University of New Mexico Press, 1985.

Linebaugh, Peter, and Marcus Rediker. *The Many-Headed Hydra: Sailors, Slaves, Commoners, and the Hidden History of the Revolutionary Atlantic*. Boston: Beacon Press, 2000.

Lockhart, James, and Enrique Otte, ed. *Letters and People of the Spanish Indies: Sixteenth Century*. Cambridge: Cambridge University Press, 1976.

López, Adalberto. *The Colonial History of Paraguay: The Revolt of the Comuneros, 1721–1735*. New Brunswick, NJ: Transaction Publishers, 2005.

López de Velasco, Juan. *Geografía y descripción universal de las Indias*. Ed. Marco Jiménez de la Espada. Madrid: Atlas, 1971.

López y Sebastián, Lorenzo E., ed. *Alemanes en América*. Madrid: Historia 16, 1985.

Lorcin, Patricia M. E. *Imperial Identities: Stereotyping, Prejudice and Race in Colonial Algeria*. London: I. B. Tauris; Distributed by St. Martin's, 1999.

Lorimer, Joyce. *English and Irish Settlement on the River Amazon, 1550–1646*. London: Hakluyt Society, 1989.

Louis, William Roger, and Nicholas P. Canny. *The Oxford History of the British Empire*. 5 vols. Oxford: Oxford University Press, 1998.

Loveman, Brian, and Thomas M. Davies, eds. *The Politics of Antipolitics: The Military in Latin America*. Wilmington, DE: Rowman and Littlefield, 1997.

Lupher, David A. *Romans in a New World: Classical Models in Sixteenth-Century Spanish America*. Ann Arbor: University of Michigan Press, 2003.

Lyall, Alfred Comyn. *Asiatic Studies, Religious and Social*. London: J. Murray, 1882.

MacCormack, Sabine. *On the Wings of Time: Rome, the Incas, Spain, and Peru*. Princeton, NJ: Princeton University Press, 2007.

MacDonald, Robert A., ed. "Introduction: Part II" to *Leyes de los Adelantados Moyores: Regulations, Attributed to Alfonso X of Castile, Concerning the King's Vicar in the Judiciary and in Territorial Administration*. New York: Hispanic Seminary of Medieval Studies, 2007.

MacLachlan, Colin M. *Spain's Empire in the New World: The Role of Ideas in Institutional and Social Change*. Berkeley: University of California Press, 1988.
MacMillan, Ken. *Sovereignty and Possession in the English New World: The Legal Foundations of Empire, 1576–1640*. Cambridge: Cambridge University Press, 2006.
Maconochie, Alexander. *Australiana Thoughts on Convict Management and Other Subjects Connected with the Australian Penal Colonies*. London: J. W. Parker, 1839.
Maier, Charles S. "Consigning the Twentieth Century to History: Alternative Narratives for the Modern Era." *American Historical Review* 105 (2000), 807–31.
______. *Among Empires: American Ascendancy and Its Predecessors*. Cambridge, MA: Harvard University Press, 2006.
Malaspina, Alessandro. *The Malaspina Expedition, 1789–1794: Journal of the Voyage by Alejandro Malaspina*. Ed. Andrew David, Felipe Fernández-Armesto, Carlos Novi, and Glyndwr Williams. London: Hakluyt Society, 2004.
Mancall, Peter C. *Hakluyt's Promise: An Elizabethan's Obsession for an English America*. New Haven, CT: Yale University Press, 2007.
Marañón, Gregorio. *Antonio Pérez*. Madrid: Espasa Calpe, 2006.
Marchant, Leslie R. *France Australe: The French Search for the Southland and Subsequent Explorations and Plans to Found a Penal Colony and Strategic Base in South Western Australia 1503–1826*. Perth: Scott Four Colour Print, 1998.
Marcos Rivas, Javier, and Carlos J. Carnicer García. *Espionaje y traición en el reinado de Felipe II: La historia del vallisoletano Martín de Acuña*. Valladolid, Spain: Diputación Provincial de Valladolid, 2001.
Mark, Peter. *"Portuguese" Style and Luso-African Identity: Precolonial Senegambia, Sixteenth-Nineteenth Centuries*. Bloomington: Indiana University Press, 2002.
Martí, José, and Celina Manzoni. *El presidio político en Cuba, último diario y otros textos*. Buenos Aires: Editorial Biblos, 1995.
Mathiasen, Joanne. "Some Problems of Admiralty Jurisdiction in the 17th Century." *American Journal of Legal History* 2, no. 3 (1958): 215–36.
Mbembe, Achille. "Necropolitics." *Public Culture* 15, no. 1 (2003): 11–40.
McAlister, Lyle N. *The "Fuero Militar" in New Spain, 1764–1800*. Gainesville: University of Florida Press, 1957.
McDonald, Kevin P. "Pirates, Merchants, Settlers, and Slaves: Making an Indo-Atlantic Trade World, 1640–1730." Ph.D. diss., University of California-Santa Cruz, 2008.
McKeown, Adam. *Melancholy Order: Asian Migration and the Globalization of Borders*. New York: Columbia University Press, 2008.
McLaren, Martha. *British India and British Scotland, 1780–1830: Career Building, Empire Building, and a Scottish School of Thought on Indian Governance*. Akron, Ohio: University of Akron Press, 2001.
McLeod, Bruce. *The Geography of Empire in English Literature, 1580–1745*. Cambridge: Cambridge University Press, 1999.
McLeod, John. *Sovereignty, Power, Control: Politics in the State of Western India, 1916–1947*. Leiden: Brill, 1999.

McPherson, Kenneth. "Trade and Traders in the Bay of Bengal: Fifteenth to Nineteenth Centuries." In Subramanian, *Politics and Trade in the Indian Ocean World*, 196.

Meinig, D. W. *The Shaping of America: A Geographical Perspective on 500 Years of History*. Vol. 1. New Haven, CT: Yale University Press, 1986.

Merwick, Donna. *Possessing Albany, 1630–1710: The Dutch and English Experiences*. Cambridge: Cambridge University Press, 2003.

Metcalf, Thomas R. *Imperial Connections: India in the Indian Ocean Arena, 1860–1920*. Berkeley: University of California Press, 2007.

Milanich, Jerald T. *Florida Indians and the Invasion from Europe*. Gainesville: University Press of Florida, 1995.

Miquelon, Dale. "Envisioning the French Empire: Utrecht, 1711–1713." *French Historical Studies* 24, no. 4 (2001): 653–770.

Mirow, Matthew C. *Latin American Law: A History of Private Law and Institutions in Spanish America*. Austin: University of Texas Press, 2004.

Mollat, Michel. *Europe and the Sea*. Oxford, U.K.: Blackwell, 1993.

Moore, James F. H. *The Convicts of Van Diemen's Land, 1840–1853*. Hobart: Cat and Fiddle Press, 1976.

Morgan, Gwenda, and Peter Rushton. *Eighteenth-Century Criminal Transportation: The Formation of the Criminal Atlantic*. New York: Palgrave Macmillan, 2004.

Morris, Norval. *Maconochie's Gentlemen: The Story of Norfolk Island and the Roots of Modern Prison Reform*. New York: Oxford University Press, 2002.

Muldoon, James. *Popes, Lawyers, and Infidels: The Church and the Non-Christian World, 1250–1550*. Philadelphia: University of Pennsylvania Press, 1979.

______. *The Americas in the Spanish World Order: The Justification for Conquest in the Seventeenth Century*. Philadelphia: University of Pennsylvania Press, 1994.

______. *Empire and Order: The Concept of Empire, 800–1800*. New York: Macmillan, 1999.

______. "Who Owns the Sea." Paper presented at "Sea Changes: Historicizing the Oceans," Universität Greifswald, Germany, July 2000.

______. "Discovery, Grant, Charter, Conquest, or Purchase." In *The Many Legalities of Early America*, ed. Christopher L. Tomlins and Bruce H. Mann, 25–46. Chapel Hill: University of North Carolina Press, 2001.

Mulford, Elisha. *The Nation: The Foundations of Civil Order and Political Life in the United States*. New York: Hurd and Houghton, 1871.

______. *The Republic of God. An Institute of Theology*. Boston: Houghton Mifflin, 1881.

Mundy, Barbara E. *The Mapping of New Spain: Indigenous Cartography and the Maps of the* Relaciones Geográficas. Chicago: University of Chicago Press, 1996.

Navarro Brotóns, Víctor, and William Eamon, eds. *Más allá de la leyenda negra: España y la revolución científica*. Valencia, Spain: Instituto de Historia de la Ciencia y Documentación López Piñero, Universitat de Valencia, 2007.

Nelson, William. *The Common Law in Colonial America*. New York: Oxford University Press, 2008.
Nerhot, Patrick, ed. *Legal Knowledge and Analogy: Fragments of Legal Epistemology, Hermeneutics, and Linguistics*. Dordrecht, The Netherlands: Kluwar, 1991.
Neuman, Gerald L. "Anomalous Zones." *Stanford Law Review* 48, no. 5 (1996): 1197–1234.
Newitt, M. D. D. *A History of Portuguese Overseas Expansion, 1400–1668*. New York: Routledge, 2005.
Nowell, Charles E. "The Loasa Expedition and the Ownership of the Moluccas." *The Pacific Historical Review* 5:4 (1936): 325–36.
Ocko, Jonathan, and David Gilmartin. "State, Sovereignty, and the People: A Comparison of the 'Rule of Law' in China and India." *Journal of Asian Studies* 68, no. 1 (2008): 1–46.
Ohlmeyer, Jane H. "'Civilizinge of those Rude Partes': Colonization within Britain and Ireland, 1580s–1640s." In Canny, *The Origins of Empire*, 124–47.
Oldham, James. "Insurance Litigation Involving the *Zong* and Other British Slave Ships, 1780–1807." *Journal of Legal History* 28 (2007): 299–318.
Olmedo Bernal, Santiago. *El dominio del Atlántico en la Baja edad media: Los títulos jurídicos de la expansión peninsular hasta el Tratado de Tordesillas*. Valladolid, Spain: Sociedad V° Centenario del Tratado de Tordesillas, 1995.
Oppenheim, L., ed. *The Collected Papers of John Westlake on Public International Law*. Cambridge: Cambridge University Press, 1914.
Orr, D. Alan. *Treason and the State: Law, Politics and Ideology in the English Civil War*. Cambridge: Cambridge University Press, 2002.
Otero Lana, Enrique. *Los corsarios españoles durante la decadencia de los Austrias: El corso español del Atlántico peninsular en el siglo XVII (1621–1697)*. Madrid: Editorial Naval, 1992.
Oviedo y Valdés, Gonzalo Fernández de. *Historia general y natural de las Indias*. Vol. 5. Madrid: Ediciones Atlas, 1992.
Pacheco Pereira, Duarte. *Esmeraldo de situ orbis*. Translated by George H. T. Kimble. London: Hakluyt Society, 1937.
Padrón, Ricardo. *The Spacious Word: Cartography, Literature, and Empire in Early Modern Spain*. Chicago: University of Chicago Press, 2004.
Pagden, Anthony. *Spanish Imperialism and the Political Imagination: Studies in European and Spanish-American Social and Political Theory, 1513–1830*. New Haven, CT: Yale University Press, 1990.
———. *European Encounters with the New World from Renaissance to Romanticism*. New Haven, CT: Yale University Press, 1993.
———. *Lords of All the World: Ideologies of Empire in Spain, Britain and France c. 1500–c.* 1800. New Haven, CT: Yale University Press, 1995.
———, ed. *Facing Each Other: The World's Perception of Europe and Europe's Perception of the World*. Burlington, VT: Ashgate/Variorum, 2000.
———. "The Struggle for Legitimacy and the Image of Empire in the Atlantic, to c. 1700," in Canny, *The Origins of Empire*, 34–54.
———. "Law, Colonization, Legitimation, and the European Background." In Grossberg and Tomlins, *The Cambridge History of Law in America*.

Panikkar, K. M. *The Indian Princes in Council: A Record of the Chancellorship of His Highness, the Maharaja of Patiala, 1926–1931* and *1933–1936*. London: Oxford University Press, 1936.
Pares, Richard. *War and Trade in the West Indies, 1739–1763*. Oxford: Clarendon Press, 1936.
Pearson, M. N. *Port Cities and Intruders: The Swahili Coast, India, and Portugal in the Early Modern Era*. Baltimore, MD: Johns Hopkins University Press, 1998.
Pennell, C. R., ed. *Bandits at Sea: A Pirates Reader*. New York: New York University Press, 2001.
Pérez, Joseph. *The Spanish Inquisition: A History*. Translated by Janet Lloyd. New Haven, CT: Yale University Press, 2005.
Pérez-Mallaína, Pablo E. *Spain's Men of the Sea: Daily Life on the Indies Fleets in the Sixteenth Century*. Translated by Carla Rahn Phillips. Baltimore: Johns Hopkins University Press, 1998.
Pérotin-Dumon, Anne. "The Pirate and the Emperor: Power and Law on the Seas, 1450–1850." In *The Political Economy of Merchant Empires*. Ed. James D. Tracy. Cambridge: Cambridge University Press, 1991.
Perruso, Richard. "The Development of the Doctrine of *Res Communes* in Medieval and Early Modern Europe." *Tijdschrift voor Rechtsgeschiedenis* 70 (2002): 69–94.
Peters, Edward. *Inquisition*. Berkeley: University of California Press, 1989.
Peters, Rudolph. *Crime and Punishment in Islamic Law: Theory and Practice from the Sixteenth to the Twenty-First Century*. Cambridge: Cambridge University Press, 2005.
Petit, Jacques-Guy. "La colonizzazione penale del sistema penitenziario francese." In *Le colonie penali nell'Europa dell'Ottocento: Atti del Congegno internazionale... Porto Torres, 25 Maggio 2001*, ed. Mario Da Passano, 37–65. Rome: Carocci, 2004.
Petit-Breuilh Sepúlveda, María Eugenia. *Naturaleza y desastres en Hispanoamérica: La visión de los indígenas*. Madrid: Sílex, 2006.
Pfining, Ernst. "Contrabando, ilegalidade e medidas políticas no Rio de Janeiro de século XVIII." *Revista Brasileira de História* 21, no. 42 (2001): 397–414.
Picó, Fernando. *El día menos pensado: Historia de los presidiarios en Puerto Rico, 1793–1993*. Río Piedras, Puerto Rico: Ediciones Huracán, 1994.
Pieroni, Geraldo. *Vadios e ciganos, heréticos e bruxas: Os degredados no Brasil-Colônia*. Rio de Janeiro: Berstrand Brasil, 2000.
Pigafetta, Antonio. *The Voyage of Magellan: The Journal of Antonio Pigafetta*. Translated by Paula Spurlin Paige. Englewood Cliffs, NJ: Prentice Hall, 1969.
Pike, Ruth. *Penal Servitude in Early Modern Spain*. Madison: University of Wisconsin Press, 1983.
Pimentel, Juan. "Baroque Natures: Juan E. Nieremberg, American Wonders, and Preterimperial Natural History." In Bleichmar, *Science in the Spanish and Portuguese Empires*, 93–111. Stanford, CA: Stanford University Press, 2009.
______. *Testigos del mundo: Ciencia, literature y viajes en la ilustración*. Madrid: Marcial Pons, 2003.
Pitts, Jennifer. "Legislator of the World? A Rereading of Bentham on Colonies." *Political Theory* 31, no. 2 (2003): 200–34.

Plank, Geoffrey Gilbert. *An Unsettled Conquest: The British Campaign against the Peoples of Acadia*. Philadelphia: University of Pennsylvania Press, 2003.

Portuondo, María M. "Spanish Cosmography and the New World Crisis." In *Más allá de la leyenda negra: España y la revolución científica*, ed. Victor Navarro Brotóns and William Eamon, 383–97. Valencia, Spain: Instituto de Historia de la Ciencia y Documentación López Piñero, Universitat de Valencia, 2007.

———. "Cosmography at the *Casa*, *Consejo*, and *Corte* During the Century of Disovery." In Bleichmar, *Science in the Spanish and Portuguese Empires*.

———. *Secret Science: Spanish Cosmography and the New World*. Chicago: University of Chicago Press, 2009.

Prakesh, Om. "European Corporate Enterprises and the Politics of Trade in India, 1600–1800." In Subramanian, *Politics and Trade in the Indian Ocean World*, 174.

Prichard, M. J., and D. E. C. Yale, eds. *Hale and Fleetwood on Admiralty Jurisdiction*. London: Selden Society, 1993.

Prucha, Francis Paul. *The Great Father: The United States Government and the American Indians*. Lincoln: University of Nebraska Press, 1984.

Pulsipher, Jenny Hale. *Subjects unto the Same King: Indians, English, and the Contest for Authority in Colonial New England*. Philadelphia: University of Pennsylvania Press, 2005.

Raffield, Paul. *Images and Cultures of Law in Early Modern England: Justice and Political Power, 1558–1660*. Cambridge: Cambridge University Press, 2004.

Raleigh, Walter. *The Discoverie of the Large, Rich, and Bevvtiful Empire of Gviana with a Relation of the Great and Golden Citie of Manoa (Which the Spanyards Call El Dorado) and the Prouinces of Emeria, Arromaia, Amapaia, and Other Countries, with Their Riuers, Adioyning*. London: By Robert Robinson, 1596.

———. *Sir Walter Rawleigh His Apologie for His Voyage to Guiana*. London: Printed by T. W. for Hum. Moseley, 1650.

Ramusack, Barbara N. *The Indian Princes and Their States*. Cambridge: Cambridge University Press, 2004.

Redding, Sean. *Sorcery and Sovereignty: Taxation, Power, and Rebellion in South Africa, 1880–1963*. Athens: Ohio University Press, 2006.

Redfield, Peter. *Space in the Tropics: From Convicts to Rockets in French Guiana*. Berkeley: University of California Press, 2000.

Rediker, Marcus. *Between the Devil and the Deep Blue Sea: Merchant Seamen, Pirates, and the Anglo-American Maritime World, 1700–1750*. Cambridge: Cambridge University Press, 1987.

———. *Villains of All Nations: Atlantic Pirates in the Golden Age*. Boston: Beacon Press, 2004.

Reid, John Phillip. *Law for the Elephant: Property and Social Behavior on the Overland Trail*. San Marino, CA: Huntington Library, 1997.

Rela, W. *Portugal en las exploraciones del Río de la Plata*. Montevideo, Uruguay: Academia Uruguaya de Historia Marítima y Fluvial, 2002.

Reynolds, Susan. "Empires: A Program of Comparative History." *Historical Research* 79, no. 204 (2006): 151–65.

Rhode Island (Colony). *A Court Martial Held at Newport, Rhode Island, in August and September, 1676, for the Trial of Indians, Charged with Being Engaged in King Philip's War*. Albany, NY: Printed by J. Munsell, 1858.

Richardson, J. S. "Imperium Romanum: Empire and the Language of Power." *Journal of Roman Studies* 81 (1991): 1–9.

Richardson, Philip L. "The Benjamin Franklin and Timothy Folger Charts of the Gulf Stream." In *Oceanography: The Past*, ed. Mary Sears and Daniel Merriman, 703–17. New York: Springer-Verlag, 1980.

Richter, Daniel. "Dutch Dominos: The Defeat of the West India Company and the Reshaping of Eastern North America." Paper presented at "Transformations: the Atlantic World in the Late Seventeenth Century," Harvard University, March 30–April 1, 2006.

Ritchie, Robert C. *Captain Kidd and the War against the Pirates*. Cambridge, MA: Harvard University Press, 1986.

Ritsema, Alex. *A Dutch Castaway on Ascension Island in 1725*. Netherlands: A. Ritsema, 2006.

Robins, Benjamin. *An Address to the Electors, and Other Free Subjects of Great Britain; Occasion'd by the Late Secession. In Which Is Contain'd a Particular Account of All Our Negotiations with Spain*. 3rd ed. London: Printed for H. Goreham, 1739.

Robinson, O. F. *The Criminal Law of Ancient Rome*. Baltimore: Johns Hopkins University Press, 1995.

Rodríguez, Linda Alexander, ed. *Rank and Privilege: The Military and Society in Latin America*. Wilmington, DE: Rowman and Littlefield, 1994.

Rosen, Deborah A. *American Indians and State Law: Sovereignty, Race, and Citizenship, 1790–1880*. Lincoln: University of Nebraska Press, 2007.

Ross, Richard. "Legal Communications and Imperial Governance: British North America and Spanish America Compared." In Grossberg and Tomlins, *The Cambridge History of Law in America*.

Rothschild, Emma. "A Horrible Tragedy in the French Atlantic." *Past and Present*, no. 192 (2006): 67–108.

Rubin, Alfred P. *The Law of Piracy*. Newport, RI: Naval War College Press, 1988.

Rubio, Julián María. *Exploración y conquista del Río de la Plata, siglos XVI y XVII*. Barcelona: Salvat Editores, 1942.

Rushbrook Williams, L. F. *The British Crown and the Indian States: An Outline Sketch Drawn up on Behalf of the Standing Committee of the Chamber of Princes by the Directorate of the Chamber's Special Organisation*. London: P. S. King and Son, 1929.

Russell, Conrad. "The Theory of Treason in the Trial of Strafford." *English Historical Review* 80 (1965): 30–50.

Russell, P. E. *Portugal, Spain, and the African Atlantic, 1343–1490: Chivalry and Crusade from John of Gaunt to Henry the Navigator and Beyond*. Brookfield, VT: Variorum, 1995.

———. "Castilian Documentary Sources for the History of the Portuguese Expansion in Guinea, in the Last Years of the Reign of Dom Afonso V." In Russell, *Portugal, Spain, and the African Atlantic*, XII, 1–23.

———. "New Light on the Text of Eustache de la Fosse's *Voiaige à la Guinée* (1479–1480)." In Russell, *Portugal, Spain, and the African Atlantic.*

———. "White Kings on Black Kings." In Russell, *Portugal, Spain, and the African Atlantic*, XVI, 153–63.

Sack, Robert David. *Human Territoriality: Its Theory and History*. Cambridge: Cambridge University Press, 1986.

Sahlins, Peter. *Boundaries: The Making of France and Spain in the Pyrenees.* Berkeley: University of California Press, 1991.

Salazar, S. Gabriel. "Brief Description of the Manché: The Roads, Towns, Lands, and Inhabitants." In Feldman, *Lost Shores*, 22–54.

Salmond, Anne. *The Trial of the Cannibal Dog: The Remarkable Story of Captain Cook's Encounters in the South Seas*. New Haven, CT: Yale University Press, 2003.

Salvatore, Ricardo Donato. "Death and Liberalism: Capital Punishment after the Fall of Rosas." In *Crime and Punishment in Latin America: Law and Society since Late Colonial Times*, ed. Ricardo Donato Salvatore, Carlos Aguirre, and G. M. Joseph, 308–41. Durham, NC: Duke University Press, 2001.

Samuel, Geoffrey. *Epistemology and Method in Law*. Burlington, VT: Ashgate, 2003.

Sandman, Alison. "Controlling Knowledge: Navigation, Cartography, and Secrecy in the Early Modern Spanish Atlantic." In Delbourgo, *Science and Empire in the Atlantic World*, 31–52.

Sassen, Saskia. *Territory, Authority, Rights: From Medieval to Global Assemblages* (Princeton, NJ: Princeton University Press, 2006).

Sastry, Kadayam Ramachandra Ramabhadra. *Indian States and Responsible Government*. Allahabad: Allahabad Law Journal, 1939.

Schama, Simon. *Landscape and Memory*. New York: Vintage, 1995.

Schmitt, Carl. *The Nomos of the Earth in the International Law of the* Jus Publicum Europeaum. New York: Telos Press, 2003.

———. *Political Theology: Four Chapters on the Concept of Sovereignty.* Chicago: University of Chicago Press, 2005.

Scott, James C. "La montagne et la liberté, ou pourquoi les civilizations ne savent pas grimper." *Critique Internationale* 11 (2001): 85–104.

Scott, Robert B. *The Military Law of England (with All the Principal Authorities): Adapted to the General Use of the Army, in Its Various Duties and Relations, and the Practice of Courts Martial.* London: T. Goddard, 1810.

Sears, Mary, and Daniel Merriman, eds. *Oceanography: The Past.* New York: Springer-Verlag, 1980.

Seed, Patricia. *Ceremonies of Possession in Europe's Conquest of the New World, 1492–1640.* Cambridge: Cambridge University Press, 1995.

Segurado, Eva Maria St. Clair. "'Vagos, ociosos y malentretenidos': The Deportation of Mexicans to the Philippines in the Eighteenth Century." Paper presented at the Conference of the American Historical Association, Atlanta, January 4–7, 2007.

Semple, Ellen Churchill. *Influences of Geographic Environment, on the Basis of Ratzel's System of Anthropo-Geography*. New York: H. Holt, 1911.

Sen, Satadru. *Disciplining Punishment: Colonialism and Convict Society in the Andaman Islands*. Oxford: Oxford University Press, 2000.

Sen, Sudipta. *Distant Sovereignty: National Imperialism and the Origins of British India*. New York: Routledge, 2002.

Serrano y Sanz, Manuel, ed. *Relación de los naufragios y comentarios de. Alvar Núñez Cabeza de Vaca (ilustrados con varios documentos inéditos)*. 2 vols. Madrid: Liberería General de Victoriano Suárez, 1906.

Serulnikov, Sergio. *Subverting Colonial Authority: Challenges to Spanish Rule in Eighteenth-Century Southern Andes*. Durham, NC: Duke University Press, 2003.

Shapiro, Barbara J. *"Beyond Reasonable Doubt" and "Probable Cause": Historical Perspectives on the Anglo-American Law of Evidence*. Berkeley: University of California Press, 1993.

______. *A Culture of Fact: England, 1550–1720*. Ithaca, NY: Cornell University Press, 2003.

Shapiro, Scott J. "What is the Rule of Recognition (and Does it Exist)?" Yale Law School, Public Law Working Paper No. 184. Available at SSRN: http://ssrn.com/abstract=1304645

Shaw, A. G. L. *Convicts and the Colonies: A Study of Penal Transportation from Great Britain and Ireland to Australia and Other Parts of the British Empire*. London: Faber and Faber, 1966.

Sheehan, Jonathan, and Dror Wahrman. "Matters of Scale: The Global Organiztion of the Eighteenth Century." Paper presented at "Geographies of the Eighteenth Century: The Question of the Global," Indiana University, May 19–22, 2004.

Shoemaker, Nancy. *A Strange Likeness: Becoming Red and White in Eighteenth-Century North America*. New York: Oxford University Press, 2004.

Silver, Peter. *Our Savage Neighbors: How Indian War Transformed Early America*. New York: W. W. Norton, 2007.

Silver, Timothy. *A New Face on the Countryside: Indians, Colonists, and Slaves in South Atlantic Forests, 1500–1800*. New York: Cambridge University Press, 1990.

Simón, Pedro. *The Expedition of Pedro de Ursua and Lope de Aguirre in Search of El Dorado and Omagua in 1560–1*. Translated by William Bollaert. Boston: Adamant Media, 2001.

Singha, Radhika. *A Despotism of Law: Crime and Justice in Early Colonial India*. New York: Oxford University Press, 1998.

Siskind, Clifford. *Blaming the System: Enlightenment and the Forms of Modernity*. Chicago: University of Chicago Press, forthcoming.

Skaria, Ajay. *Hybrid Histories: Forests, Frontiers and Wildness in Western India*. Oxford: Oxford University Press, 1999.

Smail, Daniel Lord. *Imaginary Cartographies: Possession and Identity in Late Medieval Marseille*. Ithaca, NY: Cornell University Press, 1999.

Smith, Abbot Emerson. "The Transportation of Convicts to the American Colonies in the Seventeenth Century." *American Historical Review* 39, no. 2 (1934): 232–49.

Spieler, Miranda. "Empire and Underworld: Guiana in the French Legal Imagination c. 1789–1870." Ph.D. diss., Columbia University, 2005.

______. "The Legal Structure of Colonial Rule during the French Revolution," *William and Mary Quarterly* 66 (2009), 365–408.

Spruyt, Hendrik. *The Sovereign State and Its Competitors: An Analysis of Systems Change*. Princeton, NJ: Princeton University Press, 1996.

Stark, Francis R. *The Abolition of Privateering and the Declaration of Paris [1897]*. Honolulu: University Press of the Pacific, 2002.

Starkey, David. "Pirates and Markets." In *Bandits at Sea: A Pirates Reader*, ed. C. R. Pennell, 107–24. New York: New York University Press, 2001.

Steele, Ian Kenneth. *The English Atlantic, 1675–1740: An Exploration of Communication and Community*. New York: Oxford University Press, 1986.

Steffen, Lisa. *Defining a British State: Treason and National Identity, 1608–1820*. New York: Palgrave, 2001.

Steinberg, Philip E. *The Social Construction of the Ocean*. Cambridge: Cambridge University Press, 2001.

Stern, Philip. "British Asia and British Atlantic: Comparisons and Connections." *William and Mary Quarterly* LXIII: 4 (2006), 693–712.

______. "'A Politie of Civill & Military Power': Political Thought and the Late Seventeenth-Century Foundations of the East India Company-State," *Journal of British Studies* 47 (April 2008): 253–83.

Stoler, Ann Laura. "On Degrees of Imperial Sovereignty." *Public Culture* 18, no. 1 (2006): 125–46.

Straumann, Benjamin. "'Ancient Caesarian Lawyers' in a State of Nature: Roman Tradition and Natural Rights in Hugo Grotius' *De Iure Praedae*." *Political Theory* 34, no. 3 (2006): 328–50.

______. "The Right to Punish as a Just Cause of War in Hugo Grotius' Natural Law." *Studies in the History of Ethics* 2 (2006): 1–20.

Streets, Heather. *Martial Races: The Military, Race and Masculinity in British Imperial Culture, 1857–1914*. Manchester, U.K.: Manchester University Press, 2004.

Stuchtey, Benedikt, and Eckhardt Fuchs, eds. *Writing World History, 1800–2000*. New York: Oxford University Press, 2003.

Subramanian, Lakshmi, and Rudrangshu Mukherjee, eds. *Politics and Trade in the Indian Ocean World: Essays in Honour of Ashin Das Gupta*. Delhi: Oxford University Press, 1998.

Sulivan, Richard Joseph. *Thoughts on Martial Law, with a Mode Recommended for Conducting the Proceedings of General Courts Martial... By Richard Joseph Sulivan, Esq.* 2nd ed. London: Printed for T. Becket, 1784.

Sylvest, Casper. "The Foundations of Victorian International Law." In *Victorian Visions of Global Order: Empire and International Relations in Nineteenth-Century Political Thought*, ed. Duncan Bell, 47–66. Cambridge: Cambridge University Press, 2007.

Tamanaha, Brian Z. *On the Rule of Law: History, Politics, Theory*. Cambridge: Cambridge University Press, 2004.

Taylor, E. G. R. *Late Tudor and Early Stuart Geography, 1583–1650: A Sequel to Tudor Geography, 1485–1583*. London: Methuen, 1934.

Teng, Emma. *Taiwan's Imagined Geography: Chinese Colonial Travel Writing and Pictures, 1683–1895*. Cambridge, MA: Harvard University Asia Center, 2004.

Theal, George MacCall, ed. *Basutoland Records: Copies of Official Documents of Various Kinds, Accounts of Travellers . . . [Etc.]*. Cape Town: W.A. Richards & Sons 1883.

Thomson, Janice E. *Mercenaries, Pirates, and Sovereigns: State-Building and Extraterritorial Violence in Early Modern Europe*. Princeton, NJ: Princeton University Press, 1994.

Tierney, Brian. *The Idea of Natural Rights: Studies on Natural Rights, Natural Law, and Church Law, 1150–1625*. Grand Rapids, MI: William B. Eerdmans, 2001.

Tilly, Charles. *Coercion, Capital, and European States, AD 990–1992*. Cambridge, MA: Wiley-Blackwell, 2007.

Tittoni, Tommaso, Bernardo Quaranta di San Severino, and Maggiorino Ferraris. *Italy's Foreign and Colonial Policy: A Selection from the Speeches Delivered in the Italian Parliament by the Italian Foreign Affairs Minister, Senator Tommaso Tittoni, During His Six Years of Office (1903–1909)*. London: Smith, Elder, 1914.

Tod, James. *Annals and Antiquities of Rajast'han, or the Central and Western Rajpoot States of India*. London: Smith, 1829.

Tomlins, Christopher. "The Legal Cartography of Colonization, the Legal Polyphony of Settlement: English Intrusions on the American Mainland in the 17th Century," *Law and Social Inquiry* 26, no. 2 (2001): 315–72.

______. "Law, Population, Labor." In Grossberg and Tomlins, *The Cambridge History of Law in America*, 1:211–52.

Towle, Dorothy S., ed. *Records of the Vice-Admiralty Court of Rhode Island, 1716–1752*. Washington, D.C.: American Historical Association, 1936.

Tracy, James D., ed. *The Political Economy of Merchant Empires*. Cambridge: Cambridge University Press, 1991.

Travers, Robert. *Ideology and Empire in Eighteenth-Century India: The British in Bengal, 1757–93*. New York: Cambridge University Press, 2007.

Tupper, Charles Lewis. *Our Indian Protectorate. An Introduction to the Study of the Relations between the British Government and Its Indian Feudatories*. London: Longmans, 1893.

Tupper, Charles Lewis, ed. *Indian Political Practice. A Collection of the Decisions of the Government of India in Political Cases. Compiled by C. L. Tupper. [1895]*. Delhi: B. R. Publishing, 1974.

Twiss, Travers. *The Law of Nations Considered as Independent Political Communities: On the Rights and Duties of Nations in Time of Peace [1884]*. Littleton, CO: Fred B. Rothman, 1985.

Tyacke, Sarah. "English Charting of the River Amazon c. 1595–1630." *Imago Mundi* 32 (1980): 73–89.

Tyler, Lyon Gardiner, ed. *Narratives of Early Virginia, 1606–1625*. New York: Charles Scribner's Sons, 1907.

Tytler, Alexander Fraser. *An Essay on Military Law, and the Practice of Courts Martial*. Edinburgh: Printed by Murray and Cochrane, 1800.

Vaidik, Aparna. *Imperial Andamans: A Spatial History of Britain's Indian Ocean Colony, 1858–1921*. New York: Palgrave MacMillan, 2009.

Valverde, Nuria and Antonio Furtado. "Space Production and Spanish Imperial Geopolitics." In Bleichmar, *Science in the Spanish and Portuguese Empire*, 198–215.

Van Ittersum, Martine Julia. *Profit and Principle: Hugo Grotius, Natural Rights Theories and the Rise of Dutch Power in the East Indies, 1595–1615*. Leiden: Brill, 2006.

______. "Dating the manuscript of De Jure Praedae (1604–1608)," *History of European Ideas*, 35:2 (2009), 125–193.

______. "Preparing *Mare liberum* for the Press: Hugo Grotius' Rewriting of Chapter 12 of *De iure praedae* in November-December 1608," in Blom, *Property, Piracy and Punishment*, 246–80.

Van Nifterik, Gustaaf, "Grotius and the Origin of the Ruler's Right to Punish," in Blom, *Property, Piracy and Punishment*, 396–416.

Vas Mingo, Marta Milagros del. *Los consulados en el tráfico indiano*. Madrid: Fundación Histórica Tavera, 2000.

Virginia Company of London. "Instructions Given by Way of Advice by Us Whom It Hath Pleased the King's Majesty to Appoint of the Counsel for the Intended Voyage to Virginia, to Be Observed by Those Captains and Company Which Are Sent at This Present to Plant There [1606]." Thomas Jefferson Papers, Virginia Records Manuscripts, 1606–1737; Virginia, 1606–92, Charters of the Virginia Company of London. Library of Congress, Manuscript Division, http://memory.loc.gov/cgi-bin/ampage?collId=mtj8&fileName=mtj8page062.db&recNum=0017.

Virginia Company of London and Susan M. Kingsbury. *The Records of the Virginia Company of London: The Court Book, from the Manuscript in the Library of Congress*. 4 vols. Washington, D.C.: Government Printing Office, 1906.

Waley-Cohen, Joanna. *Exile in Mid-Qing China: Banishment to Xinjiang, 1758–1820*. New Haven, CT: Yale University Press, 1991.

Ward, Kerry. *Networks of Empire: Forced Migration in the Dutch East India Company*. New York: Cambridge University Press, 2008.

Warren, Christopher. "Literature and the Law of Nations in England, 1585–1673." D. Phil. thesis, University of Oxford, 2007.

Washburn, Wilcomb E. *The Governor and the Rebel: A History of Bacon's Rebellion in Virginia*. New York: W. W. Norton, 1972.

Weaver, John C. *The Great Land Rush and the Making of the Modern World, 1650–1900*. Montreal: McGill-Queen's University Press, 2006.

Webb, Stephen Saunders. *The Governors-General: The English Army and the Definition of the Empire, 1569–1681*. Chapel Hill: University of North Carolina Press, 1987 [1979].

Werner, Patrick S. "El régimen legal de actividad marítima del imperio hispánico: El libro nuevo de la Recopilación." *Nicaraguan Academic Journal* 3 (2002): 39–62.

Wey Gómez, Nicolás. *The Tropics of Empire: Why Columbus Sailed South to the Indies*. Cambridge, MA: MIT Press, 2008.

Whitman, James Q. *Harsh Justice: Criminal Punishment and the Widening Divide between America and Europe*. New York: Oxford University Press, 2003.

Wigen, Kären. "Discovering the Japanese Alps: Meiji Mountaineering and the Quest for Geographical Enlightenment." *Journal of Japanese Studies* 31, no. 1 (2005): 1–26.

Wijffels, Alain. "Sir Julius Caesar and the Merchants of Venice." In Battenberg and Ranieri, *Geschichte Der Zentraljustiz in Mitteleuropa*.

Wilkinson, Charles F. *American Indians, Time, and the Law: Native Societies in a Modern Constitutional Democracy*. New Haven, CT: Yale University Press, 1987.

Williams, Megan. "Dangerous Diplomacy and Dependable Kin: Transformations in Central European Statecraft, 1526–1540." Ph.D. diss., Columbia University, 2008.

Wood, Malcolm. "Rule, Rules, and Law." In *The Jurisprudence of Orthodoxy: Queen's University Essays and H. L. A. Hart*. Ed. Philip Leith and Peter Ingram. New York: Routledge, 1988, 27–60.

Woodward, Ralph Lee. *Robinson Crusoe's Island: A History of the Juan Fernández Islands*. Chapel Hill: University of North Carolina Press, 1969.

Worster, Donald. *Rivers of Empire: Water, Aridity, and the Growth of the American West*. Oxford: Oxford University Press, 1992.

Ziarek, Ewa Plonowska. "Bare Life on Strike: Notes on the Biopolitics of Race and Gender." In *The Agamben Effect*, ed. Alison Ross, 89–105. Durham, NC: Duke University Press, 2007.

Zouch, Richard, and Edward Coke. *The Jurisdiction of the Admiralty of England Asserted against Sr. Edward Coke's Articuli Admiralitatis, in XXII Chapter of His Jurisdiction of Courts*. London: Printed for Francis Tyton and Thomas Dring, 1663.

Index

abolition
 of convict transportation, 196
 of slavery, 35, 209–210
Acadians, 175
Acosta, Juan de, 232, 233
Act for the More Effectual Suppression of Piracy, 147
Acuña, Cristóbal de, 54
adelantado, 68
 Cabeza de Vaca as, 72, 74–76
 legal role of, 68–69
admiralty law
 in colonies, 146–147, 150
 common law and, 127, 145–146
 Gentili and, 124–131
 piracy and, 146, 147
 prize cases and, 124, 145, 148
 in Rhode Island, 155–156
Africa
 Basutoland, 266–271
 disease in, 45
 North, 126, 171, 176
 Portuguese in, 22, 44, 48–49, 57
 rivers in, 43–45
 settlements in, xii
 slave trade from, 164
 trading posts in, 44
 West, 25, 44, 150
Agamben, Giorgio, 39, 282–287
Aguirre, Lope de, 79–81
Aitchison, Charles, 244
Almadén, 176
Alpujarras, 228
Amazon River, 46, 48, 54
 imperial rivalry and, 46, 54, 58
 interior sea and, 49–50, 69
 Pizarro on, 26, 53, 79
 Spanish chronicles and, 79–81
Ancient Law (Maine), 246
Andes, 68–71, 233
Anghie, Antony, 238, 264–265, 284, 296–297
Angola, 170, 235
Annals and Antiquities of Rathast'han (Tod), 241
anomalous legal zones, 6, 9, 30, 298–299
 islands and, 165
 quasi-sovereignty and, 227, 243, 266
Antequera, José de, 88–90
Arabian Sea, 148. *See also* Indian Ocean
Araucanians, 233–234
Arbousset, Thomas, 266–267
Asia, 14
 Central, 236
 European trade in, 106–108, 141–142
 Southeast, 224
asiento, 151. *See also* slave trade
astronomy, 10, 55
Asunción, 71–75, 77–78, 86, 87–90, 100
Atlantic Ocean
 campaign against pirates in, 150, 158
 Dutch in, 140
 European voyages in, xii
 geographic imagination and, 15
 as legal region, 137–149
 navigation map of, 107

Atlantic Ocean (*cont.*)
prize courts in, xii, 19, 145–147, 158
rivers and, 33–34, 40–103
audiencia, 68–71, 88, 183
Austin, John, 246
Avery, Henry, 118, 119, 142
Avilés, Pedro Menéndez de, 54
Ayolas, Juan de, 71

Bacon, Nathaniel, 96–99
Bacon's Rebellion, 96–99
bagnes, 175
banishment, 35, 167. *See also* convict transportation; penal colonies
China and, 167
of clergy, 168
islands and, 163–164
Ottoman empire and, 167
Portugal and, 167
Roman law and, 166–167
slavery and, 209
in Spain, 168
in Spanish empire, 168, 170
Banks, Joseph, 188
Barbados, 152, 209, 210–211
Barbary states, 124–127
Baroda, 250–260
bastides, 229
Basutoland, 266–271
jurisdiction in, 227
quasi-sovereignty in, 227
bays. *See* harbors
behetría, 232, 233
Bello, Andrés, 214–216
Bentham and, 214–216
Bellomont, Earl of, 117, 118
Bemoim (king), 65
Bentham, Jeremy, xiv, 29, 191–196, 297
Bello and, 214–216
martial law and, 192, 196
Berkeley, William, 96–99
Bhils, 241, 264
Blackbeard. *See* Teach, Edward
Blackstone, William, 201
Bligh, William, 190
Bodin, Jean, 287–288
Bombay, 247, 253
Bordeaux, 43
borderlands, 37–38, 229
Botany Bay, 165, 175, 188, 189. *See also* New South Wales
Braudel, Fernand, 4, 222–223
Brazil, 78, 129, 235
convicts in, 170
geography of, 51
slavery in, 235
Brisbane, Thomas, 205
British empire, 236. *See also* England
admiralty law in, 117–120, 146–147, 148, 150
Bacon's Rebellion and, 96–99
Basutoland and, 266–271
campaign against piracy in, 150, 158
convict transportation in, 169, 172–174
Indian princely states and, 227, 237, 238–240, 242–264
mapping and, 2, 10–11, 13–14
martial law in, 211–212
navy in, 150
North America and, 10–11, 13–14, 90–101
treason in, 81–85
Buenos Aires, 69, 71–72, 87–88, 90
Bureau of Indian Affairs, 272
Burma, 242, 259

Cabeza de Vaca, Alvar Nuñez, 48, 52, 68–79
Cabral, Pedro Álvares, 168
Cáceres, Felipe, 87
Cádiz, 20, 155, 179, 180
Calcutta, 260
California, 181
Calvin's Case, 29, 194
Cambrensis, Giraldus, 228
Camões, Luís de, 104, 105
Canada, 211. *See also* New France
Canary Islands, 22, 78
canon law, xiv, 22–23, 24, 25, 36, 62
Cão, Diogo, 44, 57
Cape Coast Castle, 189
Cape Colony, 211, 267–270
captains. *See* ship captains
cartaz (permit to sail), 141
cartography. *See* mapping
Castro, João de, 1
Catholicism, 23, 63
Jesuits, 88–90
papal authority and, 22–23
treason and, 63, 80

Ceylon, 211
Champlain, Samuel de, 66–68
Charles I (king), 63
Charles River, 91
The Charles the Second (ship), 119
Chesapeake Bay, 83
Chile, 186, 217, 233
  constitution in, 214–215
  penal colonies and, 215–216
China, 167
  banishment and, 167
chorography, 18
  settlements and, 229
Christianity. *See also* Catholicism
  conversion to, 65, 222
  Indians and, 91
  Reconquest and, 229
Cicero, 123
citizenship, 29, 274, 297
  imperial, 289, 293
  in Rome, 166
civility
  law and, 58
  towns and, 56, 229
  vs. wildness, 32, 296
claims, 4, 10–11, 152
  rivers and, 54–55
  Roman law and, 55–56
clergy. *See also* Jesuits
  banishment of, 168
  benefit of, 173
  jurisdiction over, 62
Cochin, 257, 265–266
Coke, Edward, 29, 66, 98, 146, 194
Collins, David, 195
Columbus, Christopher, 106
  harbors and, 20, 46
  rivers and, 19
Commentaries (Blackstone), 201
commissions. *See also* letters of marque
  to privateers, 113–116, 140
common law
  admiralty law and, 127, 145–146
  in empire, 29, 145
  martial law and, 212
  piracy and, 66, 146–147
  treason and, 63
comuneros, 62, 73, 86, 89, 186
Congo River, 44, 45, 57
Connecticut River, 91, 96, 100
Conrad, Joseph, 40–41
constitutions
  in Chile, 214–215
  imperial, 164, 166, 175, 208–217
  in Spain, 213–214
  United States, 273
consulados (Spanish merchant courts), 145
contraband, 151, 152, 153, 177
convict transportation. *See also* penal colonies
  abolition of, 196
  England and, 169–174, 187–197
  France and, 169, 174–175
  islands and, 162–221
  to Maryland, 173
  to New South Wales, 187–197
  Peru and, 179
  in Portuguese empire, 168–169, 170, 171–172
  Spain and, 165–166, 169
  to Virginia, 169, 173
  VOC and, 170
Cook, James, 16, 197, 198
corridors, 2, 3, 10–23, 34, 149–158. *See also* rivers; sea lanes
  law and, 8–9
  ocean passages as, 106–108
cosmography, 1, 11, 18, 21, 28
Council of the Indies, 74, 79, 170
courts martial. *See* martial law
crosses, 56
  at Jamestown, 57
  on Mississippi River, 58
  on St. Lawrence River, 57
Cuba. *See also* Havana
  penal colonies in, 177, 216–217
  piracy and, 115
currents, 106, 108
  in oceans, 108–110
Cusack, George, 114

Dampier, William, 114
Dangs, 263
Daston, Lorraine, 20
Davis, Edward, 114
Dawes Act, 272
De iure belli ac pacis (Grotius), 124, 131, 132, 135
De iure praedae (Grotius), 131, 132, 133–135
DeBry, Theodore, 47
Defoe, Daniel, 162, 163

degredado (convict), 169, 171–172
  slave trade and, 171
Delaware River, 90
delegated legal authority, 3, 30–31, 209, 217
Demerara, 209–210
derottas (routes), 106
descriptive geography, 18
desert, 15
desertion, 66, 179, 181, 184
despotism
  on islands, 163
  sovereignty and, 225
  Turkish, 223
destierro, 168, 170. *See also* banishment; convict transportation
The Discovery of the large, rich, and beautiful Empire of Guiana (Raleigh), 81
dominium, 5, 11
  definition of, 4–5
donatario, 172
Downes v. Bidwell, 274
Durand, H. Mortimer, 244
Dutch
  Amazon River and, 46, 58
  in Atlantic Ocean, 140
  in East Indies, 133–134
  England and, 128–129, 140
  Indian Ocean pass system and, 141–142
  mercantile law and, 145
  Portugal and, 106–108, 133
  ship captains, 138
  Spain and, 124, 133, 155–156
Dutch East India Company (VOC), 124
  convict transportation and, 170
Duval, Jean, 67

East India Company (EIC), 143, 148, 241
  Mughal empire and, 143–144
Ecuador, 233
Edward III (king), 94
EIC. *See* East India Company
El Dorado, 51
Elphinstone, Mountstuart, 241
emergency, law of, 218–219
empires. *See also specific empires*
  anomalies of, 1–9
  bare sovereignty and, 256, 294, 299
  competition among, xiii, 8, 108, 177, 198
  international law and, xii, 8
  islands and, xiii
  mapping and, 1–3, 13–15
  oceans and, xi
  pirates and, xi–xii
  Rome and, 231
  rule of law in, 286–294
  slave trade and, 239
  sovereignty and, xii, 279–280
  subjecthood in, xiii, 28–31
  territoriality and, xii, 1–2, 3–5, 11–12, 280–281, 282
enclaves, 3, 10–23. *See also* hills; islands; mountains
  along corridors, 2
  in colonies, xiii
  quasi-sovereignty and, 222–278
Endeavor Bay, 16
England, 2, 229. *See also* British empire
  Catholicism in, 63
  common law in, 29, 145
  convict transportation and, 169, 172–174, 187–197
  Dutch and, 128–129, 140
  garrisons in, 229
  hills and, 228
  hulks in, 187
  law of nations and, 157
  martial law in, 201–202
  in New World, 54
  Northwest Passage and, 50, 108
  pirates and, 110
  Spain and, 124, 150–156
  treason in, 61, 63
  Zanzibar and, 237
epistemology, 9, 16
  geography and, 18–21
  law and, 21–22, 26–28
escribanos, 25–26, 77
ex parte Crow Dog, 272
exile. *See* banishment
extraterritoriality, 238
eyewitness testimony, 17, 19, 27
Eyre, Edward, 211

Falkland Islands, 216
Fernando Po, 216
Florida
  France in, 46–47
  harbors in, 49
  rivers in, 46

Spain in, 46–48, 53–54, 68
forced labor, 168, 176, 208–217
on galleys, 168
in presidios, 177, 179
Roman law and, 167
Foreign Office, of British government of India, 242, 244, 257
forts, 56, 58. *See also* garrisons
on Amazon River, 58
Fosse, Eustache de la, 26
Foster, George, 197
Foveaux, Joseph, 204–205
Fradera, Josep, 214
France, 112, 145
in Angola, 235
convict transportation and, 174–175
in Florida, 46–47
garrisons in, 229
Guiana and, 175
Indian Ocean pass system and, 141–142
New Caledonia and, 174, 219
treason in, 61
French Guiana, 175
Frobisher, Martin, 169
fuero militar (military jurisdiction), 213
fueros (local law codes), 62, 229

gaekwar, 176, 247, 251–256, 258–260
galleys, 168
Gambia River, 44, 188–189
Ganj-I Sawai (ship), 142
Garcia, Aleixo, 71
garrison government, 34, 163, 299
garrisons, 2. *See also bastides*; forts; presidios
in England, 229
in France, 229
on rivers, 58
Genoese, 123
Gentili, Alberico, xiv, 122, 124–131, 297
geographic imagination, xii, 7–8, 15–21, 87, 100, 103, 110
rivers and, 43–59
geography, 1–2, 11, 7–8, 15–21
chorography and, 18
descriptive geography and, 18
rivers and, 43–59
Germanic law, 60, 81
Gilbert, Humphrey, 66
Gillis, John, 15
Gironde River, 43
globalization, 12–13, 104
Goa, 170
Gordon, George, 211, 271
Great Swamp Fight, 96
Greaves, John, 108
Grotius, Hugo, 124, 131–137, 297
prize courts and, 111
Guadalquivir River, 43
Guaraní Indians, 71
Guantánamo Bay, 6, 299
guardacostas (coast guards), 150–155
guides, 27, 41, 51–53, 71, 76, 85
Gujarat, 247

Habeas Corpus Act, 169, 173, 195
Hakluyt, Richard, 28
Hale, Matthew, 201
Hall v. Campbell, 193
harbors, 19
Columbus and, 20, 46
in Florida, 49
rivers and, 43
settlements and, 20
Havana, 152, 155–156, 177–180. *See also* Cuba
Heart of Darkness (Conrad), 40
heresy, treason and, 62
high seas, 15, 34, 110
Hill Tipperah, 258
hills, 227–236, 296
England and, 228
in India, 241–242
Spain and, 228
Hispanica advocatio (Gentili), 124, 126–131
Historia natural y moral de las Indias (Acosta), 232
Holy Roman Empire, 237
Honduras, 189, 209
Hudson River, 90
hulks, 187–188
Hussain, Nasser, 284
Hyderabad, 242, 256
hydrography, 108–109
hydrology, 49, 50, 51

imperium, 5, 235
behetría and, 233
definition of, 5
Incas, 233

India
  British empire in, 238–245
  mountains of, 241–242
  princely states in, 227, 237, 238–240, 242–260
  subjecthood in, 256–257
  territoriality in, 240, 260–264
Indian Ocean
  as legal region, 137–149
  piracy in, 116–117
  privateering in, 139–140
  prize courts in, 118, 148
  sea lanes in, 137, 144–145, 158
Indian princely states, 227, 237, 238–240, 242–264
Indians. *See also specific Indian groups*
  Bacon's Rebellion and, 96–99
  in California, 177
  Christianity and, 91
  Guaraní, 71, 74–77
  as imperial legal subjects, 75, 91, 93–95, 99
  Incas, 233
  King Philip's War and, 93–96
  as local guides, 51–53, 71, 76, 85, 91–96
  Spain and, 29, 69, 231–235
  territory and, 13–14
  treason and, 64, 75, 95
  in United States, 272–276
indigenous peoples, 14–15
  mapping by, 11, 14–15, 229
indirect rule, 29
  quasi-sovereignty and, 226, 243, 268, 271
Inquisition, 62
Institutes, of Justinian, 55, 122
Instructions for the intended voyage to Virginia, 50
insular cases, 274–275
international law, xii, xiii, 8, 297. *See also* law of nations
  Europeans and, xiv
  mountains and, 223–224, 225
  natural law and, 5–6, 131–132
  oceans and, 105, 110, 120–137
  piracy and, 112–113
  quasi-sovereignty and, 226
  sovereignty and, 9–10, 35–36, 121
  Spain and, 22–23, 158
Irala, Domingo de, 68, 72, 74, 75, 77
Ireland, 64, 228
  convicts from, 204
Isla de Pinos, 186, 216–217
Islam. *See* Muslims
islands, 15, 296
  anomalous legal zones and, 165
  banishment and, 163–164
  convict transportation and, 162–221
  empires and, xiii
  garrison government on, 34, 163, 299
  legal imagination and, 164
  military law and, 162–221
  penal colonies on, 35
  sovereignty of, 163, 164
  wildness of, 296
isolarios, 18
itineraries. *See* tours
ius gentium (law of nations), 120, 235. *See also* law of nations

Jamaica, 115, 146–147
  martial law in, 211–212
  slavery in, 235
James I (king), 82–83, 169
James River, 96
Jamestown, 54, 83–85
  claims at, 57
Jesuits, 88–90
John of Fordun, 228
Johnson, Charles, 149
Johnson, Samuel, 222
Juan Fernández Islands, 178, 186, 215–216
jurisdiction
  in Basutoland, 227
  criminal, 146
  imperial authority and, xii, 6, 31
  Indian princely states and, 227, 250–260, 261–262
  military, 185, 213
  in oceans, xii, 111, 121–123, 128–129, 130–131, 134–136
  vs. ownership, 29, 123, 135–136
  on rivers, 34, 101
  in Roman law, 31, 122
  sea lanes and, 106, 123, 137–138
  ship captains and, 112
Justinian's *Institutes*, 55, 122

Kabyles, 235–236
Kathiawar, 247–248
Keene, Benjamin, 153

Kercher, Bruce, 190
Khoi, 169
Kidd, William, 116–120, 143
King, Philip Gidley, 198–199, 200–201, 202–203
King Philip's War, 93–96
Kircher, Athanasius, 108, 109
Krasner, Stephen, 281

lançados. *See* Luso-Africans
Lane, Frederick, 123
Las Casas, Bartolomé de, 234
law of nations
  English law and, 157
  Gentili and, 129
  natural law and, 120
  oceans and, 111, 120, 149–158
  prize courts and, 34, 157
The Law of Nations (Twiss), 272
lawlessness, 25, 28–32
  in England, 229
  oceans and, 105
  zones of, 30–32, 102, 282–283, 284
laws of Oléron, 66
Le Moyne, Jacques, 47
legal culture, 3, 23, 25. *See also* legal imagination
  pirates and, 112–120
legal imagination, 8, 9, 25
  islands and, 164
legal posturing, 24–25, 34, 211
  of pirates, 113–116, 150
Leisler, Jacob, 94
Leith, James, 210
Lemain, island of, 188–189
lèse-majesté, 61. *See also* treason
Lesotho, 268
letters of marque and, 113, 140
  Santa Catarina and, 140
lex mercatoria, 146
Lisbon, 43
Locke, John, 58
Loire River, 43
London, 43, 117, 124, 126, 207, 214, 228
Louisiana, 179
L'Ouverture, Toussaint, 180
Luso-Africans, 45, 101
Lyall, Alfred, 244

Maconochie, Alexander, 197, 206–207
Madagascar, 116
magistrates, 112, 167, 185, 187, 192, 270, 288
Magna Carta, 194
Maier, Charles, 7
maiestas, 60–61. *See also* lèse-majesté
Maine, Henry Sumner, xiv, 244–246, 297
Maine (colony), 91
Major Crimes Act, 273
Málaga, 180, 181
Malhar Rao, 251–256, 258–260. *See also* gaekwar
Manipur, 289
Mansfield, Edward, 115
mapping
  by Asians, 14
  empires and, 1–2, 10–12
  by indigenous people, 14–15, 229
  of Massachusetts, 92
  by Muslims, 14
  of oceans, 2, 105–106
  rationalization of space and, 14
  of rivers, 2, 83–84
  sketch-maps, 18
  of South America, 70
  of Spanish empire, 14, 18
  to stake claims, 56
  tours and, 16–17
  way-finding maps, 18
  world map, 1
Marathas, 142, 241
Mare liberum (Grotius), 124, 131, 132
maritime law. *See* admiralty law; prize courts
Marshall, John, 272
Martí, José, 216
martial law, 94, 211, 283, 290. *See also* military law
  in Barbados, 209, 210–211
  Bentham and, 192, 196
  Blackstone and, 201
  in British empire, 211–212
  constitutions and, 166
  in Demerara, 60–61, 209–210
  in England, 94, 201–202
  in Jamaica, 211–212
  in New South Wales, 190–191
  on Norfolk Island, 199–200, 291
  penal colonies and, 35, 164
  rebellion and, 94
  slavery and, 209–211
Maryland, convict transportation to, 173

Más-a-Tierra. *See* Juan Fernández Islands
Massachusetts
  King Philip's War and, 93–96
  Massachusetts Bay Colony and, 91, 92–93
  rivers and, 92
Massachusetts Bay Colony, 91, 92–93
May, William, 119, 148
Mello, João de, 172
Mendoza, Pedro de, 46, 71
Merrimack River, 91, 92
Mexico, 233. *See also* New Spain
military law, 34. *See also* fuero militar; martial law
  islands and, 162–221
  in Spanish presidios, 213–214
Mill, John Stuart, 211
Mississippi River, 51, 58
Mobile Bay, 49
Molucca Islands, 10, 52, 170
Montemorcency, Florys de, 62
Morgan, Henry, 115–116
moriscos, 228
Moshoeshoe, 266–270
Mosto, Ca' da, 45
mountains, 222–227. *See also* hills
  Andes, 233
  of India, 241–242
  international law and, 223–224, 225
  Mediterranean, 223
  slavery and, 235
  sovereignty and, 225
  wildness of, 263
Mughal empire, 141–145
  EIC and, 143–144
  Europeans and, 144
  piracy and, 142–143
Muldoon, James, 234
Muslims
  banishment and, 167
  mapping by, 14
mutiny, 33, 66, 67, 76, 83, 205, 218, 220
Mysore, 242

naming, 16
Nantes, 43
Narragansetts, 92, 93, 95
natural law, 131–132
  international law and, 5–6
  law of nations and, 120
  Mare liberum and, 132
  oceans and, 106
  vs. positve law, 29
  Roman law and, 55, 121
nature, 9, 17, 20–21, 132, 163
  admiration of, 267
  taming of, 229
Netherlands. *See* Dutch
New Caledonia, 174, 219
New England. *See also specific colonies*
  Indians in, 91–96, 99
New France, 169
New Granada, 179, 180
New Hampshire, 91
New Laws (1542), 78
New Netherland, 90
New South Wales, 187–197, 297
New Spain, 179, 235
New Zealand, 16, 198
Niger River, 44, 48
Nile River, 49–50
Nipmucks, 93, 96
Norfolk Island, 35, 197–208
  martial law on, 199–200, 291
Northwest Passage, 50, 108

oaths, 92, 96, 99, 289
occupation, 122, 123, 135
oceans, xi, xii, 15, 104–161. *See also specific oceans*
  currents in, 108–110
  globalization and, 104
  international law and, 105, 110, 120–137
  jurisdiction in, xii, 111, 121–123, 130–131, 134–136
  law of nations and, 111, 149–158
  lawlessness and, 105
  natural law and, 106
  territoriality and, xi, 10
Opechancanough, 51, 85
Orange River Sovereignty, 267
Orellana, Francisco de, 26, 79, 80
Orinoco River, 83
Ottoman empire, 125, 127
  banishment and, 167
outports, 43

Pacific Ocean, imperial rivalries in, 198
padrão, 57
Paraguay. *See* Asunción

Paraguay River, 71–72, 74, 76–77, 100
paramountcy, 245, 260, 272
Paraná River, 88
  headwaters of, 69
pardons, 42, 81, 83, 97–98, 149, 168, 171, 173, 203–204
Paris Evangelical Missionary Society, 266
Park, Katherine, 20
pass system, in Indian Ocean, 141–142
Peace of Utrecht, 149
Pelly, Lewis, 259–260, 261
penal colonies, 209–211, 217–221, 290. *See also* convict transportation
  on Falkland Islands, 216
  in French Guiana, 174–175
  on islands, 35, 164–166, 219–220, 221
  martial law and, 35, 164, 190–191, 199–200
  on Norfolk Island, 35, 197–208
  presidios as, 176–187
Pensacola Bay, 49
perduelli, 60. *See also* treason
Pérez, Antonio, 62
Peru, 58, 90
  convict transportation and, 179
  exile in, 170
  mountains in, 233
  rebellion in, 78–79
peshwa, 247
Phayre, Robert, 250–256, 258–260
Philip II (king), 62, 80, 81
  privateers and, 151
Philippines, 170, 179, 214
piracy, 34, 66
  admiralty law and, 117–120, 146
  Barbary states and, 124–127
  campaign against, 110, 150, 158
  empires and, xi–xii
  international law and, 112–113
  legal culture and, 112–120
  Mughal empire and, 142–143
  pardons and, 149
  privateering and, 113, 130
  Spain and, 150
Pizarro, Gonzalo, 26, 53, 78–79, 170
  on Amazon River, 26
A Plea for the Constitution (Bentham), 191–195
Pocahontas, 84
policía, 231
political law, 242
Portugal
  in Africa, 22, 44, 48–49, 57
  Amazon River and, 46
  astronomy and, 1, 10
  Atlantic Ocean and, 10
  in Brazil, 235
  convict transportation and, 167
  Dutch and, 106–108, 133
  factories and, 44
  Spain and, 10, 22–23
  treason in, 65
positive law
  international law and, 5–6
  vs. natural law, 29
possession, 55–59
  ceremonies of, 51
  of rivers, 34
  in Roman law, 41, 56
  settlements and, 57
postliminium, 126
Poverty Bay, 16
Powhatan, 51, 84, 85
presidios
  in California, 177, 181
  in Cuba, 177–180
  forced labor and, 177, 179
  in North Africa, 176
  as penal colonies, 176–187
  in San Juan, 177–180, 181, 183
  Spain and, 176–187, 213–214
Príncipe, 172
privateering, 153
  commissions and, 113–116, 140
  in Indian Ocean, 139–140
  Philip II and, 151
  piracy and, 113, 130
Privy Council, 256
prize courts, 145, 148
  in Atlantic, 145–147, 158
  Grotius and, 111
  in Indian Ocean, 118, 148
  law of nations and, 34, 157
  in Spanish empire, 145, 151–156
  treaties and, 152
probanzas, 26
protectorates, 266
Puerto Rico, 179, 184, 274. *See also* San Juan
Punjab, 245

quasi-sovereignty, 226, 293–294, 297
  anomalous legal zones and, 227, 243, 266
  in Basutoland, 227
  enclaves and, 222–278
  indirect rule and, 226
  international law and, 226, 236–250
  treaties and, 264
Quebec, 42, 66, 67
Quedah Merchant (ship), 117, 137, 143

Rajputana, 244–245, 261, 262
Raleigh, Walter, 83
Raper, George, 199
Rappanhanock River, 96
rationalization of space, xii, 1, 9, 10–15, 16
  mapping and, 14
rebellion
  martial law and, 94
  in Peru, 78–79
  treason and, 64–65
reconquest, 229
Relaciones de Indias, 27
Relaciones Geográficas, 18
relegatio in insulam (relegation to an island), 166
Report on the Territories Conquered from the Paishwa (Elphinstone), 241
res communes (common things), 122
res nullius (things without owners), 58–59, 122
res publicae (public things), 122
res universitatis (community things), 122
Resolution (ship), 197
Revenge and Success v. Welhelm Gally, 155
Rhode Island, 95–96
Río de la Plata, 46, 57, 68, 69–71, 86, 87–88
rivers, 34, 40–103, 57–58. *See also specific rivers*
  in Africa, xii, 43–45
  of Atlantic, 40–103
  Columbus and, 19
  danger on, xiii
  Europeans and, xii, 19
  in Florida, 46
  garrisons on, 58
  harbors and, 43
  jurisdiction on, 34
  mapping of, 2, 83–84
  in New World, 45–48
  possession of, 34
  settlements on, 58
  in South America, 51, 69–71
  subjecthood and, 296
  treason and, 40–103
Roanoke, 54
Robben Island, 169
Robinson Crusoe (Defoe), 162, 163
Roman law, xiv, 8, 25, 28, 31, 58, 235
  banishment and, 166–167
  Europeans and, 297
  forced labor and, 167
  jurisdiction in, 31, 122
  natural law and, 55, 121
  possession and, 41, 55–56
  settlements and, 8
  treason and, 41, 59–60
rule of law, 283, 286–294
Rum Rebellion, 190
Russell, P.E., 65

Sable Island, 169
Salazar, Gabriel, 17, 53
San Juan, 177–180, 181, 183. *See also* Puerto Rico
sanads, 244
Santa Catarina (ship), 124, 131, 134, 139
  Grotius and, 124
  letters of marque and, 140
Santo Domingo, 152, 153, 179
São Tomé, 171–172
Scheduled Districts Act, 262
Schmidel, Ulrich, 70
Schmitt, Carl, 282–287
science, 19, 21, 27. *See also* epistemology
Scott, James, 224
Scottish Highlands, 228
sea lanes, 2, 105–106, 157
  in Atlantic, 107
  in Caribbean, 152–153
  as corridors, 295–296
  in Indian Ocean, 137, 144–145, 158
  jurisdiction and, 105–106, 123, 137–138
  Pacific routes and, 177, 197
  settlements and, 2
Selkirk, Alexander, 163
Senegal River, 44, 45
servitude, law and, 35, 164
settlements. *See also* garrisons; penal colonies
  in Africa, xii

on Amazon River, 58
in British North America, 231
chorography and, 229
harbors and, 20
political uncertainty in, 42
possession and, 57
on rivers, 58
Roman law and, 8
sea lanes and, 2
in Spanish empire, 229
to stake claims, 56
subjecthood in, xiii
Seven Years' War, 175, 177
Seville, 43
Shakespeare, William, 162
ship captains, 112
Dutch, 138
from England, 112
from France, 112
as legal authorities, 26, 31, 112, 134, 136
as pirates, 66
from Spain, 112
Shivaji, 142
Signaty, 144
singularity, 16, 19–21
Sirius (ship), 200
sketch-maps, 18
slave trade
from Africa, 164
degredados and, 171
empires and, 239
slavery, 291–292. *See also* forced labor
abolition of, 35
banishment and, 209
in Brazil, 235
hill regions and, 235
in Jamaica, 235
martial law and, 209–211
treason and, 95, 101–103
Smith, John, 51, 83–85
Solís, Juan de, 57, 71
Soto, Hernando de, 52
South America. *See also specific colonies and countries*
map of, 70
rivers in, 51
sovereignty
bare, 256–257, 294, 299
divisible, 5, 244, 246, 248, 258, 279–280, 297–298
domestic, 281
imperial, 4–5, 31, 37, 132, 176, 212, 225, 279–280
international, 281
international law and, 9–10, 35–36, 121
layered, 31, 295
national, 4, 279
partial, xiii
quasi-sovereignty, 222–278, 297
rule of law and, 286–294
state, 279
territoriality and, xii, 1–4, 11–12, 103, 280–281, 282
Westphalian, 281
Spain. *See also* Spanish empire
constitution in, 213–214
convict transportation and, 165–166, 176–187
Dutch and, 124, 155–156
England and, 150–156
in Florida, 46–48, 53–54, 68
mercantile law in, 145
mountains in, 228
Portugal and, 22–23
ship captains from, 112
sworn statements and, 26
towns and, 56–57
Spanish empire, 24. *See also* Spain
convicts in, 170
Indians and, 29, 231–235
international law and, 158
mapping in, 14, 18
militarization of, 212–214
presidios in, 176–187, 213–214
prize courts in, 145, 151–156
towns in, 229
treason and, 64, 68–79
treaties and, 152
Treaty of Tordesillas and, 10, 13, 22–23
spatial history, 38
Spelman, Henry, 85
St. Domingue, 209
St. Johns River, 54
St. Lawrence River, 51
Champlain on, 66
crosses at, 57
St. Vincent, 211
state of exception, 218, 284
subjecthood, 3, 29, 94, 286, 297
in empires, xiii, 28–31, 288, 289
in India, 256–257
of Indians, 75, 91, 93–95, 99

subjecthood (*cont.*)
 mariners and, 129, 133–134
 rivers and, 296
 in settlements, xiii
 treason and, 65, 101–102
Swan, Charles, 114

Tagus River, 43
Talton v. Mayes, 273
Teach, Edward, 149–150
Tebicuary River, 88
Teixeira, Pedro, 54
The Tempest (Shakespeare), 162
terra nullius, 58
territoriality, 7, 14–15, 282
 empires and, 1–2, 4–5, 11–12, 280–281, 282
 in India, 240, 260–264
 oceans and, 10, 128–129
 sovereignty and, xii, 1–5, 12, 280–281, 282
Thames River, 43
Theal, George, 268–270
Tift, Joshua, 95
Topography of Ireland (Cambrensis), 228
tours
 geography and, 16
 mapping and, 16–17
towns. *See* settlements
trading posts, 2, 44
Transportation Act of 1718, 172
Travancore, 265–266
travel literature, 25
treason, xiii, 40–103
 British empire and, 81–85, 97–99
 empire and, 63–65
 in England, 61, 63
 in France, 61
 heresy and, 62
 Indians and, 64, 75–76, 93–95
 petty, 60, 66, 75
 in Portuguese empire, 65
 punishment for, 61
 rebellion and, 64–65
 Roman law and, 41, 59–60
 slavery and, 95, 101–103
 in Spanish empire, 64, 68–79
 subjecthood and, 65
treaties, 130
 prize courts and, 152
 quasi-sovereignty and, 264
 Spain and, 10, 13, 22–23, 152
 suspension of, 238
Treaty of Tordesillas, 10, 13, 22–23
Treaty of Westphalia, 4
Triangulation Survey of British India, 11
Tunis, 126–127
Tupper, Charles Lewis, 243–245, 248
Twiss, Travers, 272

United Provinces. *See* Dutch
United States. *See also specific states*
 Constitution of, 273
 Indians in, 272–276
United States v. Kagama, 273
Ursúa, Pedro de, 79

vacuum domicilium, 58
Van Diemen's Land, 197, 207
Van Heemskerck, Jacob, 139–140
Vaz da Cunha, Pero, 65
Velasco, Juan López de, 27
Venice, 123, 126–128
vice admiralty courts. *See* admiralty law
viceroys, 31, 64, 80, 89
Virginia, 91, 100
 Bacon's Rebellion and, 96–99
 convict transportation to, 169, 173
Vitoria, Francisco de, 234
Vivar, Gerónimo de, 233
VOC. *See* Dutch East India Company
Voiaige à la Guiné (Fosse), 26

Wampanoags, 93
Ward, John, 127
Wecopeak, John, 95
West Indies, 154, 169, 187
Westlake, John, 239–241
Westphalian sovereignty, 281
wildness, 32, 229
 of islands, 296
 of mountains, 263
Williams, Isaac, 204
world map, 1, 109

yerba mate, 88, 89
York River, 96

Zanzibar, 237
zones, of law, 28–32, 38, 281–286, 294–298. *See also* anomalous legal zones

Breinigsville, PA USA
15 February 2011
255482BV00008B/1/P